SUPER-INFINITE

'What a delightful book *Super-Infinite* is: companionable, astute, intimate in tone and clear-eyed in judgment, it brings Donne and his milieu to glorious life.'
 Nick Laird

'There can be no better companion than Rundell in a bracing pursuit of John Donne. Throughout this sure-footed and eloquent biography, she encourages us to listen attentively to his many voices, and to the voices of those around him.'
 Diarmaid MacCulloch

'Storytelling genius . . . Her sizzling prose blows away the cobwebs of academia and makes this a deeply satisfying, joyful read.'
 Lucy Jago

'[A] brilliant leap into literary history . . . Her skill as a novelist shows us John Donne the man, so real, so eccentric, fizzing with talent, weird as hell; while her attention to detail makes her a historian of the first rank.'
 Dan Snow

SUPER-INFINITE

The
Transformations
of
JOHN DONNE

KATHERINE RUNDELL

faber

First published in 2022
by Faber & Faber Ltd
Bloomsbury House
74–77 Great Russell Street
London WCIB 3DA

Typeset by Faber & Faber Ltd
Printed and bound by CPI Group (UK) Ltd, Croydon, CR0 4YY

A CIP record for this book
is available from the British Library

ISBN 978–0–571–34591–5

6 8 10 9 7 5

To Bart van Es, whose teaching changed
the course of my life

CONTENTS

INTRODUCTION

I

The power of John Donne's words nearly killed a man. It was the late spring of 1623, on the morning of Ascension Day, and Donne had finally secured for himself celebrity, fortune and a captive audience. He had been appointed the Dean of St Paul's Cathedral two years before: he was fifty-one, slim and amply bearded, and his preaching was famous across the whole of London. His congregation – merchants, aristocrats, actors in elaborate ruffs, the whole sweep of the city – came to his sermons carrying paper and ink, wrote down his finest passages and took them home to dissect and relish, pontificate and argue over. He often wept in the pulpit, in joy and in sorrow, and his audience would weep with him. His words, they said, could 'charm the soul'.

That morning he was not preaching in his own church, but fifteen minutes' easy walk across London at Lincoln's Inn, where a new chapel was being consecrated. Word went out: wherever he was, people came flocking, often in their thousands, to hear him speak. That morning, too many people flocked. 'There was a great concourse of noblemen and gentlemen', and in among 'the extreme press and thronging', as they pushed closer to hear his words, men in the crowd were shoved to the ground and trampled. 'Two or three were endangered, and taken up dead for the time.' There's no record of Donne halting his sermon; so it's likely that he kept going in his rich, authoritative voice as the bruised men were carried off and out of sight.

Donne the preacher: engraving by Pierre Lombart,
after an unknown painting

II

Just fifteen years before that, the same man finished a book and immediately put it away. He knew as he wrote it that it could be dangerous to him were it to be discovered. He was living in obscurity in Mitcham, in a cold house with thin walls and a noxious cellar that leaked 'raw vapours' to the rooms above, distracted by a handful of gamesome and clamouring children. It was a book written in illness and poverty, to be read by almost no one. The book was called *Biathanatos*; a text which has claim to being the first full-length treatise on suicide written in English. It laid out, with painstaking precision, how often its author dreamed of killing himself.

III

A decade or so before, the same man, then about twenty-three years old, sat for a portrait. The painting was of a man who knew about fashion; he wore a hat big enough to sail a cat in, a big lace collar, an exquisite moustache. He positioned the pommel of his sword to be just visible, an accessory more than a weapon. Around the edge of the canvas was painted in Latin, 'O Lady, lighten our darkness'; a not-quite-blasphemous misquotation of Psalm 17, his prayer addressed not to God but to a lover. And his beauty deserved walk-on music, rock-and-roll lute: all architectural jawline and hooked eyebrows. Those eyebrows were the author of some of the most celebratory and most lavishly sexed poetry ever written in English, shared among an intimate and loyal group of hyper-educated friends:

License my roving hands, and let them go
Behind, before, above, between, below!
O my America! My new-found land!
My kingdom, safeliest when with one man manned!

The Lothian Portrait, artist unknown, c.1595

Sometime religious outsider and social disaster, sometime celebrity preacher and establishment darling, John Donne was incapable of being just one thing. He reimagined and reinvented himself, over and over: he was a poet, lover, essayist, lawyer, pirate, recusant, preacher, satirist, politician, courtier, chaplain to the King, dean of the finest cathedral in London. It's traditional to imagine two Donnes – Jack Donne, the youthful rake, and Dr Donne, the older, wiser priest, a split Donne himself imagined in a letter to a friend – but he was infinitely more various and unpredictable than that.

Donne loved the *trans-* prefix: it's scattered everywhere across his writing – 'transpose', 'translate', 'transport', 'transubstantiate'. In this Latin preposition – 'across, to the other side of, over, beyond' – he saw both the chaos and potential of us. We are, he believed, creatures born transformable. He knew of transformation into misery: 'But O, self-traitor, I do bring/The spider love, which transubstantiates all/And can convert manna to gall' – but also the transformation achieved by beautiful women: 'Us she informed, but transubstantiates you'.

And then there was the transformation of himself: from failure and penury, to recognition within his lifetime as one of the finest minds of his age; one whose work, if allowed under your skin, can offer joy so violent it kicks the metal out of your knees, and sorrow large enough to eat you. Because amid all Donne's reinventions, there was a constant running through his life and work: he remained steadfast in his belief that we, humans, are at once a catastrophe and a miracle.

There are few writers of his time who faced greater horror. Donne's family history was one of blood and fire; a great-uncle was arrested in an anti-Catholic raid and executed: another was locked inside the Tower of London, where as a small schoolboy Donne visited him, venturing fearfully in among the men convicted to death. As a student, a young priest whom his brother had tried to shelter was captured, hanged, drawn and quartered. His brother was taken by the priest hunters at the same time, tortured and locked in a plague-ridden jail. At sea, Donne watched in horror and fascination as dozens of sailors burned to death. He married a young woman, Anne More, clandestine and hurried by love, and as a result found himself thrown in prison, spending dismayed ice-cold winter months first in a disease-ridden cell and then under house arrest. Once married, they were often poor, and at the mercy of richer friends and relations; he knew what it was to be jealous and thwarted and bitter. He was racked, over and over again, by life-threatening illnesses, with dozens of bouts of fever, aching throat, vomiting; at least three times it was believed he was dying. He lost, over the course of his life, six children: Francis at seven, Lucy at nineteen, Mary at three, an unnamed stillborn baby, Nicholas as an infant, another stillborn child. He lost Anne, at the age of thirty-three, her body destroyed by bearing twelve children. He thought often of sin, and miserable failure, and suicide. He believed us unique in our capacity to ruin ourselves: 'Nothing but man, of all envenomed things,/Doth work upon itself with inborn sting'. He was a man who walked so often in darkness that it became for him a daily commute.

But there are also few writers of his time who insisted so doggedly and determinedly on awe. His poetry is wildly delighted and captivated by the body – though broken, though doomed to decay – and by the ways in which thinking fast and hard were a sensual joy akin to sex. He kicked aside the Petrarchan traditions of idealised, sanitised desire: he joyfully brought the body to collide with the soul. He wrote: 'one might almost say her body thought.' In his sermons, he reckoned us a disaster, but the most spectacular disaster that has ever been. As he got older he grew richer, harsher, sterner and drier, yet he still asserted: 'it is too little to call Man a little world; except God, man is a diminutive to nothing. Man consists of more pieces, more parts, than the world doth, nay, than the world is.' He believed our minds could be forged into citadels against the world's chaos: he wrote in a verse letter, 'be thine own palace, or the world's thy jail.' Tap a human, he believed, and they ring with the sound of infinity.

Joy and squalor: both Donne's life and work tell that it is fundamentally impossible to have one without taking up the other. You could try, but you would be so coated in the unacknowledged fear of being forced to look, that what purchase could you get on the world? Donne saw, analysed, lived alongside, even saluted corruption and death. He was often hopeless, often despairing, and yet still he insisted at the very end: *it is an astonishment to be alive, and it behoves you to be astonished.*

¶

How much of Donne remains to us? Those who love Donne have no choice but to relish the challenge of piecing him together from a patchwork of what we do and do not know. He is there in his work, always; but there are moments in his life where we must work out from fragments and clues what it was that he was doing: there is a long gap in his childhood, another after university, more after his marriage, and in his later years he flickers in and out of sight. Time eats your paperwork, and it has eaten some of his. We have, for instance, not yet discovered any diaries, no books of household notes or accounts. There are no manuscript drafts of poems – we have only one English poem in his own handwriting – and so no evidence of him at work, building the verse from false starts and scratches. He burned all his friends' letters to him after they died; a letter was, for him, akin to an extension of the living person, and should not exist without its parent – so we have no gossipy to-and-fros in the letter archive.

But what remains is a miracle; because a colossal amount of Donne's work has been rescued from time's hunger, remarkable in the period for its variety and sweep.

There are two long prose treatises on religious questions,

one of which – an attack on the Jesuits called *Ignatius His Conclave* – is racy and explosive and delicious, and the other of which – an argument that Catholics must take the Oath of Allegiance to the King, called *Pseudo-Martyr* – is so dense it would be swifter to eat it than to read it. There are thirty-one pieces of half satirical, half serious prose writing called the Problems and Paradoxes: essays with stings in them, and the *Essays in Divinity*, which are hyper-learned disquisitions on various books of the Bible. There is *Biathanatos*, his treatise on suicide, an interrogation of sin and conscience. There are the *Devotions upon Emergent Occasions*, a collection of twenty-three meditations on humanity, written at breakneck speed during a near-fatal illness in the very teeth of what Donne believed was going to be his death. (Having published them within weeks of writing them, he went on to survive another eight years.) There are 160 sermons, dating from 1615 to 1631 – six of which were published during his lifetime, the rest collected by his son into three great luxurious folios after his death.

There are 230 letters, to his friends, patrons and employers, the majority of which were also collected and published posthumously by his son, John Donne junior. John junior had a bad habit, when editing the letters, of removing all dates and changing the names of the addressees to make his father's early acquaintance seem more high-flying and high-society, so dating and attributing them is an ongoing and gargantuan task. Anyone turning to the prose letters seeking disquisitions on politics or news of his love affairs would be disappointed; Donne lived under a state which both censored and spied on its citizens, and his letters are largely – though not solely – practicalities. Will you come for dinner? I am ill. Might you give me money? Can you find me work? (Or, more accurately, because a significant portion of the letters are outrageous pieces of flattery: you are so ravishingly exquisite, can you find me work?)

And there are the poems: about two hundred of them, totalling just over 9,100 lines. In among those lines are epithalamia – poems written to salute a marriage – and obsequies – poems written to mourn a death. There are satires, religious verse, and about forty verse letters, a tradition he loved; poems of anything from twelve to 130 lines, carrying news, musings on virtue and God, and declarations of how richly he treasures the friend to whom he is writing. The idea of writing letters in verse wasn't his own – Petrarch did it, and the tradition dates all the way back to Ovid, whose *Heroides* are imagined verse letters by the wronged heroines of Roman and Greek myths – but Donne seems to have used the form more than any other poet of his lifetime. There was something in the way a verse letter could elevate the details of the day-to-day and render it sharp-edged and memorable that he cherished. It appealed to the part of him that wanted his own brand of intense precision to suffuse everything he touched.

And then there is the work Donne is most famous for; the love poetry and the erotic verse. To call anyone the 'best' of anything is a brittle kind of game – but if you wanted to play it, Donne is the greatest writer of desire in the English language. He wrote about sex in a way that nobody ever has, before or since: he wrote sex as the great insistence on life, the salute, the bodily semaphore for the human living infinite. The word most used across his poetry, apart from 'and' and 'the', is 'love'.

This body of surviving work is enough, taken together, to make the case that Donne was one of the finest writers in English: that he belongs up alongside Shakespeare, and that to let him slowly fall out of the common consciousness would be as foolish as discarding a kidney or a lung. The work cuts through time to us: but his life also cannot be ignored – because the imagination that burns through his poetry was the same which attempted to manoeuvre through the snake pit of the Renaissance court. This book, then, hopes to do both: both to tell the story of his life, and to point to the places in his work where his words are at their most singular: where his words can be, for a modern reader, galvanic. His work still has the power to be transformative. This is both a biography of Donne and an act of evangelism.

§

You cannot claim a man is an alchemist and fail to lay out the gold. This, then, is an undated poem, probably written for Anne More, some time in his twenties, known as 'Love's Growth' –

I scarce believe my love to be so pure
As I had thought it was,
Because it doth endure
Vicissitude and season as the grass;
Methinks I lied all Winter, when I swore
My love was infinite, if Spring make't more.

But if this med'cine, love, which cures all sorrow
With more, not only be no quìntessence,
But mixed of all stuffs paining soul or sense,
And of the Sun his working vigour borrow,
Love's not so pure and abstract as they use
To say, which have no mistress but their Muse;
But, as all else being elemented too,
Love sometimes would contèmplate, sometimes do.

And yet not greater, but more eminent,
Love by the Spring is grown,
As in the firmament
Stars by the Sun are not enlarged but shown.
Gentle love-deeds, as blossoms on a bough,
From love's awakened root do bud out now.

If as in water stirred more circles be
Produced by one, love such additions take;
Those, like to many spheres, but one heaven make,
For they are all concentric unto thee;
And though each Spring do add to love new heat—

As princes do in times of action get
New taxes, and remit them not in peace—
No winter shall abate the spring's increase.

Read the opening stanza and all the oxygen in a five-mile radius rushes to greet you. It's a poem with gleeful tricks and puns in it. 'But if this med'cine, love, which cures all sorrow/With more' is a small, private gift for Anne More; no matter how many millions of other people have read it since, the poem was different for her. Donne baked time's accumulation and love's accumulation with it into the structure of the poem: twenty-four ten-syllable lines, plus four of six (equalling twenty-four): the hours in the day. Seven rhymes per stanza: the days in the week. Twenty-eight lines in the poem: the days in a lunar month, each day part of love's growth.

Love, he writes, is a mixture of elemental things: 'as all else being elemented too' – and so 'love sometimes would contemplate, sometimes do.' Donne is more daring than he sounds: the thirteenth-century theologian Thomas Aquinas's ideal was the 'Mixed Life', one of contemplation and action. Donne hijacks the Aquinian ideal for his own erotic purpose: the *do* is sex. It's the same impulse as in another poem, 'The Ecstasy', where bodies must join as well as minds, 'else a great prince in prison lies.' True sex, he insists, is soul played out in flesh.

'Love's Growth' hangs on the idea of apparently infinite love, made more – which, once you have read all that he wrote, is wholly unsurprising. John Donne was an infinity merchant; the word is everywhere in his work. More than infinity: super-infinity. A few years before his own death, Donne preached a funeral sermon for Magdalen Herbert, mother of the poet George Herbert, a woman who had been his patron and friend. Magdalen, he wrote, would 'dwell bodily with that righteousness, in these new heavens and new earth, for ever and ever and ever, and infinite and super-infinite forevers'. In a different sermon, he wrote of how we would one day be with God in 'an infinite, a super-infinite, an unimaginable space, millions of millions of unimaginable spaces in heaven'. He loved to coin formations with the *super-* prefix: super-edifications, super-exaltation, super-dying, super-universal, super-miraculous. It was part of his bid to invent a language that would reach beyond language, because infinite wasn't enough: both in heaven, but also here and now on earth, Donne wanted to know something larger than infinity. It was absurd, grandiloquent, courageous, hungry.

That version of Donne – excessive, hungry, longing – is everywhere in the love poetry. Sometimes it was worn lightly: who has yet written about nudity with more glee, more jokes? In 'To His Mistress Going to Bed', written in his twenties, the speaker attempts to coax his lover out of her clothes:

Full nakedness! All joys are due to thee:
As souls unbodied, bodies unclothed must be
To taste whole joys.

The poem could be seen as one of domineering mascu-linity, except that at the end of it there's a joke: only the man stands naked. 'To teach thee, I am naked first; why then/ What need'st thou have more cov'ring than a man?'

Then there is the wilder, defiantly odd Donne, typified by the poem for which most people know him, 'The Flea'. The speaker watches a flea crawl over the body of the woman he desires:

Mark but this flea, and mark in this
How little that which thou deny'st me is;
Me it sucked first, and now sucks thee,
And in this flea, our two bloods mingled be.

When the poem was first printed in 1633, the typogra-phers used the 'long s', a letter that looks almost identical to an f, for the words 'sucked' and 'suck': which offers readers of the third line another, more extravagant rendering.

In 'Love's Progress', he summons up the outlandish edge of sex. He describes a woman's mouth:

There in a creek, where chosen pearls do swell,
The remora, her cleaving tongue doth dwell.

The remora is a sucking fish; it was supposed, according to Pliny the Elder, to have the ability to haul ships to a stop in the ocean. Not many women dream of having their tongues compared to semi-mythical sea creatures – but, as with his flea, it's his way of embodying the strangenesses of human fleshy desire. He allows himself to end on a major chord, a switch to bawdy lusting:

Rich Nature in women wisely made
Two purses, and their mouths aversely laid:
They, then, which to the lower tribute owe,
That way which that exchequer looks must go;
He which doth not, his error is as great
As who by clyster gives the stomach meat.

Donne seems to deserve the questionable recognition of being the first to so use 'purse' for female genitalia. The 'exchequer' implies that those who travel down the body must pay a tax: and ejaculate is the fitting tribute. (Men were believed to need a huge amount of blood to form sperm within the body: a ratio of 40:1.) A 'clyster' is an enema tube which was used to carry nutrients to the body via the rectum. The argument – that those who don't consummate love are as mad and upside-down as those who try to nourish the body via the anus – has teeming desire in it, but very much resists the tradition of Petrarchan flowers. It refuses to be pretty, because sex is not and because Donne does not, in his love poetry, insist on sweetness: he does not play the 'my lady is a perfect dove' game beloved by those who came before him. What good is perfection to humans? It's a dead thing. The urgent, the bold, the witty, the sharp: all better than perfection.

There is the meat and madness of sex in his work – but, more: Donne's poetry believed in finding eternity through the human body of one other person. It is for him akin to sacrament. *Sacramentum* is the translation in the Latin Bible for the Greek word for mystery: and Donne knew it when he wrote, 'We die and rise the same, and prove/Mysterious by this love.' He knew awe: 'All measure, and all language, I should pass/Should I tell what a miracle she was.' And in 'The Ecstasy', love is both a mystery and its solution. He needed to invent a word, 'unperplex', to explain:

'This ecstasy doth unperplex,'
We said, 'and tell us what we love . . .'

But as all several souls contain
Mixture of things, they know not what,
Love these mixed souls doth mix again,
And makes both one, each this and that.

'Each this and that': his work suggests that we might voyage beyond the blunt realities of male and female. In 'The Undertaking', probably written around the time he met Anne, the body can take you to a grand merging:

If, as I have, you also do
Virtue attired in woman see,
And dare love that, and say so too,
And forget the 'he' and 'she' . . .

His poetry sliced through the gender binary and left it gasping on the floor. It's in 'The Relic', too: 'diff'rence of sex no more we knew/Than our guardian angels do' – for angels were believed to have no need of gender. He offered the possibility of sex as transformation: and we are more tempted to believe him when he says it, because he is the same man who acknowledges, elsewhere, feverishness, disappointment and spite in love. He is sharp, funny, mean, flippant and deadly serious. He shows us that poetry is the thing – perhaps the only thing – that can hold love in words long enough to look honestly at it. *Look: love.*

¶

He took his galvanising imagination and brought it to bear on everything he wrote: his sermons, his meditations, his religious verse. In the twenty-first century, Donne's imagination offers us a form of body armour. His work is protection against the slipshod and the half-baked, against anti-intellectualism, against those who try to sell you their money-ridden vision of sex and love. He is protection against those who would tell you to narrow yourself, to follow fashion in your mode of thought. It's not that he was a rebel: it is that he was a pure original. They do us a service, the true uncompromising originals: they show us what is possible.

To tell the story of Donne's life is to ask a question: how did he, possessed of a strange and labyrinthical mind, navigate the corresponding social and political labyrinths of

Renaissance England? What did his imagination look like when he was young, and how was it battered and burnished as he grew older? Did it protect him from sorrow and fury and resentment? (To spoil the suspense: it did not.) Did it allow him to write out the human problem in a way that we, following on four hundred years later, can still find urgent truth in? This book argues that it did. 'Dark texts', he wrote to a friend, 'need notes' – and it is possible to see his whole body of work as offering us a note on ourselves. This book aims to lay out that note as clearly as possible: how John Donne saw us with such clarity, and how he set down what he knew with such precision and flair that we can seize hold of it, and carry it with us. He knew about dread, and it is therefore that we can trust him when he tells us of its opposite, of ravishments and of love.

THE PRODIGIOUS CHILD

In one way, and one way only, it was an auspicious beginning: John Donne was born on Bread Street in central London, from one end of which you have a clear and easy view of St Paul's Cathedral. He was born in sight of both his future job and his final resting place, which must be rare. In every other way, it was a hard time to come into the world. It was 1572 – month unknown – and a Catholic plot to assassinate Queen Elizabeth I had just been foiled. The Duke of Norfolk was executed for treasonous Popish machinating, and it was a bad year in which to be an English Catholic.

Donne's mother, Elizabeth Heywood, was the great-niece of the Catholic martyr Thomas More. She sounds to have been formidable, unafraid to assert herself: a woman of whom it was whispered (erroneously) that she carried the head of Thomas More in her luggage when she travelled. Donne's father, also John Donne, was an ironmonger, though not of the horny-handed, rugged variety; he was warden of the Ironmongers' Company. The family had once owned magnificent estates, before they had been confiscated by the Crown in the various Tudor shake-downs of Catholic landowners. He married, in Elizabeth, the daughter of a musician and epigrammatist who had played for Henry

VIII; so Donne was born into a family who had known the smell and touch of a king.

What was his childhood? When London burned in 1666, a colossal chunk of history burned with it; the house in which Donne was born was reduced to cinders, along with 13,200 other homes; the cathedral he would later preach in, and eighty-seven parish churches; and, too, catastrophic amounts of paper across the city, carrying records of the details of thousands of ordinary lives. Whole libraries' worth of paper: accounts, disputes, wills, play texts and poems, postmasters' trunks, bills, love letters folded so intricately into paper locks that you couldn't open them without leaving a telltale tear; all gone. Time and fire together have laid waste to so much of the paper that might have told us about Donne. The names and lives of his siblings, for instance, are blurry; there were at least two before him, Elizabeth and Anne, then John, and after him Henry and then we aren't so sure. But to fill the gaps, we have the account written by Izaak Walton, Donne's friend and first biographer, and a man with a claim to have written the first literary biography in English.

Walton was a gentle, retiring kind of man. He was younger than Donne by two decades, and had been Donne's adoring parishioner in London. Best known in his lifetime as the author of *The Compleat Angler*, an ecstatic poetic celebration of fishing, he was at his most perceptive when talking about trout – but in taking time off fish to set out the facts of his friend's life, Walton created one of the most valuable resources we have. All Donne scholars must be profoundly grateful to him: but, equally, rarely has a man been so keen to make his subject appear a shining example to all humanity. Walton didn't subscribe to the sceptical school of biographer, who carry a pen in one hand and a knife in the other. He was eager from the very outset to reassure his readers about Donne's worth. 'Though [Donne's] own learning and other multiplied merits may justly appear sufficient to dignify both himself and his posterity; yet the reader may be pleased to know, that his father was masculinely and lineally descended from a very ancient family in Wales, where many of his name now live, that deserve, and have great reputation in that country.' Born high enough to merit some small awe, Walton wants us to know. (Donne's connection to the Welsh Dwns has never, in fact, been proven.)

Donne came of stock that valued literary flourishes. Donne's maternal grandfather John Heywood had his own line in ironical verse. In his *Play Called the Four PP*, the four Ps (a pardoner, a palmer, a 'pothecary and a pedlar) hold a competition to see who can speak the biggest lie. The palmer wins:

I have seen women five hundred thousand
Wives and widows, maids and married
And oft with them have long time tarried
Yet in all places where I have been
Of all the women that I have seen
I never saw nor knew, in my conscience
Any one woman out of patience.

22

Years later, Donne would write with exactly the same sceptical eyebrow:

If thou beest born to strange sights,
Things invisible to see,
Ride ten thousand days and nights,
Till age snow white hairs on thee:
Thou, when thou return'st, wilt tell me,
All strange wonders that befell thee,
  And swear,
  'Nowhere
Lives a woman true, and fair.'

Donne's family prized good jokes in extremis (and, evidently, casual sexism as a comic trope). His grandfather became famous for his deathbed comedy: his confessor, repeating over and over that 'the flesh is frail', to which Heywood: 'Marry, Father . . . it will go hard but you shall prove that God should a made me a fish.'

When Donne was four, his father died and his mother married again to a John Syminges, a physician who had been several times the President of the Royal College of Physicians. It might sound a gentle, upper-middle kind of upbringing: but to be born a Catholic was to live with a constant, low-level, background thrum of terror.

England had been so shot through with religious violence in the sixteenth century that there was ample evidence to cast either side as villain. Mary I, a Catholic, had burned at least three hundred Protestants, and now with Protestant Elizabeth on the throne a concerted effort was made to channel national ire at the Catholic minority. John Foxe's *Book of Martyrs* had been published in 1563, nine years before Donne's birth, and its frontispiece illustration served well to remind those in doubt of where the country stood: on one side Catholics with bulbous noses are seized by gleeful demons, while on the other Protestants with aquiline profiles burn in the fires of persecution and rise to glory.

It was in the spring of 1574, when Donne was a toddler, that disaster first came for the family. His mother's uncle Thomas Heywood was suddenly and without warning arrested. A house on Cow Lane, close to Donne's own home, was raided; officials discovered Thomas, a priest and former monk, along with 'divers Latin books, beads, images, palms, chalices, crosses, vestments, pyxes, paxes and such like'. (A pyx was the box used for wafers: a pax was a piece of engraved wood which was kissed by Catholics during the Peace. Before the invention of the pax the congregation used to kiss each other, until it was felt this was unreasonably intimate – and plaguey – for church.)

At the time, the penalty for being a Catholic priest was to be hanged, drawn and quartered – which meant being stretched, hung until almost dead, and then having the arms and legs severed from the body while crowds looked on. One Richard Simpson was caught by a priest hunter – not unlike a bounty hunter – in 1588, and was hanged, drawn and quartered in the company of two other men. A bystander

24

remarked that he 'suffered with great constancy, but did not evince such signs of joy and alacrity in meeting death as his two companions'. (This evokes Samuel Pepys's laconic note of 1660: 'I went out to Charing Cross to see Major General Harrison hanged, drawn, and quartered – which was done there – he looking as cheerful as any man could do in that condition.') It's unclear from the Privy Council records exactly what happened to Thomas – but tradition holds that he was executed as his family looked on.

The punishments of Catholics were designed to be as performative as they were cruel. In response, the loyalty of families like Donne's, necessarily driven underground, took on correspondingly strange and lurid shapes. The Thomas More tooth, and the head it came from, is a vivid example. After More's death, his head was put on a pike for several weeks at London Bridge; his formidable daughter, Margaret Roper, bribed the executioner, whose job it was to take down the heads and throw them into the Thames, to give it to her instead. She pickled it in spices; and when one of the teeth worked loose she gave it as a sacred relic to Jasper and Ellis Heywood, Donne's uncles, both of whom were Jesuits, a then-newish Catholic missionary order founded in 1540 by Ignatius of Loyola. There was a story that once, when the two uncles were going on separate journeys, unable to decide who got to take the tooth, it 'fell asunder and divided of it self'. Not just Catholic, then, but super-Catholic: the kind of Catholic which relishes the theatre and paraphernalia of martyrdom.

Sir Thomas More, after Hans Holbein the Younger

Donne would have been familiar with all the legends of More, the one-time Lord Chancellor of England: with his many works of hyper-learned prose, his asceticism (More liked to wear a grey goat's hair shirt next to his skin, now enshrined at Buckfast Abbey) and his insistence on educating

26

his daughters to almost unheard-of levels of female erudition. His mother's proud Catholicism meant he would have heard from his cradle about More's steadfast refusal to acknowledge Henry VIII as supreme head of the Church of England, and about his subsequent death by beheading. More's wit was inexhaustible, uncompromising, and with him to the very last breath: 'I pray you,' he was supposed to have said to the executioner as he mounted the scaffold, 'master Lieutenant, see me safe up, and for my coming down let me shift for myself.' And, once settled: 'Pluck up thy spirits, man, and be not afraid to do thine office; my neck is very short; take heed therefore thou strike not awry.' The Undersheriff of London wrote: 'I cannot tell whether I should call him a foolish wiseman, or a wise foolishman.' Donne grew up knowing you were supposed to meet death with a flourish: he never forgot it, right to the very end.

Elizabeth I had hoped to let Catholicism fade quietly away, starved to death without a public institution; but in 1570, two years before Donne's birth, a papal bull excommunicated her, calling her 'the pretended Queen of England', 'the servant of crime'. In response the English government's attitudes to the Catholic population became more anxious, more repressive, more bloody. But Catholics with living memory of Mary I were unlikely to forget that if the fate of a religion could wane, it could also wax. Donne was taken by the adults around him to witness the blood and suffering of his religion. Much later, he wrote that in the past he had seen executions of Catholic priests, and around their bodies 'some bystanders, leaving all old Saints, pray to him whose body lay there dead; as if he had more respect, and better access in heaven.' It's likely that his Catholic tutors would have shepherded him to the deaths, to show him the brutality of the world and the possibility of rising through it to the heavens; a front-row view of a dark and scarring kind of theatre.

Donne was once taken right into the heart of the fear, inside the Tower of London to visit his uncle Jasper. Jasper, another man whom Donne was brought up to honour, was an unexpected candidate for the wild adventure that his life became. His early education had taken place in the royal court, alongside Princess Elizabeth – the most useful connection of his life, and one that would save it. He should, really, have been a scholar with a quiet, paper-bound life, chewing on swan-feather quills (Elizabeth's preferred writing pen: popular at court) and disputing the finer points of religious heresy. He had been made a Fellow of All Souls College, home of the incurably bookish, where he produced three translations of plays by Seneca. But he had to leave Oxford, unable to negotiate the ever more stringent reforms against Catholics, and became a Jesuit priest. He felt the strain of it: he suffered night terrors and underwent an unsuccessful exorcism. For all that, he did not lack bravery: he attempted to convert some of the country's most powerful earls (the 'big fish', he said) to Catholicism, and in doing so caused a scandal so loud he had to make a break for France. He was almost in sight of Dieppe when a storm blew his boat, drenched and battered, all the way back to England. He was arrested, tried, indicted for treason and locked in the Tower of London.

It was there that his sister Elizabeth, Donne's mother, came to minister to him, and to secretly carry messages between Jasper and another Jesuit, William Weston. If caught, Elizabeth would not have been safe from punishment by virtue of her sex: in 1592 a Mrs Ward was hanged, drawn and quartered for helping a Catholic priest to escape his pursuers in a box; a Mrs Lynne was put to death for harbouring a priest in her home. Once, Weston disguised himself in other clothes and came with Elizabeth into the Tower, an act of astonishing bravery or stupidity or both, to go into arms' reach of the jailers. Weston was terrified: 'I accompanied her to the Tower, but with a feeling of great trepidation as I saw the vast battlements, and was led by the warder past the gates with their iron fastenings, which were closed behind me.' Donne, aged twelve or thereabouts, accompanied them, perhaps as a way of making the party seem innocent and familial; he wrote, later, that he was once at 'a Consultation of Jesuits in the Tower, in the late Queen's time'. Heywood petitioned his one-time playmate the Queen for leniency. She granted it: he was deported to France, and from there to Rome, never returning to the country of his birth, where they were so liable to cut him into four.

Self-bifurcating molars and state-endorsed torture: these were the things of Donne's early years. It was a darkly particular way to grow up; not only the terror and injustice, but the *strangeness* of it: how unhinged the world must feel, that you are persecuted for professing that which you believe to be the most powerful possible truth. Not 'strange' as in 'unfamiliar', for being killed for your religion was hardly new; strange as in unmoored from all sense, reason, sanity.

John Donne's mother almost certainly did not, in truth, carry Thomas More's head in her accoutrements: Margaret Roper had it until she died in 1544, when she left it to her husband, who was buried with it: it's unlikely that he would have loaned it out like a library book. But Donne's internal baggage was piled high with skulls: with persecuted family members, with the wounds of his mother and uncles. He felt his family had been tried beyond almost any other: 'I have been ever kept awake in a meditation of martyrdom, by being derived from such a stock and race, as, I believe, no family (which is not of far larger extent, and greater branches) hath endured and suffered more in their persons and fortunes, for obeying the teachers of the Roman doctrine, than it hath done.'

His family would haunt him for life: and nothing in his writing gives the impression he was surprised that it should be so. We are haunted animals: ghosts, Donne's work and life suggest, should be treated as the norm. He accepted it as such. To read him is to know that we cannot ever expect to shake off our family: only to pick up the skull, the tooth, and walk on.

THE HUNGRY SCHOLAR

Donne worked on words his entire life. It was a time in which prodigal talent among the young was common – his near contemporary, the poet Katherine Philips, claimed to have 'read the Bible thorough before she was full four years old', and his biographer Izaak Walton calls Donne 'another Picus Mirandula' – the Italian philosopher and child prodigy who was made a protonotary by the Pope at the age of ten (a protonotary was the highest grade of monsignor, entitling him to wear a lot of purple velvet). Even reckoning that Walton is beamish and over-saucing with his praise (and that Pico della Mirandola was murdered at the age of thirty-one by arsenic poisoning, and thereby provides a sad ideal), Donne was born hungry, a lifelong strainer after words and ideas. He sought to create for himself a form of language that would meet the requirements of someone who watched the world with careful and sceptical eyes.

Donne was not sent to school. He was missing very little; the schools of sixteenth- and seventeenth-century England were grim, ice cold metaphorically and literally. Eton's dormitory was full of rats; at many of the public schools at the time, the boys burned the furniture to keep warm, threw each other around in their blankets, broke each other's ribs and occasionally heads. The Merchant Taylors' school had in its rules the stipulation, 'unto their urine the scholars shall go to the places appointed them in the lane or street without the court', which, assuming the interdiction was necessary for a reason, suggests the school would have smelled strongly of youthful pee. Because smoking was believed to keep the plague at bay, at Eton they were flogged for the crime of not smoking. Discipline could be murderous. It became necessary to enforce startling legal limits: 'when a schoolmaster, in correcting his scholar, happens to occasion his death, if in such correction he is so barbarous as to exceed all bounds of moderation, he is at least guilty of manslaughter; and if he makes use of an instrument improper for correction, as an iron bar or sword . . . he is guilty of murder.'

Instead, Donne was educated at home. Walton tells us that he learned fluent Latin – as would have been requisite, for a gentleman's son – though he makes no mention of Greek; Donne learned that later, under his own tutelage, with a tenacity that is characteristic of him. In 1584 he enrolled with his younger brother Henry at Hart Hall, Oxford University; their ages were given as eleven and ten respectively, although in fact they were both a year older. All students over sixteen were required to take an oath acknowledging royal supremacy over all questions of religion: but it was thought that a child under sixteen couldn't be expected to understand the nature of the oath, and therefore the young brothers could live under the radar in Hart Hall, a place with a reputation for nurturing and protecting Catholics. There was less burning in the quiet streets of Oxford than in London (at least since Archbishop Thomas Cranmer, condemned under Mary for refusing to acknowledge papal supremacy, had met a fiery death in 1556). There were more books in Oxford, more people his own age, less dying.

Both Oxford and Cambridge were, at the time, just edging into fashionability: until shortly before Donne arrived, both places had been looked at with sceptical eyes by anyone with claim to any class. In 1549, Oxford students were 'mean men's children set to school in hope to live upon hired learning'. It was only as the century wore on that more gentry started to pass through the doors – by the time Donne came to live there, it had started to have a little cachet. There were various attempts to give it more of a gleam: when the antiquary William Camden published the *Life of King Alfred* by the medieval monk Asser, he added notes of his own, putting into the mouth of the monastic the fake claim that the University of Oxford had been founded by Alfred the Great. And the city would have been very beautiful in 1584, yellow-stoned and with the River Isis nearby. Its spires soared less ecstatically skywards than today, as most of the colleges were not yet fully formed, and the great Bodleian Library did not open until 1602, but it was still a place worth loving.

Some students at Oxford worked formidably. Donne, according to Walton, was one of them: 'in the most unsettled days of his youth his bed was not able to detain him beyond the hour of four in the morning.' If this is true, he was not wildly unusual. In 1550, a student at Christ Church sketched out his day: from 6 to 7 a.m., he studied Aristotle's *Politics*; then Roman law; then further study, dinner at 11 a.m., then studying some Cicero, then from 1 to 3 p.m. 'I exercise my pen, chiefly in writing letters, wherein as far as possible I imitate Cicero', then civil law, 'which I read aloud so as to commit them to memory'; then after supper, 'walking up and down some part of the college, we exercise ourselves in dialectical questions'. Others, almost certainly, were less impressively dedicated. Among the treasures of unstudied manuscripts in Britain's university archives, there is one from the early seventeenth century which pokes fun at the idea of hard work:

The Oxford Scholar

As I was riding on a day
One chanced to ask me by the way
How Oxford scholars pass their time
And thus I answered all in rhyme

Item for Homer poor blind poet
Oh, if our tutors did but know it
For old tobacco we make free
Till smoke makes us as blind as he.

Donne was unlikely to have been lonely. He had Henry, his familiar companion, to bicker with and protect. They had a well-off aunt, a Mrs Dawson, whose husband Robert kept the Blue Boar Inn, on the corner of what is now Blue Boar Street and St Aldate's. The Dawsons would have welcomed the boys, Catholicism and all. They may have been Catholic themselves: certainly, they were known for having as their long-term guest one Mr Henslowe, 'once of New College and expelled out of that house for popery, who lieth now at the sign of the Blue Boar'. The boys' souls, and rapacious young stomachs, would both have been catered for.

And, soon, Donne had friends: he was a contemporary, though younger, of the poet John Hoskins, who was a rebel and a wit, and would have called to those corresponding rebellious parts in Donne. Hoskins was elected to the role of *terrae filius* ('son of the soil') – a role which allowed him to be the licensed jester at the university's ceremonies, making jokes against senior officials – which would have appealed to Donne's sceptical, satirical streak. Hoskins, though, took it too far – his more personal attacks on the university's grandees were badly received, and he was abruptly expelled from Oxford. There was Richard Baker, grandson of the first ever Chancellor of the Exchequer, who arrived at Hart Hall on the same day as the Donne brothers and who wrote approvingly that as Donne grew older he was 'not dissolute, but very neat; a great visitor of ladies, a great frequenter of plays'. Above all, it was here Donne met

Henry Wotton, Baker's roommate. With his fine blue eyes and aquiline nose, Wotton was to prove a true ally: a swift talker, a natural diplomat, a great introducer of men. He was to end up an ambassador, and it showed young. It was to Wotton that Donne wrote, 'Sir, more than kisses, letters mingle souls,/ for, thus friends absent speak.'

¶

During this time we know Donne was collecting his fascinations in a book: a collection of scraps and shards of knowledge known as a commonplace book. Its current whereabouts are mysterious: Donne gave it to his eldest son, who left it to Izaak Walton's son in his will, who left all his books and papers to Salisbury Cathedral. If it is ever found, it will cause great and joyful chaos among the Donne community. Because, simply, Donne wouldn't be Donne if he hadn't lived in a commonplacing era; it nurtured his collector's sensibility, hoarding images and authorities. He had a magpie mind obsessed with gathering. In his work, as Samuel Johnson said disapprovingly, you find the 'most heterogeneous ideas are yoked by violence together'. The practice of commonplacing – a way of seeking out and storing knowledge, so that you have multiple voices on a topic under a single heading – colours Donne's work; one thought reaches out to another, across the barriers of tradition, and ends up somewhere fresh and strange. It's telling that the first recorded use of the word 'commonplacer' in the *Oxford English Dictionary* is Donne's.

The commonplace book allowed readers to approach the world as a limitless resource; a kind of ever-ongoing harvesting. It was Erasmus, the Dutch scholar known as 'the prince of the humanists', who codified the practice. The compiler, he wrote, should 'make himself as full a list of place-headings as possible' to put at the top of each page: for instance, beauty, friendship, decorum, faith, hope, the vices and virtues. It was both a form of scholarship and, too, a way of reminding yourself of what, as you moved through the world, you were to look out for: a list of priorities, of sparks and spurs and personal obsessions. Donne's book must surely have had: angels, women, faith, stars, jealousy, gold, desire, dread, death. Then, Erasmus wrote

whatever you come across in any author, particularly if it is especially striking, you will be able to note it down in its appropriate place: be it a story or a fable or an example or a new occurrence or a pithy remark or a witty saying or any other clever form of words . . . Whenever occasion demands, you will have ready to hand a supply of material for spoken or written composition.

As always with any intellectual pursuit, there were those who were anxious about achieving the ideal commonplace book, and, as it always does, the market seized on a way to monetise that anxiety. It became possible to buy ready-prepared commonplace books with the quotations already filled in: years' worth of work achieved without lifting a quill. Buying a ready-made text meant that you avoided the potential pitfalls: for instance, of making a heading and then finding either too much or not enough to fit. Sir Robert Southwell (there are many famous Robert Southwells of the period: in this case, the President of the Royal Society rather than the saint who was disembowelled) had a commonplace book in which some headings were confidently set down and then left forever blank (*Academia* and *Tedium*), while others (*Authoritas* and *Error*, *Religio* and *Passio*) left him scribbling in increasingly tiny handwriting at the foot of the page, and scoring out other headings to make space. Crucially for Donne, though, the commonplace book wasn't designed to be used for the regurgitation of memorised gobbets: it was to offer the raw material for a combinatorial, plastic process.

The ideal commonplacer is half lawyer, building up evidence in the case for and against the world, and half treasure hunter; and that's what Donne's mind was in those early days. This is a poet who in one single poem could pass through references to Aristotelian logic and Ptolemaic astronomy, to Augustine's discussion of beauty, and Pliny's theory on poisonous snakes being harmless when dead.

T. S. Eliot, a man who had in common with Donne both poetic iconoclasm and good clothes, loved his writing. He said: 'When a poet's mind is perfectly equipped for its work, it is constantly amalgamating disparate experience,' whereas 'the ordinary man's experience is chaotic, irregular, fragmentary.' For Donne, apparently unrelated scraps from the world were always forming new wholes. Commonplacing was a way to assess material for those new connections: bricks made ready for the unruly palaces he would build.

Donne's heterogeneity, which so annoyed Johnson, wasn't a game: it was a form of discipline. Commonplacing plucks ideas out of their context and allows you to put them down against other, startling ones. So, with Donne, images burst from one category into another; when he writes in ribald, joking defence of sexual inconstancy, he compares women to foxes (fairly normal in the poetry of the day) and ruminants (not normal):

Foxes and goats, all beasts change when they please:
Shall women, more hot, wily, wild then these,
Be bound to one man?

Love is a fish: a 'tyran pike, our hearts the fry'. Birds are lassoed to justify infidelity: 'Are birds divorced, or are they chidden/If they leave their mate, or lie abroad a-night?' In 'The Ecstasy', love is cemented, a balm, concoction, mixture, allay: terms stolen from alchemy. The writing is itself a kind of alchemy: a mix of unlikely ingredients which spark into gold. Images clash up against each other, and the world looks, however briefly, new.

¶

After about three years at Oxford, Walton said, Donne took his magpie mind to Cambridge; and although no record of Donne being enrolled there for a degree exists, the records are so imperfect that it's very possible. Donne would have arrived at a time when poetic war was being waged by his seniors. The poet and pamphleteer Thomas Nashe (about five years older than Donne) and the Harvey brothers Richard and Gabriel (about two decades older) swaggered over the city, feuding on literary battlefields. The Harvey brothers wanted to shake up English literary traditions, to bring the laws of Latin hexameters to English verse; Nashe mocked them for it: '[Gabriel Harvey] goes twitching and hopping in our language like a man running upon quagmires, up the hill in one syllable, and down the dale in another.' Gabriel Harvey was also an inventor of words: 'jovial', 'notoriety', 'rascality'. So the idea that language might be bent into different shapes was all around Donne in that year, as well as the idea that poetry was something you might care enough to physically fight about. Poetry for those young men was more than a way to show off the brightest sparks of their wit, or a way to pass the evenings (though of course it was that too: the evenings were long, and you couldn't be drunk all the time). It was a way to challenge political and social convention under the careful shield of metaphor; if you were going to criticise, do it in verse. (Spenser's *Mother Hubberd's Tale* was well known to be a veiled attack on

Lord Burghley, the Lord High Treasurer.) And it was part of the great humanist project: it allowed you to step into a tradition of chroniclers and visionaries, celebrants and beauty merchants. Poetry mattered more, then, than at almost any other time since.

It's possible, though, that he didn't go to Cambridge at all: some biographers have had it that he left Oxford and made a bolt for Europe – because for all its hushed libraries and broad quads, Oxford was not safe for Donne. His uncle Jasper had been made aware, via his intricate networks of those in and out of the court, that the Privy Council had resolved to start rounding up selected students as young as twelve, and make them swear the Oath of Supremacy. Any who refused risked being taken from their parents and forced to become 'school hostages', educated under 'good schoolmasters'. That this hyper-cautious surveillance was spreading to such little children was, in part, Jasper's own fault. Jasper had been attempting to recruit scholars in their teens at Oxford and Cambridge and coax them into studying at continental seminaries. He shuttled twenty students from English universities to the English seminary at Rheims in 1582, and then another fifty in 1583. From there, some went to Rome, others to France where the Duke of Guise, a luxuriously coiffed nobleman with hair down to his fourth vertebra, was planning to recruit them into a military arm: so Elizabeth's anxiety about something being afoot at the universities was entirely well founded. Heywood was suspected of gathering ranks for a full-scale

'Enterprise' – an invasion of England. Donne must have been closely watched, lest he appear to be a young accomplice to his uncle's 'perpetual aqueducts' of young people being siphoned off across the water.

Jasper was not the only one making waves of Catholic obstinacy: Donne's mother was also courting trouble. Donne's stepfather had died suddenly, and Elizabeth soon remarried, this time to Richard Rainsford, 'gentleman, dwelling in Southwark' – but grief did not seem to have muted her. In 1589 'Mistress Symones Mr Doctor Symone's wife late deceased' was brought up before the parish and fined 'for not coming to church to receive the communion'. Possibly the news of the fine, or of the death, hastened his return – or perhaps he felt himself ready for the noise and scope of the capital – but when we next see Donne he is in London, in 1591. He chose to follow in the footsteps of his magic-toothed ancestor Thomas More by enrolling at the Inns of Court.

The four Inns of Court, established in the fourteenth and fifteenth centuries, remain to this day the starting point for every barrister in England, and many more for whom the bar is just a stepping stone; through their libraries and dining halls have passed Thomas Cromwell, Francis Bacon, William Pitt the Younger, Margaret Thatcher, hordes of bishops and archbishops, enough MPs to start a war. Donne went, very briefly, to Thavie's, a feeder institution for Lincoln's Inn, into which he was duly fed. Lincoln's Inn had glamour: it had housed Francis Walsingham, Elizabeth I's spymaster.

Original thought was possible there: it had tutored John Fortescue, the Lord Chief Justice under Henry VI, who was the first to argue the then-radical principle that 'one would much rather that twenty guilty persons should escape the punishment of death, than that one innocent person should be condemned'. But the twenty-year-old Donne did not go to the Inns intending to become a lawyer; he went to be among rich, sharp-witted young men who also did not intend to become lawyers.

The Inns of Court were close to the other, royal court, and it was expected that some of the graces and smoothness of the latter would transfer to the hopeful student at the former. When Donne arrived with his ghost of an adolescent moustache and his crucifix earring, Lincoln's Inn had a membership of around 150 – of those, less than a third would be called to the bar to practise law professionally. You went to the Inns to learn the ways of the world – particularly if you had money or were expected to come into some. The Chief Secretary for Ireland declared that the study of law 'concerns noblemen and gentlemen above others, as they have great estates, and great trusts in government; in which ignorance of the laws will not well set them off'. They learned the law in order to protect their land and large houses against it, and Donne learned alongside them.

Donne seems to have joyfully erupted out of the solemn hardships of his youth and into the delight and noise of London. Though not rich, he had come into a moderate fortune from his father; enough to eat and drink and dress well. The Inns were beautiful: at Lincoln's Inn there was green space all around him, planted with elm trees with 'fair walks' among them; and he was a fifteen-minute walk from Covent Garden, back when it was truly a garden, belonging to the Earl of Bedford. The Lincoln's Inn lands included a site called Coney Garth: conies were rabbits reared with a view to eating them; in 1572, the Inns of Court decreed that 'it shall be lawful from henceforth for any man to destroy the conies' in the garden, so Donne's legal studies would have been punctuated with the occasional sight of a man and a dog in pursuit of dinner.

Technically, no women were allowed in the Inns, except for the 'laundresses' who cleaned, and who had to be under the age of twelve or over forty in order to prevent romantic entanglements. (It's tempting to find this implication – that there is no such thing as a beautiful forty-one-year-old woman – a personally provoking one.) But in fact a certain amount of mayhem seems to have been expected; in 1560, at Lincoln's Inn, a man called Dilland was 'fined 13s 4d for having a woman at night in Nugent's chamber'. Meanwhile Nugent's 'chamber fellow', Talbot, was 'fined 40s for drawing his sword and hurting Nugent', and tempers ran high over academic debate: one young man was charged with hitting one of the Benchers, a Governor of the Inn, because said Bencher had 'found fault with his study of astronomy'.

Donne learned formidably, somehow: but he didn't want his friends to know it. He was so keen not to be seen by his

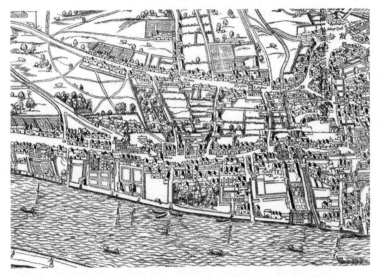

Lincoln's Inn, 1561: surrounded by fields and green spaces

peers as a future drudging middle-class man of law that he wrote to one friend, asking him to quash rumours that he intended to take the degree: 'For my purpose of proceeding in the profession of the law, so far as to a title you may be pleased to correct that imagination, wheresoever you find it.' He sounds like a boy self-conscious about his image: about his cutting the right kind of dash. Law was, he says, never more than 'my best entertainment, and pastime'; he was there for the pleasure of it. He excelled at the joyful business of frivolity: he was elected the Inn's Master of the Revels, in charge of putting on pageantry and wild parties for his fellow scholars, with raucous singing and drinking and dancing of the galliard, the finest fashion at the time. (The dance, which involved a series of enormous leaps and small hops, kicks and spins, was Elizabeth's favourite: she was said, even in her fifties, to dance 'six or seven galliards in a morning'.) But his later writing is so peppered with confident and accurate legal terminology that he must have either worked hard on the sly, or had a staggeringly retentive memory. The law's language and structures stuck with him all his life; near the end of it, he would make lawyer jokes from the pulpit: 'If any man will sue thee at law for thy coat, let him have thy cloak too . . . for if thy adversary have it not, thine advocate will.' (The pulpit Donne sounds very pleased, from where he stands, not to be a lawyer.)

The space in which Donne lived would have been small: he shared his bedroom, and probably the bed itself, with a friend, Christopher Brooke, but each had a tiny study of his own, little more than a cell, with a set of shelves for books, a stool and a table. During his time at the Inns, he began the writing of five long satirical poems, mocking with a young man's fury the corruptions of the Church, the bar, the court: and they give a good sense of what his life looked like. Satire I imagines a fellow student bursting in on him:

Away, thou changeling, motley humorist!
Leave me, and in this standing wooden chest,
Consorted with these few books, let me lie
In prison, and here be coffined when I die.

Here he reads: not just law, but philosophy, theology and poetry.

Here are God's conduits, grave divines; and here
Nature's secretary, the Philosopher;
And jolly statesmen, which teach how to tie
The sinews of a city's mystic body;
Here, gathering chroniclers, and by them stand
Giddy, fantastic poets of each land.

In comparison, the intruder, coming to lure him away, is an uncertain bet: 'Shall I leave all this constant company,/ And follow headlong, wild, uncertain thee?' In the poem, he does go, though: he heads out into the street, to seek out what the irresistible world has left out for them.

It was from that room, tiny as a 'standing wooden chest', that some of Donne's earliest poetry came. His earlier poems are often shot through with throwaway jokes, sallies against boredom which allowed him to show to his new-found friends that, though he might have less money and fewer acres than them, yet he had a faster wit. The voice is more conventional than the later verse would be, but even in the early work there is that same presence, bold and ornery and intricate, that we find later. There was already, in those early poems, the impression he was laying down what he knew about the world in the form that would be most memorable, and would seize hold of the reader most tenaciously and irreversibly.

It was a time in which blandishments were the fashion: many of the early poems are elaborate compliments to members of his coterie. He writes to Thomas Woodward, the younger brother of his friend Rowland whom he probably met through his beloved Wotton, to say how much he envies Thomas's talent in verse. It takes a lot of saying. 'All hail, sweet poet, more full of more strong fire,/Than hath or shall enkindle any spirit!' It deems all those souls unfortunate who fall into the not-Thomas-Woodward category: 'I', writes Donne, 'do thee envy;/O wouldst thou, by like reason, pity me!'

There's a joke in 'pity me'. Even in the early 1590s, Donne's verse was thought remarkable. The dramatist Ben Jonson, gossiping tipsily over dinner with the Scottish diarist William Drummond of Hawthornden, said that Donne had 'written all his best pieces ere he was 25', which would have been 1597. Donne knew that he had the seeds of something original – that what he was doing with the English language was fresh and different: in a sonnet to Samuel Brooke, his roommate Christopher's little brother, he writes, 'I sing not siren-like, to tempt, for I/Am harsh'. His voice was starting to take shape.

Donne sounded like nobody else. The majority of his fellow poets were obedient to forms and rhyme schemes inherited from the classical greats and from European traditions of courtly verse. Think of Walter Raleigh writing to Queen Elizabeth:

If love could find a quill
drawn from an angel's wing
or did the muses sing
that pretty wanton's will.

Many of Donne's readers who came after him have, for
this reason, disliked his work in the way you would dislike
a tooth in a basket of flowers. Samuel Taylor Coleridge, for
one: 'Donne, whose muse on dromedary trots,/Wreathe iron
pokers into true-love knots.' And John Dryden: 'Would not
Donne's satires, which abound with so much wit, appear
more charming if he had taken care of his words, and of his
numbers [i.e. his scansion]? . . . I may safely say it of this
present age, that if we were not so great wits as Donne, yet
certainly we are better poets.'

But for Donne, divergence from the accent and peculiar
breaks in form contain the very stamp of what he meant:
they were never aimless. The world was harsh and he needed
a harsh language.

Donne's five Satires are among the hardest to scan and
read aloud: deliberately so: they sound exclamatory, darting
from expostulation to fluency and back again, poetry that is
quick on its feet and angry at you. Donne opened his second
Satire with a joke about poets, and the way the desire to
write verse catches hold of you:

Though poetry indeed be such a sin,
As I think, that brings dearths and Spaniards in;

Though, like the pest'lence or old-fashioned love
It riddlingly catch men, and doth remove
Never till it be starved out; yet their state
Is poor, disarmed, like papists, not worth hate.

A hundred and thirty years later, the poet Alexander Pope read those lines and winced. Pope believed in the moral and aesthetic superiority of poetic balance and restraint: so much so that he took Donne's Satires and 'versified' them, so that they scanned and made what he thought was nice, proper sense. In his hands Donne's line, 'Sir, though (I thank God for it) I do hate/Perfectly all this town' becomes, 'Yes; thank my stars! As early as I knew/This Town, I had the sense to hate it too.' The spike of the 'hate/Perfectly' is gone.

Pope wasn't the only one: there was also Thomas Parnell, an Anglo-Irish contemporary of Pope's, a man unafraid to rhyme 'love' and 'dove'. He was inspired by his friend's lead; he chose Donne's Satire III, an attack on all authority, a furious bark of a poem which orders us to 'doubt wisely'. Donne's eye took in the sweep of the world's corruption, and began:

Kind pity chokes my spleen; brave scorn forbids
These tears to issue which swell my eyelids;
I must not laugh nor weep sins and be wise;
Can railing, then, cure these worn maladies?

50

Parnell mangled it: 'Compassion checks my spleen, yet Scorn denies/The tears a passage thro' my swelling eyes.' But 'compassion' and 'kind pity' aren't the same thing, at all. Donne was perfectly capable of using the word compassion – a swift count turns up at least a dozen cases in the poetry alone – but meant exactly what he said: pity laced with kindness is still pity; harsh and generous at once, angular and vulnerable.

Parnell and Pope and their many allies were men who believed that art had rules: that poetry was a monovocal exercise; that there was one poetic voice, and we should stick to it. Years later, when Samuel Johnson compared Donne's 'false wit' with Pope's 'true wit', it wasn't a throwaway comment: it was real anxiety that Donne might be nigh-on insane. His work, for Johnson, was improper and ugly and broken – it was 'produced by a voluntary deviation from nature in pursuit of something new or strange'.

But that was exactly it. Donne did not want to sound like other poets. Human experience exceeds our capacity to either explain or express it: Donne knew it, and so he invented new words and new forms to try. He created new rhythms in poetry: Jonson said that Donne, 'for not keeping of accent, deserved hanging'. He was an inventor of words, a neologismist. He accounts for the first recorded use in the *Oxford English Dictionary* of around 340 words in the English language. Apprehensible, beauteousness, bystander, criminalist, emancipation, enripen, fecundate, horridness, imbrothelled, jig. (And, for those who bristle against the loose use of 'disinterested' to mean 'not interested' rather than 'lacking a vested interest': Donne was the first to do so, and we must take it up with him.)

He wanted to wear his wit like a knife in his shoe; he wanted it to flash out at unexpected moments. He is at his most scathing writing about originality, and those who would steal the ideas of better men:

> But he is worst who, beggarly, doth chaw [i.e. chew]
> Others' wits' fruits, and in his ravenous maw
> Rawly digested doth those things outspew
> As his own things . . .

Donne imagined his own words taken by another. He imagined them chewed up and expelled:

> And they're his own, 'tis true,
> For if one eat my meat, though it be known
> The meat was mine, the excrement's his own.

Why should we all sound the same? There are parts of us which can be expressed well in neatly rhyming couplets: there are 'love/dove' pockets in each human heart. But there are elements of each of us so particular, unwieldy, so without cliché, that it is necessary for each poet to invent his own language. It is necessary for us all to do so; owning one's own language is not an optional extra. The human soul is so ruthlessly original; the only way to express the distinctive pitch of one's own heart is for each of us to build our own way of using our voice. To read Donne is to be told: kill the desire to keep the accent and tone of the time. It is necessary to shake language until it will express our own distinctive hesitations, peculiarities, our own uncertain and never-quite-successful yearning towards beauty. Donne saves his most ruthless scorn for those who chew other wits' fruit, and shit out platitudes. Language, his poetry tells us, is a set, not of rules, but of possibilities.

ANNO DNI. 1591
ÆTATIS SVÆ 18

This was for youth, Strength, Mirth, and wit that Time
Most count their golden Age; but t'was not thine.
Thine was thy later yeares, so much refind
From youths Drosse, Mirth, & wit; as thy pure mind
Thought (like the Angels) nothing but the Praise
Of thy Creator, in those last, best Dayes.
  Witnes this Booke, (thy Embleme) which begins
  With Love; but endes, with Sighes, & Teares for sins.

Will: Marshall sculpsit.   IZ: WA:

Donne aged approximately eighteen

THE EXQUISITELY CLOTHED
THEORISER ON FASHION

It was as he enrolled in the Inns of Court that Donne sat for his first painting. The portrait itself, a painted miniature probably by Nicholas Hilliard, didn't survive, but there's an engraving of it, which was deemed sufficiently handsome and lifelike to be used on the frontispiece of his collected verse after his death. In it he looks very young, and every particular of his outfit, down to the buttons, was chosen with sharp-eyed care. Clothing in sixteenth-century England was carefully regulated – a 1597 proclamation had decreed that only earls and above could wear cloth of gold, while nobody ranking below a knight could parade town in the ostentatious silk stockings known as 'netherstocks'. In addition to those laws, the Inns of Court wielded against their students a litany of sumptuary regulations, to keep the men looking as serious externally as they were presumed to be internally. All gowns were to be 'of a sad colour', and there was a formidable list of forbidden accessories and styles, including ruffs, hats, boots, spurs, swords, daggers, long hair, beards, and 'foreign fashions' generally; overall, the Inns' legislation stated that each student should ensure 'his apparel pretend no lightness, or wantonness in the wearer'.

The Donne in the 1591 engraving, in contrast, is wanton to the hilt; his hair almost reaches his shoulders, and he holds in his right hand a sword. It is the look of a man who revels in self-fashioning. He was beautiful: 'of stature moderately tall, of a strait and equally-proportioned body, to which all his words and actions gave an unexpressible addition of comeliness'. He was tall, dark, handsome, still new at the business of living.

It is possible to turn to the young Donne's work for a theory of fashion, for he understood that when we get dressed we ask something of the world. All clothes speak: they say *desire me*, or *oh ignore me*, or *endow my words with greater seriousness than you would were I not wearing this hat.* When he mocks the dress of his compatriots, he is mocking the shoddiness and lack of imagination of what they are asking for. And, he knew, the beautiful are rarely beautiful without effort. (The best-dressed people spend a secretly enormous amount of time thinking about line and shape and cloth, and imagining themselves into three dozen possible outfits before they put on their trousers.) Donne's appearance must have taken a lot of thought: it was another part of the theatricality of his work across his entire life. He understood that presentation, voice and look are not frivolities to be dismissed, but weapons to be harnessed.

The other painting of the young Donne – the one with the hat and moustache – was painted in about 1595 and is known as the Lothian portrait. (It's so named because it was in the collection of the Marquess of Lothian, mis-labelled until the 1950s as a portrait of John Duns Scotus.

Duns Scotus was a poet from the thirteenth century who, in portraits, looked as unlike Donne as it is possible to look and still be of the same species.) In both portraits, he wears a moustache so thin you could fit it under your fingernail – and it would be a mistake to assume that even the moustache came easily. Moustaches were at the time, like clothing, subject to surveillance, though by society rather than the state: Simion Grahame, a Scottish courtier, insisted in his *Anatomy of Humors* that a man should have 'his beard well brushed and always his upper lip well curled . . . For if he chance to kiss a gentlewoman, some rebellious hairs may happen to startle in her nose and make her sneeze.' He adds an interdiction against 'snotty nosed gentlemen, with their drooping moustaches covering their mouth and becoming a harbour for meldrops . . . He will drink with anybody whatsoever, and after he hath washed his filthy beard in the cup . . . he will suck the hair so heartily with his under lip.' But Donne's moustache, particularly in the Lothian portrait, is exemplary. It is careful: the moustache of a man who understands that even facial hair has to it an element of performance. To see his moustache is to know: *almost nothing is easy.*

Performance, and the clothes that accompany it, remained an interest all Donne's life. From his youth, when he posed exuberantly for images, until his death, before which he demanded that he be sketched for his statuary dressed only in his winding-sheet, Donne knew this: that to get dressed is to make both a statement and a demand. There's no such thing as neutral clothing: to attempt neutrality is itself a statement of style. Donne's poetry suggests he watched the world, a critic of dress and haircuts and behaviour. His verse from his Inns of Court period laughs at those who get it wrong, and those who care too much about getting it right: he had the world in a double bind. In 'The Anagram', he stabs at the idea of fad-fashion: 'One like none and liked of none fittest were,/For, things in fashion every man will wear.' In 'The Perfume', a satire on love poetry, the courtier, attempting to hide from his mistress's father, attempts to quieten his ridiculous fashionable clothes: 'I taught my silks their whistling to forbear;/E'en my oppressed shoes dumb and speechless were'. Some of the looks at the time would truly have been startling: a fashion for melancholia led to flowing sleeves and open shirt-necks in portraiture, while women used pads and wires to make large heart-shaped frames of hair around their heads. King Christian of Denmark had a medical condition which made his hair matt, so he wore it cropped short, but with a single rat-tail that reached down to his nipple, threaded with a pearl. The look caught on, and soon London streets were dotted with men and some women wearing a single long strand of hair, dubbed a lovelock, over the left shoulder and down over the heart.

In his Satire I, Donne conjures an imaginary companion: a vain fellow student on the make, come to tear him from his studies. The fellow student, dressed in 'motley' (the costume of a jester), is fashionable before anything else: ready to leave if someone better dressed comes along. The speaker demands,

> First swear by thy best love in earnest
> (If thou which lov'st all, canst love any best)
> Thou wilt not leave me in the middle street
> Though some more spruce companion thou do meet . . .

Donne – or at any rate, the speaker of the Satire – imagines being abandoned for some naval captain, dressed in gold-plated armour, 'bright parcel-gilt with forty dead men's pay', or a 'brisk, perfumed, pert courtier'. Donne did not admire the kind of glamour his fellow students pretended to. Glamour for Donne is a kind of neediness; one cannot be glamorous sitting alone on one's own, glamour requires witnesses: and how far can something which exists only in the presence of others really exist at all? Donne's speakers in his Satires provide witness against their will, and rail against it. He raises both eyebrows at the always-changing fashions:

> And sooner may a gulling weather-spy
> By drawing forth heav'n's scheme tell certainly
> What fashioned hats or ruffs or suits next year
> Our supple-witted, antic youths will wear.

His ire is for those who, without the protective armour that is given by wit, are easily conned into seizing on the newest hat or ruff or suit as a form of progress. Do not,

Donne's poetry would argue, buy too readily into that which the world wants to sell you. Your outward presentation has unavoidable power, and so must be engaged in with the full force of your intelligence.

There was only one time when you could escape the language of clothes: one place in which the rich pleasures of velvet and lace were superseded. He wrote in 'The Undertaking' –

But he who loveliness within
Hath found, all outward loathes,
For he who colour loves and skin,
Loves but their oldest clothes.

Their oldest clothes: the skin they were born in. Clothes had a power and a thrill to them: but they were not as good as their absence.

BROTHER TO A DEAD MAN

Donne's pleasure in Lincoln's Inn – in teasing his fellow students, in testing the scope of his linguistic virtuosity – lasted roughly a year. It was shattered by a double bill of disaster: by persecution and by plague.

Unless you're currently living through one yourself – as the AIDS generation did, and as we have done with the coronavirus pandemic that began in 2020 – it's hard to truly believe in the plague. Petrarch knew it; he wrote in a letter to his brother during a plague epidemic in 1348, 'Oh happy people of the future, who have not known these miseries and perchance will class our testimony with the fables!' After so much time and so many jokes, the idea of plague becomes exactly that: a fable, or a punchline – something that happens to people far away from us, with fewer teeth and less intricate souls. We are now a generation who knows a small something of its horror and fear: but Donne lived through a plague with mortality rates at sixty per cent and higher. (Covid-19 has a global mortality rate of about three per cent. In 1603, there were 22,819 plague deaths in London in ten weeks. The population of the city was two hundred thousand: if you reckon the current population of London is about eight million, it would be the equivalent of 880,000 dead Londoners in less than three months.) If you fell ill, your house was boarded up with both patient and family inside for twenty days, and a paper reading 'Lord have mercy upon us' nailed to the door. The playwright Thomas Dekker wrote, 'What an unmatchable torment were it for a man to be barred up every night in a vast silent charnel-house! . . . Where all the pavements should, instead of green rushes, be strewed with blasted rosemary, withered hyacinths, fatal cypress and yew, thickly mingled with heaps of dead men's bones.' It was said that a man could 'dine with his friends and sup with his ancestors'. Dekker wrote of a man who 'felt a pricking in his arm . . . and upon this, plucking up his sleeve, he called to his wife to stay; there was no need to fetch him anything from the market; for see (quoth he) I am marked; and so showing God's Token, died a few minutes later.' The symptoms were as grim as they were swift: a racing pulse, pain in the back and stumbling was followed by agonising buboes – hard red swellings, plague sores, some cherry-size, some as large as an apple. Students who could afford it left London during the worst of it, making a dash for the countryside as cases rose in their part of the city; as far as we know, Donne, whose family were London-based, stayed. He would have seen plague rage through the schools and prisons, leaving hundreds dead and scarred, and then fall quiet again.

In 1593, cases began to grow exponentially: the theatres were closed. The bear-baiting was forced to shut, and the bears were allowed to rest easy. The brothels emptied. In the streets officials wielded three-foot-long marshal wands, to swat at people who weren't maintaining social distancing. William Shakespeare, who across the river was just beginning to make his name as a playwright, found his livelihood temporarily overturned, swiftly switched to poetry and wrote *Venus and Adonis*, an epic which abruptly made him famous at court. Donne's friend from the Inns of Court, Everard Guilpin, was a satirist whose raucous verse boasted about shunning love poetry – 'whimpring sonnets, puling elegies' – and it was to him that Donne wrote his lament for the city's swagger:

Now pleasure's dearth our city doth possess:
Our theatres are fill'd with emptiness;
As lank and thin is ev'ry street and way
As a woman delivered yesterday.

Many years later, during the outbreak of 1626, Donne preached a plague sermon which became famous for its brutality. It spares nothing. The days had an apocalyptic note to them: the ground in London was heaving with bodies, and rains occasionally brought corpses floating up to the surface of the soil. The graveyards became so full that graves had to be reopened to cram in more: 'in this lamentable calamity, the dead were buried, and thrown up again before they were resolved into dust, to make room for more.' Donne tells his audience that the ground they walk on is 'made of the bodies of Christians'. So many people have been buried and dug up again to be rearranged in tighter and tighter proximity that their bodies are in the air: 'every puff of wind within these walls, may blow the father into the son's eye, or the wife into her husband's, or his into hers, or both into their children's, or their children's into both.'

Donne was rare in that he faced the plague without offering explanation or excuse. It was as though it was only by facing it in detail, by fully delineating it, that he could stay upright. Most men offered rationalisations, the majority of which were moral rebukes: the plague, they roared, was condemnation for England's past ills, and particularly those of sordid, money-and-flesh-hungry London. One poet wrote:

Fair London that did late abound in bliss
and waste our Kingdom's great Metropolis . . .
The hand of Heaven (that only did protect thee)
thou hast provoked most justly to correct thee.

Donne rejected it: he would not blame those who died of plague. He refused to speculate. He said in his sermons that a plague could not 'give a reason how it did come'. It was 'not only incurable, uncontrollable, inexorable, but undisputable, unexaminable, unquestionable'. He laid out the scale of the tragedy like a shopkeeper lays out his wares: looked at it, turned it over and over, held it up to the light, but did not attempt the arrogance of hypothesising. He had an urgent, personal reason for his refusal to join in the clamorous condemnation of those who died of the disease; a reason which dated back to his Lincoln's Inn days.

¶

Donne had been at Lincoln's Inn for a year when his brother
Henry was arrested. Henry was John's junior by a year, and
had followed him after Oxford to Thavie's Inn. Given the
geography of the two Inns – Thavie's just on the edge of
Holborn Circus and Lincoln's Inn less than ten minutes
away on Chancery Lane – they would have lived a short
walk from each other: brothers who held each other close,
heart-wise and geographically.

In the spring of 1593, Henry took a young priest called
William Harrington into his chambers. He planned to hide
him from Elizabeth's priest hunters, and feed him and care
for him in secret. He was still barely more than a child, or
he would have seen the impossibility of it; Henry's fellow
scholars would have been all around, eating and working
and gossiping. How did he expect to get food to him? How
did he expect to wash Harrington's clothes, to dispose of his
waste, to keep friends away, to steer clear of the laundresses?
In May, without warning, Henry's chambers were raided.
A man called Richard Young – close friend of the famed
Richard Topcliffe, Elizabeth's chief enforcer and torturer
– hunted through his rooms and found Harrington inside.
Both William and Henry were arrested, but Harrington,
trained to withstand pain, at first steadfastly denied being
involved in the Catholic Church.

Henry betrayed him. He broke under questioning and
admitted that Harrington had 'said he was a priest, and did

shrive him'. Henry and Harrington were sent first to the Clink prison, and then to Newgate.

Newgate jail had been rebuilt in 1423 on a bequest from the famous Dick Whittington, Lord Mayor of London and hero, along with his cat, of many folk tales: but it had nothing of folk-tale sweetness to it. Built just inside the City of London, between Newgate Street and Old Bailey, it was notorious for its dirt and cruelty. By the time Henry was sent there, it was a grotesque place, cold and dark and humiliating. In 1500 and again in 1550, prison inspectors enquired into the conditions and issued a command that the prison be run lawfully: that it had to be told to do so was proof that it was not. Corruption and bribery were accepted as the norm; prisoners were kept in leg irons and forced to pay for their own board. The mayor himself would not set foot in it for fear of disease. The floor was said to crunch because of the carpet of lice, dead and alive. And the lice themselves could be deadly; in the city's Bill of Mortality one man has the cause of death listed as 'eaten of lice'.

It was from Newgate that Harrington was tried and found guilty of high treason, on 18 February 1594. He was subjected to the death of a traitor; he was 'drawn from Newgate to Tyborne; and there hanged, cut down alive, struggled with the hang-man, but was bowelled, and quartered'. It was recorded later that he had given 'proofs of unusual constancy and noble-mindedness in prison, at the bar, and on the scaffold'.

Henry never saw his friend leave Newgate for the scaffold. The plague was running untrammelled through the cells. A contemporary Catholic claimed that Henry was transported from the Clink to Newgate in a bid to murder him indirectly with the disease, before he could be tried; there isn't evidence to bear the rumour out, but it would have looked true to the terrified friends who saw him go in. More likely, he was moved out of institutional bloody-minded aggression: his parents lived near the Clink, in Southwark down by the river, and the commissioners for recusancy were told to move their prisoners away from any prison where they might 'have favour shown them': where relatives might have visited daily, brought food, fresh clothes, small gifts. It was explicit policy to be cruel.

Donne did not visit his brother in jail. He delayed a few days – perhaps he was afraid of the plague, or perhaps there was nobody who could tell him there was an urgency. He may not have known what was happening to the boy with whom he had gone, small and alone, to face the older, taller undergraduates of Oxford. Within days of arriving in Newgate, Henry was feverish, tortured by buboes. He died fast. He was nineteen years old.

§

Donne barely wrote about his brother's death in the letters that we have, but fever and corruption and plague got into his writing. There was the major outbreak in 1593 (more than ten thousand victims in London alone), followed by 1603 (23,045 London plague burials) and 1625, and smaller flare-ups in other years: from 1606 to 1610, plague was responsible for at least ten per cent of deaths a year. It became the constant hunter that stalked the city.

Donne was often ill in later life: his body was handsome but not strong. Henry's death must have made it more terrifying: to have lost his brother to plague would have made every one of Donne's own itches or coughs a terror. Later in life, Donne repeatedly fell ill with what's now thought to have been relapsing fever, a tick-borne infection which killed up to seventy per cent of those who contracted it. The symptoms were exactly those of the early stages of plague. Each time he felt it rise in him, there would be the question: was it the old familiar fever, or had Henry's contagion come for him?

There's a kind of imaginative ferocity to Donne's writing about death, after Henry, and it grows over time, as he loses more and more of the people he loves and their ghosts pile up around him. He becomes a pedlar of the grotesque, a forensic scholar of the entropy of the body. The word 'decay' appears a dozen times in his verse, and that Old Norse, *rot*, is scattered through his work: of an imagined love rival, he writes, 'in early and long scarceness may he rot'; in an elegy he demands of us, 'think that thy body rots'. He wrote, of death: 'Now wantonly he spoils, and eats us not,/But breaks off friends, and lets us piecemeal rot.' He invited those around him to a fleshy thought experiment: to imagine yourself as daily mouldering a little more, and see if it colours where you stand.

The body is, in its essentials, a very, very slow one-man horror show: a slowly decaying piece of meatish fallibility in clothes, over the sensations of which we have very little control. Donne looked at it, saw it, and did not blink. He walked straight at it: no explanation, justification, no cheerful sallies. There was just the clear-eyed acknowledgement of the precise anatomy and scale, the look and feel, the reality of ruin.

It was his superpower, that unflinching quality. It allowed him clarity of vision. He would, throughout his life, write to the very brink of his terror: 'I have a sin of fear, that when I've spun/My last thread, I shall perish on the shore.' But the same clarity would also allow him a fierce intensity with which to imagine himself: 'I am a little world made cunningly/Of elements and an angelic sprite.'

THE CONVERT (PERHAPS)

How much blood is too much blood to bear? Between Thomas More's execution in 1535 and Henry's death in 1593, we can count eleven members of Donne's family who died in exile or in prison for their Catholicism. There was some majesty and glory, as with Thomas More, who ended by being canonised by the Catholic Church – but also plenty of humiliation and muddy uncertainties. Donne's grandfather John Heywood had been sentenced to death over a Catholic plot, and saved himself from death at the last moment when he read a public recantation, which was then written up, extremely unflatteringly, in Foxe's *Book of Martyrs*. Donne attempts to jab back at him, much later, referring to 'the art of copying out within the compass of a penny all the truthful statements made to that end by John Foxe': a small and furious sally, not liable to wound Dr Foxe, he being dead.

Exactly when Donne turned from Catholicism to Protestantism is the central boxing ring of Donne studies: how, when and why the young man decided to turn away from the rituals and well-loved rites of his childhood. In 1593, at Henry's death, Donne was still Catholic, and when he married he was not. What happened in between? It is possible that he licked a finger and held it to the political wind, and saw that no man could advance while remaining a Catholic: it's possible there was never a change of heart, only of expedience. But if the conversion was real, there was probably no single burst of light or dark that caused it; like almost everything in our rusty-hinged, slow-moving world, it happened in pieces. There was the power of his ambition, and his understanding that promotion and success would not be compatible with open Catholicism, but there would also have been new books and new conversations, drinking with Protestants, flirtations with Protestants. There would have been the pull of other allegiances over denominational ones – to the monarch and to the idea of nationhood, which slowly took on the shape of national loyalism and led him towards the Church of England. His priorities shifted, realigned, took on new shapes. You, too, have experienced time.

And what happened to Henry must have been part of it. Donne wrote nothing that explicitly names his brother – in part because he wrote very little about any of his family. There are far more of his words to be found about eagles, dust, the suburb of Mitcham, and tax, than his own mother. But around the time of Henry's death, he wrote a verse letter to his friend Rowland Woodward, in which he confessed his heartbreak, though he never names the cause:

Grief which did drown me; and, half-quenched by it,
Are sàt'ric fires which urged me to have writ
In scorn of all.

In that lack of naming, you can hear the guilt that must have haunted him: he would have known that Henry was sheltering Harrington. It's been suggested Donne may even have helped shelter the man himself, although there's no evidence for it except the bond of closeness between the two brothers. The loss shaped him. It seemed to clarify his sense of the necessity of seizing control of your own self and own fate. He told a friend in a verse letter in the 1590s: 'be then thine own home, and in thyself dwell.'

There were rumours, at the time, that the Jesuits were in some way implicated in Henry's arrest. There were rifts between Jesuits and seminary priests – many Catholic priests saw the increasingly extreme positions of the Jesuits, who advocated various degrees of violence against the monarchy, from deposing to beheading, as over-much and ungodly. Harrington, the priest discovered in Henry's rooms, was one of those who had begun to feel doubts – he had written of his need to be 'answerable to my father's estate', which required loyalty to queen and country and the system into which he had been born – and when the priest hunters came crashing in through the door, whispers ran through London that Harrington had been betrayed because of his weakening stance.

It is very possible that Donne felt the Jesuits were in part to blame for the death of his brother. William Clark, a seminary priest, wrote that the Jesuits 'indirectly . . . cause Priests to be apprehended', which they did by spreading false rumours accusing the priests of being 'espialls' (spies

working against the Catholics), 'sometimes termed sedi-
tious', making them vulnerable within their own community. Clark singled out Harrington as one such: a man who
was driven by the Jesuits to be like a rat in a trap, unable
to access the usual channels for help, and putting all those
who supported him in danger. One of the most prominent
seminarists of the time, Christopher Bagshaw, wrote in
1601 about the Jesuits, seemingly with Harrington in mind:
'They do not indeed directly cause Priests to be apprehended, but indirectly. That is, having spread some reports
of them, whereby their good name is taken away . . . no
Catholic entertaineth them, and so consequently, they are
driven to poverty' – or, in Harrington's case, driven to ask
the help of a teenager who proved disastrously ill equipped
to provide it.

There's a poem, probably written this same year, 'The
Bracelet', which reads like a coded reference to Henry. It's
a poem about the loss of a mistress's gold chain, but the
despair in the poem is wildly disproportionate to the loss; it
is a 'bitter cost'. It's not that it's a straightforward metaphor
– Henry = chain – but the outsized dread makes a poem
that embodies loss. It's a veiled horror-poem. Donne issues
a curse on the finder of the chain: 'But oh, thou wretched
finder, whom I hate/So much that I almost pity thy state';
he leaves open the ghost of a possibility that 'finder' refers
to those who found the priest in Henry's rooms. And as the
speaker casts his gold 'angels' (gold coins: a pun with a lot of
space for interpretation) into the fire, to make another chain:

. . . such anguish, as her only son
The mother in the hungry grave doth lay,
Unto the fire these martyrs I betray.

It's a strange image – a poem about a piece of jewellery, ending on an image of a dead boy. It reads like a man forcing misery into the small space of a poem, which warps and stretches under the pressure. It reads like the work of a man with a broken heart, and nowhere to lay it down and rest.

THE (UNSUCCESSFUL)
ADVENTURER

Henry was dead, and the delight of London was dead too. By 1596, Donne was keen to get away: he was finished with the law, and with the life he had led.

At the same time, preparations for an expedition against Spain had begun. For several years, England had been in a watery conflict with its Papist enemy – Donne makes jokes about the two worst afflictions, 'dearths and Spaniards'. King Philip II of Spain had been husband to Mary I, making him *jure uxoris* ('by right of marriage') King of England, and English Protestants lived in constant fear that he might mount an attack on England and carry it off into the bosom of Rome. He had, in 1588, sent his Armada of 130 ships over the water in an attempt to overthrow Elizabeth; he was defeated by flaming English fireships laden with gunpowder, and by storms, but the English suspicion was that the passion for unthroning remained. As a result, any attempts to weaken the Spanish were seen as acts of valiant national devotion. The battle had been waged for the past years, not by armies, but by individuals: state-sponsored pirates. They were known as privateers, but it was absolutely piratical in nature: the Queen offered her subjects 'letters of reprisal', which would allow a ship's captain to loot any Spanish ships on the water, including the heavily laden trade vessels set for the Americas, and call it legal.

Now, in 1596, there were rumours that Philip was building another armada, to attempt the invasion again. In London, a pre-emptive counter-strike was being planned, to take as many ships and as much of their gold as could be seized: boats were being outfitted, men being gathered. The Earl of Essex, Robert Devereux, first cousin twice removed to the Queen and generally reckoned to be the most dashing man in England, was at the forefront of it, seeking men. His secretary was young Henry Wotton; he may have introduced his employer to his friend. Donne presented himself and offered his services as a sailor – and untrained and inexperienced though he was, they needed bodies to man the boats: he was accepted.

There's a manuscript which claims to contain 'A Journal of all the particularities that fell out in the voyage under the charge of the two Lord Generals, the Earl of Essex and the Lord Charles Howard, Lord High Admiral of England, and also the names of all the commanders and great officers with the captain and voluntary gentlemen that appertain to the army' – but alas the pages which should contain the list are blank, the compiler having had more initial enthusiasm for the task than follow-through, and so we don't know which ship he leapt aboard, so young and questing and ready for the sea.

In early June they set out, dressed in their finest clothes, silver and lace gleaming, cheered by crowds. Their weapons shone, and they were some of the best-equipped men to have departed England's docks for many years. George Carew, a captain, declared in pride that 'they are strong enough at sea to abide the proudest fleet that ever swam'. There was one brief hiccup, when the ships were blown straight back into the harbour at Plymouth the same day they sailed: but then they were on the high seas and truly away.

The first portion of the expedition was an admiral's dream; after just over two weeks, the English sailed in sight of Cadiz, where they launched a cannon attack on the Spanish ships in harbour. It was a great success, but the kind of success that was terrible to watch. Walter Raleigh wrote of the Spanish soldiers that, seeing their cause was lost, 'they all let slip and ran aground, tumbling into the sea heaps of soldiers so thick as if coals had been poured out of a sack, [from] many ports at once, some drowned, some sticking in the mud . . . many, half burnt, leapt into the water . . . if any man had a desire to see hell itself, it was there most lively figured.'

Donne wrote about the moment in his epigram '*Naue Arsa* (A Burnt Ship)', composed in the 1590s: one of the most blunt-edged of his poems, it's part lament, part fascination. It has a cruelty to it – there's pleasure in the wordplay, of men on a ship drowning in fire:

Out of a fired ship which by no way
But drowning could be rescued from the flame,
Some men leaped forth, and ever as they came
Near the foe's ships, did by their shot decay:

So all were lost which in the ship were found,
They in the sea being burnt, they in the burnt ship
    drowned.

It was here, though, that the expedition took a turn and went rogue. The British were supposed to send their own smaller ships into the harbour to capture the Spanish fleet. Instead, Essex, his blood high, went roaring ashore to sack the city and everyone followed. Cadiz fell that same day, 30 June, and the troops set about looting, taking forty-two hostages – among them the Mayor of Cadiz, several members of the council and a number of priests – for ransom. While they were busy sacking and pillaging, the Duke of Medina Sidonia ordered his own ships in the inner harbour be burned before the British could seize them. The English demanded 120,000 ducats for their hostages; when that was refused, they set fire to Cadiz and sailed home with the hostages in tow. The hostages were not freed until July 1603, when James I negotiated their return – but not before the mayor, Antonio Giron, was said to have reached English soil, lain down and died of grief. They, along with the burning soldiers, got the very worst of the enterprise.

Donne did not write about the sacking of the city; so much of war, he found, was in reality just waiting about, and he wasn't in the thick of the fighting. A contemporary wrote drily that his only achievement was 'to march into the market place with an armour on my back and a pike on my neck in an extreme hot day'.

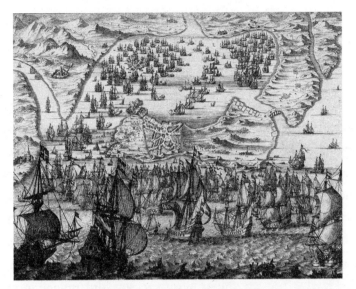

An etching of the Battle of Cadiz, 1596

The Storming of Cadiz

They arrived home to cheering crowds. It had technically been a financial failure – because they hadn't seized the Spanish ships, the Queen was able to recoup only £8,359 against her initial investment of £50,000. But it was a grand symbolic coup; it had been one of the worst Spanish defeats in the Anglo-Spanish war, a cause for bonfires and feasting. It was good enough that the Queen laid out plans for another attack, on Ferrol, where yet another fleet was being gathered by the Spanish; and Donne stepped forward to rejoin the crew. On 17 August 1597, after much waiting about in Plymouth, Donne was one of the sailors who again set out for Spain.

He did not go aboard with a straightforward heart. Nothing suggests he loved his time on the ocean, and there's an element of self-scorn in the poem 'The Calm', one of the rare poems we can easily match to a very specific moment and time in Donne's life. He wrote, of this voyage:

Whether a rotten state and hope of gain,
Or to disuse me from the queasy pain
Of being beloved and loving, or the thirst
Of honour or fair death out-pushed me first,
I lose my end: for here as well as I
A desperate may live and a coward die.

'Hope of gain' nods to his need, constant at the time, for money; and it is possible that there was a woman somewhere in it. War, after all, is a cure for love in Ovid.

The second expedition was, for Donne, hell. Almost immediately a violent storm broke out, and the fleet of more than a hundred ships was strewn across the ocean along the south coast. Raleigh remembered how 'we thought to yield ourself up to God, having no way to work that offered any hope.' Donne wrote, 'it rained more/than if the Sun had drunk the sea before': the sky spits out a sea's worth of water, and:

Some coffined in their cabins lie, equally
Grieved that they are not dead and yet must die.

A storm at sea, when boats were splintering and there was no possible hope of rescue until the water was calm again, was a terrifying thing. The seventeenth century produced several published collections of accounts of graphic disasters (our desire for in-depth reporting of plane crashes and our Hollywood films about ruined ocean liners are not new); one, titled 'Memorable accidents, and unheard of transactions containing an account of several strange events: as the deposing of tyrants, lamentable shipwrecks [and] dismal misfortunes', reports how the waves and noise and tearing of the ship together bring absolute certainty of death: 'It would be a hard task to represent the astonishment, terror and consternation that seized up on every heart on the ship. Nothing now was heard but cries sighs and groans: Some prostrate upon the deck implored the assistance of Heaven.' Some years later, another voyager,

William Hickey, would write of a storm, 'at this awful hour did it occur to me what I had somewhere read that death by shipwreck is the most terrible of deaths.' Donne would have known, in those hours, what the most terrible of deaths might look like.

In total chaos, they made it back to shore. Slowly, the ships were repaired. The sailors loitered about in the port, waiting to begin again, though some thought better of it, found horses and galloped home. A fellow sailor at the time noted with scorn that 'a great many of our young gentlemen (who seeing that the boisterous winds and merciless seas, had neither affinity with London delicacy, nor Court bravery) . . . secretly retired themselves home, forgetting either to bid their friends farewell, or to take leave of their General.' The smell of so many men and so little washing was awe-inspiring: a letter once ascribed to Donne, now doubted, ran, 'it is true that Jonas was in a whale's belly three days, but he came not voluntary as I did, nor was troubled with the stink of 150 land soldiers as we.' Donne was tougher than the boys who went riding home for warm fires and clean clothes, but he was undelighted by the way the days were going.

In late August the fleet prepared to set out again for Spain, but the crew was depleted, dirty and sick. Walter Raleigh's fleet, which almost certainly contained Donne, was separated from Essex's when the latter's ship started leaking, mid-sea. There were misleading reports of the position of the Spanish Armada, restless cruising in wrong directions;

and then, just before the two fleets were able to unite again, Raleigh's fleet hit a period of utter calm. 'We were very much becalmed for a day or two, and the weather extremely hot, insomuch as the wind could not bear the sails from the masts.' The finery of the ship became squalid; 'all our beauty and our trim decays.' Sailors hung their clothing from the masts and collapsed around the deck. Donne wrote: 'The fighting-place now seamen's rags supply,/And all the tackling is a frippery.'

The rest of the expedition was chaotic; the ships communicated largely by musket fire, and it's difficult to be specific with a musket. The Spanish fleet evaded the English. The English could find no viable way to attack it: they seized a few straggling ships, but failed to take several larger ones. They returned home, rocking and tipping through huge waves, to a royal reception as stormy as the weather. Nobody gathered at the dock to cheer. Sailors had foot-rot and suppurating wounds. Donne did not attempt the privateering life again.

¶

Perhaps, though, voyaging had got into his blood: or perhaps it was always there. His poetry, after his sally on the sea, is shot through with images of exploration, discovery, fresh territory: 'O my America! My new-found land!' New-found lands were at the forefront of the Renaissance mind; that, and maps of lands. Maps weren't neutral objects. On the one hand they could be weapons – and on the other, they could be something very like pornography. The first accurate map of England and Wales was surprisingly late, Christopher Saxton's Atlas of 1579. It was – perhaps – created in response to the potential threat of the Belgians. Mapping could be, if not an act of aggression in itself, then one that made aggression possible: in 1564, Flemish cartographer Gerard Mercator had created the *Britanniae* map, a beautiful engraving, as large as a child's bed, made up of eight great copper plates of the British Isles. In it, the outline of Wales's coastline is significantly improved compared to any maps that had gone before – the Bay of Cardigan appears for the very first time in cartographic history – and the shape of Scotland is so much more accurate that it remained the model for subsequent maps for a hundred years. Should Catholic forces choose to invade from Europe, the new map of the coast would be invaluable.

It was unthinkable that Europe should have a better record of the coast of the British Isles than the British Isles themselves, and so the Saxton Atlas was commissioned by the Secretary of State, Lord Burghley (the same Lord Burghley who persuaded Elizabeth to execute Mary Queen of Scots: not a man who was comfortable, strategically, with leaving things open to chance). The subsequent Atlas became a kind of talisman; a revelation of the land, when for the first time people were able to trace their own familiar rivers across paper; to know that their portion of the land had been counted. Donne would have seen one, and would have known how a map could stand for life and death. Years later, near the end of his life, he would imagine himself a paper-thin chart:

> Whilst my physicians by their love are grown
> Cosmographers, and I their map, who lie
> Flat on this bed.

And just as west and east, when the map is folded, meet and touch and become the same, so West, death, becomes the East, rebirth:

> As West and East
> In all flat maps (and I am one) are one;
> So death doth touch the Resurrection.

Before that, though – before he knew about pain and fever – there was for Donne the thrill of exploration. Maps could be the sexiest paperwork. In around 1330, the Lombardian Opicinus de Canistris was making an anthropomorphic map: a scribe in the papal office of the Apostolic Penitentiary, Opicinus drew maps in which landmasses took on eyes and fingers. Opicinus used maps to transform and unfix; in one map, Spain and Italy make the leg and head of a female figure, with Avignon, the French seat of the Pope, as the heart; Corsica and Sardinia are small turds, while the top of Africa is the head of its female interlocutor. Elsewhere, Venice is a vulva alongside a sea of sperm. In one plate the female country/woman speaks an inscription, almost impossible to read; it appears to say *'venite commiscemini nobiscum'*, 'come, copulate with me'. Donne knew the same thing: his verse insists, over and over, that we approach another body with the same awe with which we would step onto unknown earth. In 'The Good Morrow', from around 1602, he wrote it out, step-by-step instructions:

Let sea-discov'rers to new worlds have gone,
Let maps to others, worlds on worlds have shown,
Let us possess one world, each hath one, and is one.

THE INEXPERIENCED
EXPERT OF LOVE

Home from exploring, Donne was introduced to a man who would change his life for ever. One handshake, and the way was set to shift the whole course of his days.

(They probably didn't actually shake hands. The history of the handshake is contested: some say it dates from medieval Europe, where knights grasped each other's hands as a show that their sleeves were weaponless; others that it was part of a wider move away from the deferential hierarchical gestures of bowing and curtsying; others that it was introduced to the Tudor court by Sir Walter Raleigh, and it is for this, rather than for the potato which he absolutely did not discover, that he should be famous.)

One of the hopeful young sailors voyaging alongside Donne to the Azores was Thomas Egerton junior, a boy five years younger than Donne. They would have known each other by sight, at least, from Lincoln's Inn, that holding-pen of ambitious strivers. Thomas was himself undistinguished and barely formed, but he was the son of one of the most swiftly rising men in England. Born the Catholic illegitimate son of a minor squire, Thomas Egerton senior had risen to be a powerful lawyer, was prosecutor at the trial of Mary Queen of Scots, and, by the time Donne was introduced to him, was the Lord Keeper of the Great Seal.

Sir Thomas Egerton, 1st Viscount Brackley

The Lord Keeper was by definition one of the most influential men in the country: he sat atop the legal hierarchy of England. The holder of the post was said, in the Lord Keeper Act of 1562, to have 'like place, pre-eminence, jurisdiction, execution of laws, and all other customs . . . as the Lord Chancellor'. He was also very literally the person who had to keep the Great Seal safe, carrying it in an elaborately gold-beaded purse of the kind coveted by high school girls at prom. James II would, years later, destroy his own Great Seal while fleeing to France in 1688, supposedly casting it into the Thames in the hope it would bring government to a halt; such was the importance of the seal's role in law-making.

Donne saw in Egerton a glittering chance; for London life, for connection, for purpose, for promotion in the world. He wrote to him: 'I had a desire to be your Lordship's servant, by the favour which your good son's love to me obtained.' Egerton, Walton tells us, 'took him to be his chief Secretary, supposing and intending it to be an introduction to some more weighty employment in the State; for which, his Lordship did often protest, he thought him very fit'. (Walton is as ever inflating Donne's importance: it's very unlikely that Donne would have been Egerton's chief secretary, for Egerton had two other, far more experienced and senior men working in the same position. But it's true that he was propelled right into the middle of Egerton's life, and that the relationship between secretary and master was an intimate one, of daily closeness and confidences.)

Egerton's plan was to reform the country's legal procedures, which were in a state of such untrammelled complexity as to be incomprehensible even to the most educated lawyers. Donne, in Satire V, condemns those who 'adulterate law' and salutes Egerton's fight to 'know and weed out this enormous sin'.

The Lord Keeper was traditionally given York House for his home; a long stone pile with rear gardens opening directly onto the River Thames, from where you could leap on a boat over the water to the Globe Theatre. (These days, there are public gardens on the site, equal parts roses and cigarette butts, and nearby the Embankment tube.) Donne would have accompanied Egerton to the palace at Whitehall, where he worked: twenty-three acres and two thousand rooms, with the Privy Chamber at the very heart of it, where

York House, engraved after an original drawing by Wenceslaus Hollar

very few could enter in. 'The court' was not one single place; rather, it was a Pied Piper-like procession, in which the monarch would move between multiple palaces – from St James's Palace in London to Hampton Court, with its kitchen that could cook a thousand meals a day – and the entourage would follow: law-makers, advisers, allies, ladies in waiting, carriers of news, jesters, petitioners, hopefuls, poets. Donne would have been one of their number.

He became, in his spare time, a young man about town. There's little that remains to give us clues about his day-to-day life, but we know what kinds of entertainment the city had laid out waiting for him. Happily for a man whose verse is so peppered with animal imagery, the city was full of wild beasts. (He loved in particular 'nature's great masterpiece, an elephant/The only harmless great thing': one came to London in the 1620s.) A visiting Italian recorded how, at the Bankside, one could witness a monkey mounted upon a horse and chased by dogs around a ring: 'it is wonderful to see the horse galloping along, kicking up the ground and champing at the bit, with the monkey holding very tightly to the saddle, and crying out frequently when he is bitten by the dogs.' There was bear-baiting: one of Elizabeth's courtiers recorded how the bear would go after the dogs 'with biting, with clawing, with roaring, with tossing and tumbling', then turn to 'shake his ears twice or thrice with the blood and the slather hanging about his physiognomy'. At the Tower there was the menagerie, where you could pay to see lions so tame they kissed their keepers. Donne wrote enviously: 'Oh! Cannot we/As well as cocks and lions jocund be.'

'Nothing whereat to laugh my spleen espies/But bear-baitings or law-exercise.' – To Mr Everard Guilpin

And there were women. Lists were routinely published of the most famous and sought-after London prostitutes; one, *The Wand'ring Whore*, told of a woman, Priss Fotheringham, who would give performances known as 'chucking'. She would stand on her head, while men were encouraged to place coins in her 'commodity': 'Whereupon the sight thereof French dollars, Spanish pistols, English half-crowns are plentifully poured in . . . as she was showing tricks upon her head with naked buttocks and spread legs in a round ring.' Possibly Donne had a similar trick in mind when he wrote,

'Rich nature hath in women wisely made/Two purses, and their mouths aversely laid'; just as his work is coloured by London's plague, so too it has in it all the raucous colour and ribaldry of the city.

Donne was born into a moment in which sex was comedy and scandal, sacrosanct and commonplace: a time in which extramarital sex could be prosecuted by law, but where the law was transgressed so frequently that the consistory courts came to be known as 'bawdy courts'. Shakespeare's daughter Susanna appeared before one, bringing a furious slander case against a man who had claimed she 'had the running of the reins and had been naughty with Rafe Smith at John Palmer's'. Puritans denounced children cavorting around maypoles as frivolling in the presence of phallic symbols and 'stinking idols', but no sooner were you a boy born in the sixteenth century than the world began to plot for your sexual prowess. The French surgeon Jacques Guillemeau recorded the general belief that the length of umbilical cord left uncut on the male baby would determine the length of both his tongue and his penis.

The navel must be tied longer or shorter, according to the difference of the sex, allowing more measure to the males: because this length doth make their tongue, and privy members the longer, whereby they may both speak the plainer and be more serviceable to ladies . . . the gossips commonly say merrily to the midwife; if it be a boy, make him good measure; but if it be a wench, tie it short.

You barely tasted air before your midwife was vexing over you like a genital sommelier. On the female side – in refutation of those who believe that female pleasure was not considered until Clark Gable cracked his first half-smile – it was widely believed that female orgasm was necessary for conception.

Was, then, the young Donne a great tumultuous lover: a conqueror of swathes of women? After so much time and so much entropy, we can only guess: but, almost certainly, not. Women of his class would have been hard to seduce – they were fiercely and carefully protected. Make a mistake, they knew, and you could be punished for life. For instance: when beautiful eighteen-year-old Mary Fitton was sent in 1595 to wait on Queen Elizabeth, she found herself captivated by William Herbert, the Earl of Pembroke. She was reported 'proved with child, and the Earl of Pembroke being examined confesseth a fact but utterly renounceth all marriage'. Mary and the earl were both threatened with the Tower; in the end Herbert was thrown in the Fleet prison and Mary banished from court. She had two further illegitimate children with a naval officer, and then married twice over, but was never forgiven by her family. It would have been better, her mother wrote to Mary's sister, if she had died at birth: 'if it had pleased god when I did bear her that she and I had been buried [together], it had saved me a great deal of sorrow . . . Write no more to me of her.'

Of course, there were those who risked it – women who calculated their fertile moments, who practised coitus interruptus or gambled on prophylactic penis baths made of ginger and vinegar. Some women tried pessaries of blanched almonds inserted into the vagina; others used castoreum (from a beaver's secretions) mixed with ground lily roots and rue – all of which sound painful and extremely likely to provoke yeast infections. There were those, moreover, who were independent and established enough for it not to destroy them. The poet Lady Mary Wroth was one, who lost her drunkard of a husband to gangrene in her late twenties and went on to have two illegitimate children with her cousin – the very same William Herbert. But by and large, the risk wasn't worth the gain.

There were, too, the brothels lining the river; in the liberties of Whitefriars to the west, and along Petticoat Lane to the east, set among the taverns and alehouses of Billingsgate and in Ave Maria Alley – now office blocks – close by St Paul's Cathedral. But that came with its own dangers, and even high prices weren't a guarantee of safety; in the pamphlet *Look on Me London* (1613) 'the young novice payeth 40 shillings or better' – a huge amount – for 'a bottle or two of wine, the embracement of a painted strumpet and the French welcome': that is, syphilis. Syphilis was rife, and could only be treated with mercury rubbed on the skin, or eaten in chunks which could cause whole mouthfuls of teeth to drop out. At its worst, the disease caused disfigurement and nasal collapse, and artificial noses – some made of plated metal, some of ivory – were marketed to replace them. A twenty-one-year-old Donne wrote with scorn and disgust about men who paid for sex: those who 'in rank, itchy lust, desire and love/The nakedness and bareness to enjoy/Of thy plump, muddy whore'.

Woodcut, artist unknown, *An Elizabethan Whore House*

The idea that Donne's poetry would give you, of a beautiful young man cutting through swathes of London's finest female population, would have been difficult – though not impossible – to pull off. It's more likely that Donne had many flirtations and dalliances (he was, after all, 'a great visitor of ladies'), and occasional intimate brushes with women – but that he wrote the early swaggering erotic poetry for which he is so famous for a small coterie of male friends, Henry Wotton and Samuel Brooke among them. Donne's early lusting verse is part of an epistolary and literary merry-go-round in which poems changed hands over and over. Donne was almost certainly an exhausted over-sexed lover in the imagination only, but he caught that voice of the libertine and exploded it, made it his own. There's a lot of poetry, from around this period, in which Donne gleefully takes on the pose of the rake. If you are looking for a masterclass in how to look and sound like a womaniser, he offers it.

For instance: you could appear to be so sated and overwhelmed by your own exploits that you are exhausted: caught somewhere between the suggestive eyebrow and the yawn. In 'Community', the poet takes on the rueful pose of the exhausted conqueror, one who has to only think of love to wither with ennui: 'changed loves are but changed sorts of meat,/And when he hath the kernel eat,/who doth not fling away the shell?' Women, strange hybrids that they were, were to be seized and then discarded:

If then at first wise Nature had,
Made women either good or bad,
Then some we might hate, and some choose,
But since she did them so create
That we may neither love nor hate
Only this rests: all all may use.

Or, alternatively, if you were seeking to appear wise in the ways of women, you might, like Donne, write about being battered by excess of love. Love, he proclaims, is only for those who are willing to be eaten alive. In 'The Broken Heart', he writes:

All other griefs allow a part
To other griefs, and ask themselves but some;
They come to us, but us Love draws;
He swallows us, and never chaws.

The man is chewed, like meat, while the heart is smashed like tableware: 'Love, alas/At one first blow did shiver it as glass.' One step further, he casts himself as so swamped in desire that he has dropped dead, a love-corpse – thirty-two of Donne's fifty-four Songs and Sonnets make some reference to death. In the opening lines of 'The Damp', he imagines that those who come to find his dead body, on seeing his lover's likeness, die too: a domino stack of lust-struck bodies:

When I am dead, and doctors know not why,
And my friends' curiosity
Will have me cut up to survey each part,
When they shall find your picture in my heart,
You think a sudden damp of love
Will thorough all their senses move,
And work on them as me, and so prefer
Your murder to the name of massacre.

Donne, ever stretching, ever extravagant, takes the pose to the furthest possible extreme: in 'The Apparition' he imagines his ghost taking revenge on a lover whose coldness tormented him into the grave. The poem, gleefully excessive, ends with a hope the woman 'bathed in a cold quicksilver sweat wilt lie/A verier ghost than I': 'since my love is spent,/ I'd rather thou should'st painfully repent.'

But, because he is Donne, even the poetry which seems straightforwardly about world-weary out-loved lovers twists out of your hands. 'Farewell to Love' begins in the well-trodden tradition of poetry about disillusionment with romantic courtly striving. It appears to end with a resolve to renounce all love:

I'll no more dote and run
To pursue things which, had, endamage me;
And when I come where moving beauties be,
As men do when the summer's sun
   Grows great,
Though I admire their greatness, shun their heat:
Each place can afford shadows. If all fail,
'Tis but applying worm-seed to the tail.

Donne's poems have fault-lines – they slip away from you. Worm-seed was a concoction made of flower heads, an anti-aphrodisiac. The 'tail' is a Latin dick joke (because the Ciceronian Latin for 'tail' is *penis*). The lines are Donneanly ambiguous: they could mean, if all else fails, the speaker can simply apply worm-seed to the penis to cool their ardour. But it could be the opposite. Worm-seed only worked when taken orally, a fact which Donne, the stepson of a physician, would have known. The meaning could be, it's as useless to make such resolutions against love as putting worm-seed in the wrong place: passion overwhelms. Even when he is working in the same tradition as his allies, offering up imagined conquests for his friends, his verse is different. His poetry will not hold still. It tussles and shifts, the way desire does.

THE ERRATIC COLLECTOR OF
HIS OWN TALENT

Exactly what Donne did for Egerton is something of a
mystery – he never says, in his letters, what precisely his
job was. He calls himself 'your Lordship's secretary', but
his handwriting, beautiful and erratic, didn't have the fine,
regular clarity of the men trusted with copying out Chancery
records. His signature appears on a bond that Egerton drew
up for a man from the Inns of Court, so he may well have
been a glorified clerk, dealing with legal detail. One thing
we do know, though: in among his work, whether it was
arduous or whether he was largely ornamental, he was still
writing poetry.

It would be a mistake, though, to imagine that all this
time Donne was filing his verse away, keeping it safe,
copying it by candlelight into leather-bound tomes in his
bedroom in the great house. Donne's early writing life was
one of papery disarray. He made very little effort to keep
versions of his work; he did not write with an eye to future
fame, immortality. Poetry was the best possible way to set
down the unwieldy human truth as he saw it, but it was
for himself and his close allies. He allowed almost none of
his work to go to the press in his lifetime; Izaak Walton
described the poems as having been 'scattered loosely (God
knows too loosely)'. When, at one point, did Donne briefly

think of printing his verse, he had to cast around, writing to friends to retrieve poems of which he'd kept no copies, complaining it 'cost me more diligence to seek them than it did to write them'. He was often dismissive of his poetry; they were, he'd tell his friends, 'a rag of verses' or 'light flashes': nothing worth very much. There were poets who wrote with enduring fame in mind – Edmund Spenser was one, Milton another. Donne was different. He was the kind of man of whom George Puttenham remarked, 'I know very many notable gentlemen in the court that have written commendably, and suppressed it again, or else suffered it to be published without their own names to it: as if it were a discredit for a gentleman to seem learned, and to show himself amorous of any good art.' The thought that thousands of people from across the world would gather in hotel conference rooms to discuss poems which Donne himself had perhaps forgotten by the time he died; that hundreds of years later it would be possible to buy a mug printed with his face and the legend *let's get metaphysical*: it would have been unfathomable.

Because of this devil-may-care attitude to his own work, when you quote a Donne poem, you are in fact quoting an amalgamation, pieced together over four hundred years from an array of manuscripts of varying degrees of scrappiness. His poems were folded into small squares and passed from hand to hand, posted between friends of friends of friends: read it and pass it on. The only surviving holograph copy – which is to say, in Donne's own handwriting – of an English

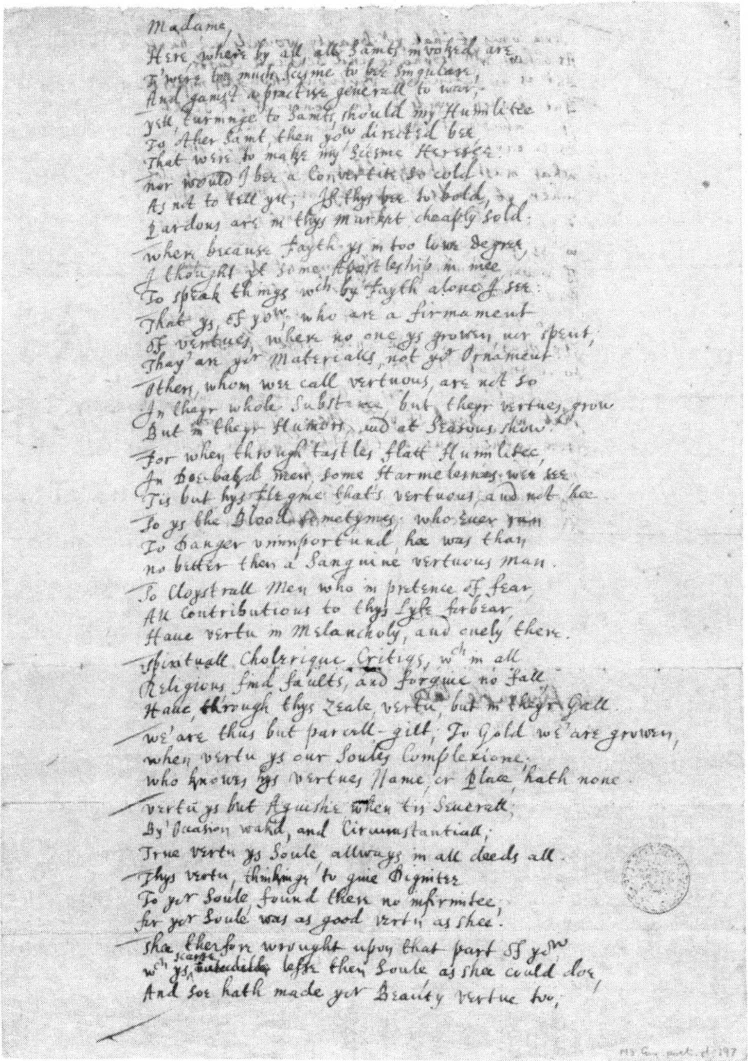

Madame,
Here where by all, all Saints invoked are,
T'were too much Scisme to bee singular,
And gainst a practise generall to war,
yet, turninge to Saints, should my Humilitee
To other Saint, then yow directed bee,
That were to make my Scisme Heresee.
Nor would I bee a Convertite so cold
As not to tell yt; If thys bee too bold,
Pardons are in thys markett cheaply sold.
where because Fayth ys in too lowe degree,
I thought yt some Apostleship in mee
To speak things wch by fayth alone I see:
That ys, of yow, who are a firmament
Of vertues, where no one ys growen, nor spent,
They'are yor Materialls, not yor Ornament.
Others, whom wee call vertuous, are not so
In theyr whole Substance, but theyr vertues grow
But in theyr Humors, and at Seasons show.
For when through tastles flatt Humilitee
In dow-bak'd men some Harmelesnes wee see
Tis but hys flegme that's vertuous, and not hee:
So ys the Blood sometymes; who ever ran
To danger vnimportund, hee was than
no better then a Sanguine vertuous man.
So Cloystrall Men who in pretence of fear
All contributions to thys Lyfe forbear,
Haue vertu in Melancholy, and onely there.
Spirituall Cholerique Critiqs, wch in all
Religions find faults, and forgiue no fall
Haue, through thys Zeale, vertu, but in theyr Gall.
We'are thus but parcell-gilt; To Gold we'are growen,
when vertu ys our Soules Complexione;
who knowes hys vertues Name, or Place, hath none.
vertu ys but Aguishe when tis Severall,
By'occasion wak'd, and Circumstantiall;
True vertu ys Soule, allways in all deeds all.
Thys vertu, thinkinge to giue dignitee
To yor Soule, found there no infirmitee,
for yor Soule was as good vertu as shee.
Shee therfore wrought vpon that part of yow
wch ys scarse lesse then Soule as shee could doe,
And soe hath made yor Beauty vertue too;

The only poem in Donne's handwriting: 'To the Lady Carew'

poem written by him is a verse letter 'To the honourable
lady the Lady Carew' (1612): his hand is beautiful, the italic
hand of a Courts-trained man, with elaborately swooping
'y's. All the other poetry we have by him was copied out by
other people: some written into large vellum-bound collections with great care, fine handwriting at its most looped
and elaborate, Donne nestling against the compiler's other
favourites; others were scribbled into corners of a nearly-full
page in a booklet, or carried in a single sheet amid bits of
pocket debris until they were worn into almost nothing.

It was not only Donne's poetry that was read in this way
– he was one among hundreds, at a time when it would be
unusual to be an educated ambitious man and not occasionally try your hand at verse. Poetry could be made to
function as entertainment, news, flirtation, insinuation,
slander, religious contemplation, invoice, in-joke, thank-
you note, apology, profound meditation of love, scurrilous
sex dream. Like everything else, it had crazes and fashions:
someone invented a joke or an image or a metrical scheme,
and someone else wrote a response to it; it multiplied.

But Donne's poetry was different in one thing: once it
escaped from his immediate grasp, it spread like fire. There
are more than four thousand copies of his individual poems,
in 260 manuscripts – and it's extremely likely there are more
out there, in archives and private collections, waiting for
us to discover them. Without having any way of knowing
it, he became one of the most popular manuscript poets of
his generation. A fair number of the copied-out poems are

unattributed, so men and women didn't necessarily know who they were writing out into their books, whose poetry they were sending to a sweetheart or carrying around for luck: they only knew they loved and coveted it.

Because his poetry flew so far and so wide, Donne is one of the hardest Renaissance writers to pin down textually. Inevitably, the poems vary from copy to copy – sometimes just a letter or two, sometimes whole lines – and are often almost impossible to date. 'Slumbered' in one text will be 'snorted' in another; 'reclaimed' will be 'redeemed'. The poems we know as 'by John Donne' have in fact been constructed by editors, piecemeal, from the best of the manuscripts and the seventeenth-century print editions: the title page should, were it to be bluntly literal, read, 'Poems, by John Donne and by educated guesswork'.

On the other hand, titles of Donne's verse are plain, descriptive and uncomplicated. This is because they were largely not written by him. We know that some titles – for instance, some of the wedding-celebration epithalamia – were given by Donne, and in cases where the same title occurs in all collated manuscripts we tend to tentatively assume it's his own. 'A Nocturnal upon St Lucy's Day, Being the Shortest Day' is one. Some titles win out over rivals with greater textual authority simply because we prefer them; 'The Sun Rising' is called 'Ad Solem' in two of the three most famous manuscript groups, but was given its current title in the first printed edition of Donne's work in 1633, and will now forever be 'The Sun Rising', puzzled over by children in schools. Most, though, appear to have been added by manuscript scribes during Donne's life; there are exceptions, but by and large it looks like quicksilver Donne didn't make a habit of anything as solid as a title. His poetry left his hands unnamed, allowing it to gather up titles and edits and little flourishes from each poem's new owner. The poems were akin to living organisms, changing shape and colour as they were copied and recopied.

There is something astonishing in that: that he wore his skill so very lightly. He was willing to lose his work, perhaps because he knew there was more to come. Imagination will beget imagination, and more readily so if it is flung out instead of dragon-hoarded. At no point in his life did Donne come to an end of himself.

THE WITNESS OF
DISASTROUS INTRIGUE

Donne and his poetry would have occupied one room in the Egerton house; but there were many more, and Egerton had a household large enough to fill them all. Just before Donne was appointed, Egerton married for a second time. His wife was a woman named Elizabeth Wolley, and she had style and gloss. She had been married twice already, and had been one of the most active of the Queen's ladies of the Privy Chamber, accompanying her out on royal hawking trips to catch partridges. She brought money with her, a large household of servants and a number of striving young hangers-on. She also had a son, Francis, from a previous marriage – but not wanting her son to be in her new husband's way while he was educated, she and her brother performed a swap. She would send Francis to live with his uncle, Sir George More – an MP and owner of the beautiful Loseley Park, a manor house built with stone heisted from an abbey. George More had a reputation for munificence ('he kept 50 liveries, spent every week an ox and 12 sheep') and for a sharp temper. In return for taking Francis, he would send his third daughter to live at York House and learn the ways of the city and the court. She was fourteen, or thereabouts: her name was Anne More, and something in her face or manner bludgeoned John Donne in the heart.

She was said to be beautiful. (Although, they said the same of Anne Boleyn, a woman who in paintings looks like an unimpressed headmistress.) There is a portrait which goes by the name *An Unknown Woman*, by Nicholas Hilliard, dating from 1602, which might, or perhaps more likely might not, be of her: if it is, she is round-faced, matronly, sweet-smiling, a little exhausted. We have portraits of her father, who has a long strong nose, good space between the eye and eyebrow, and a small mouth; if that resemblance passed down to the girls, she would have looked like the profile on a Roman coin.

An Unknown Woman, attributed to Nicholas Hilliard

Donne, in and out of York House all day, would have met Anne often at the dinner table. Even though he was a paid employee, Walton tells us, 'nor did his Lordship in this time of Master Donne's attendance upon him, account him to be so much his servant, as to forget he was his friend; and, to testify it, did always use him with much courtesy, appointing him a place at his own table, to which he esteemed his company and discourse to be a great ornament.' Anne was learning the ways of London for the first time; he, to her eyes, must have seemed endlessly glamorous, with his reputation for brilliance, his swiftly summoned eloquence and his fine-crafted face.

If you were out courting, you gave gifts. In 1641, one courtship was laid out: 'he perhaps giveth her a ten-shilling piece of gold, or a ring of that price . . . then the next time, or the next time after that, each other time, some conceited toy or novelty of less value.' If you weren't rich, you could give a corset stay, carved by hand and inscribed with a message. If he gave her anything, it would perhaps have been poetry. In 'A Valediction: Of My Name in a Window', written in 1599, Donne imagines etching his name with a diamond ring on a window and his lover seeing her own reflection and his name intermingled:

'Tis much, that glass should be
As all-confessing and through-shine as I;
'Tis more, that it shows thee to thee,
And clear reflects thee to thine eye.

But all such rules love's magic can undo:
Here you see me, and I am you.

'You this entireness better may fulfil,' he wrote, 'Who have the pattern with you still' – a sly numerological joke. Using the then-popular Latin and Hebrew process of *gematria*, in which numbers are assigned to letters, 'my name', 'John Donne', and 'Anne More' all add up to sixty-four. It was the kind of coincidence that Donne – always seeking connections between things not obviously connected, always hunting out symmetries and unexpected felicities – would have relished.

But Anne was not the only exciting member of the household. There was also, at the table, the man Donne had admiringly dubbed in his poetry 'our Earl' – the Earl of Essex. He was there under duress.

¶

The Earl of Essex had been manoeuvring to become one of the most powerful men in England. The Queen loved his company and his flair for talk and games – when the two sat down together to talk, they were in for the night: 'my lord is at cards or one game or another with her, that he commeth not to his own lodging till the birds singe in the morning.' He was beautiful, book-hungry, martial-minded and extravagantly well dressed (he spent £40 on two suits of clothes for his sister's wedding: for comparison, the house Shakespeare bought in 1597 cost £60). But he couldn't

Robert Devereux, Earl of Essex, with a map of Cadiz,
the Azores and Ireland in the background

afford to be complacent – for all Essex was Elizabeth's
current favourite, Walter Raleigh was always waiting in the
wings, hoping he might slip up. Raleigh knew the chances
were good: Essex was quick-tempered, vain and liable to
explode in tantrums. Once before he had quarrelled with
the Queen over her fondness for Raleigh, storming out in
a fury that his affections were 'so much thrown down, and
such a wretch as Raleigh highly esteemed'. The Queen liked

his bumptiousness enough to laugh at him and summon him back, but nobody knew how long it would last. More, despite the fact that his seafaring had made him the adored darling of the public, his determination to continue to wage war on Spain was beginning to be distasteful in court, where the talk was of peace. His insistence on a consistently aggressive foreign policy was losing ground with the Queen – and the only person who seemed not to know how thin was the ice on which he skated was Essex himself.

In 1598, the Privy Council held a debate about Irish policy; the Great Earl Hugh O'Neill was leading a rebellion against English rule. Essex urged the necessity of war, while the Queen's principal secretary argued for peace. The Queen dismissed one of Essex's arguments and, insulted, he deliberately turned his back on her. Exasperated, she slapped him round the head and told him to go and be hanged; Essex half-drew his sword, and had to be held back by a Lord Admiral. He roared to the Queen that 'he neither could nor would put up so great an affront and indignity, neither would he have taken it at King Henry the Eighth his hands.' Legend – and the gossiping Earl of Clarendon – suggests he said to Elizabeth's face that 'she was as crooked in her disposition as in her carcass', which wouldn't have been particularly winning. He stormed out, refusing to return. Thomas Egerton was there to witness it, so Donne would have had a first-hand account.

Egerton, fearing chaos, sent a letter to Essex begging him to see his foolishness and impudence, his 'unseasonable discontentment', and to think of his employees who risked being ruined by his behaviour; Essex sent back a letter made up almost entirely of irate rhetorical questions: 'cannot princes err? And cannot subjects receive wrong? Is an earthly power or authority infinite?'

Donne, frequently called to Whitehall with Egerton, saw the gossip that ran through the rooms, where word could pass between dozens of courtiers in a single day. He was unimpressed. He wrote a verse letter 'To Mr Henry Wotton', who as Essex's man would have been urgently keen to hear the gossip. The poet was uninspired by the scandals: 'here's not more news, than virtue':

> here no-one is from th' extremity
> Of vice by any other reason free
> But that the next to'him still is worse than he . . .

The people of court, he wrote, could dish out slander but not take it:

> Suspicious boldness to this place belongs,
> And to'have as many ears as all have tongues;
> Tender to know, tough to acknowledge wrongs.

Despite the acrimony and the insults, the Council and the Queen could not fully function without Essex. In March 1599, he was sent to Ireland to quell the rebels, taking with him more than a thousand horses and sixteen thousand troops;

the largest expeditionary force ever sent across that stretch of water. Among his young men went Thomas Egerton junior and Henry Wotton, leaving Donne behind to write notes edged with discontent at his own stay-at-home days.

His envy would have grown during the start of the campaign. Wotton wrote home to Donne, enamoured of his earl, 'for our wars, I can only say we have a good cause and the worthiest gentleman of the world to lead it.' Essex knew the power that comes with knighting your allies, and he tapped people with abandon; young Egerton became young Sir Thomas. The Irish rebels mocked that 'he never drew sword but to make knights' – and Elizabeth later was so annoyed by the sea of Sirs he was creating that she threatened to demote some of them.

But despite a strong beginning, the Irish resistance was unexpectedly tenacious. Essex's men struggled to seize the upper hand; two key battles were lost, and amid the blood and confusion and waning optimism, young Thomas Egerton was wounded. Thomas was taken to Dublin Castle, for what rough and ready care was possible. It wasn't enough, and he died there, far from home. His body was sent back home, a long, disintegrating kind of journey for a corpse, for a funeral at Chester Cathedral. Donne travelled to Chester to carry his sword in procession before the coffin. The edge of envy for the excitement of the field disappeared from his letters to Wotton.

In September 1599 Essex, in direct defiance of the Queen's orders, made an uneasy truce with O'Neill. Wotton helped draft the articles of peace, working as one of two chief negotiators: a thrilling kind of task for so young a man – but when Essex returned home it was to a stony welcome. Rumour said that he ran, covered in mud from his ride, straight into the Queen's bedchamber before she had her wig on, bursting in on her wisps of hair and unpainted, ravaged face. Elizabeth, livid, ordered that Essex was to be banished from court and held captive somewhere safe until she could decide what she would do with him. As for Wotton, word reached him that the Queen was displeased with him, too, for those peace articles: pragmatically, he fled the country and headed towards Europe to watch and wait.

Elizabeth chose York House for Essex's house arrest – much to Egerton's disgust – and so in the autumn he became part of the Egerton household. He was confined to its walls; Donne would have encountered him often, full of angry plans for how to recover his footing. Very swiftly, though, the earl's health began to falter; by December 1599, he was very ill. His family asked the Queen if he might be 'removed to a better air, for he is somewhat straitly lodged in respect the Lord Keeper's household is not great'. Elizabeth, her amusement at her old unruly charmer finally exhausted, refused.

Christmas came, and Essex seemed certain to die. Donne was shocked by how jaunty everyone was, as if nothing was amiss. He wrote to a friend that the court was 'as merry as if it were not sick': the Queen came forth every night, to see 'the ladies dance the old and new country dances'. Each day was, Donne said, 'full of jollity and revels and plays' – and among them was the first performance of Shakespeare's *Twelfth Night.*

§

(It's often asked – did Donne know Shakespeare? The response, as with so much of the period, is a seesaw of maybes: probably not, but it's possible, but there is no proof, but perhaps. There's a chance they could have encountered each other this Christmas, at court; both there, both watching with careful eyes. Donne could easily have seen Shakespeare on the stage throughout his London years. Donne enjoyed the theatre, and Shakespeare was an actor in both his own and others' work; in 1610 Donne's friend John Davies wrote that 'Good Will' played upon the stage in 'kingly parts' – and they had a mutual acquaintance in Ben Jonson, who relished opining about both men at regular, waspish intervals. On the one hand, Donne was class-conscious: in 'Love's Alchemy' he took pains to refer to the fact that he kept a manservant – 'my man' – something hard to find in any other poet's work; and he may well have dismissed any notion of knowing Shakespeare, who was then a mere player. On the other, there is the ghost of a book which might link them together. For a fee of about sixpence, a publisher could register his right to a work in the Stationers' Register, an early and slightly haphazard form of copyright law; and in January 1600 was entered: 'A book called Amours by J.D., with certain other Sonnets by W.S.' by one Eleazar Edgar. Many have hoped that it might be John Donne and William Shakespeare, yoked in print. It's possible: Donne had an acquaintance called Berkeley, an ally from Cadiz, who might have passed some of Donne's poetry along to his half-brother Thomas Russell, who was a friend of Shakespeare's and later the executor of his will. Russell might, in turn, have planned to parcel up the verse and turn a swift pound on it: perhaps. But the book, if it was ever printed, no longer exists, and the W.S. could just as readily have been William Smith, a sonneteer and disciple of Edmund Spenser's, while the J.D. could have been John Davies, or indeed a misprint for M.D., Michael Drayton, whose sonnets had been published under the subtitle 'Amours' in their first edition in 1594: it's tantalisingly impossible to know.)

§

All the while that Christmas the earl languished. If he comforted himself with the thought that the Queen missed him and that his absence was a ghost at her feast, he was wrong. 'My Lord Essex', Donne writes, 'and his train are no more missed here than the angels which were cast down from heaven, nor (for anything I can see) likelier to return.' Donne writes about his former martial leader with compassion and pity, but also a new strain of exasperation: he 'withers still in sickness . . . that which was said of Cato, that his age understood him not, I fear may be averted of your lord, that he understood not his age . . . such men want [i.e. lack] locks for themselves and keys for others.' Some, though, still loved him: some churches within earshot of York House rang their bells for him, to the Queen and Egerton's distaste.

In the early days of 1600, there was a sudden loss at York House, but not Essex: Lady Egerton died, wholly unexpectedly. It hit Egerton hard: harder than was thought seemly at the time. A looker-on wrote, 'my Lord Keeper sorrows more than so great a man ought. He is discontented that his house is made a prison of so long continuance.' Egerton's household was immediately broken up, and Anne was sent back home to Loseley Park, away from Donne and their clandestine romance.

Loseley Park, Anne's home

That spring, letters spilled out of York House. Donne wrote surreptitiously to Anne, declarations in the grand style: 'I will have leave to speak like a lover,' he said, for 'I love more than any yet.' Essex's letter, in contrast, was to the Queen, full of lamb-like submission – and he was at last allowed to leave Egerton's household for his own home, Essex House. The whole of London, though, was still uncertain as to whether the Queen planned to reinstate him in his former place of glory. He needed her to renew his grant on sweet wines, which earned him thousands of pounds, without which his extravagant living – the banquets, the music, the trousers that cost the same as a cottage – would be impossible, and he'd be ruined. But Elizabeth's patience was dead; in October 1600, she announced she wouldn't renew the grant: and abruptly Essex became a man with nothing left to lose.

As the autumn turned to winter, a furious Essex filled Essex House with dissatisfied minor aristocrats and army officers with time on their hands, and began to plan unlikely schemes to gain back his old place in court. On 3 February 1601, Essex packed Drury House in London – a house Donne would later come to know intimately – with his allies, conspiring to overthrow his enemies and re-establish himself where he felt he belonged, at the Queen's right hand. On the 7th, it became clear to the Queen that he was planning something drastic. She called a council: twice Essex was summoned, and twice he refused.

A sub-group of Essex supporters hastened to the Globe to see Shakespeare's *Richard II*, to hear the clash of (real) swords and see (fake) blood – usually made out of vinegar and sheep's blood – in a bid to make themselves feel suitably warlike. On the 8th, Thomas Egerton, along with three other nobles and their entourages, appeared at Essex House, demanding parley in the name of the Queen: it's conceivable that Donne, having lived so close alongside the earl for so long, was in tow – if not, he would later have had a full and furious telling of the day from Egerton.

Essex let the four nobles in, but left the minor figures to loiter outside. He ushered the four men into his study, shut the door on them and locked them in. Then, with fanfare but with very few firearms, Essex led his three hundred followers, including numerous other earls, into the City, heading for Whitehall. His hope was that people in the street would rally to his side: there would be a joyful uprising, and together they would seize control of the capital.

It was a disaster. The Lord Mayor shut the gates against them: the expected support did not flood the streets. Forces loyal to the Queen surrounded them, and Essex fought his way home that same afternoon with less than a hundred of his men, followed and besieged by the Lord Admiral's troops. That evening he surrendered and was taken to the Tower of London.

The Sunday after his insurrection, all the preachers in London were required by order of the Queen to give sermons condemning him; Elizabeth knew that he was still held dear by many, and that it wouldn't pay to have a beloved man beheaded. His trial was followed by thousands, with word passed by gossip, letters and dozens of manuscript copies of the prosecution and defence: Donne would have had access to every word spoken. Essex, worn out, and counselled by his own chaplain to abase himself, gave up on his swash-buckling stance of battered heroism and became a penitent. He was found guilty of treason, and went to his death with a piety so impressive that it was reported across the country. On 25 February 1601, the Queen's former favourite was beheaded in the courtyard of the Tower, watched by a small crowd. The witnesses' names were not recorded, but years later, Donne wrote a poem featuring a beheading in which he dwelt, hard, on the blood: and on the way the dying cling feverishly to life.

> Or as sometimes in a beheaded man,
> Though at those two red seas which freely ran,
> One from the trunk, another from the head,
> His soul be sailed to her eternal bed,
> His eyes will twinkle, and his tongue will roll
> As though he beckoned and called back his soul,
> He grasps his hands, and he pulls up his feet,
> And seems to reach and to step forth to meet
> His soul . . .

Donne was ideally placed to assess fallout from Essex's death, as later that same year he was suddenly made an MP. Egerton had the borough of Brackley, Northamptonshire sewn up, and he made Donne the gift of the parliamentary seat. Donne wasn't naïve; he would have known that the power that came with being a Member of Parliament was not his to wield according to his own desire; he was there as Egerton's man, to pick up information and glean snippets of news. Parliament sat for only a brief time, from October to December 1601, just enough to grant, among stormy mutterings, a new injection of supplies for the war in Ireland. There is no evidence that the young Donne, still not yet thirty, took part in any debates, spoke in public, sat on a committee or indeed participated in any way at all in the process of government; but he would have been able to gather gossip in the aftermath of the rebellion; he would have seen how deeply it had shaken the men who ruled England.

It was probably around this time that Donne wrote one of his longest, strangest poems, 'Metempsychosis'. It is so peculiar and arduous that almost nobody has read it, including some professors of John Donne: it's a semi-epic about a soul which migrates from body to body, starting with the forbidden apple in Eden, to a mandrake, several assorted fish, a sparrow, a mouse, a wolf, and finally Eve's daughter. 'I sing the progress of a deathless soul'. It was theologically risky: according to gossipy Ben Jonson, Donne's original plan with the poem 'was to have brought in all the bodies of the heretics from the soul of Cain, and at last left it in the body of Calvin. Of this he never wrote but one sheet, and now, since he was made Doctor, repenteth highly.' Some have argued that the poem is a kind of guilty metaphor, an account of Donne's shifting and mutating sympathies

Parliament in session in the reign of King James I

away from Essex. But to find the most in 'Metempsychosis', it is best read as a poem that embodies tumult: Donne's understanding of the order of things was in chaos, and he wrote a poem not to explain, but to capture it. To read it offers some of the feeling of trying to wrestle with a world that was shifting and raw and unhinged. The body and soul, which he spent so much time longing to bind together, refuse to merge: instead, fish transmigrate into wolves who transmigrate into women. You can read it as a verdict on those who expected him to behave as though the world was sane.

The whole Essex affair was a powerful lesson for Donne, of how intricate and dangerous it was to play with power, and how swiftly the men you trusted could turn on you. If he began to fall out of love with courtly things, then it perhaps started here, with that spurt of the earl's blood. His admiration for Essex had steadily waned, but the man had been his commander and the idol of the age. He would never forget him: his sermons, years later, would be full of warnings about how easy it is to fall. There is no such thing as safety, while you are alive.

THE PARADOXICAL QUIBBLER, TAKING AIM AT WOMEN

Anne returned to London in October of 1601; her father brought her with him, to continue her education in becoming an elegant young woman. If she and her father visited York House, Donne would not have been there to greet her. Egerton, letting very little grass grow under his feet, had married for a third time, a woman of a great fortune and blueish blood named Alice Spencer. Alice – a distant cousin of the poet Edmund Spenser, and related by marriage to the Queen – brought with her three daughters and a substantial household. Donne was ousted from the newly bustling York House and moved to lodgings in the Savoy. He perhaps wouldn't have minded much: the marriage was a miserable one, and the house was soon a furious battleground. Egerton wrote later, 'I thank God I never desired long life, nor ever had less cause to desire it than since this, my last marriage, for before I was never acquainted with such tempests and storms.' In his new, sparer home, Donne would at least have had peace, in which to work and write.

It's probable, though, that Donne and Anne had been corresponding all along. There are four unattributed and undated love letters copied out into a large collection of letters, poems and accounts of table-talk known as the Burley manuscript. The manuscript, which was thought lost to fire for many decades, seems to be in the hand of Henry Wotton's secretary, William Pankhurst. The four love letters could be Donne's letters to Anne: he writes 'in all that part of this summer I spent in your presence you doubled the heat and I lived under the rage of the hot sun and your eyes'. Their correspondence was risky, and in one the man accuses the woman of depriving him of 'the happiness I was wont to have in your letters'. In another, he describes the weather's turn to cold and ice – 'the sun forsakes us' – but, he says, the heart which she melted in the summer, 'no winter shall freeze'. It does sound very like him, at his most earnest; it's the twin of his promise, in 'Love's Growth', that 'no winter shall abate the spring's increase'.

But – before the finest love poet in the English language could kneel before his love – there is the question: what had Donne, by this time, written explicitly about women? What would Anne have been able to read, had she had the inclination and ability to seek it out, that he had written about the group to which she belonged?

¶

Hope not for mind in women: at their best
Sweetness and wit, they're but mummy, possessed.
    'Love's Alchemy'

The German physicist Johann Schroeder, famous primarily for his study of arsenic, was also convinced of the panacea-like properties of 'mummy'. In 1656, his *Pharmacopoeia Medico-Chymica* suggested that, while the best mummy was of course Egyptian, when it couldn't be found home-made alternatives were also workable:

> Take the fresh unspotted cadaver of a red-headed man (because in them the blood is thinner and the flesh hence more excellent) aged about 24, who has been executed and died a violent death. Cut the flesh in pieces and sprinkle it with myrrh and a little aloe. Then soak it in spirits of wine for several days, hang it . . . let the pieces dry in a shady spot. Thus they will be similar to smoked meat and will not stink.

It was a cure for almost anything. It is to this medicinal powdered corpse that Donne compares women in his 'Love's Alchemy': 'they're but mummy possessed.' Useful, but hardly romantic.

It would be absurd to try Donne anachronistically as a misogynist; but alongside the poems which glorify and sing the female body and heart, there are those that very potently don't. This is the man who wrote, 'Like sun-parched quarters on the city gate/Such is thy tanned skin's lamentable state': 'quarters' means the bodies hung and quartered at the entrance to the city, particularly nasty coming from someone who had known people who had swung. Donne's delineation of love – his work that encompasses its hunger, evasion, fear, stoicism, joy – is a staggering thing, but he never was an uncomplicated lover of women.

'The Comparison', written in the 1590s, is a good example of how eye-wateringly extreme Donne's anti-female verse could be. Even if we decide that Donne's stance in relation to the voice of the poem is ironical and sceptical, the poem is shot through with disgust. The speaker compares his own mistress with that of a rival, and the text aligns itself loosely to the tradition of what is known as a 'counter-blazon'. A blazon was a courtly poem of the kind that people imagine when they think of ruffs and cross-gartered men with huge lutes: poems that catalogued the physical qualities of an adored figure, like Sir Philip Sidney's excessive praise in his verse 'What Tongue Can Her Perfections Tell':

And thence those arms derived are;
The phoenix's wings be not so rare
For faultless length and stainless hue.

Sidney's woman's hair is gold, her shoulders 'be like two white doves' and her whole person 'out-beauties' beauty itself. Donne's counter-blazon takes that tradition and knifes it in a dark alley. He writes how the sweat of his own mistress's brow is 'no sweat drops, but pearl carcanets', while on his companion's mistress:

Rank sweaty froth thy mistress' brow defiles,
Like spèrm'tic issue of ripe menstr'ous boils,
Or like the scum, which, by need's lawless law

Enforced, Sanserra's starvèd men did draw
From parboiled shoes and boots, and all the rest
Which were with any sovereign fatness blest.

A couple of decades earlier, beginning in 1572, the year
Donne was born, the Protestant Huguenots in Sancerre in
France had been under siege by the Catholic forces of the
King. The citizens ate any hides they possessed; hundred-
year-old parchment documents, horses' harnesses, shoes –
anything that had once been an animal was made into stew.
Children, the historian Jean de Léry wrote, ate their own
belts as if they were tripe. It was very common, in counter-
blazon verse, to suggest your rival's mistress was sweaty; it
was less common to suggest that the mistress's sweat was
like the fat eked out of the boiled shoes of the starving.

Then there is the prose. It's sometimes said that the
more you read Donne's verse, the more you love him, and
the more you read Donne's prose, the less you can bear
him. This is particularly true, for modern readers, with the
nineteen Problems and twelve Paradoxes he wrote: short
essays, written perhaps at the Inns of Court or possibly
a little later. They were never printed in his lifetime, but
they were sent out to his friends and from there rippled
outwards to eager readers and transcribers: there are 429
copies of the individual essays, in at least twenty-six different manuscripts.

Paradoxes were high fashion at the time; short pieces
of writing in which opposites were brought to co-exist,

earnestly or facetiously, with the sideways unspoken implication that such a clash of ideas might have a kind of
unhinged logic somewhere in it. Donne's had titles like
'That Nature is our worst guide'; 'That only cowards dare
die'; 'That the gifts of the body are better than those of
the mind'. They were in enormous vogue across Europe:
in Italy, the philosopher Ortensio Lando was writing neat
little pieces, *contra opinionem omnium* – 'against received
opinion' – in which he argued, for instance, that it was better to be ugly than beautiful, drunk than sober, ignorant
than wise. As Erasmus wrote to Thomas More, about his
own mock-encomium *The Praise of Folly*, paradoxes were
ancient: 'As for those who are offended by the levity and
playfulness of the subject matter, they should consider that I
am not setting any precedent but following one set long ago
by great writers: . . . Glauco praised injustice . . . Synesius,
baldness; Lucian, the fly and the art of the parasite.'

They were a controversial craze; for anyone wanting to
write anything politically inflammatory, phrasing it in a
paradox allowed for plausible deniability, but it could also
leave room for misinterpretation, for being thought more
radical than you were. The playwright Anthony Munday
wrote to his patron to apologise for not handing in his
promised 'Paradox Apology' because the 'misinterpretation of the work by some in authority', he wrote, made
it too dangerous. George Puttenham, the author of the
core Early Modern text on rhetoric and poetry, *The Arte
of English Poesie*, hated them. 'Oftentimes,' he wrote, 'we

will seem to cast perils, and make doubt of things when by a plain manner of speech we might affirm or deny him.' (Although Puttenham was himself a vile man, whose moral judgement was not worth much: he was regularly sued and counter-sued, imprisoned at least six times, excommunicated four times, and was said by his enemies to have kidnapped a seventeen-year-old girl and kept her locked up in his farmhouse for three years.)

All this is to say that Donne's Paradoxes and Problems can't be taken as straight opinion pieces. Nobody in Donne scholarship agrees on the question: what did Donne *mean* by them? Is there seriousness in them? Did he mean his misogyny to be so wild as to be an attack on those who would believe it?

The wittiest of Donne's Paradoxes was headed, 'That women ought to paint themselves'. Make-up was popular in Elizabeth's court: powders made from white lead mixed with vinegar, vermilion on the lips. Hairlines were tweezered. Blonde hair was coveted, and Donne would have seen dyes for sale made of yellow celandine flowers, honey and cumin, or of quicklime and tobacco. You left them in for a day, then rinsed off with a wash made of cabbage stalks, ashes and barley straw. Donne's Paradox, light-hearted and insouciant, takes the side of paint: 'Foulness is loathsome; can that be so too which helps it? . . . If in kissing or breathing upon her, the painting falls off, thou art angry: wilt thou be so, if it stick on? Thou didst love her: if thou begins to hate her then it is because she is not painted.'

Another of the Paradoxes, 'A Defence of Women's Inconstancy', rides to the defence of a woman's right to sleep around:

That women are inconstant, I with any man confess,
but that inconstancy is a bad quality, I against any man
will maintain . . . [Women] cannot be immutable like
stocks, like stones, like the Earth's dull centre; gold that
lieth still, rusteth; water, corrupteth; air that moveth not,
poisoneth; then why should that which is the perfection
of other things, be imputed to women as greatest
imperfection? Because they deceive men?

It's so tempting to read it as a paean to female sexual liberation – except of course that it's a paradox: the model that allows the writer to both posit and ridicule simultaneously: and it goes on, rampantly uncharmingly, 'Women are like flies which feed amongst us at our table, or fleas sucking our very blood.'

Alongside the Paradoxes, though, there are the Problems; very similar in form – short essays, rarely more than a page – but sadder, heavier, and harder to dismiss entirely as ironical intellectual games. One asks 'Why have bastards best fortunes?' – from a man who was poor and struggling. Another, 'Why did the Devil reserve Jesuits till the latter day?' – from a man who had seen a hidden Jesuit priest bring about his brother's death.

Donne used his Problems to ask this question: 'Why hath

the common opinion afforded women souls?' It's unlikely that Donne had any doubt about the besouledness of his sisters and mother and female acquaintances; but the essay is dark. There's an anger in it: women, he writes, have 'so many advantages and means to hurt us (for even their loving destroys us) that we dare not displease them'. Women, he writes, are only superior to apes because they can talk: 'we deny souls to others equal to them in all but in speech for which they are beholding only to their bodily instruments: for perchance an ape's heart, or a goat's or a fox's or a serpent's would speak just so if it were in the breast and could move the tongue and jaws.'

The question of whether women had souls had, it was widely believed, been hotly debated in the year 585 by a council of bishops at Mâcon in Burgundy. Of course, it hadn't: it was just a historical misunderstanding based on a mean little pun, in which homo means both 'human' and 'adult male'. Towards the end of the sixteenth century, Valens Acidalius, a poverty-stricken young scholar, wrote a pamphlet in which he used the double meaning of homo to 'prove' that the Bible said only adult men had souls; it gained popularity, was eventually banned by the Pope. It was into this debate that Donne waded, with this parting shot: 'Perchance because the Devil (who is all soul) doth most mischief, and for convenience and proportion, because they would come nearer him, we allow them some souls.' He ends – 'so we have given women souls only to make them capable of Damnation.'

But Donne rarely gives anyone the last word on a topic: and that very much included his own self. Years later in a sermon Donne returned to the same question. He poured scorn on anyone who would dare cast doubt on whether women have a soul: 'Some men out of a petulancy and wantonness of wit, and out of the extravagancy of paradoxes' have called the 'abilities of women in question, even in the root thereof, in the reasonable and immortal soul'. Donne glares out from the pulpit: 'No author of gravity, of piety, of conversation in the Scriptures, could admit that doubt.' He is writing about himself.

'The extravagancy of paradoxes' was the pleasure and the point of them – the possibilities that lie inside pointing out absurdity. Donne discovered that if you force together the two Venn diagram circles of reason and the absurd, in the overlap there is a weapon. He chose to level that weapon at women – or possibly at those who would be credulous enough to believe his prose – or at both. He wrote in a letter, about his Paradoxes and Problems, that 'if they make you to find better reasons against them, they do their office: for they are but swaggerers, quiet enough if you resist them.' Life among lawyers had taught him to argue; but logic, Donne's writing declares, can be brought to defend illogic. Donne knew that the more bold and extravagant your stance, the easier it is to argue you actually meant the diametric opposite. Careful sobriety is dangerous, but surrealism, ribaldry, insouciance – these have a defence mechanism built in, and he seized on them with both hands.

They're cruel, too: no amount of irony or hyperbole cuts that away. They point to something anarchic and furious in his intellectual make-up. It was mostly kept down out of sight, but that hyperbolic streak was part of his strange, remarkable intellect, with its courageous munificence and its angry, bitter corners. Just as he saw, so clearly, both marvels and corruption in the state of humanity as a whole, so Donne very much embodied those extremes. He was capable of being such a joy, and such a fount of satirical, mean snide: he was both celebrant and assassin, ever shifting between the two.

ANNE

Who was she – the very young woman with whom the complicated, furious, funny author of the Paradoxes was so in love? We know very little; we do not even know how she preferred to spell her own name, as with the capriciousness typical of the period, she is spelled both Ann and Anne. It was her second name, though, that Donne played on, over and over: 'as much more loving, as more sad'. She was likely to have been fashionable, given her father's wealth, and her clothes would have been good. Stitching elaborate needle lace was the rage – geometrical patterns and flower designs, especially – and necklines were having a moment of extremes, either rising high to the chin or scooped so low they skated close to the nipple. But his poetry never describes her clothes, or her body. Donne's metaphors are vivid, wild, evocative and potent, but they're strikingly unspecific. It never occurred to him to tell us if she curved at the hip, or jutted at the collar bone, or was taller than him: presumably it was not what was important. The hunger, and the body itself, were what mattered. Perhaps to look for Anne in Donne's verse is to misunderstand what the poems are doing: they're not representations of her, but representations of him: him watching her, needing her, inventing for her. They are trumpet blasts across a hard land, more than they are portraits.

She was almost certainly a reader: he would put it on her epitaph, and Henry Wotton once in a letter referred to 'that fair and learned hand of your mistress, than whom the world doth possess nothing more virtuous'. Female literacy, though, wouldn't be something she could have taken for granted: if she was book-hungry, it would have made her stand out. There had been moments in which female education took high priority, but the stance on educating women changed as often as the fashions for coloured garters, and Anne just missed a wave; so she was unlikely to have been surrounded in her domestic sphere by female friends who valued learning or talked with her about fashions in poetry. Anne was born too late for the burst of enthusiasm for female learning that erupted between 1523 and 1538, inspired by Catherine of Aragon: there were at least seven passionate treatises published on the theme of female classical education between those years. In 1581 – three years before Anne's birth – Richard Mulcaster, the headmaster of St Paul's, wrote, 'Do we not see in our country, some of that sex so excellently well trained' that they could be compared 'even to the best Roman or Greekish paragons be they never so much praised?' But Mulcaster was lauding a dying breed. In 1561, a translation by Thomas Hoby (a scholar married to one of the most learned women of the age) of Castiglione's *The Courtier* put forward a different vision of womanhood. Women, in Castiglione's world, should have their letters, but that was less important than their grace: their painting, dancing, ability to sew a fine seam. Restoration comedy began to make fun of the idea of 'Plato in petticoats'. In 1694, William Wotton wrote that in the sixteenth century learning 'was so very modish that the fair sex seemed to believe that Greek and Latin added to their Charms, and Plato and Aristotle, untranslated, were frequent ornaments of their closets' but that by the seventeenth, 'this humour in both sexes abated by degrees.' So when Anne read his poetry, she probably did it alone. (She does not seem to have written any verse of her own. Women of her generation absolutely wrote poetry, but rare women: lucky ones, who had been trained in its rigours and rules, mostly very rich.)

Her willingness to defy her father was a remarkable thing: she must have had in her a flash of daring in a world that insisted on obedience. She could only have met Donne in secret, and secret places were not easy to find. They might have been able to collide under the plausible deniability of public spaces: parks, popular walks, church. They might have attended events in the evening: pageants, or visits to the assembly halls at court, which could be so crowded that silk-clad bodies would press against each other. Anne would have known that fashion, too, decreed that women play hard to get: Shakespeare's Juliet frets that she was 'too quickly won', and says 'I'll frown and be perverse and say thee nay,/So thou wilt woo'. She went against the fashion; she let him win her.

The richer you were, the more you risked in defying your parents. Authoritarian parental control lasted longest in the tranches of society where there was most property and social status at stake: you might get away with a lot if you were poor, but barely a handful of upper-class children resisted their parents' dictation, and their rebellions were rarely much of a success. In the mid-fifteenth century, a young woman called Elizabeth, a daughter of one Agnes Paston, declared that she would choose her own husband. In response, she was put under effective house arrest, forbidden to talk to visitors or male servants, and was 'beaten once in the week or twice, and sometimes twice on a day, and her head broke in two or three places'. Anne would have known that Sir George More would have expected something far more impressive and gilt-edged for his daughter. So she was in a small and fiery minority when she decided to love him anyway.

She took vast risks for him: larger than he took for her. Spurred on by desire, or perhaps by Donne's urgent importuning, or by the wild optimism of youth, she risked gossip, scandal – and perhaps, at the very end, pregnancy. There are some who believe that by the winter of 1601, they would have become adept at finding brief snatched moments alone. They may well have been lovers in the weeks before they wed, hiding behind insouciant faces and very careful timing. She gave a great, recklessly romantic leap into the dark. The landing was not to be a soft one.

THE DARING OF THE LOVER,
AND THE IMPRISONED GROOM

Was he worth the sacrifice she made, when she forswore the thousand easier futures that surrounded her? The alternatives would have been right in front of her: she could have aimed for a life more like that of her cousin by marriage Elizabeth (uncle Egerton's third wife's daughter) who had that year been married off to Baron Hastings, with all the castles and gardens and wall hangings embroidered with unicorns that that involved. What was Donne, that she decided to risk her father's wrath in order to share his days, his small income, his bed?

If he took her to bed like he wrote – if he knew how to render bodily his poetry – then he was worth sacrificing all the wall hangings in England for. To read him – to read all of his love poems together – is to feel yourself change, for his is a passion which acknowledges the strangeness you are born with.

His best poetry is a triumphant call of desire, sincerity, joke, all bound into one. It's there, for instance, in 'A Valediction, Forbidding Mourning': the lovers are imagined as the two feet of a pair of mathematical compasses, joined eternally at the base.

If they be two, they are two so

As stiff twin compasses are two:
Thy soul, the fixed foot, makes no show
To move, but doth, if th'other do;

And though it in the centre sit,
Yet when the other far doth roam,
It leans, and hearkens after it,
And grows erect as it comes home.

It is so extravagantly witty, and so riotously plays only by its own rules. It needed to be clever, because he demands that sex be intelligent: it's the poem of a man who has the temerity and invention to see the human condition in a piece of metal. It loves the body, because Donne, unlike so many of the highbrow poets who went before him, never pretended not to have a body – 'grows erect as it comes home' is a pun so obvious it might as well be a little sketch of a penis. Yeats wrote, 'Donne could be as metaphysical as he pleased, and yet never seemed inhuman or hysterical as Shelley often does, because he could be as physical as he pleased.'

But it is fundamental to his love poetry that the body Donne imagines isn't just a body. It transforms, and becomes simultaneously other things: a world, a state, a city, a planetary sweep. The lover looks at the woman in 'The Good Morrow' and sees a world atlas: 'Where can we find two fitter hemispheres/Without sharp North, without declining West?' In 'To His Mistress Going to Bed', the woman's girdle becomes a constellation of stars, and her body is the entire world. 'Off with that girdle, like Heav'n's zone glist'ring,/ But a far fairer world encompassing.' And, again, 'My kingdom, safeliest when with one man manned!' And the man in 'The Sun Rising' chides the rising sun, declares, 'She all states, and all Princes I'. She becomes the world:

> since thy duties be
> To warm the world, that's done in warming us.
> Shine here to us, and thou art everywhere:
> This bed thy centre is, these walls, thy sphere.

Of course, some of that woman-as-state, woman-as-world is Donne working in a tradition. He was not anywhere close to the first poet to claim to find in woman an everything. Pierre de Ronsard, fifty years older than Donne and France's 'Prince of Poets', tells the sun, '*va te cacher*', and asks it if it has seen, in its orbiting of the world, a thing more whole than the woman of the poem.

But some of it was personal. Donne's mind was cacophonous. His relentless imagination was his single most constant feature; he wrote about his 'worst voluptuousness, which is an hydroptique immoderate desire of humane learning'. In his darker moments, it tortured him. His mind had ceaselessness built into it. It was to be, throughout his life, a site of new images, new theology, new doubts: even those who disliked his work acknowledged that he was a writer who had erupted through the old into the new. A contemporary wrote that, with him, it was 'the lazy seeds/of servile imitation thrown away/and fresh invention planted'.

But the *always* of that imagination must have been exhausting. For a mind like that, sex – real sex, true sex – would allow a singleness to hush the multitudinous mind. It's why so much of Donne's imagery around sex is so total-ising: the man and woman become one, the woman becomes a state, a country, a planet. Sex, for Donne and those like him: permission, for those who watch the world with such feverish care, to turn one person into the world and to watch only them. It was a transforming of his constant seeking for knowledge. To adore and to devour and to be devoured is its own kind of focus: a gasp of a different kind of oxygen.

¶

And so they married.

The wedding took place 'about three weeks before Christmas', in 1601, according to Donne. It was very small: no more than five guests. The fashion for brides swathed in white, popularised by Queen Victoria, had not yet begun; burgundy was popular in Italy, gold in Austria. Elizabeth's sumptuary clothing laws, still in place until James I swept them all away, would have forbidden that Anne wore tinselled satin or silk, or velvet in crimson, scarlet or blue; but it's likely, given its clandestine nature, she only wore the best of what she already had.

The couple were probably married at the Savoy. First a thirteenth-century crenellated palace belonging to Peter,

Count of Savoy, it had been rebuilt as a hospital with a chapel for the needy under Henry VII, and by the time Donne reached London part of it was let to fashionable people who had enough money to dress themselves in sweeping hats and cloaks but no need for an actual town house. With the Earls of Huntingdon, Cumberland and Northampton registered among its tenants, it had a glamour to it. But it was also, legally speaking, decreed a 'liberty', which meant it was free from the ordinary jurisdiction of the city; later it became an infamous spot for secret marriages.

Samuel Brooke – the same loved S.B. to whom Donne wrote one of his very earliest poems – performed the ceremony. He had been ordained two years before and was chaplain of his Cambridge college. The couple would have spoken almost precisely the same words that couples married in the Church of England speak today, taking their words from the 1559 Book of Common Prayer: 'I John take thee Anne to my wedded wife.' To answer the moment where Samuel asked, 'Who giveth this woman to be married unto this man?' there was Samuel's brother Christopher Brooke, who had known Donne at the Inns and had agreed to stand in. 'And the Minister receiving the woman at her father or friend's hands, shall cause the man to take the woman by the right hand, and so either to give their troth to the other.' The service takes less than half an hour, if you go fast: they wouldn't have needed much of either of the Brooke boys' time.

Nonetheless: both brothers were to have good reason to regret their generosity very soon.

After the wedding Anne returned to Loseley in the countryside with her oblivious father as if nothing had happened, and Donne went back to his lodgings, to wait and hope. To hope for what, beyond a good moment to break the news, is hard to say. The moment didn't come, so in the end, on 2 February, almost two months after the wedding day, he wrote a letter, and sent it to his father-in-law via the 9th Earl of Northumberland, Henry Percy.

It wasn't, by any reckoning, a good letter. Donne was aiming for both humility and authority; he instead succeeded in sounding at once over-confident and mildly unhinged:

> I knew my present estate less than fit for her; I knew, (yet I knew not why) that I stood not right in your opinion; I knew that to have given any intimation of it, had been to impossibilitate the whole matter. And then having these honest purposes in our hearts, and those fetters in our consciences, me thinks we should be pardoned, if our fault be but this, that we did not, by fore-revealing of it, consent to our hindrance and torment.

It is a wonderful word, 'impossibilitate'. The first date currently given for it in the *OED* comes thirty years later, so it was possibly Donne's own invention: an inauspicious beginning for a word. His aside, 'I knew, (yet I knew not why) that I stood not right in your opinion' is comically unplacatory – asking 'why don't you like me?' rarely endears the asker. He continues,

I know this letter shall find you full of passion; but I
know no passion can alter your reason and wisdom; to
which I adventure to commend these particulars: that it
is irremediably done [he spells it 'donne': a fantastically
inappropriate pun on his own name]; that if you incense
my Lord you destroy her and me; that it is easy to give
us happiness; and that my endeavours and industry,
if it please you to prosper them, may soon make me
somewhat worthier of her.

It's multiple requests rolled up in one: daughter, and a job,
and forgiveness. What Donne did not add, though, was that
he had already, in January, prepared and brought his suit
to the ecclesiastical Court of Audience. He had employed
lawyers representing him and Anne to argue before the
judge, Richard Swale, that the marriage was valid; he had,
essentially, stolen a march on his father-in-law, but had no
intention of telling him so.

From the point of view of George More, with his notoriously
quick temper and his aspirations to nobility, it was a disaster.
Anne might have formed a great alliance, have given him
titled in-laws with whom to socially machinate: now she had
bound herself to a scribbling reprobate, without property
and with a dead religious traitor for brother. Moreover,
not only was Donne, having spent most of his inheritance,
not rich – and Donne wrote that 'some uncharitable malice
hath presented my debts double at least' – but rumours had
reached Sir George that he was as sexually promiscuous as

his poetry implied: 'that fault which was laid to me, of having deceived some gentlewomen before.' Donne was also out of favour with Sir Thomas Egerton for routinely tampering with (as Egerton saw it) or improving (as Donne saw it) the letters that Egerton gave Donne to copy. The essayist Francis Osborne, looking on from a distance, used Donne's example as a warning to his son: 'it is not safe for a secretary to mend

Sir George More, whose face Anne may or
may not have inherited

the copy his master hath set him . . . lest he should grow jealous, that you valued your conceptions before his.' So to Sir George he was a glorified servant, and not even a very obedient one.

Sir George went immediately to Egerton. Anne was still a minor, so Donne had broken canon law. Donne was summarily dismissed from Egerton's household. The shock and betrayal of it would have felt colossal: the bond between master and secretary was supposed to be as strong as that between man and wife. Donne would have been even more bewildered immediately afterwards: he was thrown into the Fleet prison to await further investigation. Egerton did nothing to prevent it. The two Brooke brothers meanwhile were tracked down, arrested and locked up in prison; Christopher in the Marshalsea, and Samuel, seemingly, in Newgate. As a lawyer and a minister, they had potentially committed more serious crimes than Donne. Given they didn't even get a marriage out of it, the loyal brothers undoubtedly proved the losers of the day: they tried to be the heralds of love, and got only rats in return.

The Fleet prison was simultaneously disgusting and expensive: a debtor's prison, it didn't have even the dignity and royal tinge of the Tower. It stood on the banks of the River Fleet in east London – the same river that gave its name to Fleet Street – and had a grille looking onto the street through which prisoners could beg for alms. Prisons were profit-making enterprises: you paid for each turn of the key, paid to have your irons removed, paid for your food and lodging. The rooms were cramped and dank, fourteen and a half feet by twelve, and ceilings low enough to touch. The treatment was cruel to the point of deadly; in 1593 a bill had been sent to Parliament accusing the deputy warden of murder.

The Fleet prison

Donne's brother had died in one prison: now he was in another, and, like Henry, he was growing increasingly desperately unwell. On 11 February, locked in his cell, he got hold of ink and paper and wrote a more desperate plea to Sir George. He no longer stood upon his pride.

And though perchance you intend not utter destruction, yet the way through which I fall towards it is so headlong, that, being thus pushed, I shall soon be at bottom, for it pleaseth God, from whom I acknowledge the punishment to be just, to accompany my other ills with so much sickness as I have no refuge but that of mercy, which I beg of Him, my Lord, and you.

This new, humbler letter asked More to think of Anne: 'all my endeavours and the whole course of my life shall be bent to make myself worthy of your favour and her love, whose peace of conscience and quiet I know must be much wounded and violenced if your displeasure sever us.' Donne's fall from nuptial rebellion to obeisance was very swift: fast enough to overturn his whole understanding of what you could and couldn't talk your way around.

Sir George sent word in return that he would leave the matter up to Egerton. It was then to Egerton that Donne wrote, in full obeisance: More, 'whom I leave no humble way unsought to regain', he said, 'refers all to your Lordship'. He was, he said, now cognisant of how he had sinned: 'your justice hath been merciful in making me know my offence, and it hath much profited me that I am dejected.' But since the accumulation of pain had worked upon him, he begged that Egerton might 'be pleased to lessen that correction which your just wisdom hath destined for me'. Egerton unhardened his heart a little and ordered that Donne should be allowed to return to his lodgings. He stayed there, under house arrest in dark midwinter, while the legality of his marriage to Anne was decided by the city's Commissioners.

Donne's health began to improve as soon as he was out of the jail, but his life was still in chaos. While the High Commission deliberated, he continued to send out flocks of letters. Some were to Sir George – in one, he reiterated his passion for Anne, and begged permission to send a note to her:

> My conscience, and such affection as in my conscience becomes an honest man, emboldens me to make one request more, which is that by some kind and comfortable message you would be pleased to give some ease of the afflictions which I know your daughter in her mind suffers; and that (if it be not against your other purposes) I may with your leave write to her; for without your leave I will never attempt any thing concerning her.

'Without your leave I will never attempt any thing concerning her' – a bold statement, it must have sounded to Sir George, all things considered. If he was permitted to write to his newly made wife, the letters alas don't survive. But there was also the question of the Brooke brothers. Walton says he 'neither gave rest to his body or brain, nor to any friend in whom he might hope to have an interest, until he had procured an enlargement for his two imprisoned friends'. He lobbied Egerton. In the end, Christopher Brooke – who would go on, eventually, to live down his brief stint in jail and become an MP for multiple constituencies

– marshalled all his lawyerly ability and wrote to Egerton himself. He was good at it: he apologised, and pleaded a need to be in York, where he had a legal practice and court session had begun four days ago. His love for Donne is strong in the letter – he ends it, 'and pardon me a word for him [Donne], my lord; were it not now best that every one whom he any way concerns, should become his favourer or his friend, who wants (my good lord) but fortune's hands and tongue to rear him up and set him out.' The letter, coupled with Donne's own importuning, worked, and the brothers were at last allowed to leave their prison cells and dust down their briefly halted lives.

Very slowly, George More began to come round. Walton puts his eventual change of heart down to Donne's trans-formative charm, the kind of personality that could heat a cold room by force of will – Donne, Walton says, when he worked to 'entice, had a strange kind of elegant irresist-ible art'. It's equally probable, though, that it was looking increasingly certain that the marriage would be a legal fait accompli, and so Sir George was grudgingly accepting the inevitable. By the time the court decision was to be made, he was mollified enough to agree to try to help Donne recover his position with Egerton.

Donne wrote a letter to his former employer, full of a kind of hopeful despair: 'I was four years your Lordship's secretary, not dishonest nor greedy. The sickness of which I died is that I began in your Lordship's house this love. Where I shall be buried I know not.' The urgency of his position was not just in the immediate need for money, but also that if Egerton wouldn't have him back, it would be taken as a sign that he was completely unemployable. 'To seek preferment here with any but your Lordship were a madness. Every great man to whom I shall address any such suit, will silently dispute the case, and say, would my Lord Keeper so disgraciously have imprisoned him, and flung him away, if he had not done some other great fault, of which we hear not.'

Egerton – perhaps remembering the hints that had been given him, during Donne's imprisonment, of Donne's diffi-cult Catholic family, perhaps remembering his secretary's inability to stop correcting his grammar – would not be persuaded. According to Walton, Egerton felt 'unfeignedly sorry for what he had done, yet it was inconsistent with his place and credit, to discharge and re-admit servants at the request of passionate petitioners'. Donne remained fired.

On 27 April 1602, Donne's marriage was declared good and sufficient. Richard Swale, the judge to whom Donne's lawyers had so swiftly hurried to make their case, issued a decree from the Court of Audience of the most emphatic kind. Donne's case, Swale decreed, was 'reliable and from top to bottom to be pronounced well-founded and proved', and, nothing could be 'excepted, argued, proposed, alleged or proved that would negate the accusation of the said John Donne in this case, or in any way weaken it': it was a very unambiguous victory. 'A true and pure marriage', he declared, had been contracted 'between the said Anne

Moore alias Donne and John Donne'. Donne was allowed to take up his wife.

¶

One of the things most people know about Donne, along with 'no man is an island', is the pun: 'John Donne, Anne Donne, Undone.' It's supposed to come from these dark days, just after his marriage. But it is characteristic of everything to do with Donne that it isn't at all straightforward: it's very possible the pun was never Donne's, or, if it was, it wasn't meant to mean what we think it means. The primary source for it is slippery Walton: 'Immediately after his dismission from [Egerton's] service, he sent a sad letter to his wife, to acquaint her with it: and, after the subscription of his name, writ, *John Donne, Anne Done, Un-done*. And God knows it proved too true.' Walton calls the wedding 'the remarkable error of his life' and this version of the story is the one that fits best with his version of what Donne was.

The pun appears before that, though, in several other places: one, the anonymous 1658 collection *Witty Apophthegms*, suggests, wildly improbably, that Donne wrote the words to his father-in-law: he 'took his pen and writ (and sent it to the old man) in this manner, John Donne, Anne Donne, undone, which wrought good effects on the old man'. Another version, William Winstanley's *England's Worthies*, has Donne scratching the words into the window of his jail: 'In the time of Master Donne's melancholy imprisonment, how true I know not, only I have heard it often discoursed, that he writ on the window with the point of his Diamond, reflecting the then present affliction of his Marriage with these words, John Donne, done and undone.'

These all agree at least in this: that Donne, miserable and alone, made his pun in the midst of his sorrow. There is, though, an entirely different rendering of the pun, in *A Choice Banquet*, a jest book written by Archibald Armstrong in 1660, which has just as much claim on the truth as any of the others: 'Doctor Donne after he was married to a maid, whose name was Anne, in a frolic (on his Wedding day) chalked this on the back-side of his kitchen door, *John Donne, Anne Donne, Un-done*.' In this version, the un-done refers not to the dramatic overturning of his hopes and the loss of his job and position, but something gladder, a sexual undoing. It's kinder, and has in it a kind of carnival spirit of new discovery. It's traditional, and probably more likely, to believe the sadder, more despairing version – but this book chooses to believe in the possibility, too, of a man floored and upended by desire.

THE ANTICLIMACTICALLY
MARRIED MAN

He had his teenaged bride in his arms – but where exactly to go with her was the difficulty. His prison debts for himself and the two Brooke brothers now reached to £40 – a huge sum, at a time when a schoolmaster might be paid £20 a year. Anne had a dead aunt who had left her £100, but beyond that they had very little bar their clothes and their wits.

At the last moment they had sudden, rich luck: a young cousin of Anne's, Francis Wolley, a godson of the Queen, offered a place in his manor house at Pyrford. Francis was about nineteen and a gifted gambler – it was said that he once won £800 in a single night, betting with royalty and earls. His house was eight miles out of Guildford, more than twenty miles from London, handsomely set in large grounds, and amply 'adorned with paintings of fowl and huntings, etc.' Whether Anne and Donne liked the hearty decor or not, they gladly moved in. It was here, as guests of a charming boy gamester, that they spent the first three years of their married life.

It was probably at Pyrford that Donne wrote 'The Sun Rising'. While it's a love poem you would eat your own heart for, it's also not entirely what it seems. First of all, there's a hidden spike in it, levelled at Donne's father-in-law. In 1597, George More had published a little treatise called *A Demonstration of God in His Works*, an attempt to prove unequivocally the existence of God. In it he, like his son-in-law, writes about the sun rising, a mixture of Psalm 19 and his own muscular enthusiasm: 'who seeth not the glorious arising of the sun his coming forth as a bridegroom out of his chamber, and his rejoicing like a mighty man to run his race?'

Donne refuses to rejoice like a mighty man; instead he heckles it:

> Busy old fool, unruly Sun,
> Why dost thou thus
> Through windows, and through curtains call on us?

He appears to be laughing at his father-in-law's more conventional efforts; and by extension, at George More's text more widely, which is not a piece of rhetorical wizardry: it argues that an atheist is akin to a stone, or a monster not fully human. It doesn't sound dull, but does manage to be; it opens with a preface addressed 'England, my dear country give me leave, out of love and duty, a dutiful and loving servant to speak unto thee.' (England chose not to listen. It wasn't by any stretch a bestseller.)

There's also a joke and an equivocation in it which is often missed: at the end of the poem the sun does rise, of course, because suns do. But then Donne could claim that he wanted it to rise all along:

Shine here to us, and thou art everywhere:
This bed thy centre is, these walls, thy sphere.

It's not a straightforward adoration poem – it's also a poem about bravado; about a young man visibly conjuring good out of necessity. If you are battered and thwarted in your day-to-day life, still in your poetry you can pretend the sun only rises because you allow it. The poem knows the speaker is being absurd, but it also knows that he shines.

§

'We can die by it,' he wrote, 'if not live by love'. There had been the great leap of desire and hope: and then there was reality. Pyrford, on the banks of the River Wey just outside Woking, in Surrey, was a long ride from London and the theatres and bear pits: a good thirty miles on hard roads. When Donne looked back at these days, at the prison and the time that followed, he wrote: 'I died at a blow then, when my courses were diverted.' He discovered very swiftly – as many men and far, far more women have discovered before and since – that domesticity had neither the outside witnesses necessary for glamour nor the drill-down intensity of private study.

Worse, every day he was away from London, a friend wrote, his chances of making something grand of himself grew smaller. 'Your friends are sorry that you make yourself so great a stranger, but you best know your own occasions.

Howbeit, if you have any designs towards the Court, it were good you did prevent the loss of any more time . . . the places of attendance . . . grow daily dearer.'

Donne had no obvious employment in these years. He studied and read widely, but there was very little money. Meanwhile, his friends were moving into the fast stream of Renaissance politics. Henry Wotton, who had retreated so prudently to Europe to wait out the Queen's fury (or her life, whichever ended first), was in Tuscany in 1602 when he was given a mission. The Grand Duke of Tuscany had intercepted letters detailing a plot to poison King James VI of Scotland. The King had to be warned, and Wotton – quick-witted, eager to please and fluent in Italian – was chosen to go, carrying letters to James and vials of antidotes prepared by the Italians. In order to evade the suspicion of the would-be regicides, Wotton travelled under the name Ottavio (or Octavio) Baldi.

Izaak Walton, who came to know and love Wotton in later life through Donne, told the story of his arrival at James's Scottish court: 'When Octavio Baldi came to the Presence-chamber door, he was requested to lay aside his long rapier – which, Italian-like, he then wore.' Wotton delivered his message to the King, who was in the company of a handful of his courtiers, officially and in Italian: then 'after a little pause, Octavio Baldi steps to the table, and whispers to the King in his own language, that he was an Englishman, beseeching him for a more private conference with his Majesty, and that he might be concealed during his stay in that nation.' Wotton stayed with the King, living as Baldi, for three months, after which 'he departed as true an Italian as he came thither.' For Donne, living amid someone else's horse portraiture, surviving on the charity of a man a decade younger, the difference between their two lives must have been hard. His letters to Wotton were remarkably unjealous, but they were full of yearning. The love was constant: when Wotton was about to depart on another journey, as ambassador to Venice, Donne wrote asking if he would be long enough in London for him to dash down to town so that 'such a one as I may yet kiss your hands'. But in the same letter, he included a verse, stoic and wry and mournful –

For me (if there be such a thing as I)
Fortune (if there be such a thing as she)
Spies that I bear so well her tyranny
That she thinks nothing else so fit for me.

Another friend of Donne's, Sir Henry Goodere, sent weekly news of life amid the jostle and plotting of the court. Goodere was the son of a well-off landowner and had been knighted, like young Egerton, in Ireland. Sweet-natured and profligate, he was intent on cutting a figure at court, and throughout his life spent far more money than he had. They were an unlikely pairing, and it's not clear how they met – but if Donne had a best friend, it was Goodere. His letters to Donne didn't survive – Donne carefully burned

Sir Henry Wotton

them after Goodere's death, as was his custom – but at least forty-eight of Donne's to him are extant: letters in which Donne is, by turns, sympathetic, loving, wry and full of exasperated advice. Several times during their lifelong friendship he would stay up late after an already long day, rewriting Goodere's formal letters for him, to save him from embarrassing himself in his work. Goodere's weekly letters would have been full of news: he took part in court masques, attempted business deals that went haywire, was a keen hawker.

In return for Goodere's news, Donne had nothing to send but poetry, which he dismissed even as he packed it into the packet of paper:

> I accompany [this letter] with another rag of verses,
> worthy of that name for the smallness and age, for it hath
> long lain among my other papers, and laughs at them
> that have adventured to you: for I think till now you saw
> it not, and neither you nor it should repent it. Sir, if I were
> any thing, my love to you might multiply it, and dignify
> it: but infinite nothings are but one such.

They were hard years for Donne and Anne. There were many moments in which the flashes of his old relishing self flared up again – some of the love poetry certainly dates from this period, though it's impossible to say how much. There were days with glee in them, but also days in which his new, unfamiliar work of marriage and consistency and obligation felt as onerous as any job he had ever done. A letter written a few years later to Goodere catches exactly the up-and-down sweep of Donne's mood:

> Sometimes when I find my self transported with jollity, and love of company, I hang leads at my heels; and reduce to my thoughts my fortunes, my years, the duties of a man, of a friend, of a husband, of a father, and all the incumbencies of a family: when sadness dejects me, either I countermine it with another sadness, or I kindle squibs [fireworks] about me again, and fly into sportfulness and company.

It was a difficult, emotionally volatile task; Donne was attempting, still young and stumbling, to find his footing in a world which was not welcoming him with open arms.

THE AMBIVALENT FATHER

Donne very swiftly became a father. His daughter Constance was born in the beginning of 1603, in the dark depths of the Surrey winter. In London, the Queen was growing frail, and another wave of plague was rising.

As far as we can tell, Donne was not an exemplary parent; or at least, he wasn't a father who seemed to garner much joy from his children. Renaissance filial relations among the upper classes were carefully choreographed affairs: all lifted hats and hinging knees. The great biographer and antiquary John Aubrey, author of a collection of biographies called *Brief Lives*, wrote, disapproving:

> Gentlemen of thirty and forty years old were to stand like mutes and fools bareheaded before their parents; and the daughters (grown women) were to stand at the cupboard-side during the whole time of their proud mother's visit, unless (as the fashion was) leave was desired, forsooth, that a cushion should be given them to kneel upon, brought them by the serving man after they had done sufficient penance in standing.

Donne, in contrast, relished that theatrical element of the status quo: 'children', he noted with approbation in a sermon,

'kneel to ask blessing of parents in England; but where else?'
Everything that made him so spectacular a poet made him
ill-suited to being a father: having a parent whose mind is
riddling, intense and recalcitrant of easy comfort is rarely
what a child dreams of.

In those early days of marriage, Donne found himself
almost housebound: he wrote to Goodere, 'I have not been
out of my house since I received your packet. As I have much
quenched my senses, and disused my body from pleasure,
and so tried how I can endure to be mine own grave, so I
try now how I can suffer a prison.' The monotony of home
life chipped away at his ability to rouse himself: 'if I ask
myself what I have done in this last watch, or could do in
the next, I can say nothing.' He describes his domesticity as
stagnant water: 'When I must shipwreck, I would do it in
a sea, where mine impotency might have some excuse; not
in a sullen weedy lake, where I could not have so much as
exercise for my swimming.'

He did at least have the grace to be guilty that he was
dissatisfied. Donne's letters very rarely painted domestic
scenes – but there is one letter, to Goodere, which does.

I write not to you out of my poor library, where to
cast mine eye upon good authors kindles or refreshes,
sometimes, meditations not unfit to communicate to near
friends; nor from the highway, where I am contracted,
and inverted into my self, which are my two ordinary
forges of letters to you. But I write from the fire side in

my parlour, and in the noise of three gamesome children; and by the side of her, whom because I have transplanted into a wretched fortune, I must labour to disguise that from her by all such honest devices, as giving her my company and discourse; therefore I steal from her all the time which I give this letter, and it is therefore that I . . . gallop so fast over it.

There's affection in it, but heavily laden with exasperation: it's one of the moments in his letters in which Donne is most suddenly human.

He does not seem, though, to have gone hunting for other sexual partners. For all the monotony, and all the drudgery, Donne was – if we believe him – faithful to Anne. He wrote, in an undated essay: 'Thou hast delivered me, O God . . . from the Egypt of lust, by confining my affections, and from the monstrous and unnatural Egypt of painful and wearisome idleness, by the necessities of domestic and familiar cares and duties.' In 'confining my affections', Donne claims fidelity to Anne. It could just be a piece of showy rhetoric – or even a way of staring down guilt – but Donne was addressing God: perhaps unlikely to lie. Anne wouldn't necessarily have thanked him for it, given her whole adult life became the bearing and mourning of children – but the poet who found ten dozen ways to write the joy and sorrow of sex, once hers was – if we take him at his word – hers alone.

That's not to say, though, that there weren't flirtations;

most particularly, with a woman of substance, intelligence and high style, Magdalen Herbert. Magdalen was five years older than Donne, the mother of a brood of poets and philosophers. They first established a relationship over a chance meeting in around 1599, but in the early years of the new century the acquaintance kindled into a more intimate friendship. It's often suggested, by Walton among others, that Donne wrote his 'Autumnal' for Magdalen. The poem begins beguilingly: 'No spring, nor summer beauty hath such grace,/ As I have seen in one autumnal face.' It goes on, though, less flatteringly: 'But name not winter faces, whose skin's slack,/ Lank as an unthrift's purse, but a soul's sack.' Donne would have to have been spectacularly off in his assessment of what he could venture (which, given his miscalculation of his wedding, is not completely impossible) to have thought the poem would charm an older woman. It's more likely that Donne kept to letters and verse epistles: she was, he wrote in his most courtly mode, 'a world alone', he was 'your servant extraordinary'. What sets it apart from his other friendships was that Walton thought it necessary to state outright that though Donne was struck with 'the beauties of her body, and mind', yet it 'was not an amity that polluted their souls'; the need to say it suggests there might, perhaps, have been rumours. Donne's fidelity may possibly have been absolute, but he certainly allowed himself space, in his relationship with his patronesses, for a certain linguistic leeway. What Anne thought, of his vaunting praise of other women, we can't know; she would have been worldly enough to know that a great deal of Donne's flourish was convention – but it can't have been her most treasured thought, as she moved through the house, inevitably pregnant.

Anne was pregnant twelve times in their sixteen years of marriage. She would have spent her entire adult life either pregnant or recovering from childbirth, and often both at once. Her physical pain must have been relentless. After Constance there was John in 1604 and George in 1605. Life at Pyrford was growing increasingly crowded, and Francis Wolley was increasingly attracting scandal. He had been married at the age of eleven to his mother's ward, Mary; they had no children, but he had a daughter by his mistress, whom he insisted on calling Mary, and bringing into the family; it must have been strained for the Donnes. So, in 1606, Donne moved his family to a house in Mitcham, to the south of London, where Francis, Lucy, Bridget and Mary were born.

The house in Mitcham was a two-storey cottage, with a pretty garden but a chill in winter: Donne wrote of 'the incommodity of a little thin house'. He called it his hospital, a dungeon, his prison. It was, though, far closer to London – two hours' brisk horse ride to London Bridge. Donne told Goodere of how often he would compose his letters in his head on horseback, to put on paper later: that the road was one of his main 'ordinary forges of letters to you'. Because he had the kind of mind that values putting things well and then putting them better, he wrote it out in a verse epistle, 'To Sir Henry Goodere':

Riding, I had you though you still stayed there,
And in these thoughts, although you never stir,
You came with me to Mitcham and are here.

The days would have been a little easier for the whole
family, despite the chill and the thinness of the walls. Two
of Anne's sisters lived a carriage ride away from the new
house, one at Peckham and one in Beddington, so family
visiting was more possible. Donne, though, spent as much
time as he could escaping his brood. From 1607 to 1611,
he took lodgings in the Strand, riding often to London and
not returning for days: in London, he could be a dashing
youngish man again, dining and gossiping, and not a stuck-
at-home parent.

For a man so emphatic, and capable of such fervent
enthusiasm, he never did manage to enthuse very emphatically about his offspring while they were alive. The closest
he ever gets to writing enthusiastically about them as a
group is in one riotously uneffusive note to Henry Wotton:
'I am a Father as well as you, and of children (I humbly
thank God) of as good dispositions.' He heralds the birth of
his daughter Margaret (his fifth daughter, and tenth child)
with an unflattering note to a friend, three days before she
was baptised: 'I must beg of you to christen a child, which
is but a daughter.' There is, on the one hand, real joy in
the announcement of his son Nicholas in 1613: 'The newest
thing that I know in the world, is my new son'. Everything
with a fresh-born baby becomes re-possible. But he writes

in the same letter, 'I stand like a tree, which once a year bears, though no fruit, yet this mast of children.' 'Mast' is a weight, but is also a fruit from forest trees that is inedible to humans but was used as food for swine. So his children, in this mood, are unwholesome and burdensome produce. Few warm details of Donne's children pepper his letters; he wrote, as far as we know, no poetry for or about them. Queen Elizabeth's court astronomer John Dee noted his child's first word in his diary, but Donne mentions them when they are born and then for three reasons: when they are ill; when they are loud, 'gamesome', or expensive; and when they are dead.

Death marched in and out of the house for the whole of his and Anne's life together. Three of their children died before their tenth birthday; another two were stillborn – and it is in recording their deaths that his love of them flares into life. He wrote, in the winter of 1614, of Anne, who has just miscarried: 'I have already lost half a child, and with that mischance of hers, my wife [has] fallen into an indisposition, which would afflict her much, but that the sickness of all her other children stupefies her.' Donne is readying himself for another loss: 'of one of which [children], in good faith, I have not much hope . . . if God should ease us with burials, I know not how to perform even that: but I flatter myself with this hope, that I am dying too; for I cannot waste faster than by such griefs.' He lost no children to that epidemic: but, in March 1614, wrote:

Perchance others may have told you that I am relapsed
into my fever; but that which I must entreat you to
condole with me, is, that I am relapsed into good degrees
of health; your cause of sorrow for that, is, that you are
likely to be the more troubled with such an impertinency
as I am; and mine is, that I am fallen from fair hopes of
ending all; yet I have 'scaped no better cheap, than that I
have paid death one of my children for my ransom.

It is a strange mix of half-achieved comedy ('your cause
for sorrow', he says, that he is alive) and misery: the baby
was his Mary, just over three years old. 'Because I loved it
well, I make account that I dignify the memory of it, by
mentioning of it to you.'

How did Donne take such deaths? Infant mortality was a
blunt fact of life – depending on the region, anything from
one hundred to four hundred out of a thousand live-born
babies did not live to their first year, and children could be
taken at any time by dysentery – known as 'bloody flux' –
whooping cough, smallpox, 'scarlatina' (scarlet fever) and
myriad other unidentified fevers. The death of children was
so much more common that today there's often an assump-
tion that the loss of each child was less strongly felt. But
that seems implausible – even though it was very differently expressed. In the early seventeenth century, stone effigies
of lost babies began appearing on the tombs of the families. Donne's contemporary Ben Jonson lost his eldest son,
Benjamin, at the age of seven. He wrote, in the poem 'On

My First Son': 'Rest in soft peace, and, asked, say, "Here doth lie/Ben Jonson his best piece of poetry."'

And there are other, vivid accounts of loss. Lady Mary Carey wrote a prose dialogue on the loss of her boy that has at its heart a keening cry: 'the Lord hath taken from me a Son, a beloved Son, an only son, an only Child, the last of three, and it must needs affect me; can a woman forget her suckling child?' Gertrude Aston Thimelby's poem 'On the Death of Her Only Child' summons up the blame, embraces it:

Dear infant, 'twas thy mother's fault
So soon inclosed thee in a vault
And father's good, that in such hast
Has my sweet child in heaven placed.

The poems that are saddest have a tooth-gritted hope in them: the effort involved in attempting to turn misery into possibility is so palpable and so unconvincing. Elizabeth Egerton's epitaph 'On My Boy Henry' begins, 'Nor can I think of any thought, but grieve/For joy or pleasure could not me relieve.' It ends, though: 'But you art happy, sweet'st on high/I mourn not for thy birth, nor cry.' Marcel Proust – a man whose love for provocative metaphors has much in common with Donne's – said: 'people of bygone ages seem infinitely remote from us. We do not feel justified in ascribing to them any underlying intentions beyond those they formally express: we are amazed when we come across an emotion more or less like we feel today in a Homeric hero.'

The details of grief are different across time, and the places where the suffering laid their blame and guilt were different, and suppression and expression were different, and the attempts at comfort were different. But rage and sorrow and loss are rage and sorrow and loss.

Donne knew what it was to be haunted by that sorrow. Several years later, in 1612, under very different circumstances, he would go to Paris, leaving his wife in London. She was by then pregnant with their eighth child. Walton writes about this moment in his biography far more vividly than any other:

Two days after their arrival there, Mr Donne was left alone, in that room in which Sir Robert [Drury], and he, and some other friends had dined together. To this place Sir Robert returned within half an hour; and, as he left, so he found Mr Donne alone; but, in such ecstasy, and so altered as to his looks, as amazed Sir Robert to behold him: insomuch that he earnestly desired Mr Donne to declare what had befallen him in the short time of his absence? To which, Mr Donne was not able to make a present answer: but, after a long and perplexed pause, did at last say, I have seen a dreadful vision since I saw you: I have seen my dear wife pass twice by me through this room, with her hair hanging about her shoulders, and a dead child in her arms: this, I have seen since I saw you. To which, Sir Robert replied; Sure Sir, you have slept since I saw you; and, this is the result of some melancholy dream, which I desire you to forget, for you are now awake. To which Mr Donne's reply was: I cannot be surer that I now live, then that I have not slept since I saw you: and am as sure, that at her second appearing, she stopped, and looked me in the face, and vanished.

Donne never managed to show much effervescence about his children, but they were shot through his nerves and sinews. He sent a messenger to London the next morning; the man returned twelve days later. Anne, he said, had borne a stillborn child 'the same day, and about the very hour that Mr Donne affirmed he saw her pass by him in his Chamber'. For all his bluntness about his children, the thought of them literally haunted him. To read Walton's account is to be reminded that it is not only the effusive who feel the heavy weight of love.

HOW TO PRETEND TO HAVE READ
MORE THAN YOU HAVE

Queen Elizabeth died, aged sixty-nine, in the spring of 1603. Quick-witted and quick-tempered to the very grave, she refused to go to bed; when Robert Cecil told her she must, she was said to have slapped him back: 'Must! Is *must* a word to be addressed to princes? Little man, little man!' London put on black and unleashed a funeral procession of splendid sorrow and extravagant dolour. The historian William Camden sketched a drawing of her funeral procession, labelling the groups like a map: 'children of the chapel', 'poor women to the number of 266', 'countesses and viscountesses' in one group, 'Earls' daughters and baronesses' in another, and at the end, the Queen's effigy on a canopied four-horse chariot, flanked by six barons. All of the women have the same nose, as does Sir Walter Raleigh. Donne would write about her, much later: 'In the death of that Queen, unmatchable, inimitable in her sex; that Queen, worthy, I will not say of Nestor's years, I will not say of Methusalem's, but worthy of Adam's years, if Adam had never fallen; in her death we were all under one common flood, and depth of tears.'

King James I – previously James VI of Scotland, son of Mary Queen of Scots, thin legs but broad shoulders, quick-witted but poor table manners – took the throne. Poets

The funeral procession of Queen Elizabeth.

poured forth their praise. (The verse produced for new monarchs is traditionally known as Ascension Literature, and James inspired some of the most remarkably boring poetry of the period. If Donne joined in, his offering has not survived.) Precisely what kind of monarch James was is still, four hundred years later, up for debate; in the nineteenth century he was said to be 'indeed made up of two men – a witty, well-read scholar, who wrote, disputed and harangued, and a nervous drivelling idiot who acted'. Within months of his coronation a letter had gone out to the Venetian Doge from a secretary: 'The new king . . . seems to have forgotten that he is a king except in his kingly pursuit of stags, to which he is quite foolishly devoted.' Donne jokes about it in 'The Sun Rising', 'go tell court huntsmen that the king will ride.' More recently, his reputation has been reassessed; he treasured peace, and learning – known as the 'Scholar King', he wrote at just eighteen a literary manual, 'Some Rules and Cautions to be Observed and Eschewed in Scottish Prosody', and published two books of not-awful poetry while King

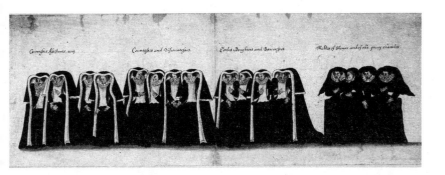

of Scotland. Married with seven children, James also loved men, and had intense, probably sexual relationships with a small number of beautiful and accomplished courtiers who rose to power under him.

A new king was a cause for optimism among England's finest under-employed; Donne would have hoped that he might yet find his way to the stipend and the favour-swapping, quid-pro-quo lucrativity that the best court jobs allowed for. There was a great spate of knightings: Egerton became Baron Ellesmere, Anne's brother Robert was knighted along with other friends of Donne's – Francis Bacon and Richard Baker from the university days – and Henry Goodere was made a Gentleman of the Privy Chamber. James, coming upon Wotton for the first time since their Ottavio Baldi days, seized him in his arms with a roar of delight, declared 'he was the most honest, and therefore the best dissembler that he ever met with', and knighted him apparently on the spot.

Nothing, though, was forthcoming for Donne. James had heard via court gossip about the marriage and the prison spell; he doesn't seem to have been inclined to risk polluting his beginning by associating with a recently fired ex-Catholic jailbird. So Donne kept writing: letters, some poems, tracts – and a text which showed how forensically and beadily he was watching and judging the world.

Donne knew intimately the power of books. Both their real power, and the easier, less arduous power that comes with putting on the language of scholarship like a disguise. Reading – even just the appearance of it – can be wielded as a weapon, and in 1604 Donne wrote an entire text that imagines that wielding and takes it to its absurd end point. In 2016, the Keeper of the Muniments at Westminster Abbey was sorting through a tin trunk of scrappy bits of manuscripts, and found that he held in his hands, entirely without warning, a new version of one of Donne's works: 'The Courtier's Library'. The new text allows us to date the work to the moment in his life when Donne was casting about for what he should become. He knew, though, what he should not be: a pretender. Its full Latin name translates to 'Catalogue of incomparable courtly books, not for sale', but Donne referred to it in his letters as his *Catalogus*: a satirical list of books that the striving courtier can introduce into conversation to make himself seem wiser, keener, sexier. The advantage is that, because none of the books exist, the courtier can't be cross-examined on them: the only way to be a true, unassailable authority on a text is for it not to exist.

The titles of the books add up to an assassin's hit list: of intellectual sloppiness, of two-faced hypocrisy and ethical ugliness in religious debate, of the pliancy of the law and of lazy humanist scholarship of the time: the misuse of something that should be treated as terrifyingly precious. The text tells us a colossal amount about Donne: which human foibles he found funny, which he found more serious. For instance, he lists an imaginary book by Sir Edward Hoby, a non-imaginary diplomat and courtier known for having liquid lunches and laying down the law at them: 'Sir Edward Hoby's Afternoon Belchings: or, a Treatise of Univocals, as of the King's Prerogative, and Imaginary Monsters, such as the King's Evil and the French Disease'.

Elsewhere its jibes are more seriously derogatory. For instance, Matthew Sutcliffe, Dean of Exeter, is treated thus: '32. *What Not? or, a Refutation of all the errors, past, present and future, not only in Theology but in the other branches of knowledge, and the technical Arts, of all men dead, living and as yet unborn*: put together in a single night after supper, by Doctor Sutcliffe.' Sutcliffe was technically an ally, in that by the time Donne was writing the *Catalogus* both he and Sutcliffe ostensibly shared a religiously conformist stance, but Sutcliffe's confident dogmatism goes against the grain of Donne's suppler mind. It gives a key to understanding Donne: the emphasis in his work on the need for rigorous attention to the world around you. The desire for totalitarian certainty, in a refutation of all the mistakes 'of all men dead, living and as yet unborn', is from a man like Donne a damning accusation.

The structure of the *Catalogus* is itself a joke. Donne

is laughing at the ability of scholarly erudition to expand into infinity; there are 141 volumes, 60,047 authors, editors, translators, amanuenses, patrons – and an unspecified horde of servants, who help the great scholarly drive by providing soiled toilet paper to use as copy-texts. Donne goes after multiple targets at once: those who enjoy religious persecution, those whose zeal blinds them to religious nuance, the pretensions of the courtier, and the power that scholarly bloviating and stupid writing has to expand upon itself, like paper rabbits.

But the book was more than a witticism – it was also a sideways political jab at the new king. Soon after he wrote his *Catalogus*, Donne panicked. In a Latin letter to Goodere (the only Latin letter we have of his), he asks for the return of his 'rag', and says he is desperately trying to recall any 'others of them have crept out into the world without my knowledge'. The book, he knew, risked being read as he intended it: a criticism of the new order. It had become very quickly obvious to Donne that the new 'Scholar King', though he stood officially on the side of learning and scholarship, was not over-fond of dissent or discussion. In 1604 (the year of the *Catalogus*) James summoned the Hampton Court Conference, ostensibly as a moment for consultation with his new subjects. Rather than nurturing free speech, though, James had crushed any theological positions which might threaten his absolute power. The King, Donne saw, was swiftly surrounding himself with those who would offer elaborate scholarly justifications for whatever political moves he had already decided on. The *Catalogus* was a how-to for those who wanted to thrive under James: if you wanted to get ahead in the new system, Donne implied, you would need to disguise your sycophancy in the most learned jargon you could invent: talk like a 141-volume book, but don't say anything at all. Scholarship itself, he feared, would have to bend before the will of the King; reduced to the value of Book 23 in the *Catalogus*, 'On the Nothingness of a Fart'.

The *Catalogus*, then, is not a dismissal of learning: it's a ferocious sally in its defence. Read, the spoof catalogue tells us, carefully, sceptically, with all your wits worn like armour against those who care more for the look of knowledge than the meat of it. Donne read prodigiously. We still have some of his own books, and the marks he made in them. They might look, the little pencil jabs along the margins, like respectful acts of attention, but to read the *Catalogus* is to know that they could just as well have been marks of condemnation or irony: little jabs of disapprobation.

Donne's scepticism was more than a wit's pose; it was a fundamental ordering principle, faced with a world in which erudition could be faked by snake oil men who smelled of ink, and charlatans would sell you false certainties between hardback covers. He valued the pursuit of knowledge too highly to watch it being bastardised without lashing out.

THE SUICIDAL MAN

I begin to be past hope of dying . . . Death came so fast
towards me that the over-joy of that recovered me.
   Letter to Robert Ker

The years between 1607 and 1610 are biographically murky.
The letters are hard to date and hard to decipher, and the
best historical records we have are of jobs that didn't happen. He failed to get a position in the Queen's household in
1607, and there are references in the letters to his application to jobs in Ireland or, even more remotely, Virginia, but
neither came to anything, if they were ever serious prospects
to begin with. It's equally likely that they were an attempt
on his part to look industrious, both to his friends and to
himself; neither Ireland nor Virginia were at all desirable
places at the time.

We do have, though, some of his weekly letters to
Henry Goodere, letters filled with attempts at counsel and
spiritual comfort, ironical gripings at Donne's own days,
money worries, and a great deal of letter-writing about
letter-writing: frequent apologies for the scrappiness of
the letter itself and of the exigencies of the carrier. This
was before Charles I's 1635 postal reforms, so his letters
crossed the city and country, haphazard and often lost, in

hands of merchants, personal servants, friends, and messenger boys who seemed always to be hovering at Donne's shoulder, ready to snatch the paper away. As the years went on, more and more letters carried accounts of sickness and pain – he grew ill, and each illness refused to fade entirely. One spring, he wrote, bluntly, 'The pleasantness of the season displeases me. Everything refreshes, and I wither, and I grow older and not better.'

As his pain grew, so too did his dream of being dead and rid of it all. In one particular undated letter, the pain was greater than normal:

I have contracted a sickness which I cannot name nor describe. For it hath so much of a continual cramp, that it wrests the sinews . . . but it will not kill me yet; I shall be in this world, like a porter in a great house, ever nearest the door, but seldomest abroad: I shall have many things to make me weary, and yet not get leave to be gone.

In the same letter, he writes:

The day before I lay down, I was at London where I delivered your letter for Sir Ed. Conway, and received another for you, with the copy of my book, of which it is impossible for me to give you a copy so soon, for it is not of much less than 300 pages. If I die, it shall come to you in that fashion that your letter desires it. If I warm again . . . you and I shall speak together of that . . . At this time I only assure you, that I have not appointed it upon any person, nor ever purposed to print it.

The book he referred to was *Biathanatos*. Its title is taken from the Greek for 'violent death': it was, the title page announced when it was published years after his death, a 'Paradox, or thesis, that self-homicide is not so naturally sin, that it may never be otherwise'. In it, Donne lays out a startling argument. The majority of suicides, he writes, are committed from positions of fear, pain, self-protection or spiritual despair: those are sinful, and failures of the soul. But there is an exception: suicides which stem from a single-minded desire to advance God's glory. Donne digs from the Bible to argue that it's not against nature, but along its grain, to lean towards self-slaughter: that there is in all of us a keening towards it. He quotes Paul's letter to the Corinthians: 'Though I give my body that I be burned, and have not love, it profiteth nothing' – from it, he argues, you can conclude two things: 'first, that in a general notion and common reputation, it was esteemed a high degree of perfection to die so, and therefore not against the law of nature; and secondly, by this exception, "without charity", it appears that with charity it might well and profitably be done.'

To write *Biathanatos* was an extraordinary decision. It was dangerous, and potentially illegal, because to attempt suicide in England was a sin punishable by death. This relationship between crime and punishment always sounds like a wry and self-defeating irony, but it was darker than that: doctrine and fear together leaking out in the form of state violence. Successful suicides were buried at a crossroads, pinned through the chest with a stake to stop the spirit escaping. In France under Louis XVI, they were dragged through town face down in the dust. In the same century, there were cases of adults murdering young children as a roundabout form of suicide. The theory was that if you murdered a baby, the child would go to heaven and, once you were arrested, you would have time to repent in the presence of a priest before your execution and therefore reach heaven too: it was a cultural and legal interdiction of such strength that it created murderers.

Donne conjured up examples from the most theatrically vivid stories in Church history – the ones with dramatic reversals, sudden sweeps of bravery and drama. There's the tale, for instance, of Nicephorus of Antioch. Nicephorus, in Donne's telling, knew a church elder named Sapritius, who was to be executed for his Christian faith. At the last minute, faced with the executioners, Sapritius lost confidence, recanted and was saved: 'And Nicephorus, standing by, stepped in to his room and cried, "I am also a Christian!" and so provoked the magistrate to execute him, lest from the faintness of Sapritius the cause might have received a wound or a scorn.' This, Donne reasoned, was 'giving of his body': a form of suicide. This free-jazz interpretation of the Nicephorus hagiography wouldn't have seemed, really, terrifyingly radical, but it was only preparation for his central, inflammatory premise: that Christ's death was a suicide.

Christ could have struck down those who crucified him, but instead he sped up his last breath on the cross; 'many martyrs having hanged upon crosses many days alive', and yet Christ died swiftly, while the thieves either side of him were still breathing. '[He] said, "No man can take away my soul, and I have power to lay it down."' Therefore the cause of Christ's death, Donne writes, was no 'other than His own will'.

There are many astonishments in it: things which sound startlingly modern. For instance, Donne argues that the fact we are very sure of something is not proof that we are right. Aristotle, he writes, was certain about the immutability of the stars; certainty which is now 'utterly defeated'. If we can be wrong about the stars in the sky, we can be wrong about anything, including the ethics of suicide. Even more astonishing, though, was Donne's radical boldness in his willingness to offer up his own horrors: because he writes personally and urgently about his own death wish. There was nobody else who had written anything like it, only him.

He lays it out, his terror and dread, like a filleted body. He probes his own suicidal desires. Perhaps, he wrote, his own questing towards death was down to his early years amid the furtive, death-haunted Catholic community: 'because I had my first breeding and conversation with men of a suppressed and afflicted religion, accustomed to the despite of death, and hungry of imagined martyrdom'. But then he goes on to offer other suggestions, spilling them out in a tumble; perhaps he was just somehow born less well protected – 'the common enemy find that door worst locked against him in me'. He is only sure of the strength of the pull within towards his own oblivion: 'whensoever any affliction assails me, me thinks I have the keys of my prison in mine own hand, and no remedy presents it self so soon to my heart as mine own sword.'

As soon as he had written *Biathanatos*, Donne began to worry about it. It was an inflammatory thing, the kind of book that might burn your career right in front of you. He did not want it read; but nor did he want it destroyed. Many years later, about to embark on a voyage, he sent a copy to his friend Robert Ker, a sophisticated and well-connected courtier, asking him to keep it safe.

It was written by me many years since, and because it is upon a misinterpretable subject, I have always gone so near suppressing it, as that it is only not burnt: no hand hath passed upon it to copy it, nor many eyes to read it . . . It is a book written by Jack Donne, and not by Doctor Donne: Reserve it for me, if I live, and if I die, I only forbid it the press, and the fire: publish it not, but yet burn it not; and between those, do what you will with it.

The book was not published until after Donne's death, when he was out of reach of the possible whispers and exclamations, of both the condemnations and the potential over-enthusiasms.

¶

How, then, did he stay alive: this man whose pain urged his thoughts towards self-slaughter? His letters show the way. On the one hand, they are a laundry list of his agonies: he demanded of his friends a high tolerance for vomit-talk. He complains of 'a stomach colic as kept me in a continual vomiting, so that I know not what I should have been able to do to dispatch this wind, but that an honest fever came and was my physic'. And, another time, sick alongside Anne, 'it hath pleased God to add thus much to my affliction, that my wife hath now confessed her self to be extremely sick; she hath held out thus long to assist me, but is now overturn'd, and here we be in two beds, or graves; so that God hath marked out a great many of us, but taken none yet.' Still, though, he attempts to joke: 'I have passed ten days without taking [i.e. eating] any thing; so that I think no man can live more thriftily.'

Elsewhere, his uvula swells in his throat and he is rendered dumb; his eyes falter. He shudders with coughs; his teeth plague him. The latter was a common enough affliction – made worse by the most popular recipes to remove tooth stains, which included the powder from a burned rabbit's head, or an abrasion made from ground brick, egg shells and myrrh. (The rich suffered it most, having eaten the most sugar; so much so that there was a brief fashion among the poor for colouring one's own teeth black in order to look glamorously prosperous.)

But in answer to his pain, Donne's letters also show him seizing hold of it and re-conceiving of it as a kind of travel. He writes to a friend: 'this advantage you and my other friends have by my frequent fevers, that I am so much the oftener at the gates of heaven, and this advantage by the solitude and close imprisonment that they reduce me to after, that I am thereby the oftener at my prayers; in which, I shall never leave out your happiness.' To be ill, then, is to journey closer to the reality of death, to be closer to the ear of God in order to importune him. And the closer to death, the more clearly you see the richness of living; Donne used his illness to demand from God's ear happiness for his friends.

More than that, though: for Donne, to be so deathly ill so frequently was to be accelerated into readiness for the world that might be to come. He wrote to a close female friend:

> I am not alive because I have not had enough upon
> me to kill me, but because it pleases God to pass me
> through many infirmities before he take me either by
> those particular remembrances, to bring me to particular
> repentances, or by them to give me hope of his particular
> mercies in heaven . . . All this mellows me for heaven,
> and so ferments me in this world, as I shall need no long
> concoction in the grave, but hasten to the resurrection.

Ferment. To be alive is to stew in readiness: illness is a clarifying marinade, through which he might forestall the pause of the grave and leap into eternity.

They were heavy metal, Donne's letters: there is little romance in them, and a great deal of twisting and hammering at his pain to force it to take on the shape of some meaning. It is one more kind of *making*. It's a furious kind of focus, an instance of feverish, counter-intuitive seeking for good; an insistence that it must show you the truth of mortality, and allow you to see more clearly: to see the hopeless, transitory, pained soul, suffused in glories. It says a great deal about him, that he was the kind of man who demanded of pain that it shunt you closer to infinity.

§

Donne's anxieties about *Biathanatos* turned out to be true. Perhaps. In the 1650s, twenty years after Donne's death, the Regius Professor of Divinity at Cambridge, Anthony Tuckney, declared that he believed Donne's book had led a convicted criminal to attempt to poison himself. It was also said that the classical translator Thomas Creech used to hold and twist in his hands a rope while reading Donne's text: and eventually hanged himself. Correlation, of course, is not causation. But the philosopher Charles Blount wrote approvingly of *Biathanatos* in 1680: 'wherein, with no weak arguments, he endeavours to justify out of scripture, the legality of self-homicide'; then, later, he killed himself. His friends seemed to think the very possibility of suicide was first sparked by his reading of Donne, who had overturned seemingly perpetual truth and, one of Blount's friends wrote, 'found that self-preservation was not so general a precept, but it met with various limitations and exceptions'. This was possibly less significant than the fact that thirteen years had passed since his reading, and Blount had just been forbidden to marry the sister of his dead wife; but, still, it has been laid at Donne's door. To write about death in the way he did – to send a suction pump down into the gap between what we know and what we fear – was to risk chaos. Donne knew it and did it anyway.

And perhaps he never really meant to kill himself. Do those who plan to do it write so extensively about it? Or is the writing a form of exorcism? If you write down the desire, if you forensically dissect it, it cannot take you by surprise. Perhaps it is a way of stopping it from creeping up on you: perhaps it was a way of staying alive.

THE FLATTERER

And they who write to lords rewards to get –
Are they not like boys singing at doors for meat?
  Satire II

It was in around 1607 that Donne was first asked if he would turn towards the Church. Thomas Morton, former chaplain to the Earl of Rutland and now the Dean of Gloucester, offered Donne a job on the spot, if he would take holy orders. He said no. He wrote, we are told: 'I may not accept of your offer: but, sir, my refusal is not for that I think myself too good for that calling, for which kings, if they think so, are not good enough.' He must have known, even then, that his imagination would be suited to the discipline and invention of sermon writing; but, he wrote, his past dogged him. He had not yet managed to exorcise, in the public imagination, the ghost of his youthful reckless marriage and his Catholicism:

> Some irregularities of my life have been so visible to some
> men, that though I have, I thank God, made my peace
> with him by penitential resolutions against them, and by
> the assistance of his grace banished them my affections;
> yet this, which God knows to be so, is not so visible to

man as to free me from their censures, and it may be that
sacred calling from a dishonour.

And, of course, there was still the question of money.
The difficulty of history is that we must, to some extent
at least, take men at their word; we must assume that they
planned to do what they said they planned to do, and for
roughly the reasons they said they did. We cannot read
disingenuousness into every single speech, or the whole of
history would be eaten alive by scepticism. But equally, the
specific job Morton was offering was not a lucrative one –
more than half of the country's clergymen earned less than
£10 a year – and Donne had a family to feed, and good hats
and ruffs to buy.

Donne urgently needed other work. The route to preferment in Early Modern England – the route to jobs and
elite posts which put you in the same room as power – was
byzantine, labyrinthine, often unpredictable, and luck and
strategy and talent all played a part: but the one element
you couldn't do without was contacts. It was imperative,
therefore, if you weren't born at the top of the ladder of
power, to be as universally charming as you had it in you
to be, and many writers' letters of this period are peppered
with protestations of the recipients' unquenchable glories.

Donne's letters though are extraordinary, even in a time
in which compliments were core currency, for the high-
flown grandiloquence of their blandishments. Some of the
letters were carefully politic: addressed to wealthy women,

who could be sources of both gifts of money and work, such as Lady Kingsmill, doyenne of Sydmonton Court (currently owned by Andrew Lloyd Webber): 'your going away hath made London a dead carcass . . . when you have a desire to work a miracle, you will return hither and raise the place from the dead.' Similarly, in a verse epistle to the Countess of Huntingdon, wife of the fifth earl, he writes, 'from you all virtues flow'; 'To some you are revealèd as a friend,/And as a virtuous prince far off to me.' One anonymous critic of Donne wrote of his verse letters, in 1823, that 'they are disfigured . . . by an extravagance of hyperbole in the way of compliment that often amounts to the ridiculous – and by an evident want of sincerity that is worse than all.'

But Donne's flattery was more than just politically savvy ground-laying – because it wasn't only to the rich and famous that he wrote his mad fountains of praise. He saved some of his greatest encomiums for the least important. He wrote, for instance, to Martha Garrard, the wholly insignificant sister of his friend George: 'I am not come out of England if I remain in the noblest part of it, your mind, yet I confess it is too much diminution to call your mind any part of England or of this world, since every part even of your body deserves titles of higher dignity.' The Garrards were a family of London merchants, and Martha was a woman of no power or influence; she could give him nothing in return but her pleased laughter.

It's there so often with Donne, that doubleness: there was his canny, cautious, political side, planting his sycophantic adjectives in the hope they would seed money; and then there was also something else: pleasure in extravagance. There must have been real satisfaction for him somewhere in lavishing compliments. Perhaps because it was something he could offer: he could not host fine dinners, but he could send fine idioms. Or, you could read it as a wariness of the world (tame it with lavishments, before it bites you) – or you could read it as an enthusiasm for admiration itself: that he valued the hyperbole of praise and the game it set in motion. There is some of that old delight, in the extravagance of desire, in the courtly letters he sent out, heavily freighted with his praise.

One of the key targets for his charm was Lucy, Countess of Bedford. Lucy had been born the daughter of a knight, and was married off at just thirteen to the Earl of Bedford. She grew up canny and witty, and knowing the court like her own territory: on the coming of James to the throne she took daring measures, at the age of twenty-four, to secure a position in his consort's retinue. She skipped Queen Elizabeth's funeral and galloped several horses – some said to death – in order to be the first lady to greet James's bride, Anna of Denmark, as she came down from Scotland. Anna made her Lady of the Bedchamber on the spot, and she became at a stroke one of the most powerful women in England. Donne met her through his friend Goodere, and she became his most important patron, passing sums of money to him throughout his life. In exchange, multiple verse letters proclaim Lucy's beauty: 'I had never known/

Lucy Russell, Countess of Bedford

virtue or beauty but as they are grown/In you'. (Lucy was indeed very beautiful: although in the most famous portrait, she has a look of scepticism powerful enough to burn rubber.) He named his newborn Lucy after her in 1608: he wrote of 'that favour which my Lady Bedford hath afforded me, of giving her name to my daughter'.

Despite the enormous imbalance of wealth and power when it began, their friendship seems to have been both a real and a productive one. They exchanged poems, and without the countess we wouldn't have his 'Twickenham Garden', named for the garden she had had laid out on the blueprint of the Ptolemaic universe: concentric rows of trees, walks mirroring the orbits of the planets. Mixed in with his verse, though, came the begging letters, particularly after she had inherited property on her brother Lord Harington's death. Donne sent her a long memorial verse, 'Obsequies to the Lord Harington', and with it, riding pillion on his poetry, a begging letter. Faced with the problem of asking for money without appearing to, he attempted a sort of elaborate sideways pointing, to indicate-by-denying his neediness. It wasn't even slightly convincing: 'I have learned by those laws wherein I am a little conversant, that he which bestows any cost upon the dead, obliges him which is dead, but not the heir; I do not therefore send this paper to your Ladyship that you should thank me for it, or think that I thank you in it.' Lucy offered in response to pay his debts, but then – perhaps annoyed by the limited praise her dead brother garnered in the poem, perhaps because her own debts were mounting – offered up only £30, which Donne took badly. He wrote to Goodere, 'I confess to you, her former fashion towards me had given a better confidence.' A coolness began to enter in, which he, dismayed, tried to melt with another, escalatingly sycophantic, poem: in 'To the Countess of Bedford', a poem which appears at first reading to go on for ever, she is 'virtue's temple', and 'a new world doth rise here from your light'. But then, after sixty lines, Donne pauses, to say his words 'Taste of poetic rage, or flattery,/And need not where all hearts one truth profess.'

That, he knew, was the best form of flattery: the flattery of denying the need for flattery. (Shakespeare's Decius, plotting to murder Julius Caesar, reminds us: 'when I tell him he hates flatterers,/He says he does, being then most flattered.') Donne writes to Lady Bedford – quoted here in full, for the convolutions of compliment it bends through:

> [I] tell you truly (for from me it sucked no leaven of flattery) with what height or rather lowness of devotion I reverence you: who besides the commandment of noble birth, and your persuasive eloquence of beauty, have the advantage of the furniture of arts and languages, and such other virtues as might serve to justify a reprobate fortune and the lowest condition: so that if these things whereby some few other are named are made worthy, are to you but ornaments such might be left without leaving you unperfect.

It could read as ironic, then, that years later in the pulpit Donne came down so hard and so often on flattery. Some of his finest thunder was reserved for sycophants:

A man may flatter the best man; if he do not believe himself, when he speaks well of another, and when he praises him, though that which he says of him be true yet he flatters; so an atheist, that temporizes, and serves the company, and seems to assent, flatters. A man may flatter the saints in heaven, if he attribute to them that which is not theirs; and so a papist flatters.

The most foolish, he said, attempt to flatter God. Flattery, he told his listeners, done often enough, created an opacity of oneself to oneself: it skewed your inner compass dial.

This, given Donne's letters, would seem a little rich: but, in the Renaissance, not all flattery was the same. Some of it was the custom – a tradition of air and sugar in prefaces and in commendatory verse: a ritual, designed to produce patrons of the arts sufficiently well fed on compliments to keep the literary world afloat. Some of it was, like a few of Donne's letters, a blatant attempt at money-whispering. But some was the way you situated yourself politically, or gave hints to the rich and powerful who if met with face-on criticism might cut your head off. Donne knew it – and in 1610 and 1611, just as his cause was starting to look desperate, he set about writing two books. *Pseudo-Martyr*, dedicated to King James, is an obsessively detailed tome, setting out the thesis that the Catholic recusants who risked their lives by refusing to take James's new Oath of Allegiance, instigated in the crackdown following the Gunpowder Plot, were committing suicide. They were deluded pseudo-martyrs, who didn't deserve a true martyr's crown. (Walton claims it took Donne six weeks to write – which should be taken with a pinch of salt, in part because it is a work of minutely detailed scholarship citing hundreds of authorities, of more than four hundred pages, and in part because such a number of writers through history have lied about how long their books took to write.)

It begins with a dedication of white-hot ingratiation:

The influence of those your Majesty's books, as the sun which penetrates all corners, hath wrought upon me, and drawn up and exhaled from my poor meditations these discourses: which, with all reverence and devotion, I present to your Majesty, who in this also have the power and office of the Sun, that those things which you exhale, you may at your pleasure dissipate, and annul; or suffer them to fall down again, as a wholesome and fruitful dew, upon your Church & Commonwealth.

This, though, wasn't purposeless fawning: it was a way Donne could signal unambiguously his allegiance to James's religious policies, and flag his devotion to serving the King. Though the wariness of the King's intellectual integrity that Donne had shown in his *Catalogus* still remained, time, expediency and experience had modified it. Before *Pseudo-Martyr*, the best-known treatise defending the oath was by James himself: it was the flattery of imitation and nuance, flattery as political allegiance – and it was a success. Donne had written a book so dry and relentless that it has a dust-storm quality to it – as one great Donne scholar said, 'who but a monomaniac would read *Pseudo-Martyr* through?' – but James loved it. He made Donne an honorary MA of Oxford, and this time (according to Walton) it was the King himself who suggested that he should consider taking religious orders. Donne again refused, 'apprehending it', Walton tells us, 'such was his mistaken modesty' to be still 'too weighty for his abilities'; but the book had set him, for the first time, squarely under James's approving eye.

The year following, Donne wrote a book in which he sets out a defence of flattery: *Ignatius His Conclave* – a text of brilliant and rampant oddnesses. Appearing anonymously first in Latin as *Conclave Ignati* in 1611, and then in Donne's own English translation, it's as though all the explosive energy in his religious thinking has been allowed to burst free in a one-man jousting match levelled at the Jesuits. In the book, Ignatius of Loyola, founder of the Jesuits, finds himself in hell and in dialogue with Lucifer. Ignatius is a fawner and flatterer: 'Ignatius rushed out, threw himself down at Lucifer's feet, and grovelling on the ground adored him.' Ignatius takes a dual stance on flattery. On the one hand, it can be a kind of backwards one-upmanship: 'whosoever flatters any man, and presents him those praises which in his own opinion are not due to him, thinks him inferior to himself and makes account that he hath taken him prisoner, and triumphs over him.' But, on the other hand: whoever flatters '(at the best) instructs. For there may be, even in flattery, an honest kind of teaching, if Princes, by being told that they are already endued with all virtues necessary for their functions, be thereby taught what those virtues are, and by facile exhortation excited to endeavour to gain them.'

Ben Jonson made a similar claim in his verse: that some-times the only way to instruct might be through ascribing to someone good qualities which they don't possess, in the hope that it might spur them to acquire them. 'Whoe'er is rais'd/For worth he has not, he is tax'd, not prais'd.' Jonson was himself notorious for sycophancy and occasional bouts of delicious backbiting: he wrote a gushing epigram about the writer Francis Beaumont – casting himself as 'not worth/ The least indulgent thought thy pen drops forth' – and then complained to a friend that Beaumont 'loved too much himself and his own verses'.

But if you take what Donne and Jonson are saying seri-ously, it was something that mattered: that those who read high-flown praise as *only* flattery were not approaching the written word with the care it demanded – that sycophancy should always be examined to see if it had in it a prescrip-tion. Language makes demands. It is an excavatory skill; each word needs to have its surface dusted, to see if below there is gold or snakes. Those who did not understand that language was multi-layered and subtle – those who read it lazily, who failed to imagine the demands it daily makes – deserved very little in return.

¶

The thing about Donne's flattery was that it *worked*. Perhaps Donne's greatest tour de force in adulation were his two poems in elegy for a young woman, Elizabeth Drury, the 'First' and 'Second Anniversary', written in the two immediate years after *Ignatius*. We do not know precisely how Donne met Sir Robert Drury – Gentleman of the Privy Chamber, a former ally of the Earl of Essex, and one of the Drurys of Drury Lane. It may well have been via Donne's sister's husband, William Lyly, who had been one of Drury's many protégés until his sudden death. (Lyly was virulently anti-Roman, and had been instrumental in catching Catholic agents of Mary Queen of Scots, which, given Donne's mother was still Catholic, would have made family gatherings awkward.) Donne's relationship with the Drurys was to be a life-shaping and real-estate-shaping boon to him.

In 1611, Robert Drury's daughter Elizabeth died in her fifteenth year, and Donne was employed by her father to write two funeral elegies. Her cause of death was rumoured and disputed. It was said she was grief-stricken after the death of a lover; elsewhere it was said she had had her ears boxed too hard and died on the spot. Donne may have heard tell of her from his sister, but had almost certainly never met Elizabeth; the girl he conjured in his elegies was one of his own invention.

They are strange, excessive, convoluted poems – often beautiful, though rarely very sad, for poems about death – and full of mad statements of the lost young woman's glory: Donne proclaims that the earth could 'have better spared the Sun or Man'. The riotous praise of them raised some eyebrows across literary London. Donne wrote that 'I hear from England of many censures of my book of Mistress Drury'; embarrassed and defensive, he regretted, he said, that he had 'descend[ed] to print anything in verse'. Ben Jonson said, eyebrows high, that 'if he had written it of the Virgin Mary it had been something.' Donne defended himself: in writing his 'Anniversary' poems, he had held up the '*Idea* of a woman'. Besides, he added waspishly, 'if any of those ladies think that Mistress Drury was not so, let that lady make herself fit for all those praises in the book, and it shall be hers.' (It's much, much less polite than it sounds: the implication being that, firstly, the women complaining aren't virtuous enough to merit his praise and, secondly, let them fuck off and die, as Elizabeth had so recently done, thereby 'making themselves fit'.)

It was not, for him, so much about the girl as it was about language: about what poetry can do in the art of praising. How far could he force poetry to *embody* the most extreme ideas that can be conceived of? 'For since I never saw the gentlewoman, I cannot be understood to have bound myself to have spoken just truths.'

It wasn't an exercise in truth: it was an exercise in testing how far he could extend his imagination of what perfection might look like. He wrote:

> Her pure and eloquent blood
> Spoke in her cheeks, and so distinctly wrought
> That one might almost say, her body thought.

It was the same old desire that had resounded through his youth, before the complexities and compromises of marriage and family, and it was still there: the thinking body. A completed meshing of body and imagination: that would be the thing most worth having. The Donne of the 'Anniversaries' is still the same Donne as the young man in 'The Ecstasy' who declared 'love's mysteries in souls do grow,/ But yet the body is his book.' When the mind can be made to infuse every inch of the body; that is when living becomes most possible. It hadn't, Donne implied, yet been achieved, but its achievement would transform the experience of moving through the world: it would cut back at the chaos.

The poems also paid off financially. Robert Drury belonged to a once wealthy, still fairly powerful family who claimed to have come over from France with William the Conqueror (in their case, this was probably even true: although to accommodate every English family who makes this claim, the Conqueror would have had to come over with a fleet the size of Belgium). Robert Drury asked Donne – who, as a more experienced and fluent linguist, would be helpful – to join him and his family on a journey to Europe. In Paris they witnessed the engagement of Louis XIII, amid enormous pomp and French poetry; in Frankfurt, they saw the election of the new Holy Roman Emperor, amid enormous pomp and Latin poetry. On their return in 1612, the Drurys installed the Donnes in a house close to their own on Drury Lane at very reasonable rent. Donne's capacity for imaginative excess and his extravagance in linguistic pyrotechnics had, finally, secured him a home.

He had solid, comfortable ground beneath his feet – no more noxious cellars – and Westminster School a walk away for his boys. All that he lacked was clarity, about what exactly he should be doing with his life, as the time ran through his hands.

THE CLERGYMAN

Donne was now in the very heart of London, no longer having to make the long journey on horseback to and from his family, and it was alive with bite and noise and possibility. Dekker wrote of the roiling city:

> at every corner men, women and children meet in such shoals, that posts are set up on purpose to strengthen the houses lest with jostling one another they should shoulder them down . . . Here are porters sweating under burden, there merchants' men bearing bags of money. Chapmen (as if they were at leap frog) skip out of one shop into another. Tradesmen (as if they were dancing galliards) are lusty at leg and never stand still.

Donne, best dressed among the poets, would have been passing good outfits daily. A German visitor to London, Frederick of Mompelgard, wrote:

> The inhabitants are magnificently appareled, and are extremely proud and overbearing . . . the women have much more liberty than perhaps in any other place . . . they also know well how to make use of it, for they go dressed . . . in exceedingly fine clothes, and give all

attention to their ruffs and stuffs . . . whilst at home perhaps they have not a piece of dry bread.

(Mompelgard was not, overall, a fan of the English and our tradition of jauntily violent xenophobia: 'they care little for foreigners, but scoff and laugh at them; and . . . one dare not oppose them, else the street-boys and apprentices collect together . . . and strike . . . unmercifully without regard to person; and because they are the strongest, one is obliged to put up with the insult as well as the injury.')

More children came: little Nicholas arrived in 1613. Money grew tighter. Donne had to give up his horse, and beg or borrow one whenever he needed a mount. Walton paints Donne in these days as caught between two desires: he had been living for so long in 'expectation of a state-employment' that the hope was engrained; but in him other, different desires were growing strong; a pull at him to work for 'God's glory' in 'holy orders'. Donne was urgently aware, always, of the fleeing time, and the question of how to pass his days almost crippled him. From 1607 to 1615, he hesitated. In 1608 he had written a letter to Goodere:

I would fain do something; but that I cannot tell what is no wonder. For to choose, is to do: but to be no part of any body, is to be nothing. At most, the greatest persons are but great wens and excrescences [lumps and protuberances on the skin]; men of wit and delightful conversation, but as moles for ornament, except they be so incorporated into the body of the world, that they contribute something to the sustentation of the whole.

Donne knew himself to be a man of 'wit and delightful conversation', and knew that it would, by itself, ultimately be worth no more than a drawn-on beauty spot: it had no real purchase on the world.

This I made account that I begun early, when I understood the study of our laws: but was diverted by the worst volup-tuousness, which is an hydroptique immoderate desire of humane learning and languages: beautiful ornaments to great fortunes; but mine needed an occupation, and a course which I thought I entered well into, when I sub-mitted my self to such a service [i.e. Egerton's service], as I thought might [have] employed those poor advantages, which I had. And there I stumbled too [he is referring to his marriage], yet I would try again: for to this hour I am nothing, or so little, that I am scarce subject and argument good enough for one of mine own letter.

That need to 'try again', and start afresh, became more pressing in London. He had known both loss and gain – the ghosts of his dead children stood alongside his swiftly-growing living ones, as his family grew older and more expensive in their needs. In the city he found himself amid the whirl of so many purposeful people; his hairline began to recede and he knew himself to be stepping into middle age; a decision had to be made. Slowly, in both doubt and hope, Donne's eyes turned towards the Church.

One reading of Donne's turn to the priesthood is that it was an expediency: a second-best. Many people, looking over his life, have believed that his heart and ambition lay always with the court, which, Virginia Woolf's father Leslie Stephen wrote, 'still charm[ed] and fascinat[ed] the strong accomplished flatterer'. The Church was a compromise: a road to public respectability and reliable money, and a way to finally scrub out the stain of what Walton called the 'remarkable error' of his marriage. And there must have been some truth in that; he had always known himself to be rare, and he wanted his talents to be recognised. The court had been the most obvious place to go, for any youth who hankered to have a sharp and remunerative spotlight shone on his intelligence.

But Donne had been hunting for God since his thirties. In around 1604 he had written 'The Cross', which is the poem of a man profoundly engaged in a project of reading the world like a book, seeking in the smallest things clues about the nature of the divine:

> Look down, thou spy'st out crosses in small things;
> Look up, thou seest birds raised on crossèd wings;
> All the globe's frame, and sphere's, is nothing else
> But the meridians crossing parallels.

The physical world was made up of symbolic meaning, and could, through relentless attention, be decoded. Your own body, stretched out in the water, could become a reminder of the crucifixion. He wrote:

Who can deny me power and liberty
To stretch mine arms, and mine own cross to be?
Swim, and at every stroke thou art thy cross.

(It's hard to picture exactly what stroke he's doing here, to mimic the cross. The first English treatise on swimming, in 1587 by Everard Digby, describes something akin to breaststroke with intervals of doggy-paddle: presumably not that.) The point, though, holds: the whole world could be mined for knowledge of the God he sought everywhere.

The idea that Donne chose the Church only because his ambition had failed elsewhere elides one fact: Donne had to fight to get there. In the last decade, a new reading of Donne's journey to the priesthood has emerged, based on new information surrounding five letters that he wrote to the man who became his patron: the most notorious courtier in London – Robert Carr, Viscount Rochester, Earl of Somerset.

Carr was the great shining star of the Jacobean court: beautiful, flaxen-haired and delicate-featured. A few years before, he had been riding in a tournament in London at which the King was present when, galloping at full tilt, he tumbled off his horse and broke his leg. James ran to him: it was said he knelt and cradled Carr in his arms until help was found. A contemporary wrote, 'if any mischance be to be wished, 'tis breaking a leg in the King's presence, for this fellow [Carr] owes all his favour to that bout.' From that happy accident, Carr had been made a Gentleman of the Bedchamber, where his intimacy with the King allowed him to grow rich. They may have been lovers – an epigram went round London, '*Rex fuit Elizabeth: nunc est regina Jacobus*' – 'Elizabeth was King: now James is Queen.' One man wrote at the time: '[James] constantly leaneth on his arm, pinches his cheek, and smoothes his ruffled garment . . . I tell you, this fellow is straight-limbed, well-favoured, strong-shouldered, and smooth-faced, with some sort of cunning and show of modesty; though God wot, he well knoweth when to show his impudence.'

Despite some muttering from the wider court, James appointed Carr a Knight of the Garter and granted him a place on the Privy Council. The difficulty was that Carr doesn't seem to have been an intellect suited to paperwork. He had no head for the detail of politics, so he appointed a close friend – Sir Thomas Overbury, a poet, essayist and man of letters – to be his secretary.

At the time Donne first collided with him, Carr was pulling strings in a bid to wed the dazzling young Frances Howard, who was herself married to the Earl of Essex (son of the beheaded) but was seeking an annulment. Essex had retaliated by accusing Frances of witchcraft – specifically, of cursing his penis. (Jacobean England feared witchcraft, and the fear was remarkably genital-centric. One writer, Reginald Scot, in *The Discovery of Witchcraft*, recorded

The pourtraicture of Robert Car Earle of Somerset Vicount Rochester, Knight of the most noble order of the Garter &c. And of the Ladie Francis his wife

Robert Carr, 1st Earl of Somerset, and Frances, Countess of Somerset

the belief that witches could magic away a man's entire groin: 'that men had had their genitals taken from them by witches, and by the same means again restored.') London society, both high and low, was agog; equal parts scandalised and delighted. James's court was already seen by those who stood outside it as a hotbed of bed-hopping: Lady

213

Anne Clifford, of whom Donne said she 'knew well how to discourse of all things, from Predestination to slea-silk', declared that 'all the ladies about the Court had gotten such ill names that it was grown a scandalous place.' But even in the context of a place in which gossip was rife – in which the 3rd Earl of Pembroke was said to be 'immoderately given up to women', the 3rd Earl of Dorset 'much given to women', and the Earl of Cambridge to be 'more subject to his pleasures and company of women than priests', and in which the King of Denmark had gone rogue and called the Countess of Nottingham a whore – the Carr–Howard match was still by far the most exciting and shocking. Carr's erstwhile best friend Thomas Overbury was particularly vocal against the match.

It made Carr a complicated figure for a potential patron: especially for Donne, given the history of his own marriage and his blotted romantic copybook. But Carr simply could not be bypassed. For any who sought a court-centred religious position – any Church position that did not mean being ejected to the far reaches of rural England – Carr was the route: he had come to dominate the system of ecclesiastical appointments. On a good day he could achieve almost anything, and so, in the spring of 1613, Donne wrote to Carr.

He had made his decision, he said. He had fought within himself for clarity, for many years, and the time had come to seize hold of what certainty there was before it fled.

For, having obeyed at last, after much debatement within me, the inspirations (as I hope) of the Spirit of God, and resolved to make my profession divinity: I make account that I do but tell your Lordship what God hath told me, which is, that it is in this course, if in any, that my service may be of use to this church and state.

Carr's side of the correspondence hasn't survived, but he must have responded with some warmth, because Donne either offered, or was asked, to compose a wedding poem for Carr's prospective wedding to Frances Howard. (Frances's previous marriage, it had been decreed with the King's help, was to be annulled.) Donne offered, too, to level all his legal training into writing a justification of the annulment: 'perchance this business may produce occasions wherein I may express my opinions of it in a more serious manner . . . out of a general readiness and alacrity to be serviceable and grateful in any kind.' There's an implication in Donne's letter of quid pro quo: that Carr would help him find a position in the Church, in return for Donne acting as his pen for hire.

Carr, though, had other plans. It's very likely that he wanted to make use of Donne himself; his relationship with Thomas Overbury was increasingly strained (exactly how strained would become vividly clear soon after), and he had space for a sharper, swifter counsel by his side. He sent money – thereby placing Donne in his debt – and suggested Donne apply for a handful of secular posts, for which

Donne was wholly unsuited and inexperienced. He steadfastly failed to help Donne into the Church.

Meanwhile, preparations for the wedding continued. The ceremony was slated to take place in December 1613; and Thomas Overbury died, very conveniently, just before the grand day, thereby silencing the loudest opponent to the union. But Donne's promised poem became a problem. Opinion was slowly curdling against the bride: the words 'witch' and 'whore' were beginning to attach themselves to Frances. In mid-January 1614, the poem still hadn't been completed, and he wrote to Goodere, in reference to the promised epithalamion: 'by my troth, I think I shall not scape.' In the end he could see no way out, and he sent the poem to Carr at the end of January, a month late. It was framed as a conversation between two rustic figures, as if Donne was hiding anxiously behind his two speakers: ducking out of sight of any public hiss and spittle that might come his way. It condemned 'unjust opinion' and asked, 'should chance or Envy's art/Divide these two, whom nature scarce did part?' Whether or not the bride wanted the world's gossip rehearsed in her wedding song is unrecorded by history: poets' subjects rarely get a say in the matter.

Carr accepted the poem, but continued to block Donne's way to ordination and preferment. As the year went on, Donne wrote to Carr, difficult, circular letters, expressing thanks for 'benefits already received' from Carr but pain that Carr had put 'distractions, or diversions, in the ways of my hopes'. In 1614, the post of ambassador to Venice came up, and Donne wrote to ask if his name might be put forward. Donne knew, though, that he was not remotely qualified (he had no experience in diplomacy) and his tone shows he knew it – 'I humbly beseech your Lordship to pardon my boldness of asking you, whether I may not be sent thither?' – the implication in his letter to Carr is: if you forestall my journey to the Church, then what?

In the spring of 1614, Donne had a brief sally back into the world of politics, when he was again installed as an MP, this time for Taunton; older and wiser than his first outing in 1601, he was put on four committees. But we have no record of his ever participating in debates, and if he was biding his time for a chance, it would never come: King James dissolved Parliament after just eight weeks, in disgust that they would not allow him to raise taxes: he was 'surprised that my ancestors should have allowed such an institution to come into existence'. James ruled the next seven years without summoning Parliament. Any lingering dream Donne may have harboured of politics, left over from his first abortive foray into government in his twenties, fell dead.

It may have been the abrupt folding of Parliament that provoked Donne to speak his exasperation more bluntly to Carr: 'It is now somewhat more than a year, since I took the boldness to make my purpose of professing Divinity known to your Lordship.' He demanded that Carr either help him with some other, plausible employment, if that was what Carr was so set on, or allow him to 'pursue my first purpose' of divinity, or leave him to 'abandon all'. This letter, now dated to September 1614, means it had been a full sixteen months in which Donne, taking what bits of 'court business' he could find to get by, had yet been waiting, nudging and cajoling Carr to help him. Meanwhile his in-laws had been clamouring at him to more actively seek court preferment; Donne wrote to his brother-in-law that he would go to court 'if I find it necessary to go', but to follow its train without obvious purpose would be 'a treason against myself'. There was a tenacity in his desire to reach the Church; though it was not straightforward, it had grit in it.

What changed, and pushed Donne to navigate the last steps to the pulpit? In part, the deaths of two of his children, Mary aged three in May 1614, and Francis aged seven in November, acted as a knife and a spur all at once. They galvanised him into both misery and more urgent action. And, simultaneously, Carr's star began to decline; first slowly, throughout 1614, and then it crashed out of the sky altogether. In August 1614, a beautiful young gallant caught James's eye during a hunt – George Villiers, the Duke of Buckingham, 'the handsomest-bodied man in all of England'. James gradually became enamoured; later, he would write to him, 'I desire only to live in the world for your sake.' Carr was shunted to second place, and as his power waned, he became vulnerable to staggering new accusations: Carr and Frances, the whispers hissed, had murdered Thomas Overbury. The gossips gathered to spread the word: they had sent him sweet tarts and jellies laced with poison.

A poem went round the city, very different from Donne's strained epithalamion:

A page, a Knight, a Viscount and an Earl
All those did love a lustful English girl
A match well made, for she was likewise four:
A wife, a witch, a poisoner and a whore.

The two would, eventually, be tried and found guilty of murder. It was a constellation of circumstance that proved enough to propel Donne forward. On 3 December, we find Donne on his way to Newmarket to discuss his 'purpose' with the King in person; there he met with 'as good allowance, and encouragement' as he could have longed for. Donne promptly gave up an unspecified piece of 'business' (probably a clerkship) he was engaged upon, and began to prepare for priesthood: he had already been working hard, he wrote, 'in the search of the eastern tongues'. He must have known the decision would shake everything in his life into a new and daunting shape – what it was not, though, was a repudiation of his bone-deep love of the strange ways that language works upon us.

We have so many brilliantly drawn images of priests in British literature – Austen, Oliver Goldsmith, Chaucer – but they tend to skew towards the comedic, the meek, the venal or the po-faced. To be a priest in seventeenth-century England, though, was to be part of a system of power and performance. A priest was charged with a vast task – both a political and spiritual marshalling – and was expected to use every weapon in his arsenal to carry it out. Donne would be expected not to tone down his rhetorical alchemy, but rather to feed it. He had always been in search of stark, fresh ways to tell the things he knew and believed; in that sense, the priesthood made perfect sense for him. It demanded of him both his gifts – for distillation and contraction ('my face in thine eye, thine in mine appears') and for unpredictable expansion and connection. It was a leap into a land at once brand new and familiar. He took it: he sent out a budget of letters to friends announcing the news.

He was greeted by no standing ovations. Lucy, Countess of Bedford, he said, 'was somewhat more startling, than I looked for from her'. He was dismayed to find she did not take his decision wholly at face value: 'she had more suspicion of my calling, a better memory of my past life, than I had thought her nobility could have admitted.' Wotton, though, wrote to congratulate him. Donne thanked him, rather defensively: that 'though better than any other you know my infirmity, yet you are not scandalized with my change of habit.'

Once he had decided on his purpose, it was easy enough to navigate. He did not need to undertake training, having so amply demonstrated his grasp of theology with his *Pseudo-Martyr*. In the bleak middle of winter, 23 January 1615, Donne went quietly to St Paul's Cathedral to be ordained by John King, the Bishop of London. He was forty-two. To mark the change in his life, he took on a new seal: his previous one, a knot of snakes, was cast aside, and replaced with Christ crucified on an anchor; he wrote, 'a sheaf of snakes used heretofore to be/My seal, the crest of our poor family' – and now, 'the cross (my seal at baptism) spread below/Does, by that form into an anchor grow.' Very swiftly, he was appointed to be a chaplain-in-ordinary to the King. James was in comparison to Elizabeth an addict of the pulpit, and had doubled the number of sermons the monarch heard preached every week. He cajoled the Vice-chancellor of Cambridge – apparently against the latter's better judgement: he refused at first, perhaps remembering Donne's Catholic beginnings, or perhaps having read some of the more vivid sex imagery – to award Donne an honorary doctorate of divinity.

When Donne did change his mind, Walton tells us, he changed it hard. He met his new calling with the energy and determination of someone who had previously lived in the relentless watchfulness of uncertainty and now cast it aside with relief: 'now all his studies, which had been occasionally diffused, were all concentred in divinity. Now he had a new calling, new thoughts, and a new employment for his wit and eloquence.' For someone without solid work for so long, the singleness of purpose would have been a gift. It's what Hamlet wanted; it's what Donne was to thrive on. He had written that letter to Goodere, 'I would fain do something; but that I cannot tell what, is no wonder.' The irrevocability of the 'something' he had picked must have had the same appeal as a sea after the weedy lakes.

Walton, though, as ever, pushes it too far: 'now, all his earthly affections were changed into divine love; and all the faculties of his own soul were engaged in the conversion of others.' Walton's version of Donne as a stained-glass saint is exactly what he wasn't. The 160 extant sermons show he was far more interesting than that. Roughly, his preaching was in step with religious orthodoxy of the early seventeenth century, and his careful political nuance showed him to be a man who had no interest in starting revolutions. But he was to become a sermoniser who spoke openly about his own failures, would enfranchise his audience in startling ways, and would offer imagery of sufficient sharp clarity that you could hook a faith upon it.

¶

Renaissance sermons were long: often upwards of an hour, some up to three. The villagers of Shadwell once rebelled and took their rector before the ecclesiastical court to complain: 'with a long extemporary prayer before and another very long prayer after them, many of which sermons and prayers have been ended so late in the evening that some of the parishioners have called for candle and lantern to go home,' and it was too late for the congregation to properly tend to their cattle. People couldn't sit or stand still for so long, so there was moving, rustling, eating. Rowdy episodes could break out: it was recorded that one of the aldermen of Norwich Cathedral suffered when 'somebody most beastly did conspurcate and shit upon his gown from the galleries above . . . some from the galleries let fall a shoe which narrowly missed the mayor's head.' But generally sermons, in Donne's day, were heard hungrily: they had breaking news in them, politics, entertainment, theatre; people gossiped about them and picked over in the week that followed. For that reason Donne would often repeat a point over and over in slightly different wording, because people took notes: they were not ephemera, but something to be carried out into the city more widely. A school system which hinged on colossal amounts of memorisation had built a population with the kind of mammoth recall which is, in retrospect, breathtaking – so listeners went home and argued over them, plagiarised them, fell out over them, made them part of the fabric of their days.

Donne's sermons almost all follow the same structure, as was common to the vast majority of preachers. He would begin by laying out what was to follow, which usually was formed in two or three parts, and each part would have branches running out from it, and each branch further branches. Donne preached without a text in front of him; he would write the sermon out in full, take notes, and memorise it. He used the classical trick, employed by orators for thousands of years, of imagining a speech as a physical structure – a memory palace, a temple – through which he could move in his imagination. He was explicit about it: he compares the sermon to a 'goodly palace' through which he guides his audience. Partway through, they will 'rest a little, in an outward Court, upon consideration of prayer in general; and then draw near the view of the palace, in a second court'.

For all their length, his sermons were never sombre or staid: they were passionate performances, attempts to strike a match against the rough walls of the listeners' chest cavities. It was a moral duty: the most popular preacher's manual at the time dictated that 'the preacher . . . standeth of no one thing more in need' than 'moving the affections'. Donne unleashed his charisma, for the first time, upon live, reactive audiences who could eat it in full and demand more: he was:

> a preacher in earnest; weeping sometimes for his auditory, sometimes with them; always preaching to himself, like an angel from a cloud, but in none; carrying some, as St. Paul was, to heaven in holy raptures . . . here picturing a vice so as to make it ugly to those that practised it, and a virtue so as to make it beloved even by those that loved it not; and all this with a most particular grace and an unexpressible addition of comeliness.

He made a speciality of conjuring infinity for his listeners: 'there shall be no cloud nor sun, no darkness nor dazzling, but one equal light; no noise nor silence, but one equal music; no fears nor hopes, but one equal possession; no foes nor friends, but an equal communion and identity; no ends nor beginnings; but one equal eternity.'

His fame spread fast. In the summer of 1616 he was made priest in charge of Sevenoaks in Kent, a sinecure in the gift of Egerton, worth perhaps £80; it was expected that he would take the money and install other priests to do the actual preaching and shepherding – although in fact he did preach there at least once. Most clerics treated the smaller parishes as something between a collectible and a cash cow, and Donne was not above following suit, gathering up smaller benefices. Within a year of his ordination, the man who had struggled so hard to extract a few pounds out of his patrons and patronesses was offered fourteen different clerical positions. In October 1616, he was made Divinity Reader of Lincoln's Inn, at £60 per annum; a good sum, for which he was to preach fifty sermons a year. The money would have been especially helpful, as that same summer his newest daughter, Elizabeth, was born. At last his prosperity was growing fast enough to meet the needs of his family.

At Lincoln's Inn, where he had once been Master of the Revels and a hunter of pleasure, Donne became not just preacher but arbiter of law. He entered into it without leaving much leeway for mercy. Perhaps his Catholic contemporaries hoped that some memory of his past would make him more gentle to anyone who sought to diverge from the Protestant path: if so, they were to be disappointed. One Anthony Hunt, refusing to attend Holy Communion at the Inns, was told 'to bring a Certificate from Mr Doctor Donne of his conformity in religion and thereupon order was made to be taken for his expulsion or continuance in the house'. Donne did not grant the certificate, and the man was expelled; his ruthless streak in vivid evidence.

In 1617 the Viscount Dorchester was writing to a friend in London, and mentioned in passing, 'I would gladly see a copy (if it were possible) of Doctor Donne's sermon whereof you make mention; which being in so great an audience, and so generally well liked, methinks should be hearkened after.' After so long at the outskirts, trying to edge in, Donne was finally being hearkened after. It was what his work had always demanded, from the days of the earliest poetry: the undiluted attention of those who read and heard him.

THE WIDOWER

It happened quickly: as his fortunes rose, tragedy rose alongside. Anne died, and it was a baby that killed her. On 10 August 1617, she gave birth to a stillborn child. The labour – her twelfth – was too long and too hard. She survived less than a week before mother and child were buried in the same grave. They lie in the graveyard of St Clement Danes, amid the rush of buses going down the Strand towards the West End's theatres. Seven of her children lived to mourn her, aged from fourteen-year-old Constance to little Elizabeth, just reaching her first birthday.

It was, for Donne, an irreversible end. He would not take another lover: she was his last. He wrote in a poem: 'my good is dead.' If pain takes the precise shape of the love you have for the dead, then his heart in those days must have been complicated and terrible.

Walton said he was crucified to the world. He preached her funeral sermon, and his tears, Walton wrote, worked on 'the affections of his hearers, as melted and moulded them into a companionable sadness'. Amid the horror, he could not resist getting in a little flourish about Donne's superiority to everyone: it was such a love and such a loss 'as common people are not capable of'.

Out of all the verse that Donne wrote, there are many

lines that are surely about Anne – 'she all States, and all Princes I' – but there is only one poem that he acknowledged unequivocally was written for her and about her: her epitaph. The epitaph is in Latin, and Donne chose words that can be translated in a multitude of ways, so that behind each Latin word there's a queue of English possibilities. For this, the end of her life, he chose words for her that unfurl. This is an attempt at giving as many terms as possible for the original:

Anne
Daughter of George More, of Loseley, Gilt/Golden Knight,
    Sister of Robert More,
Granddaughter of William More,
Great-granddaughter of Christopher More:
A woman most choice/select/read, most beloved/loving/well
    read;
A spouse most dear, most chaste/pure;
A mother most loving/merciful/pious/dutiful, most self-
    sacrificing/indulgent/tender; Fifteen years in union/covenant
    completed,
Seven days after bearing the twelfth of her children (of whom
    seven survive)
(Wherefore this stone to speak he commanded,
Himself by/beyond grief [made] speechless/infant)
Her husband (most miserable/wretched to say) once dear to
    the dear
His own ashes to these ashes pledges/weds
[in a] new marriage (may God assent) in this place joining
    together,
John Donne,

Doctor of Theology.

She withdrew in the thirty-third year of age, hers and Jesus's
  1617/In the year of her Saviour
1617,
on 15 August.

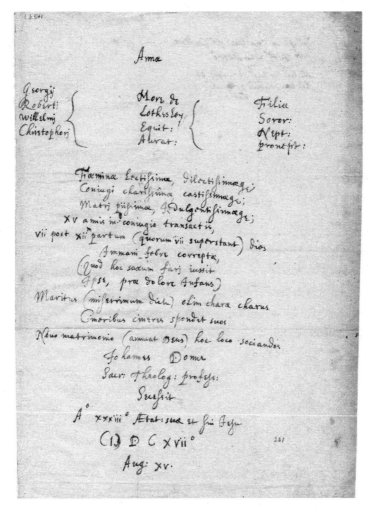

Donne's epitaph to Anne

The Latin, in Donne's handwritten version, forms, loosely, the shape of a cross. The epitaph is both a hymn and a promise: a vow never to marry again. In the Latin she is '*Faeminae lectissimae dilectissimaeque*': the words are drafted to do double work, in the Latin *lector*, so that Anne becomes Donne's best reader *and* best text. She is both well read, and read hungrily by Donne: he has studied her and tried to know her. But the Latin of the first part has a harmony which the second half abandons. It grows awkward and uneven in syntax and scansion when it talks about time, decay and loss; he broke the form of the epitaph to salute the breakdown of the heart. He had written, 'Language, thou art too narrow, and too weak/To ease us now; great sorrow cannot speak.' Words, belonging to the living, struggled to tell of death.

And for her: had it been worth it? Worth that great shining leap that she made as a teenage girl? The shame that immediately followed their marriage must have been agonising: one moment she was the beloved child of a wealthy man, dancing gavottes with boys in London, the next the wife of a jailed husband, with a disgusted father, knowing you're whispered about across the city. Then the poverty, isolation, the slow clawing back of respectability; her husband's elongated visits to London, and glowing letters to other women; the pain of relentless childbirth and of so much death. The poems suggest that they remained, at first, wildly enamoured: but the poems tapered off in the end. Anne More married the finest love poet England has ever known: but love was not, after all, enough.

THE (UNSUCCESSFUL) DIPLOMAT

The wound of Anne's loss was still sharp, and the new ordering of daily life was still in chaos. Who was to look after the children? Not him, for he surely would not have known how to care for a baby: they were probably largely in the charge of Constance, who was old enough to act as housekeeper, and the servants, with help from whichever kinswomen he could convince to come to help. Anne's sister, Lady Margaret Grymes, had a large family of her own with at least four boys, and could sometimes be persuaded to take some of his children into her home, but the disorder must have been enormous. And then, still in the middle of the hurricane of grief, Donne was finally offered a job of the kind that he had, as a young man, dreamed about.

Europe was striding towards disaster. Tensions were mounting between the citizens of Bohemia (loosely the modern-day Czech Republic and part of Poland) and the Holy Roman Empire (which, as Voltaire said, was 'neither holy, nor Roman, nor an empire': it was a Catholic, largely German-speaking patchwork of federations in western and central Europe, stretching from Hungary to Flanders and Geneva, its borders shifting like a kaleidoscope with time and war). The population of Bohemia was majority Protestant, but it was ruled by a succession of Catholic

Habsburg kings with enormous jaws and close friendships with the Pope.

In 1617, a new monarch, Ferdinand, was installed in Bohemia, much to the disgust of the Protestant masses, who knew that his fondness for the Catholic Counter-reformation wouldn't bode well for their freedoms. In May 1618, during a conflict over Protestant rights, two Catholic lords regent and one servant were turfed out of a third-floor window, in the famous 'Defenestration of Prague'. They landed on a dungheap (or at least so you were told, if you were a Protestant) or were saved by angels (if you were Catholic) and survived, but the line had been crossed. Protestant territories and the Catholic Habsburgs began to gather allies for war.

This was made more complicated for England by the fact that Frederick V of the Palatinate, who ruled over the Rhine, was James I's son-in-law. Frederick had married James's daughter Elizabeth in a political union of enormous pomp and flourish: in Heidelberg, in the grounds of the castle, there still stands an arch that Frederick was said to have had built overnight to surprise his bride in the morning. Frederick was Protestant, and it was to him that the citizens of Bohemia turned. Frederick, they said, should be their new king. The prospect horrified the Catholic Habsburgs, for whoever was King of Bohemia got one of the seven votes for the new Holy Roman Emperor. Chosen, not born, the Holy Roman Emperor was reckoned *primus inter pares* – first among equals – of the Catholic monarchs of Europe.

Into the turmoil stepped James I. James believed his own motto, appropriated from the Sermon on the Mount, '*Beati pacifici*': blessed are the peacemakers. He desperately did not want a war. He hoped he could formally mediate between his son-in-law Frederick, who was loudly calling for aid and arms from England, and the Habsburgs: and he planned to do this all while maintaining civil relations with Catholic Spain, so that he could marry his son Charles to a Spanish princess. James landed upon the charming courtier James Hay, Viscount Doncaster, as the man for the diplomatic job. Hay – whom young Elizabeth Stuart addressed as 'camel face', in part because she hoped it would deter him from passing her letters around, and in part for reasons which are obvious if you find a painting of him – knew Donne a little, and had tried to help him in his youthful job-questing days. Now, James decreed, Donne was to be his chaplain. They were to go to Germany, on a mission to stop the spread of the Bohemian troubles across the whole continent.

Considering whether or not to accept James's mediation, the King of Spain asked the advice of his ex-ambassador, who replied with unflattering candour:

The vanity of the present King of England is so great that he will always think it of great importance that peace should be made by his means, so that his authority may be increased . . . [nonetheless] it is possible and fitting to accept this mediation, since it cannot do any harm, or make things worse than they would be without it.

It was a delicate mission, and probably impossibly ambitious for anyone. But at the time Doncaster was full of hope, and planned to travel with opulence (his motto was 'Spare Nothing'); they were to have an allowance of £6 a day, and he was taking 'a great many noblemen's sons, and other personages of quality, that the Germans might admire the glory of the English'.

The chaplaincy was the kind of post that, if all went well, would inevitably lead to ecclesiastical promotion. Travel, authority, the chance to serve God, King and country: it was all Donne had been striving for during his Mitcham years, and yet now it was offered, he passionately did not want to go. His wife was dead, his children reeling, and he was in fear for his health and his safety, as the lifelong physical weaknesses that dogged him had flared again: he wrote to Goodere, 'I leave a scattered flock of wretched children and I carry an infirm and valetudinary body, and I go into the mouth of such adversaries as I cannot blame for hating me, the Jesuits, and yet I go.' He wrote a poem, while he waited, 'A Hymn to Christ, at the Author's last going into Germany', in which he bleakly resurrects the ship imagery of his youth.

> In what torn ship soever I embark,
> That ship shall be my emblem of Thy Ark;
> What sea soever swallow me, that flood
> Shall be to me an emblem of Thy blood.

In May 1619 they set off with great ceremony – and then had to halt when Doncaster realised he had left a vital letter on a window seat in Prince Charles's room (inauspicious beginnings: a theme of Donne's life). When Donne, the ambassador and his train – spending munificently wherever they went in a bid to curry favour with the locals – reached Heidelberg, the seat of Frederick V, they found he was away. Instead, his wife Elizabeth was waiting to greet her old friend with the dromedarian face. Doncaster was wary of the protocol of kissing Elizabeth's hand without the presence of her husband, and tried to make Donne and his companions lurk in the town until Frederick returned, which Elizabeth effectively scotched by forbidding anyone in the town to feed them unless they came to stay at the castle. The meeting with Frederick, when he finally arrived a few days later, went well, with Doncaster urging on him both friendship and caution – but it was to be the last of their successes. They went on to Salzburg, to seek out Ferdinand, the deposed King of Bohemia, and to press on him James's offer to negotiate a peace with the Bohemians. Ferdinand was impeccably courtly, but refused to say anything other than polite nothings to Doncaster's questions; no, he would not accept James's help; and no, thank you, he had no desire of any English interference.

Bruised and thwarted, they left, beginning a long and roundabout journey while they awaited further instructions: they swerved plague in Venice, went on to Vienna, Graz, the Hague. They arrived in the immediate aftermath of the

James Hay, Viscount Doncaster, 1st Earl of Carlisle,
alias Camel Face

Synod of Dort, a clash between the Calvinist and Arminian wings of the Dutch Church. Were some, as Calvinists argued, elected before their birth to receive salvation, while others, irrespective of their actions, were born predestined to eternal damnation? Or, as the Arminians on the liberal side of Reformed theology argued, had God foreseen which individuals would have faith in Christ, and elected all those who did? Donne would have watched with eager interest. He had always carefully refused to be drawn on predestination, but he had, once, lashed out against men who speak of 'decrees of condemnation before decrees of creation', and he would have been both unsurprised and undelighted when the Dutch Church came down on the Calvinist side.

The whole endeavour of the embassy, so visibly hopeless, must have been exhausting work – but there were moments in which Donne was able to snatch excitement from the route. In Linz, he broke free from Doncaster and made a pilgrimage to the home of Johannes Kepler.

Johannes Kepler was one of the finest astronomers of all time, a man with a revolutionary understanding of the movement of the planets, obsessed with the stars since the age of six. Their meeting was polite and formal: Kepler wanted Donne's advice on how best to get a book he had dedicated to James I into the King's hands – but it wouldn't have been polite at all, had Kepler known more about Donne's life and work.

Kepler had written a book called *Somnium* ('The Dream') in 1608, a strange, allegorical text which depicts a trip to the moon. He became fixated on the idea that malicious gossip about this book had implicated his own mother, Katharina Kepler, in a trial for witchcraft – the narrator's mother in Kepler's book summons a demon, and Kepler worried it had been taken literally. (His mother was imprisoned for fourteen months, but, though threatened with torture, refused to ever confess to witchcraft – which seems entirely reasonable, given the worst she was guilty of was, according to her son, being 'small, thin, swarthy, gossiping and quarrelsome': i.e. unpopular.) Kepler wrote, after the trial, that 'the spreading abroad of [Somnium] seems to have been . . . ominous for my domestic affairs . . . There issued slanderous talk about me, which, taken up by foolish minds, became blazing rumour, fanned by ignorance and superstition.' Among these rumour-mongers, he included the unnamed author of *Ignatius His Conclave*: he wrote in a footnote to *Somnium*, 'I suspect that the author of that impudent satire, the Conclave of Ignatius, had got hold of a copy of this little work, for he pricks me by name in the very beginning.'

Very few people on the continent knew that Donne was *Ignatius*'s creator; the book had been published anonymously, and so he was safe from Kepler making the association. In fact, Kepler gave Donne's text too much credit: he probably hadn't had a chance to read *Somnium* at all. The actual reference to Kepler in *Ignatius His Conclave* is very slight: the narrator claims the power to travel to other planets, but won't go into detail because he doesn't want to insult 'Keppler [*sic*], who (as himself testifies of himself) . . . hath received it into his care that no new thing should be done in heaven without his knowledge'. At worst, it's rather heavy-handed teasing; not enough to start bringing mothers into it.

Meanwhile, the embassy was turning into a palpable failure. While they loitered at Spa, there was a sudden rush of action: James's son-in-law, Frederick, was crowned King of Bohemia, and Ferdinand, who had been so elegantly dismissive of the English, was elected the new Holy Roman Emperor. War now looked inevitable, and Donne and Doncaster had managed to please a sum total of nobody. On the one hand, the Spaniards blamed the English embassy for helping Frederick secure the Bohemian crown; on the other side, European Protestants believed the Catholics had used the diplomatic mission as a distraction while they gathered their forces. An English diplomat at the time wrote waspishly that such 'are the inscrutable depths of his Majesty's incomparable wisdom, to amuse his son's enemies'. Doncaster and Donne returned home in a hot blaze of embarrassment, and Donne was not employed again on foreign diplomatic missions.

¶

But that stop that Donne made is tantalising: what did he and Kepler talk about? Donne had some German, and they both had impeccable Latin, so language was no barrier to speech. There's one letter that Kepler sent his sister-in-law about their meeting, but it's dry as sand, entirely about the logistics of asking Donne to 'convey and commend' his book to the King. Did Donne ask about Kepler's discoveries? It's likely – because Donne had long been fascinated and troubled by the stars.

Donne's lifetime spanned a period of astronomical discovery; every year chipped away at old assumptions. Donne's parents' generation would have been taught Ptolemy's model of the universe, which had been devised in the second century AD and had remained the standard model into the sixteenth century. In his theory, the Earth was stationary at the centre of the universe, the Sun was one of the Seven Ancient Planets, and everything was encased in a shell of stars, beyond which was the Prime Mover: God, essentially. In 1543 the Polish Nicolaus Copernicus published his model – which is, in many of its essentials, the one we use today – in which the Earth, with its crystalline sphere of stars, rotates on its axis once a day and is one of several planets that revolve about the Sun; but it was still controversial in Donne's day. (Incidentally, nobody had thought the world was flat for hundreds of years. Columbus knew it was round; the scientific arguments of the day were centred on the extent of its size and, in a few of the more vivid religious circles, whether it was going to explode.)

Some writers embraced the new order with gusto. At the end of *Cymbeline* (1611 or thereabouts) one of the most beautiful and most lunatic of Shakespeare's plays, Jupiter descends and a stage direction calls for four ghosts to dance in a circle; a reference to the planet's quartet of newly discovered moons, as described by Galileo in 1610. But Galileo's discoveries – in a world in which heliocentrism had been declared heretical in 1616 – shook Donne. Just a year after Galileo saw the moons rotate around Jupiter, and not around the Earth, Donne wrote:

> And new Philosophy calls all in doubt:
> The Element of fire is quite put out,
> The Sun is lost, and th'Earth, and no man's wit
> Can well direct him where to look for it.

It was harder to stretch the imagination wide enough, now that the universe was no longer thought to rotate around mankind.

> And freely men confess that this world's spent,
> When in the planets, and the firmament
> They seek so many new; they see that this
> Is crumbled out again t'his atomies.
> 'Tis all in pieces, all coherence gone.

It was part thrill and part anxiety: a tussle between two parts of Donne's imagination. It's part of the riddle of Donne's personality that he was at once wary of innovation and one of the greatest innovators in the English language. 'God', he wrote in a sermon, 'loves not innovations', and in *Ignatius*, the text which had made Kepler so furious, one of the main thrusts is a mockery of innovation. The place nearest Lucifer's throne in hell is reserved for whichever innovator's works have caused most confusion in the world – among the candidates are Machiavelli, Columbus, Copernicus and Paracelsus, the father of toxicology. Whoever 'gave an affront to all antiquity, and induced doubts and anxieties' should be rewarded with the devil's favour. Copernicus prides himself on rearranging the heavens: he is 'thereby almost a new Creator'.

Donne's anxiety about innovation, though, was closely bound up with a sense of the splendour of the world: the Earth, as he saw it, had been created flawless, and we could only make it worse. 'In the beginning of the world,' he told his congregation, 'we presume all things to have been produced in their best state; all was perfect.' Humans, he believed, were capable of many things: genius, but also destruction. 'For knowledge kindles calentures [burning zeal] in some,/ And is to others icy opium'. The same imagination which had tried to wrest control over the sun in his poetry also believed that we could not be trusted not to lay waste to the world: which turned out, of course, to be true. There was a dry-edged wit to it: his reckoning with our extraordinary capacities for invention, and our ability to break things. His love for the power of mankind's mind did not extend to blindness about the amount of chaos we can cause.

THE DEAN

Donne returned from Germany in January 1620, sped home to his children and waited to see what would be the results of his work in the embassy. Though the mission had been an embarrassment and a failure, Donne himself had not been; he had preached a warmly received sermon at the Hague, and was given a gold medal to mark the occasion, etched with images of disputing men. Back home, he gave sermons at Lincoln's Inn in the winter and three times at court in the spring, where the King watched him with careful eyes. He had Donne in mind for something more exacting and remarkable than chaplain; but there were delays in the usual progress of the Church. In July 1621 George Abbot, the Archbishop of Canterbury, went out hunting, aimed at a deer, missed and hit a keeper. (Lord Zouch, whose land they had been shooting on, insisted the man had been standing directly behind the deer at the time, and the animal had leapt away at the last moment. This was greeted with scepticism: it was reckoned more likely that a cleric would wreak accidental havoc with a crossbow than that a professional gamekeeper would loiter among a herd, mid-hunt.) Manslaughter was not something in which God's servants were supposed to partake, and a number of churchmen who were due to be made bishops refused to receive the consecration from his hands. The workings of the Church, therefore, were even slower than usual. But in August, when the Bishop of Exeter died, the hearts of priests around the country must have quickened with hope: for Valentine Cary, the current Dean of St Paul's, was to take his post, leaving behind him a fantastically desirable vacancy.

In 1621, according to Walton, the King sent for the forty-nine-year-old Donne and asked him to arrive at dinnertime the next day.

When his Majesty sat down, before he had eat any meat, he said after his pleasant manner, 'Dr. Donne, I have invited you to dinner; and, though you sit not down with me, yet I will carve to you of a dish that I know you love well; for, knowing you love London, I do therefore make you Dean of St. Paul's; and, when I have dined, then do you take your beloved dish home to your study, say grace there to yourself, and much good may it do you.'

This story may or may not be true: it sounds suspiciously like an almost identical anecdote told about Bishop Andrewes. If it is true, though, Donne would have had to put up with dribbles. A much-repeated report of the King told: '(His tongue) was too large for his mouth, which ever made him speak full of mouth, and made him drink very uncomely, as if eating his drink, which came out into the cup of each side of his mouth.'

How did Donne come to be given one of the most distinguished positions in the English Church? It must have been in part because he was remarkable: his sermons had a rhetorical punch that was rarely achieved by the other men, however gifted, who mounted the pulpit before the King. But there was also Donne's canny, politic side at work: he had been, for some time, putting himself in the good graces of the King's new favourite.

King James I of England and VI of Scotland

Carr and his wife were fully out of favour, though their death sentences for Overbury's murder were commuted to imprisonment, and eventually they retired to live quietly in the countryside. In Carr's place stood the Duke of Buckingham, in all his fine-limbed beauty. Donne wrote to Buckingham, offering himself up for any work that the duke might find acceptable: 'all that I mean in using this boldness, of putting myself into your Lordship's presence by this rag of paper is to tell your Lordship that I lie in a corner, as a clod of clay, attending what kind of vessel it shall please you to make of Your Lordship's humblest and thankfullest and devotedest servant.'

Buckingham may well have seen a use for Donne. The buildings of the cathedral were beginning to crumble dangerously as Donne took office as dean, and a large batch of expensive Portland stone had been bought to restore them; stone which disappeared and reappeared, quietly, in the hands of the Duke of Buckingham for use in the restoration of his own town house.

The deanship was a heavy responsibility, carrying with it the imperative to stir the hearts and mind the souls of the whole of London – but it was also a fantastic piñata of a job: hit it, and perks and favours and new connections came pouring out. Even before the deanship was made official, the riches began to come in; he wrote to Goodere, 'Though be I not Dean of Paul's yet, my Lord of Warwick hath gone so low, as to command of me the office of being Master of my game, in our wood about him in Essex.' He had to give

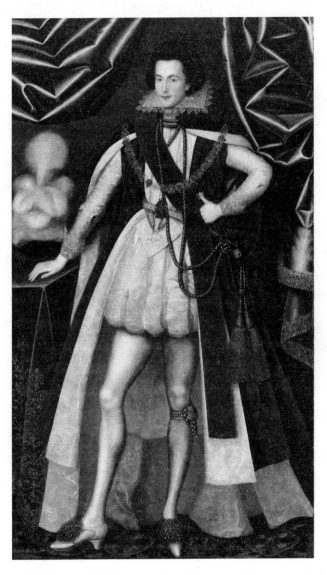

George Villiers, 1st Duke of Buckingham

The stained-glass window in Lincoln's Inn

up his post at Lincoln's Inn: but the minutes noted that he would 'be no stranger there'. (There survives today, on the west side of the church nearest the pulpit, a tiny shard of stained glass that commemorates him.) His popularity in that quarter remained enormous, almost deadly: it was there that the crush to see his sermons had nearly killed three men.

As soon as he was able, he moved his family to the Deanery, bidding farewell to those of the Drurys who still lived, for Robert Drury had since joined his daughter in death. He invited his ageing mother to move in with them. Despite her adherence to the old faith, he wrote,

> though the poorness of my fortune and greatness of my charge hath not suffered me to express my duty towards you as became me, yet I protest to you before Almighty God and his Angels and Saints in Heaven that I do and ever shall esteem myself to be as strongly bound to look to you and provide for your relief as for my own poor wife and children.

This, and the letter he sent on the death of his sister Anne, are both very formal, even for him: his new position necessitated caution. On her part, it must have been thorny – did she believe as some Catholics did, when she moved in with her rosaries and relics, that he was damned eternally?

The installation finally took place on 22 November 1621. The act-books which would tell us the details of his incumbency have vanished, but the process for becoming dean would have had an elaborate protocol. The members of the chapter of the cathedral met in person and passed their vote (a pure formality: the King had sent his letter, and Donne was waiting in a house nearby, presumably with his beard at its finest and most pointed). They gave word, whereupon Donne was ushered in like a bride, presented to the bishop and processed up into the cathedral and to the altar. A *Te Deum* was sung under the high echoing ceiling: Donne prostrated himself upon the stone ground. He kissed the altar, and rose to stand in the church that was now his own.

To picture the cathedral in which he stood in as akin to how it is now – all roped-off solemnity and Quiet Please – would be to give the wrong idea, in part because the original building burned in the Great Fire, but largely because of the noise and the smell. There were no hushed voices; rather, the church's paperwork noted, 'the boys and maids and children of the adjoining parishes . . . after dinner come into church and play as children used to till dark night.' Boys peed on the floor and used the slippery surface as an ice rink, adults scattered food or turned up drunk. If hot young gallants strode into the church still wearing their spurs, which rang out noisily against the stone floors, choirboys were allowed to chase them down and fine them 'spur-money'. One of the aisles was known as Duke Humphrey's walk, and was the place to be seen;

all the diseased horses in a tedious siege cannot show so many fashions, as are to be seen for nothing, every day, in Duke Humphrey's walk. If therefore you determine to enter into a new suit, warn your tailor to attend you in Paul's, who with his hat in his hand shall like a spy discover the stuff, colour and fashion of any doublet or hose that dare be seen there and stepping behind a pillar to fill his tablebooks with those notes, will presently send you into the world an accomplished man; by which means you shall wear your clothes in print with the first edition.

Visitors could pay to climb up to the tower and carve their names – 'or, for want of a name, the mark which you clap on your sheep' – into the leaded roof; 'and indeed the top of Paul's contains more names than Stow's Chronicle.'

The cathedral came with a large cast of churchmen over whom Donne presided: five archdeacons, a precentor to take care of the musical services, a treasurer, a chancellor, at least a dozen minor canons, six vicars choral, a host of choirboys. There were also the vergers, whose unenviable job it was to keep order in the cathedral. It was Donne's job, now, to wrangle with their personalities and their jostling for power; it was he, now, who had to decide to whom to grant the benefices in the gift of the cathedral, how to keep order: duties for which paperwork and tact were required.

He was expected, too, to entertain. He wrote to Robert Ker of how he had tried to rise to it – to the new pomp and circumstance of the dinner table: 'I have obeyed the forms of our church of Paul's so much as to have been a solemn Christmas man, and tried conclusions upon my self how I could sit out the siege of new faces, every dinner.' He asked Ker to come and see him, alone, for something more intimate – 'choose your day, and either to suffer the solitude of this place, or to change it, by such company, as shall wait upon you, and come as a visitor and overseer of this hospital of mine, and dine or sup at this miserable chezmey.' ('Chezmey' is not in the dictionary: it must be his own, joking version of chez moi. It's one of those moments that reminds us how his letters must be full of in-jokes and hark-backs and warm hat-tips to past conversations that sail straight over our heads.)

Most of all, though, he preached. Technically, Donne was bound to preach only three times a year: Christmas, Easter and Ascension Day. But he was a man who preached like others eat meat: hungrily. The Dean of St Paul's was expected to preach in multiple places: inside the church, of course, and for the King at court, but, too, in the spot outside the cathedral known as the Paul's Cross pulpit. This was where enormous crowds could gather. It was the place to be, for everyone up to and including assassins; Mary I's pet Bishop Bourne had had a knife thrown at his head while preaching at the Cross: it missed and hit the wooden pole next to him. Benches, stored in the cathedral and hauled out for the sermon days, were available to rent, seating up to about 250; servants would be sent ahead to snag a place. Everyone else had to stand or lean, and try not to be pickpocketed. There are accounts of crowds at Paul's reaching six thousand.

A question to which we still do not wholly know the answer: how did they hear him? Did they telegraph his words backwards, like a game of whispers? Recently a group of academics staged a re-enactment of the preaching conditions to test what, exactly, the crowds of thousands would have been able to hear, and discovered that the courtyard was designed to allow sound to reverberate, so Donne would have been heard relatively well by at least the nearest five hundred to a thousand people. He would only have had to go slowly, so as not to tangle with his own

A sermon preached from St Paul's Cross in 1614, by John Gipkyn

echo. It wouldn't, though, have been comfortable for his listeners: Paul's Cross sermons were held, on and off, year round, unless severe weather drove everyone inside. (One of Donne's sermons is listed as 'Intended for Paul's Cross, but by reason of the weather, preached in the Church'.) London was colder back then – the Thames froze over in 1608, and a Frost Fair was held, with nine-pin bowling and pubs on the ice. It would have been often ice-bound and windy; the coal that Londoners preferred, known as seacoal, produced great vats of sulphurous smoke which hung perpetually over the most populous parts of the city. There would, too, have been the scents of London: vegetables rotting, human waste, manure from passing horses and dogs, the stink of the Thames. It was over this never-quiet, always-moving world that Donne prepared to send his words flying.

To read the full text of a Donne sermon is a little like mounting a horse only to discover that it is an elephant: large and unfamiliar. To modern ears, they are winding, elongated, perambulating things; a pleasure that is also work. If you are a scholar, they offer notes to an A–Z of Renaissance religious flashpoints: Aquinas, bishops, casuistry, Divine Right of Kings, Erastianism, Foxe, Gnostics, heresy, incarnation, Judaism, Koran, Laudian ceremonialism, Manicheans, numerology, oaths, Plots (Gunpowder), Queen Henrietta Maria (for speaking clumsily of whom he was reprimanded), recusancy, scholasticism, Thirty-Nine Articles, utopianism, vanitas, Worms (Diet of), Xenophon, York, Zoroaster. But they can also be mined by those reading for other, less erudite and more unpindownable reasons.

You could turn to Donne's sermons for meditations on the Gospel as the bedrock of faith: less so if you are a fan of Mark (who only gets two sermons) or Luke (three), but there are sixteen on Matthew and sixteen on John; and it's

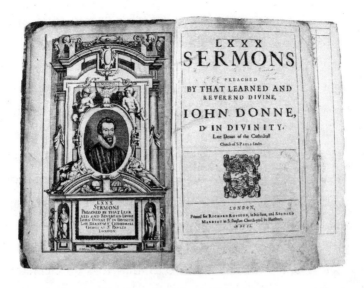

The frontispiece of Donne's *LXXX Sermons*

John, the man who trafficked in such powerful metaphors – Christ as True Light, Christ as the Word – whom Donne loves best. That, and, wholly unsurprisingly, the Psalms – of the 160 sermons, thirty-four took their text from the Book of Psalms: 'The whole frame of the poem', he wrote of one, is akin to 'a beating out of a piece of gold'.

You could turn to him for condemnations of divisions-among-allies within the Church:

Lying at Aix . . . I found myself in a house which was divided into many families, and indeed so large as it might have been a little parish, or at least, a great limb of a great one; but it was of no parish: for when I asked who lay over my head, they told me a family of Anabaptists;

255

and who over theirs? – another family of Anabaptists; and another family of Anabaptists over theirs; and the whole house was a nest of these boxes; several artificers, all Anabaptists; I asked in what room they met, for the exercise of their religion; I was told they never met: for, though they were all Anabaptists, yet for some collateral differences, they detested one another, and, though many of them were near in blood, and alliance to one another, yet the son would excommunicate the father, in the room above him, and the nephew the uncle.

Even if you have to have strong feelings about Anabaptists to really relish the humour, the thrust of his argument holds fast: that division is absurd and destructive, and very little that is destructive, he believed, is of God.

You can also find him, in the sermons, at his most authoritarian. There are places where he is harsh where his audience would have expected joy. At the wedding of the daughter of his dearest friend Henry, Lucy Goodere, to the supremely handsome diplomat Francis Nethersole, he declared, 'marriage is but a continual fornication sealed with an oath.' Sex, he bemoaned, had overtaken all else in marriage: 'few pray for the gift of continency; few are content with that incontinency which they have, but are sorry they can express no more incontinency.' His preaching left his audience in no doubt of where they stood: 'we rise poorer, ignobler, weaker, for every night's sin, than we lay down . . . We sin, and sin, and sin.' It's a long way from the gleeful rakery of his youth;

Anne was dead, he was older and in physical pain, and his thinking about sex had taken on a flinty quality. What Lucy and Francis thought of being sent in such funereal tones to their marriage bed is not, alas, recorded.

Those condemnations which ring through so many of the sermons, though, are not surprising – he always had a streak of fury in him. It is the same Donne whom we had glimpses of years earlier, when in *Biathanatos*, he condemned the practice of pulling on the feet of those who are being hanged 'to hasten their end': 'in my understanding, such an act either by an executioner or a bystander is in no way justifiable.' He had always been capable of sounding grotesque: he ordains that the death must be as agonising as possible, because it is an affront 'to the judge, who has appointed a painful death to deter others from the crime'. This, from a man whose great-uncle had been hanged in front of an eager crowd.

You could also, though, find a radical spark in his sermons. At a time in which the idea of an individual desiring an entirely unmediated relationship with God could cause riots, he speaks a bold promise of individual spiritual enfranchisement: 'at the sacrament every man is a priest . . . consider then, that to come to the communion table, is to take orders . . . There thou art a priest.'

But Donne is at his most remarkable when he speaks about how very hard it is to seek God at all. More than anyone else, he acknowledged the way that the human heart darts about like a rat. His body, he found, so readily present in desire for other humans, betrayed him when he sought the same intensity in prayer. Donne was a man so in control of his poetry that he could layer it with ten dozen references; he could write a twelve-line sonnet that would take you a week to read, but he was not in control of his mind:

> I throw myself down in my chamber, and I call in and invite God and his angels thither; and when they are there, I ignore God and his angels for the noise of a fly, for the rattling of a coach, for the whining of a door; I talk on . . . sometimes I find that I forgot what I was about, but when I began to forget it, I cannot tell. A memory of yesterday's pleasures, a fear of tomorrow's dangers, a straw under my knee, a noise in mine ear, a light in mine eye, an any thing, a nothing, a fancy, a chimera in my brain, troubles me in my prayer.

It is his lifelong quest and lifelong disappointment: that we cannot be struck daily by lightning. This is the same Donne who, in the Holy Sonnets (impossible to date for sure, but perhaps written around 1610), seeks a force so great that it will sweep away doubt, exhaustion, distraction, and leave something stripped back and certain: 'And burn me, O Lord, with a fiery zeal/Of Thee and Thy house, which doth in eating heal.' Both verse and sermons are the voice of a man seeking to have doubt torn away. In Holy Sonnet X:

> Batter my heart, three-personed God, for you
> As yet but knock, breathe, shine, and seek to mend;

That I may rise and stand, o'erthrow me, and bend
Your force to break, blow, burn, and make me new.

It is not possible, of course. It doesn't happen for him.
He remains relentlessly embodied, and therefore relentlessly
distractible, limping. But the hope remained:

We ask our daily bread, and God never says you should
have come yesterday. He never says you must again tomorrow, but *to-day if ye will hear His voice*, to-day He
will hear you . . . He brought light out of darkness, not
out of a lesser light; He can bring thy summer out of
winter, though thou have no spring; though in the ways
of fortune, or understanding, or conscience, thou have
been benighted till now, wintered and frozen, clouded
and eclipsed, damped and benumbed, smothered and
stupefied till now, now God comes to thee, not as in the
dawning of the day, not as in the bud of the spring, but as
the sun at noon, to illustrate all shadows, as the sheaves
in harvest, to fill all penuries, all occasions invite His
mercies, and all times are His seasons.

For those haltingly seeking the divine, there's no sense
in looking to those with unshakeable faith. It's no good,
for those who long for angels but also for sex, jokes, skin,
doubt, good clothes, oceans and huge appetites, looking to
the saints. Donne might be the person to turn to, if you
desired to seek God but cannot leap into the infinite. He is

the writer and the preacher for those who make their way there in gestures, symbols, flickers, errors.

And for all his bitterness and furies, he was insistent on joy. He quotes St Basil the Great, one of the Church's top ten least cheerful saints: '"But how far may we carry this joy? To what outward declarations! To laughing?" St Basil makes a round answer to a short question . . . "May a man laugh in no case."' But Donne turns on Basil:

> It is a dangerous weakness, to forbear outward declarations of our sense of God's goodness, for fear of misinterpretations . . . When David danced and leaped, and shouted before the ark; if he laughed too, it misbecame him not . . . not to show that joy, is an argument against thankfulness of the heart: that is a stupidity, this is a contempt.

The idea resonated through his life: he had written years before to Goodere, 'Our nature is meteoric . . . we respect (because we partake so) both earth and heaven; for as our bodies glorified shall be capable of spiritual joy, so our souls demerged into those bodies, are allowed to partake earthly pleasure.' We do wrong if we deliberately 'bury ourselves' in 'dull monastic sadness'. 'Heaven is expressed by singing, hell by weeping.' He knew, as Dante did, that there is a special place in hell for those who, when they could laugh, chose instead to sigh.

It is in his sermons, as it was in all his work. Donne was

able to hold two conflicting truths ever in front of him: a kind of duck-rabbit of the human condition. Humanity, as he saw it, was rotten with corruption and weakness and failure – and even so it was the great light of the universe. He gloried in mankind: if the inner world of each human was extended outwards, 'Man would be the giant, and the world the dwarf.' Few people would turn to Donne's poetry or prose, with its twisting logic and deliberate difficulty, for solace – but you might turn to him to be reminded that for all its horror, the human animal is worth your attention, your awe, your love.

THE MONIED

Donne was finally rich; if not rich enough for the kind of living he would have seen at court – where live birds erupted from pies, metre-high sugar statues decorated feasts, and roast pigs would be brought to the table mounted by little roast chickens dressed up like jockeys in paper reins and spurs – still he was rich enough to breathe easy. He could afford to stable his own horses; at some point around this time, he purchased a painting by Titian. He had enough to be extravagant in his generosity; to send £100 to an anonymous impecunious friend, and to seek out those imprisoned for debts and 'lay for their fees or small debts' (perhaps remembering his own time in the debtor's prison, and the view from the windows over the Fleet). Walton clambers into view, telling us that he was 'a continual giver to poor scholars', sending out bounty via his servants across London.

Donne's work is full of loving, semi-erotic metaphors about money. He relished puns on women and angels and the angel coin, a piece of gold worth about ten shillings and embossed with an image of an impressively muscular and topless Archangel Michael slaying a dragon. When he mounted the pulpit, the fondness remained: coinage gave him a way to talk about salvation which had the tactile, textured reality of daily life. In particular, he conjured up the imagery of salvation as purchase, over and over. Donne knew that there were merchants in his congregation, and he used their language: 'there is a trade driven, a staple established between heaven and earth . . . Thither have we sent our flesh, and hither hath [God] sent his spirit.' Christ had to be 'the nature and flesh of man; for man had sinned, and man must pay'. Money was his best way to point to value that lay beyond money: Christ was 'money coined even with the image of God; man was made according to his image: that image being defaced, in a new mint, in the womb of the blessed Virgin, there was new money coined.' Money was the perfect metaphor, being itself at once concrete and metaphysical: metal and human:

I, when I value gold, may think upon
The ductileness, the application,
The wholesomeness, the ingenuity,
From rust, from soil, from fire ever free;
But if I love it, 'tis because 'tis made
By our new nature, use, the soul of trade.

In contrast to his love for a golden metaphor, though, Donne had always claimed – before he had any – to hate the business of real-life money. He wrote to a friend, probably Wotton, in around 1607 that he loathed the strain of stumbling after cash: 'only the observation of others is my preservation from extreme idleness, else I profess, that I hate business so much, as I am sometimes glad to remember that the *Roman Church* reads that verse *A negotio perambulante in tenebris*'. He's punning: *negotium* can mean both 'business' and 'pestilence', and so, Donne writes, 'equal to me do the plague and business deserve avoiding.'

But Donne, as he grew older, had grown sharper about money. Having known the grind of relative poverty, he was determined not to return there, and he became well able to play the unshining games of money that took place among the elite. In 1623, he was looking to find a match for Constance, who was turning twenty. Marriage was a market in the most bluntly literal sense. Daughters and sons were both expensive to get rid of – an ordinary gentleman might ask for several hundred pounds, while an earl could demand many thousands be settled on his bride-to-be. Earlier, Donne had wondered about sending his girls off to be nuns, as a last-ditch desperate way to balance the books:

My daughters (who are capable of such considerations) cannot but see my desire to accommodate them in this world, so I think they will not murmur if heaven must be their nunnery, and they associated to the B[lessed] virgins there; I know they would be content to pass their lives in a prison, rather then I should macerate my self for them.

The deanship made the nunnery unnecessary; but once you were in the market, there was bidding, haggling, and occasionally bargains escaped you. There was at least one missed chance: Donne wrote to Goodere:

Tell both your daughters a piece of a story of my Con. which may accustom them to endure disappointments in this world. An honourable person (whose name I give you in a schedule to burn, lest this letter should be mislaid) had an intention to give her one of his sons, and had told it me, and would have been content to accept what I, by my friends, could have begged for her; but he intended that son to my profession, and had provided him already £300 a year, of his own gift in Church livings, and hath estimated £300 more of inheritance for their children: and now the youth (who yet knows nothing of his fathers intention nor mine) flies from his resolutions for that calling, and importunes his Father to let him travel. The girl knows not her loss, for I never told her of it: but truly, it is a great disappointment to me.

Donne's eye roved with careful intent – he wanted, as George More had wanted so many years before, a match that would secure for his daughter safety and prosperity in a hard world – and lit on fifty-seven-year-old Edward Alleyn. Alleyn: the greatest actor of the age, the man who made Faustus his own, Master of the King's Bears, and possessed, in the etchings, of a beard that looks like he cut it with a rusty ice skate.

Alleyn came round to dine and they talked terms: he wrote to Donne, after dinner in your parlour you declared your intention to bestow with your daughter Con all the benefits of your prime lease . . . worth £500 at the least, and whensoever it should rise to more, it should wholly be hers. My offer was to do as much for her as yourself, and add to that at my death £500 more . . . this gave not content and Sir Thomas persuaded me to do somewhat more, which I did, and promised to leave her at my death 2000 marks. This was accepted, and security demanded.

The marriage, which was planned as a grand and cele-bratory affair, instead took place in a rush on 3 December 1623, because Donne was suddenly struck with another sickness: perhaps with his recurring fever, or with the typhus which was sweeping London that winter. The doctor visited, and was apparently bad at disguising his feelings; Donne wrote; 'I see he fears, and I fear with him; I overtake him, I overrun him, in his fear, and I go the faster, because he makes his pace slow; I fear the more, because he disguises his fear, and I see it with the more sharpness, because he would not have me see it.'

Donne was convinced he was dying. In the depths of it, from 3 to 6 December, he was very close: so close that he was even, he said, 'barred of my ordinary diet, which is reading'. But even in the thick of illness, Donne began to write. He knew that readers give special weight to the words of those who are at the edge of life. He wrote to Robert Ker: 'though I have left my bed, I have not left my bedside';

EDWARD ALLEYN Esqr
Founder of Dulwich College

Edward Alleyn

I sit there still, and as a prisoner discharged sits at the
prison door to beg fees, so I sit here to gather crumbs. I
have used this leisure, to put the meditations I had in my
sickness into some such order as may minister some holy
delight. They arise to so many sheets (perchance 20) as

that without staying for that furniture of an epistle, that my friends importun'd me to print them, I importune my friends to receive them printed.

The book that came from it, *Devotions upon Emergent Occasions*, moved from inception to publication in a staggeringly short period of time; it was entered into the Stationer's Register on 9 January 1624 and was published almost immediately after. The writing itself took barely more than a few days: his illness had not eroded the speed of his mind.

He organised the book into a series of numbered meditations: a record of the knowledge he had gleaned, and an urgent list of what he most wanted others to know. He wrote of the isolation of illness: he had so often sought out seclusion to work, yet the inflicted loneliness of pain paralysed him. 'As sickness is the greatest misery, so the greatest misery of sickness is solitude . . . Solitude is a torment which is not threatened in hell itself . . . it is an outlawry.'

He put down, from his bed, his sharpest words about illness: on its ruthless capriciousness. He knew that bodily safety is an illusion and a fiction – a clarity that was the necessary flipside of his celebration of the bodily astonishment and urgency of sex. He looked with pitiless clear-sightedness at our precarity:

We study health, and we deliberate upon our meats, and drink, and air, and exercises; and we hew, and we polish every stone, that goes to that building; and so our health is a long and regular work. But in a minute a cannon batters all, overthrows all, demolishes all; a sickness unprevented for all our diligence, unsuspected for all our curiosity; nay, undeserved if we consider only disorder, summons us, seizes us, possesses us, destroys us in an instant.

The book burns with pain – but it is not sad. Donne's work rarely is: full of calm terror and sardonic horror, but only very rarely tears. Looking towards death, he saw the glory of what he had been: 'I am more than dust and ashes: I am my best part, I am my soul.'

¶

To read the *Devotions* is to expect that the man who emerged from his sickness would be one purified in the fire, whose moral vision was razor-sharp. But no; Donne at this point in his life is such vivid proof, if ever you find yourself in need of it, that you can be an excavator of the human soul, perceptive to the very bone marrow, and also capable of thoughtlessness and cruelty.

No sooner was he out of his sick bed than relations with Constance began to sour. Donne had promised his girl 'a little nag' which he rarely rode, but then he changed his mind without warning and sent it to Oxford, to John junior. He took from Constance a diamond ring, on the promise of replacing it with a better one which he himself wore, and then kept both. (This was particularly egregious, in that Constance as a married woman could not own property independently from her husband, but jewels and 'paraphernalia' could be hers alone.) Donne also offered to pay Alleyn a loan, which he then partially reneged on, and, according to Alleyn's furious letter, he'd promised to throw open the doors of the Deanery whenever Alleyn was in London: except, every time Alleyn attempted to take him up on his offer, Donne turned regal and told the actor that it wasn't an ideal time. Words grew heated: the revered Donne was accused of acting with 'unkind, unexpected and undeserved denial of the common courtesy afforded to a friend', and of using language more 'fitting you 30 years ago when you might be question[ed] for them, than now under so reverent a calling as you are'. Donne does not, in his reckonings with his girl, come off very magnificently, striding up to the pulpit with his daughter's ring on his finger.

(His children did not turn out much of a credit to him: John, Donne's editor after his death, without whom so much of his father's work would be lost, committed manslaughter: an eight-year-old child startled his horse, and John killed him by hitting him on the head with a riding crop. He was an incorrigible drinker who was arrested at least twice, and in 1629 was accused of having 'had about' with a young maidservant called Sara, leaving her pregnant and abandoned. The seventeenth-century antiquarian Anthony à Wood wrote, about John Donne junior, 'His nature being vile, he proved no better all his lifetime than an atheistical buffoon, a banterer, and a person of over-free thoughts.' George, like father like son, served in a spectacularly unsuccessful British siege in 1627, the Siege of Saint-Martin-de-Ré, and spent several years imprisoned at Cadiz.)

In 1624, Donne added another source of income to his slate; he became vicar of St Dunstan in the West, the tithes of which alone were worth at least £240 a year. This, added to a very tentative reckoning of his various revenues from his parishes in Sevenoaks and three other absentee benefices he held, plus the far greater sum from St Paul's, puts his annual income at close to £2,000. (For comparison: at around the same time a Norfolk knight was paying his dairy maid £2 a year, and his scullery maid £1 10s, while in Kent the yearly wage bill for a smart household of twelve servants came to £55 13s 10d.) Donne had to pay his curates' salaries out of it, but even so he was now among London's elite. St Dunstan was on Fleet Street, just along from the prison in which Donne had once been shackled. It was the same church in which William Tyndale, the great translator of the English Bible, had lectured and prayed: a church which has known more than its fair share of men who knew how to make their words grip hold of the heart. It was then that Donne met Izaak Walton; Walton, son of an innkeeper, had a linen draper's shop on Fleet Street, so St Dunstan was his local church. It was Donne who married Walton to Rachel Floud, great-grandniece of Archbishop Thomas Cranmer; it's likely to have been Donne who buried the couple's five sons, none of whom lived past four years old.

James I died in March 1625. If Donne quaked at the thought of the upheaval, and wondered if he would need to begin his careful politicking again with the new king, his tremors were unnecessary. James's son Charles I waited a week after his accession before appearing in public, when he sent out word that he wanted to hear a sermon in the chapel at St James's Palace, and that the preacher should be Dr Donne. It was testament to how securely Donne was established as the star preacher of the age; a compliment and a relief. He was at once gratified and surprisingly flustered: he wrote to Ker, asking for the loan of his rooms in the palace 'at one after noon' before he preached, so as to have enough time, like an actor, to compose himself before he made his entrance. He went to his pulpit fasting: 'I do not eat before, nor can after, till I have been at home'; nothing distracted him from focusing the full force of his mind on the sermon to come. He preached a sermon full of the nation's grief: 'The Almighty hand of God hath shed and spread a text of mortification over the land'; it was a careful compliment to the Stuart family, and Charles was sufficiently gratified that he ordered for the sermon to be published.

In 1626, there was another sermon to mark a death. This one, though, was of a very different kind of man, and it stands as some of the best evidence we have of Donne's willingness to occasionally put expediencies over moral exigencies. He was asked to give the funeral sermon of Sir William Cokayne; one-time Lord Mayor, and a man rich beyond the dreams of almost any other merchant of the time.

Cokayne had ordered, for his funeral, lavish mourning cloth and a great procession: it was one of the more elaborate death-spectacles of the year. He was also the man who had, ten years before, almost brought about the collapse of the entire English economy. It would have been not unlike being asked to preach the funeral sermon for Richard Fuld, the 'Gorilla of Wall Street' and 2008 CEO of Lehman Brothers.

In 1614 Cokayne had bribed commissioners for Treasure Affairs to prohibit the export of undyed cloth. At the time, the Dutch and Germans bought vast quantities of undyed and undressed cloth from England; some years it constituted ninety per cent of all of England's exports. The idea, Cokayne claimed, was that it would foster the English dyeing trade. The scheme went explosively badly: the Dutch, outraged, simply forbade the importing of dyed cloth and bought their undyed cloth from other countries. Customs revenues fell £6,000 in three months. The value of undyed cloth plummeted. Unemployment doubled. But Cokayne was untroubled – he simply started buying up the cloth at the reduced prices, which, when the law was (inevitably) reversed, he was able to sell on at a colossal profit: not unlike short-selling. Cokayne then cemented his position by giving James a gold basin filled with £1,000 in gold: not a million miles from those who donate selflessly to their preferred English political party, and miraculously end up in the House of Lords. He seems to have been a prototype for the destructive City boy; he also left his wife, a close friend of Donne's, in the middle of the financial chaos, and fought a fierce custody battle, causing her to squirrel her children away in several different parts of the country. And now Donne took his place in St Paul's Cathedral to speak about Cokayne's soul, with everyone waiting to see if he would thunder down visions of retribution on the heads of those listening.

He did not. Donne proclaimed that Cokayne 'did his part diligently, at least, if not vehemently, if not passionately'. He mourned him: 'you have lost a man, that drove a great trade, the right way of making the best use of our home-commodity.' And then he suggested that God, like Cokayne, would be in favour of a surplus in foreign trade: 'Out of the surplusage of His inexhaustible estate, out of the overflowing of His power, he enables his Executors to do as he did.'

Donne did touch briefly on the chaos Cokayne created: 'So great a ship, required a great ballast, so many blessings, many crosses; and he had them, and sailed on his course the steadier for them.' Donne did not spell out that the crosses made the country vastly poorer and Cokayne vastly richer: but everyone listening to him, of course, would have known. They would have heard what was going unspoken, and noted the omission.

Donne's metaphysics were married to a hard-headed practicality; he felt very sharply the appeal of the world-liness of the world. The boy who had so enjoyed a fine hat in his youth had never shaken off his love of the loveliness of things; the coveting, keep-both-diamond-rings element of existence. It might have been kin to the hunger that

endowed his verse with his own peculiar, fervent relish –
but it did require squinting at the passage in the Gospels
about the rich man, the camel and the eye of the needle.
Despite his ecclesiastical cap and cope, Donne never was the
scourge of the rich.

DONNE AND DEATH

The world is made up entirely of things that can kill you. Scarcely anything exists, Donne wrote with relish in the *Devotions*, which has not caused the death of someone once: 'a pin, a comb, a hair pulled, hath gangrened and killed.' A grim truth, and one which makes our modern attempts to avoid the topic of death look malarially unhinged. Donne lived in a time more familiar with the details and look of death than we; almost every adult was likely to have seen a dead body. They prepared intensively for it, contemplated it; Donne discussed it in letters that were otherwise about horses and dentistry. Donne had a *memento mori*, lest he forget even briefly that we are born astride the grave – he left it to a friend in his will, 'the picture called The Skeleton which hangs in the hall'.

Artists and writers especially were expected to contemplate death: there were rumours (probably mad and unfounded) that Michelangelo murdered a man and watched him die in order to be able to paint the agonies of Christ more accurately. Poets and playwrights, meanwhile, were killed and killing at a far greater rate of frequency than their percentage of the population seems to merit: Thomas Wyatt killed a man in an affray, Ben Jonson stabbed a man in a duel, Christopher Marlowe was murdered, probably in a tavern brawl, though possibly in an elaborate intrigue.

When Donne wrote about suicide there was urgent pain: but when he wrote about death *in itself*, there is great serious joy, and occasional rampant glee. Spiritually speaking, many of us confronted with the thought of death perform the psychological equivalence of hiding in a box with our knees under our chin: Donne hunted death, battled it, killed it, saluted it, threw it parties. His poetry explicitly about death is rarely sad: it thrums with strange images of living.

> Death! be not proud, though some have called thee
> Mighty and dreadful, for thou art not so;
> For those whom thou think'st thou dost overthrow
> Die not, poor Death, nor yet canst thou kill me.
> From rest and sleep, which but thy pictures be,
> Much pleasure, then from thee much more must flow,
> And soonest our best men with thee do go,
> Rest of their bones, and souls' delivery.

As a young man he had imagined his death in extravagantly sexual terms. 'The Relic' had imagined a gravedigger coming across the bodies of himself and his lover, buried together.

> When my grave is broke up again
> Some second guest to entertain . . .
> And he that digs it spies
> A bracelet of bright hair about the bone

He took tradition of the *memento mori* – a reminder of death – and injected hot desire into it. Donne's imagination was fundamentally alive, and on the side of life, on both sides of the grave. 'Death,' he wrote, 'thou shalt die.'

When Donne was talking about death he did not, unlike most of his contemporaries, yearn for the silence and stillness of the tomb. No: death was to be explosive, multicoloured, transmogrifying. He wanted ravishment: 'I would not that death should take me asleep. I would not have him merely seize me, and only declare me to be dead, but win me, and overcome me.' Donne wanted, ideally, to be struck down mid-sermon and topple down, an abrupt corpse, onto the congregation below: 'it hath been my desire (and God may be pleased to grant it me) that I might die in the pulpit.' It's telling that none of the love poems are sonnets: he kept that form for death, his other, permanent love. In Holy Sonnet VIII, Donne dared to imagine the end of all time, loud and very much awake:

> At the round Earth's imagined corners, blow
> Your trumpets, angels! and arise, arise
> From death, you numberless infinities
> Of souls, and to your scattered bodies go!
> All whom the Flood did and fire shall o'erthrow,
> All whom war, dearth, age, agues, tyrannies,
> Despair, law, chance hath slain, and you whose eyes
> Shall behold God, and never taste death's woe.

¶

He loved death in theory, and for himself: less so for others. In the very early winter days of 1627, his Lucy, nineteen and just old enough to be beginning her life as a woman, was on a visit away, probably with her sister Constance who had been widowed the year before. Donne was at home for the new year, ploughing his way ruefully through the necessary entertaining, when the message came to his door. Lucy was dead. She died with no warning, like lightning out of a blue sky – just five days before, Donne's letters had been full of amiable gripes about his social calendar. She was buried swiftly, in Camberwell on 9 January. If he wrote to tell Goodere and Wotton, the letters don't survive, but the weight of her loss leaked into his work. That Easter, he preached, and it is clear that he is preaching about her: 'If I had fixed a son in court, or married a daughter into a plentiful fortune, I were satisfied for that son and that daughter. Shall I not be so, when the King of Heaven hath taken that son to himself, and married himself to that daughter, forever?' You can hear the fixed set of his jaw in his words: 'I shall have my dead raised to life again.' It reads like a man wringing consolation by force from beliefs that had been already agonisingly hard-wrung.

His friends began dying: it must have felt like the end was setting in. Goodere went in March 1627, impoverished and untriumphant. Goodere's only son was already dead, and he left three daughters unmarriageable because of his impecuniousness: he couldn't give them dowries, and a woman without a dowry would have to be spectacularly beautiful or lucky. Goodere had loved the old chivalric code of the Henrican court, and had been beloved by Elizabeth I for his gallantry; under the more Machiavellian, less code-bound norms of the Jacobean court, he floundered, fell into debt, stumbled. Donne had told him: 'make . . . to yourself some mark, and go towards it alegrement'; but he had never been able to do it. It was almost certainly he to whom Donne gave that £100 that Walton mentions, the 'old friend'. Goodere refused it, but Donne knew very well how to be importunate; he had had long practice. He sent it back again with a note: 'my desire is, that you who in the days of your plenty have cheered and raised the hearts of so many of your dejected friends, will now receive this from me, and use it as a cordial for the cheering of your own.'

Possibly the shock of the deaths made him take his eye off the ball. His sermons had been so full of insistence on Death as liberator and translator, and yet the reality of it must have been a punch to the chest. The double loss blurred his precision, and he paid for it. On 1 April he preached a sermon for the new King Charles I. It included, as so very many of Donne's sermons had done, a long-drawn-out metaphor about the Church. Just, he said, as 'very religious Kings may have wives, that may have retained some tincture, some impressions of error, which they may have sucked in their infancy from another church,' and yet 'should not be publicly traduced to be heretics', just so the church 'may lack something of exact perfection'. Charles I's hackles rose. Word

came from Robert Ker to be on the lookout for royal fury –
and then, fast on its heels, a letter from Bishop Laud, asking
for a copy of the sermons in the name of the King. Donne
darted out instantly to visit Laud, agitated and bewildered.
His political prudence and his care around kings had been
such a fundamental feature of his rise. He had never made
a habit of being daringly inflammatory, and it must have
been alarming to face the possibility he had been so by accident. Laud would not explain what, exactly, had offended
the King, and Donne was thrown into a panic. He wrote to
Ker, 'I have cribrated [i.e. sifted: a word he himself invented,
when none other in his arsenal would do], and re-cribrated,
and post-cribrated the sermon' – and could find nothing in
it that did not 'conduce to [the King's] service'. Laud took it
upon himself to read over the text and report to the King, and
Donne was summoned into the presence to throw himself to
the ground before Charles and ask pardon. Laud wrote in
his diary, 'his Majesty King Charles forgave Doctor Donne
certain slips in a sermon.' Donne was never told exactly what
those 'certain slips' were for which he had so humbly apologised. It seems likely that Charles had bristled at the possible
aspersions Donne's simile had cast on his bride, Henrietta
Maria – daughter of the King of France – who was an ardent
Roman Catholic. Metaphors, Donne was reminded, are slippery beasts: they can escape out of your hands and bite you.

The bodies kept piling up. In May, Lucy Bedford died,
and was followed in June by his patroness Magdalen Herbert, over whose body he preached his super-infinite sermon.

Weakened by the succession of losses, he found illness sweeping in on him again; the sicknesses were more frequent, now, than the periods of health, and he was unwell a large part of that year and the next. In August 1628, his daughter Margaret fell ill with smallpox, and Donne, eager to escape the same danger, went to stay with a friend in Peckham until he was sure the risk of infection was passed. While there, he came down with a raging fever – 'complicated with squinancy', an abscess on the throat. He had to cease his preaching for a while, to protect his voice; it had happened before, and each time the fear of losing his greatest weapon shook him. He wrote, in his bone-dry joking mode, 'I should be sorry if this should make me a silenced Minister.' (A minister was said to be 'silenced' if he was suspended from the Church or excommunicated for deviating from its orthodoxies: a pun that was close to the marrow.)

We begin to lose sight of him, as he flickers in and out of the records we have: in 1629 he preached at court three times, at the cathedral three times. He appears only in his signature, signing off on churchwardens' accounts – as he grew weaker and less able to move about, the breadcrumbs by which we can trace him start to fade.

The illnesses were coming harder. In 1630, while visiting his daughter Constance in the home of her second husband, a respectable gentleman named Samuel Harvey, Donne was struck down with violent fever. Almost immediately, the gossip went out that he was dead. Donne, like Huckleberry Finn, had the immense satisfaction of discovering in life how he would be spoken of after his departure. 'A man would almost be content to die . . . to hear of so much sorrow and so much good testimony from good men as I (God be blessed for it) did upon the report of my death.'

Death came closer, and he thought incessantly about infinity. There would be no end, he decided. Even the demons in Hell, he wrote, cannot long for annihilation; he wanted to see in death the most living form of life. 'I shall not live till I see God; and when I have seen him I shall never die.' Exactly how the soul and body are anchored together teased him his entire life. He owned a library of books debating the soul's status: whether, at the start, it was formed inside the body of the mother or injected into the foetus individually by God before birth; 'whole Christian Churches', he noted testily, 'arrest themselves upon propagation from parents, and other whole Christian Churches allow only infusion from God.' He never decided: but he insisted that, whatever the beginning, there is no conclusion. We are a maze with no end.

Perhaps his love for writing about death was an attempt to transform fear into longing. He had known the dread of death: it's in Holy Sonnet I, 'I dare not move my dim eyes any way,/Despair behind, and death before, doth cast/Such terror.' Perhaps it was an attempt to convince himself when he said: 'who can fear the darkness of death, that hath the light of this world, and of the next too?' But perhaps he was, sometimes, as confident as he sounds: 'In the agonies of death, in the anguish of that dissolution, in the sorrows of the valediction, in the irreversibleness of that transmigration, I shall have a joy which shall no more evaporate than my soul shall evaporate: a joy that shall pass up and put on a more glorious garment above, and be joy super-invested in glory.' 'Invested in glory' would be enough for most of us, but not him: *super-invested*.

¶

In December of 1630, Donne knew that his body was collapsing, and he made his will. He wrote it out in his own hand, having no need of a lawyer: he had, after all, been one himself long ago. To his servants he left £5 apiece to buy mourning rings; to his friends, he left a list of paintings. Their descriptions reveal a glimpse of his artistic taste, which ran unsurprisingly religious, and of what he must have seen daily as he walked through his London home: one was of the Virgin, another of the Entombment, another of Adam and Eve, plus one of King James. The oil painting of himself in his twenties, 'the picture of mine which is taken in the shadows', all pout and hat, he left to Robert Ker, the man to whom he had trusted his *Biathanatos* all those years ago, and who had repaid his trust by keeping it safe and out of sight. His money was split evenly between his six surviving children, irrespective of gender – and provision was made for his mother, who was, like him, just clinging on to life.

As he grew weaker, he grew skeletally thin. He consulted his London doctor, Simeon Foxe – son of Foxe of the *Book of Martyrs* – who, alarmed at his swift decline, insisted that he should build his strength and gain weight. Foxe told him 'that by cordials, and drinking milk twenty days together, there was a probability of his restoration to health'. Donne loathed milk 'passionately' – to humour Foxe, he drank it for ten days, but stopped in disgust, declaring 'he would not drink it ten days longer upon the best moral assurance of having twenty years added to his life.' Donne had reached such an intimacy with death that milk held more terrors for him. His fear was not death, but slow entropy. It was his last terror, as all the other possible terrors fell away. He wrote in his final letter, to Cokayne's widow: 'I am afraid that Death will play with me so long, as he will forget to kill me, and suffer me to live in a languishing and useless age.'

¶

Donne did not get his wish; he didn't die in his pulpit – but he came close. On 25 February 1631 he preached his final sermon in the full knowledge that he was dying. Men and women who came to see him preach in London, and saw his 'decayed body, and a dying face', wondered if he might in truth be a corpse. They 'saw his tears, and heard his faint and hollow voice, professing they thought the text prophetically chosen, and that Dr Donne had preached his own funeral sermon'. He was fifty-nine: the national average life expectancy for those who made it into adulthood.

The sermon, published posthumously as *Death's Duel*, is dark as pitch, until almost the very end. Donne, standing like an ambulant *memento mori* in his church, told the listeners that their whole life was merely a movement from death to death. 'Our very birth and entrance into this life is *exitus à morte*, an issue from death': 'in our mother's womb we are dead,' he writes, or as if dead, because 'we have eyes and see not, ears and hear not,' and 'we have a winding sheet in our Mother's womb . . . for we come to seek a grave.' His own mother had died weeks before, and the grief infects the sermon: the womb from which he came was in the grave.

Worse, we can be murderers before we draw breath: if a child dies in its mother's womb it 'kills the mother that conceived it, and is a murderer, nay, a parricide, even after it is dead'. It is impossible not to think of Anne, and her childbirth death. 'There in the womb we are taught cruelty, by being fed with blood.' No other sermon by Donne is so resolutely sad.

Its ending, though, is not sad. What a person decides on matters unprovable is the surest way to know their imagination, and Donne could not write his final word without saluting the beginning.

The end of the sermon is a litany of images of life: of life 'blessed and glorious', 'that shall last as long as the Lord of Life himself'. Death would not just give life: it would give life free from his constant, relentless questing, finally solidify him and define him. Montaigne called it 'a death united in itself . . . wholly mine'. Certainty, never once available in life, is what death promised him. Donne's desire for death was a desire to see himself.

The sermon's last words – and the last Donne spoke to his congregation – were these: 'There we leave you . . . suck at [Christ's] wounds, and lie down in peace in his grave, till he vouchsafe you a resurrection.' Who is that 'we' that comes down from the pulpit: 'there we leave you'? Preachers did often use the royal 'we', but Donne in all the rest of the sermon had used 'I'.

One option: *we* is all the dozens of Donnes. He was a man constantly transforming. He was a one-man procession: John Donne the persecuted, the rake, the lawyer, the bereaved, the lover, the jailbird, the desperate, the striver, the pious, John Donne the almost dead and reporting from the front line of the grave.

Donne, though, will have meant another we. He had written years before, in another sermon, of his longing for the interlinking of God and man: 'God hath made himself one body with me.' So that 'we' is Donne imagining himself as having already made that final leap, stepped across the barrier and made a final transformation: John Donne, Jack Donne, Dr Donne, and now, finally, *we*. The 'we' is Donne and the God he has been summoning and summoning.

¶

His death came daily closer, and Donne prepared for it as others prepare for great theatrical debuts. His fascination with the dramatic silent gestures that we can make with the clothes we put on our backs lasted to the very end. In his home in London he set about designing his monument that would stand in the cathedral after his death. First he ordered a wooden urn to be carved, and a shroud to be made. He stripped naked in his study and wrapped himself in his shroud, with the knots at his feet and atop his head; then he pushed back the cloth so that only his face was showing.

The artist sketched his dying body life-size, onto a wooden plank; and the plank was set by Donne's bedside. It was entirely characteristic of him: that he forced from the fact of his dying body a final piece of art. He, of all people, was liable to insist on a *memento mori* of the most bespoke kind.

The drawing was used as the model for the stone monument that stands upright in an alcove in St Paul's Cathedral. Henry Wotton, by now the distinguished old Provost of Eton, said of it: 'It seems to breathe faintly, and posterity shall look upon it as a kind of artificial miracle.' It would be one of the only statues in the cathedral to survive the Fire of London, standing intact amid the rubble.

Donne died in his own home on 31 March 1631. Walton was close by, and ecstatic to the last:

His speech, which had long been his ready and faithful servant, left him not till the last minute of his life, and then forsook him not to serve another Master (for who speaks like him) but died before him, for that it was then become useless to him that now conversed with God on earth, as Angels are said to do in heaven, only by thoughts and looks.

Nicholas Stone's effigy, St Paul's Cathedral

As Donne felt death reach him, 'he closed his own eyes; and then disposed his hands and body into such a posture as required not the least alteration by those that came to shroud him.' Donne made himself ready; part, perhaps, of a desire to have things done exactly as he had imagined them – an artist of ferocious precision, dying precisely.

His last words – 'I were miserable if I might not die.'

The frontispiece of *Death's Duel*

SUPER-INFINITE

Donne had wanted to be buried, he said in his will, 'in the most private manner that may be': but nothing could keep the crowds away. He was buried in St Paul's, and an anonymous poet wrote on charcoal across the wall over his grave:

Reader! I am to let thee know
Donne's body only lies below
For, could the grave his soul comprise
Earth would be richer than the skies.

The bishop Henry King wrote Donne a more formal elegy, in ink and paper. It mourned that Donne couldn't have gone beyond making his own monument, and written his own epitaph: 'since but thine own/no pen could do thee justice.' King had all of a bishop's tendency to be excessively polite about the dead, but he was right. Donne, more than any other of his lifetime, understood that flair is its own kind of truth: if you want to make your point, make it so vivid and strange that it cuts straight through your interlocutor's complacent inattention. To read his verse is to hear him insist, across the gap of hundreds of years: *for God's sake, will you listen.*

¶

He was dead, but his poetry and his sermons were alive, spreading exponentially as they were copied and recopied. John Donne junior had a keen eye to a commercial endeavour, and in 1633 he produced the first printed collected works of Donne's poetry. It opened with a preface, headed 'The Printer to the Understanders': a nod to the fact that Donne was a man who required all your focus and ingenuity to untangle. For those who persevered, though, the preface said, 'a scattered limb of this author hath more amiableness in it, in the eye of a discerner, than a whole body of some other.'

Soon, those outside the literary elite were able to buy it in the marketplace outside St Paul's. Other poets and playwrights of his generation loved his work enough to lift it wholesale: Francis Beaumont, Thomas Carew, Francis Quarles and John Webster all took lines from Donne and included them, unattributed, in their own work; outright theft as the highest form of flattery. Dryden, for all his carping on Donne's scansion, stole lines from two of his obsequies and inserted them into his poem 'Eleonora'. But people wanted more. They were ravenous enough for his work to make it worth faking it, and within two decades of Donne's death, 'new' work by him began appearing.

The phenomenon – pseudepigraphy, the attribution of work to an author who didn't write it – was nothing new. People had been doing it to Shakespeare for decades; the market mushroomed with work by 'W.S.' or 'W.Sh.' – as many as ten between 1595 and 1622. In the mid-seventeenth century poems began to crop up in printed miscellanies, aping Donne's style and ascribed to a just-about-plausibly deniable 'J.D.' or 'Dr Dun'. The fakeries range from comically bad to mediocre: but all are useful, in that they revealed exactly what the forgers were thinking of as typically Donnean.

For instance: in 1654 an opportunistic young royalist called Robert Chamberlain produced *The Harmony of the Muses*, a miscellany of verses which included some real Donne poetry alongside three fakes. They show how far the idea of the glamorously woman-conquering Donne had entered the popular imagination in the twenty years after his death: 'Dun's Answer to a Lady' takes bedrooms and wordplay as Donne's hallmark.

Lady:

Say not you love unless you do,
For lying will not honour you.

Answer of the Doctor's:

Lady I love, and love to do,
And will not love unless be you.
You say I lie, I say you lie, choose whether,
But if we both lie, let us lie together.

Another, 'The Rapture', by one 'J.D.', remembers that Donne liked suns:

Just as the Sun, methinks I see her face,
Which I may gaze upon, but not imbrace:
For 'tis heavens pleasure sure she should be sent
As pure to heaven again, as she was lent
To us.

What's so telling is that although the fakers thought they knew basically what Donne was about – he liked sex, he loved a metaphor – the pastiches don't ring even slightly true. They could not step into his voice, because his voice was so constantly in motion: turbulent, shifting between triumph and anxiety, bravado and dread, irony and humility.

The other reason they don't ring true is that they're just too easy. Donne would have scoffed. It was very deliberately that he wrote poems that take all your sustained focus to untangle them. The pleasure of reading a Donne poem is akin to that of cracking a locked safe, and he meant it to be so. He demanded hugely of us, and the demands of his poetry are a mirror to that demanding. The poetry stands to ask: why should everything be easy, rhythmical, pleasant? He is at times almost impossible to understand, but, in repayment for your work, he reveals images that stick under your skin until you die. Donne suggests that you look at the world with both more awe and more scepticism: that you weep for it and that you gasp for it. In order to do so, you shake yourself out of cliché and out of the constraints of what the world would sell you. Your love is almost certainly not like a flower, nor a dove. Why would it be? It may be like a pair of compasses. It may be like a flea. His startling timelessness is down to the fact that he had the power of unforeseeability: you don't see him coming.

The difficulty of Donne's work had in it a stark moral imperative: pay attention. It was what Donne most demanded of his audience: attention. It was, he knew, the world's most mercurial resource. The command is in a passage in Donne's sermon: 'Now was there ever any man seen to sleep in the cart, between Newgate and Tyburn? Between the prison, and the place of execution, does any man sleep? And we sleep all the way; from the womb to the grave we are never thoroughly awake.' Awake, is Donne's cry. Attention, for Donne, was everything: attention paid to our mortality, and to the precise ways in which beauty cuts through us, attention to the softness of skin and the majesty of hands and feet and mouths. Attention to attention itself, in order to fully appreciate its power: 'Our creatures are our thoughts,' he wrote, 'creatures that are born Giants: that reach from East to West, from earth to Heaven, that do not only bestride all the sea and land, but span the sun and firmament at once: my thoughts reach all, comprehend all.' We exceed ourselves: it's thus that a human is super-infinite.

Most of all, for Donne, our attention is owed to one another. Donne's most famous image comes not from his poetry, but from the words he set down in extremis, in *Devotions upon Emergent Occasions*:

When one man dies, one chapter is not torn out of the book, but translated into a better language; and every chapter must be so translated; God employs several translators; some pieces are translated by age, some by sickness, some by war, some by justice; but God's hand is in every translation, and his hand shall bind up all our scattered leaves again, for that library where every book shall lie open to one another.

On his deathbed, facing down what he imagined to be the end of everything he had known, this was what he most urgently wanted to tell. We, slapdash chaotic humanity, persistently underestimate our effect on other people: it is our necessary lie, but he refused to tell it. In a world so harsh and beautiful, it is from each other that we must find purpose, else there is none to be had:

No man is an island, entire of itself; every man is a piece of the continent, a part of the main; if a clod be washed away by the sea, Europe is the less, as well as if a promontory were, as well as if a manor of thy friend's or of thine own were; any man's death diminishes me, because I am involved in mankind, and therefore never send to know for whom the bell tolls; it tolls for thee.

There's a characteristic bite in the passage, which stands as both promise and warning: death is coming for *you*. But they are glorious words. If we could believe them, they would upend the world. They cast our interconnectedness not as a burden but as a great project: our interwoven lives draw their meaning only from each other.

In his hardest days Donne wrote that his mind was a 'sullen weedy lake'. But it was fertile water: in it, things were born. From his prodigious learning, from his lust, from his fear, came work strong enough to ring through the barricade of time. Donne was honest about horror and its place in the task of living, and honest too in his insistence: joy is also a truth. Who else of his peers had been able to hold grotesqueries and delights, death and life so tightly in the same hand?

There's a scientific term, autapomorphic, which denotes a unique characteristic that has evolved in only one species or subspecies. That was him: there are ways of reckoning with the grimly and majestically improbable problem of being alive that exist only because four hundred years ago a boy was born on Bread Street to Elizabeth Donne. John Donne was super-autapomorphic.

ACKNOWLEDGEMENTS

I have built up a colossal debt, to so many for such kindness, in the long writing of this book. If you are one, please consider this a lifelong promissory note.

My first thanks are to the Warden and Fellows of All Souls College, Oxford, where this book was written – and especially to Colin Burrow, for his kindness and ruthless eradication of extraneous adjectives.

I owe a great debt to the scholars who gave their time to talk over and read this text. To John Carey, whose *John Donne: Life, Mind and Art* was the most electric piece of literary criticism I read as a teen and thereby set me on the road to Donne, and who read and commented on this text with formidable generosity. To Daniel Starza Smith, whose scholarly insight changed this book, and whose friendship spurred me on. (Good*ere,* forever.) To A. N. Wilson, who, with great kindness, read an early draft. I owe an enormous amount, too, to those who gave their expertise and time during my doctoral thesis: especially Norma Aubertin-Potter and Gaye Morgan at All Souls college library, Dennis Flynn, Arthur Marotti, Peter McCullough, Jeanne Shami and Jo Wisdom, the librarian of St Paul's Cathedral.

I owe thanks to my two wonderful editors, Alex Bowler and Mitzi Angel, and everyone at RCW: Zoe Waldie, Claire

Wilson, Peter Straus and Safae El-Ouahabi. Nic Liney expertly wrangled my dates as an independent fact-checker.

This book took more than half a decade to write, and my greatest luck is in my friends, who have put up with my talking about Donne solidly for the last ten years – especially to Susie Atwood, Chanya Button, Abi Elphinstone, Lavinia Harrington, Tom Hodgson, Ellen Holgate, Anna James, Daisy Johnson, Jessica Lazar, Kiran Millwood Hargrave, Daniel Morgan, Simon Murphy, Gerard Rundell, Adélia Sabatini, Julie Scrase, Sophie Smith, Alice Spawls, Lauren St John, Issy Sutton, Piers Torday, Katie Webber and Fred Wilmot Smith. To Mary Wellesley and Miranda Vane, donkey wardens, comrades in PhDs, joy women. To Alex Cole, for such glorious talk. To Amia Srinivasan, for such rich wisdom, about this book and so much else. Most of all to Liz Chatterjee, my most brilliant and incomparable twin, who was with me and Donne from the very start.

To Barbara and Peter Rundell I owe absolutely everything, but especially, in the context of this book, gratitude for pinning Donne poetry next to the bathroom sink when we were small.

To Charles Collier, the best and boldest editor I've ever had: it is because of you that the love poetry makes sense to me.

Finally, I have had such life-shaping good fortune in my teachers. To Professor Bart van Es, my undergraduate tutor, doctoral thesis supervisor and colleague, I owe gratitude for more than a decade of generosity and erudition: thank you.

FURTHER READING

For those seeking a wider sense of how the world has received Donne over time, the Critical Heritage series is an understated delight: a compendium of some of the many – often scathing and furious – things that have been said about Donne's work in the last four hundred years: A. J. Smith, *John Donne: The Critical Heritage* (2010).

For more on Donne and his circle of friends, and the ways in which they passed poems and jokes and knowledge between themselves: Arthur Marotti, John Donne: Coterie Poet (1986).

For the text of the letters that Donne and his in-laws exchanged during the tumultuous months of the marriage, and the four letters that are probably his love letters to Anne: M. Thomas Hester, Robert Parker Sorlien and Dennis Flynn (eds), *John Donne's Marriage Letters in the Folger Shakespeare Library* (2005).

For more on Donne's writing for Anne: M. Thomas Hester (ed.), *John Donne's 'Desire of More': The Subject of Anne More Donne in His Poetry* (1997).

For more on how Early Modern patronage functioned, as well as more on Henry Goodere: Daniel Starza Smith, *John Donne and the Conway Papers: Patronage and Manuscript Circulation in the Early Seventeenth Century* (2014).

For more on the sermons – on their structural innovations, their politics and their nuance: Peter McCullough, *Sermons at Court: Politics and Religion in Elizabethan and Jacobean Preaching* (1998) and Jeanne Shami, *John Donne and Conformity in Crisis in the Late Jacobean Pulpit* (2003).

For more on Donne's working life, and his navigation of the court and Church, David Colclough (ed.), *John Donne's Professional Lives* (2003).

For more on Donne's obsessing over the binding between the body and the soul: Ramie Targoff, *John Donne: Body and Soul* (2008).

For an electric analysis of Donne's life and work together: John Carey, *John Donne: Life, Mind and Art* (1981, revised 1990).

For those in search of where to begin with Donne's prose – the *Devotions upon Emergent Occasions* (the 1999 edition prints them with *Death's Duel* and Izaak Walton's *Life of Donne*) are relentlessly beautiful, and *Ignatius His Conclave* (ed. T. S. Healy (1969)) is genuinely funny, in ways that are revealing about the spiky, elaborate humour of the seventeenth century. For those searching for warnings against the place not to begin: for all the powerful astonishments to be found in Donne's work, it's difficult to recommend that anybody read *Pseudo-Martyr*, except under duress.

Key Manuscripts

Bodl. Rawl. poet. 117: mid-seventeenth-century quarto verse miscellany, English and Latin, including thirty-seven poems by Donne, in several hands, compiled in part by the Oxford printer Christopher Wase

BL Egerton MS 2421: mid-seventeenth-century verse miscellany, containing copy of *The Tempest*'s 'full fathoms five' alongside verse by Donne and Jonson

BL Harley MS 5110: independent quire, seven folio leaves containing three satires by Donne, in two hands, headed 'Jhon Dunne his Satires Anno Domini 1593'

BL Harley MS 6931: seventeenth-century octavo miscellany, chiefly verse in two italic hands, religious verse and prose at the reverse end in another hand, verse by Carew and Donne

The Burley manuscript, DG. 7/Lit. 2: 616 items over 373 folios, including poems, legal reports and letters, three or four of which may be Donne's love letters. The manuscript was believed lost in the devastating 1908 fire at Burley-on-the-Hill, until it was rediscovered in 1960 by I. A. Shapiro in the National Register of Archives. It then disappeared again in a series of administrative

muddles, turning up sixteen years later at the University Library
of Birmingham, and is now in the Leicestershire Record Office.
It is also printed in facsimile by Peter Redford (ed.), *The Burley
Manuscript* (2017), and so is safe for posterity for now.

Cambridge University Library MS Add. 29: verse miscellany, in
multiple hands, containing thirty-five Donne poems

Folger MS V.a.125: composite headed 'a book of verses collected
by mee R Dungaravane', including Donne verse and a number of
recipes for wine

Folger MS V.a.245: quarto verse miscellany, single secretary hand,
probably associated with Oxford and afterwards with the Inns of
Court

Folger MS V.a.262 : quarto verse miscellany, in English and Latin,
multiple hands, title 'Divers Sonnets & Poems compiled by
certaine gentil Clarks and Ryme-Wrightes', probably associated
with Oxford University and the Inns of Court

Heneage MS (private collection): early seventeenth-century
quarto miscellany, eleven texts in verse and prose, in several
hands, including seven poems by Donne in a single hand with
ornamentation

Westminster MS 41: octavo verse miscellany, including thirteen
poems by Donne, in several hands over an extended period,
associated with Christ Church, Oxford, 1620–40s

The Westmoreland Manuscript, Berg Collection, New York
Public Library, NY3: perhaps the 'canonically purest' of Donne
manuscripts, it is written in the hand of Donne's friend Rowland
Woodward and contains seventy-nine of Donne's poems, ten
prose paradoxes, and a prose letter addressed by Donne to
Woodward. Many editions of Donne's poetry have used this
manuscript as their textual starting point.

NOTES

Introduction

1 **carrying paper and ink** Francis Russell, the Earl of Bedford, filled multiple notebooks with listening notes from Donne's sermons. S. Verweij, 'Sermon Notes from John Donne in the Manuscripts of Francis Russell, Fourth Earl of Bedford', *English Literary Renaissance* 46:2 (2016), pp. 278–313.

– **charm the soul** Henry Valentine, 'An Elegy upon the Incomparable Doctor Donne', in Donne, *Poems* (1633), p. 379.

– **There was a great concourse.** Thomas E. Tomlins (ed.), *Walton's Lives, with Notes* (1852), p. 79.

3 **raw vapours** There is not yet a modern edition of Donne's letters, though *The Oxford Edition of the Letters of John Donne* is forthcoming, and has been in progress for more than fifty years. Therefore all quotations from Donne's letters, unless otherwise stated, come from the collection his son John put together and published after his death: *Letters to Severall Persons of Honour* (1651). p. 31

– **'O Lady, lighten our darkness'** In the Latin Bible, Psalm 17 reads: 'O Lord, lighten my darkness.'

4 **License my roving hands** 'To His Mistress Going to Bed', lines 25–8.

5 **But O, self-traitor** 'Twickenham Garden', lines 6–8.

– **Us she informed** 'To the Countess of Huntingdon', line 26.

7 **Nothing but man** 'An Elegy upon the Death of Lady Markham', lines 13–14.

– **one might almost say** 'The Second Anniversary', line 246.

– **it is too little.** John Donne, *Devotions upon Emergent Occasions* (1624), Meditation IV.

- **be thine own palace** 'To Mr Henry Wotton', line 52. All quotations of Donne's poetry are from Robin Robbins' brilliant edition, *The Complete Poems of John Donne* (2014). Poems are usually identified in the text of the book, but where they are not they are noted here in the endnotes, as well as in the index.

10 **just over 9,100 lines** Gary Stringer, 'The Composition and Dissemination of Donne's Writings', in *The Oxford Handbook of John Donne*, ed. Jeanne Shami, Dennis Flynn and M. Thomas Hester (2016), p. 13.

- **Donne seems to have used the form** Margaret Maurer, 'The Verse Letter', in *The Oxford Handbook of John Donne*, p. 207.

13 **twenty-four ten-syllable lines** Julia M. Walker, 'Donne's Words Taught in Numbers', *Studies in Philology* 84 (1987), pp. 44–60, 51.

14 **dwell bodily** All sermon quotations are from *The Sermons of John Donne*, ed. George R. Potter and Evelyn M. Simpson, 10 vols (1953–62). *Sermons*, Vol. VI, p. 363.

- **super-edifications, super-exaltation** All these examples are collected by John Carey, *John Donne: Life, Mind and Art* (2014), 113.

15 **more extravagant rendering** Thomas Docherty, *John Donne, Undone* (1986), p. 54.

16 **Donne seems to deserve** Robbins, *The Complete Poems of John Donne*, p. 355.

17 **akin to sacrament** Robbins notes Donne's love of words that evoke sacrament in *The Complete Poems of John Donne*, p. 355. 'The Canonisation', lines 26–7.

- **All measure, and all language** 'The Relic', lines 32–3.

19 **Dark texts** 'To the Countess of Bedford', line 11.

The Prodigious Child

20 **whispered (erroneously)** Colin Burrow, 'Recribrations', *London Review of Books*, 5 October 2006.

- **The family had once owned** M. Thomas Hester, Robert Parker

Sorlien and Dennis Flynn (eds), *John Donne's Marriage Letters in the Folger Shakespeare Library* (2005), p. 11.

22 **Though [Donne's] own learning** Izaak Walton, *The Lives of Dr John Donne, Sir Henry Wotton, Mr Richard Hooker, Mr George Herbert* (1670), p. 11. All quotations from Walton's life are from this text, unless otherwise stated.

– **I have seen women** John Heywood, *The Play Called the Four PP: A new and a very merry interlude of a palmer, a pardoner, a potycary, a pedler* (1545), unpaginated.

23 **If thou beest born** 'Go and Catch a Falling Star', lines 10–18.

– **His grandfather became famous** C. S. Lewis (ed.), *English Literature in the Sixteenth Century: Excluding Drama* (1954), p. 146.

24 **divers Latin books** John Stow, *Annales*, cited in William Bernard MacCabe, *A Catholic History of England* (1847), Vol. I, p. 322.

25 **suffered with great constancy** William E. Andrews, *Review of Fox's Book of Martyrs* (1826), Vol. III, p. 337.

– **I went out to Charing Cross** Samuel Pepys, *The Shorter Pepys*, ed. Robert Latham (1985), p. 86.

– **tradition holds** Dennis Flynn, *John Donne and the Ancient Catholic Nobility* (1995), p. 70.

– **fell asunder** ibid., p. 21.

27 **I pray you** William Roper, *The Life of Sir Thomas More, Knight*, ed. E. V. Hitchcock (1935), p. 103.

– **Pluck up thy spirits** ibid.

– **I cannot tell** Flynn, *John Donne and the Ancient Catholic Nobility*, p. 21.

– **the pretended Queen** Alec Ryrie, *The Age of Reformation: The Tudor and Stewart Realms 1485–1603* (2017), p. 228.

28 **some bystanders, leaving** John Donne, *Pseudo-Martyr* (1610), p. 222.

29 **I accompanied her** Flynn, *John Donne and the Ancient Catholic Nobility*, p. 129.

– **a Consultation of Jesuits** ibid., pp. 123–30.

30 **I have been ever kept awake** *Pseudo-Martyr*, foreword, sig 1r.

The Hungry Scholar

31 **read the Bible thorough** Katherine Philips, *The Collected Works of Katherine Philips*, Vol. I: *The Poems*, ed. Patrick Thomas (1990), p. x.

- **another Picus Mirandula** Walton, *Lives*, p. 13.

32 **unto their urine** Liza Picard, *Elizabeth's London: Everyday Life in Elizabethan London* (2013), p. 195.

- **when a schoolmaster** Richard Burn, *Justice of the Peace*, cited in Jonathan Gathorne-Hardy, *The Public School Phenomenon 597–1977* (2014), p. 97.

- **Donne learned that later** R. C. Bald, *John Donne: A Life* (revised edition, 1986), p. 40. Robert Cecil Bald's biography of Donne forms the bedrock of this book, and of every other account of Donne's life since its first publication in 1970; it's a piece of spectacularly detailed scholarship, and though many new documents have since come to light which nuance and adjust his telling, his work remains central to Donne scholarship.

33 **mean men's children** Lawrence Stone, *The Crisis of the Aristocracy, 1558–1641* (1965), p. 687.

- **in the most unsettled days** Walton, *Lives*, p. 62.

34 **I exercise my pen** James McConica and T. H. Aston (eds), *The History of the University of Oxford*, Vol. III (1986), p. 41.

- **'The Oxford Scholar'** Cambridge University Library, MS Add. 29.

35 **once of New College** Alan Davidson, 'An Oxford Family: A Footnote to the Life of John Donne', *Recusant History* 13:4 (1976), pp. 299–300.

- **not dissolute** Sir Richard Baker in Bald, *John Donne: A Life*, p. 72.

36 **Sir, more than kisses** 'To Mr Henry Wotton', line 1.

- **Izaak Walton's son** This fact has been hiding in the footnotes on page 32 of Jonquil Bevan's edition of Izaak Walton's *The Compleat Angler* (1988).

- **most heterogeneous ideas** Samuel Johnson, *Lives of the Poets*, ed. George Birkbeck Hill (1905), p. 20.

- **first recorded use** Peter McCullough notes the 'commonplacer'

coinage in his Oxford edition of Donne's sermons; cited
in Piers Brown, 'Donne, Rhapsody, and Textual Order', in
Joshua Eckhardt and Daniel Starza Smith (eds), *Manuscript
Miscellanies in Early Modern England* (2016), p. 48.

37 **make himself as full a list** Ann Moss, 'Locating Knowledge',
in Karl Enenkel and Wolfgang Neuber (eds), *Cognition and
the Book: Typologies of Formal Organisation of Knowledge*
(2005), p. 36.

– **whatever you come across** ibid.

38 *Academia* **and** *Tedium* The commonplace book of Robert
Southwell, Beinecke MS Osborn b112, pp. 470–1. Southwell
was a fan of Donne's: under *Vita*, he lists 'Lives of persons
written', including 'Dr. Donne, Sr. Henry Wotton, & Mr.
Hooker by Mr. Isaac Walton'.

– **When a poet's mind** T. S. Eliot, *Selected Essays* (3rd edn,
London, 1951), p. 287.

40 **goes twitching and hopping** Cited in *The Complete Poems of
Joseph Hall*, ed. Alexander B. Grosart (1879), Vol. VIII, p. xvi.

41 **made a bolt for Europe** Dennis Flynn, 'Donne's Education', in
The Oxford Handbook of John Donne, p. 411.

– **swear the Oath of Supremacy** Heywood to Acquaviva, n.d.,
ARSI, Anglia 30/I, fo. 118v, cited in Flynn, *John Donne and the
Ancient Catholic Nobility*, pp. 131–2.

– **school hostages** Flynn, 'Donne's Education', p. 411.

– **He shuttled twenty students** Allen to Agazzari, 5 November
1582 and 8 August 1583, *Catholic Record Society* IV (1907),
pp. 73 and 115; Flynn, 'Donne's Education', p. 412.

42 **perpetual aqueducts** ibid.

– **gentleman, dwelling in Southwark** Bald, *John Donne: A Life*, p. 50.

– **Mistress Symones** ibid.

43 **When Donne arrived** ibid., p. 55.

– **concerns noblemen and gentlemen** Stone, *The Crisis of the
Aristocracy*, p. 691.

44 **it shall be lawful** Picard, *Elizabeth's London*, p. 73.

- **fined 13s 4d** ibid., p. 207.
- **found fault with his study** ibid.
45 **For my purpose** *Letters*, p. 238.
- **my best entertainment** ibid.
46 **six or seven galliards** Suzanne Lord and David Brinkman, *Music from the Age of Shakespeare: A Cultural History* (2003), p. 9.
- **If any man will sue** *Sermons*, Vol. VIII, p. 145.
- **Away, thou changeling** Satire I, lines 1–4.
48 **written all his best pieces** 'Certain Informations and Manners of Jonson to W. Drummond', in *Notes of Ben Jonson's Conversations at Hawthornden*, cited in Gary A. Stringer (ed.), *The Variorum Edition of the Poetry of John Donne*, Vol. II: *The Elegies*, p. xciv.
49 **If love could find** Walter Raleigh, 'Now We Have a Present Made', lines 25–8; *Selected Writings*, ed. Gerald Hammond (1986), p. 50.
- **Donne, whose muse** Samuel Taylor Coleridge, 'On Donne's Poetry', cited in A. J. Smith, *John Donne: The Critical Heritage* (2010), p. 264.
- **Would not Donne's satires** John Dryden, 'Of the Original and Progress of Satire' (1693); *Of Dramatic Poesy and Other Essays*, ed. George Watson (1962), Vol. II, p. 144.
51 **produced by a voluntary deviation** Samuel Johnson, *Lives of the Poets*, ed. Robina Napier (1890), p. 42.
52 **And they're his own** Satire II, lines 25–30.

The Exquisitely Clothed Theoriser on Fashion

55 **his apparel pretend no lightness** William Dugdale, *Origines Juridiciales or Historical Memorials of the English Laws, Courts of Justice, Forms of Tryal* (1671), p. 197.
56 **of stature moderately tall** Walton, *Lives*, p. 80.
57 **his beard well brushed** Simion Grahame, *The Anatomy of Humours* (1609), p. 30.
- **snotty nosed gentlemen** ibid.

Brother to a Dead Man

61 **Oh happy people** George Deaux, *The Black Death* (1969), p. 94.

62 **If you fell ill** Picard, *Elizabeth's London*, p. 92.

– **What an unmatchable torment** *The Plague Pamphlets of Thomas Dekker*, ed. F. P. Wilson (1925), p. 160.

– **dine with his friends** Ernest B. Gilman, *Plague Writing in Early Modern England* (2009), p. 33.

– **felt a pricking** *The Plague Pamphlets of Thomas Dekker*, p. 160.

– **The brothels emptied** Antoine Joseph, *English Professional Theatre, 1530–1660* (2000), p. 84.

63 **whimpring sonnets** Everard Guilpin, *Skialetheia* (1598, 1958 facsimile reprint), sig B8.

– **in this lamentable calamity** *Sermons*, Vol. VI, p. 362.

64 **every puff of wind** ibid.

– **Fair London** John Taylor, *The Fearful Summer, or London's Calamity* (1636), sig A3r.

– **not only incurable** *Sermons*, Vol. VII, p. 80.

65 **said he was a priest** F. P. Wilson, 'Notes on the Early Life of John Donne', *Review of English Studies* 3:11 (1927), pp. 272–9.

66 **eaten of lice** Thomas Boys, *Notes and Queries*, 19 February 1859, p. 159.

– **drawn from Newgate** Stow, cited in Bald, *John Donne: A Life*, p. 58.

– **proofs of unusual constancy** Richard Simpson, *Under the Penal Laws: Instances of Sufferings of Catholics* (1930), p. 82.

67 **A contemporary Catholic claimed** See Wilson, 'Notes on the Early Life of John Donne', p. 275.

– **have favour shown them** Tom Cain, 'Elegy and Autobiography: "The Bracelet" and the Death of Henry Donne', *John Donne Journal* 23 (2004), pp. 25–57.

– **Donne did not visit** ibid., p. 33.

– **He was nineteen** Some sources have him as twenty years old; Cain, 'Elegy and Autobiography', p. 33.

68 **at least ten per cent of deaths** A. Lloyd Moote and Dorothy C.

Moote, *The Great Plague: the Story of London's Most Deadly Year* (2004), p. 10, and Paul Slack, *The Impact of Plague in Tudor and Stuart England* (1985), p. 145.

- **killed up to seventy per cent** Gilman, *Plague Writing in Early Modern England*, p. 192.

69 **I have a sin of fear** 'To Christ', lines 13–14.

- **I am a little world** Divine Meditation VII, lines 1–2.

The Convert (Perhaps)

70 **eleven members** Cain, 'Elegy and Autobiography', p. 29.

- **the art of copying** John Donne, *The Courtier's Library, Or Catalogus Librorum Aulicorum incomparabilium et non vendibilium*, ed. and trans. Evelyn M. Simpson (1930), p. 43.

71 **Grief which did drown me** 'To Mr Rowland Woodward', lines 6–8.

72 **Donne may even have helped** Cain, 'Elegy and Autobiography', p. 32.

- **be then thine own home** 'To Mr Henry Wotton', line 47.

- **answerable to my father's estate** Letter to Lord Keeper Puckering, cited in Cain, 'Elegy and Autobiography', p. 35.

- **Jesuits were in part to blame** Bald, *John Donne: A Life*, p. 67.

- **indirectly . . . cause Priests** William Clark, *A Reply unto a Certain Libel Lately Set Forth by Father Persons* (1603), 18r.

73 **They do not indeed** Christopher Bagshaw, *A True Relation of the Faction Begun at Wisbich* (1601), pp. 73–4.

- **coded reference to Henry** Cain, 'Elegy and Autobiography', p. 42.

74 **image of a dead boy** Carey, *John Donne: Life, Mind and Art*, p. 39.

The (Unsuccessful) Adventurer

75 **dearths and Spaniards** Satire II, line 6.

76 **A Journal of all the particularities** Lambeth Palace MS 250, cited in Bald, *John Donne: A Life*, p. 80.

77 **they are strong enough** R. A. Roberts (ed.), 'Cecil Papers: May 1596, 16–31', in *Calendar of the Cecil Papers in Hatfield House*

(1895), Vol. VI, pp. 183–208. John Stubbs cites George Carew in his description of the sailors setting out: 'three hundred green-headed youths, covered with feathers, gold and silver lace'. John Stubbs, *Donne: The Reformed Soul* (2006), p. 59.

– **they all let ship** Edward Edwards, *The Life of Sir Walter Raleigh* (1868), Vol. II, p. 152.

– **died of grief.** Henry Baerlein, *Spain: Yesterday and Tomorrow* (1930), p. 152.

– **to march into the market place** Cited in J. S. Corbett, *The Successors of Drake* (1900), p. 108.

81 **we thought to yield** *Calendar of State Papers (Domestic) 1595–1597*, p. 463, cited in Robbins, *The Complete Poems of John Donne*, p. 64.

– **Some coffined in their cabins** 'The Storm', lines 45–6.

– **Memorable accidents.** '*Memorable Accidents, and Unheard of Transactions*' Published in English by B.B. (1693), sig A4.

82 **at this awful hour** *Memoirs of William Hickey* (1921), Vol. II, p. 22.

– **it is true that Jonas** Edward le Comte, *Grace to a Witty Sinner: A Life of John Donne* (1965), p. 34.

83 **We were very much becalmed** Sir Arthur Gorges, Captain of the *Warspite*, in *Voyage to the Iles of Azores*, cited in Robbins, *The Complete Poems of John Donne*, p. 65.

85 **As West and East** 'Hymn to God My God in My Sickness', lines 13–15.

– **landmasses took on eyes** Noam Flinker, 'John Donne and the "Anthropomorphic Map" Tradition', *Applied Semiotics* 3:8 (1999), pp. 207–15, 208.

86 *venite commiscemini nobiscum* John Block Friedman, *Trade, Travel and Exploration in the Middle Ages* (2000), p. 459.

The Inexperienced Expert of Love

87 **history of the handshake** Peter Hall and Dee Ann Hall, 'The Handshake as Interaction', *Semiotica* 45 (1983), pp. 249–64;

Keith Thomas, 'Introduction', in Jan Bremmer and Herman Roo-
denburg (eds), *A Cultural History of Gesture* (1991), pp. 1–14.

89 **like place, pre-eminence** 5 Eliz 1 c 18; John Lord Campbell,
*Lives of the Lord Chancellors and Keepers of the Great Seal of
England, from the Earliest Times Till the Reign of King George
IV* (1868), p. 219.

– **I had a desire** Edmund Gosse, *The Life and Letters of John
Donne* (1899, reprinted 2019), Vol. I, p. 114.

– **took him to be** Walton, *Lives*, p. 17.

91 **it is wonderful** Erica Fudge, *Perceiving Animals: Humans and
Beasts in Early Modern English Culture* (2002), p. 11.

– **with biting** Edgar Innes Fripp, *Shakespeare, Man and Artist*
(1964), p. 101.

– **lions so tame** Caroline Grigson, *Menagerie: The History of
Exotic Animals in England, 1100–1837* (2016), p. 7.

92 **Priss Fotheringham** John Garfield, *The Wand'ring Whore*
(1661), in Fergus Linnane, *London, The Wicked City: A
Thousand Years of Prostitution and Vices* (2007), p. 73.

93 **had the running** E. K. Chambers, *William Shakespeare: A Study
of Facts and Problems* (1930), Vol. II, p. 12.

– **The navel must be tied** Jacques Guillemeau, *Child-birth or the
Happy Delivery of Women* (1612), p. 99.

94 **necessary for conception** Deborah Simonton (ed.), *The Routledge
History of Women in Europe Since 1700* (2006), p. 56.

– **almost certainly, not** Arthur Marotti, *John Donne, Coterie Poet*
(1986), passim.

– **proved with child** Gary Fredric Waller, *The Sidney Family
Romance: Mary Wroth, William Herbert, and the Early
Modern Construction of Gender* (1993), p. 78.

– **if it had pleased god** Brian O'Farrell, *Shakespeare's Patron: William
Herbert, Third Earl of Pembroke, 1580–1630* (2011), p. 22.

– **those who risked it** R. V. Schnucker, 'Elizabethan Birth Control
and Puritan Attitudes', *Journal of Interdisciplinary History* 5:4
(1975), pp. 655–67.

95 **brothels lining the river** Gustav Ungerer, 'Prostitution in
    Late Elizabethan London: The Case of Mary Newborough',
    Medieval and Renaissance Drama in England 15 (2003), pp.
    138–223.

– **the young novice** 'Look on Me London – a Countryman's
    Counsel Given to His Son Going up to Dwell at London'
    (1613) in *Blood and Knavery: A Collection of English
    Renaissance Ballads of Crime and Sin*, ed. Joseph Mashburn
    and Alec R. Velie (1973), p. 164.

98 **thirty-two of Donne's** Carey, *John Donne: Life, Mind and Art*,
    p. 201.

99 **The meaning could be** This is very much debated. See Noralyn
    Masselink, 'Wormseed Revisited: Glossing Line Forty of
    Donne's "Farewell to Love"', *English Language Notes* 30:2
    (December 1992), pp. 11–15.

The Erratic Collector of His Own Talent

101 **your Lordship's secretary** Stephen W. May, 'Donne and
     Egerton', in *The Oxford Handbook of John Donne*, p. 452.

– **His signature appears** ibid.

102 **cost me more diligence** Gosse, *Life and Letters*, Vol. II, p. 68.

– **a rag of verses** Carey, *John Donne: Life, Mind and Art*, p. 70.

– **I know very many** George Puttenham, *The Art of English
    Poesy: A Critical Edition*, ed. Frank Whigham and Wayne
    Rebhorn (2007), p. 112.

The Witness of Disastrous Intrigue

107 **he kept 50 liveries** Bald, *John Donne: A Life*, p. 129.

108 *An Unknown Woman* Dennis Flynn argues that the portrait
     is Anne in an as yet unpublished paper, 'Getting to Know An
     Unknown Woman'.

109 **nor did his Lordship** Walton, *Lives*, p. 17.

– **he perhaps giveth** John R. Gillis, *For Better, for Worse: British
    Marriages, 1600 to the Present* (1985), p. 35.

110 **numerological joke** Robbins, *The Complete Poems of John Donne*, p. 539.

 – **my lord is at cards** David Loades, *Elizabeth I: A Life* (2006), p. 259.

 – **he spent £40** P. E. J. Hammer, 'Robert Devereux, second earl of Essex (1565–1601), soldier and politician', *Oxford Dictionary of National Biography*.

111 **liked his bumptiousness** Loades, *Elizabeth I: A Life*, p. 260.

112 **he neither could nor would** Carole Levin, *Dreaming the English Renaissance: Politics and Desire in Court and Culture* (2008), p. 131.

 – **she was as crooked** William Oldys, *The Life of Sir Walter Ralegh* (1829), p. 329.

113 **cannot princes err** A. R. Braunmuller, *A Seventeenth Century Letter-Book* (1983), p. 66.

114 **for our wars** L. P. Smith, *The Life and Letters of Sir Henry Wotton* (1907), Vol. I, p. 309.

 – **he never drew sword** Ernest George Atkinson (ed.), *Calendar of the State Papers Relating to Ireland of the Reign of Elizabeth 1599–1600* (1899), p. 260.

115 **removed to a better air** Historical Manuscripts Commission, MSS of Lord de L'Isle and Dudley.

 – **the ladies dance** E. K. Chambers, *The Elizabethan Stage* (2000), Vol. IV, p. 112.

116 **full of jollity** Evelyn M. Simpson, *A Study of the Prose Works of John Donne* (1948), p. 310.

 – **Good Will** Samuel Schoenbaum, *William Shakespeare: A Compact Documentary Life* (1987), p. 200.

 – **A book called Amours** Bald, *John Donne: A Life*, p. 108.

117 **It's possible** ibid., p. 108 n.

 – **My Lord Essex** Simpson, *A Study of the Prose Works of John Donne*, p. 310.

 – **withers still in sickness** Bald, *John Donne: A Life*, p. 108. The attribution of this letter is disputed, but there is a strong case for it being by Donne.

118 **my Lord Keeper** Historical Manuscripts Commission, MSS of Lord de L'Isle and Dudley.

119 **I will have leave** The attribution of this letter is disputed, but Ilona Bell's argument for its being by Donne is persuasive. Ilona Bell, '"Under Ye Rage of a Hott Sonn & Yr Eyes": John Donne's Love Letters to Ann More', in Claude J. Summers and Ted-Larry Pebworth (eds), *The Eagle and the Dove: Reassessing John Donne* (1986), pp. 25–52.

121 **Or as sometimes** 'The Second Anniversary', lines 9–17.

122 **Donne's original plan** *The Works of William Drummond of Hawthornden* (1711), p. 97.

The Paradoxical Quibbler, Taking Aim at Women

125 **I thank God** *Calendar of State Papers: Domestic, 1611–18*, p. 527.

126 **in all that part** Cited in Hester et al. (eds), *John Donne's Marriage Letters*, p. 13.

  – **the sun forsakes us** Bald, *John Donne: A Life*, p. 108.

  – **the twin of his promise** Bell: '"Under Ye Rage of a Hott Sonn & Yr Eyes"', passim.

127 **Take the fresh unspotted** Karen Gordon-Grube, 'Anthropophagy in Post-Renaissance Europe: The Tradition of Medicinal Cannibalism', *American Anthropologist* 90 (June 1988), pp. 405–9.

129 **ate their own belts** Jean de Léry, *Histoire mémorable de la ville de Sancerre* (1574), cited in Robbins, *The Complete Poems of John Donne*, p. 301.

130 **enormous vogue** Peter Platt, *Shakespeare and the Culture of Paradox* (2009), p. 22.

  – **As for those who are offended** Erasmus, *The Praise of Folly*, cited in Platt, *Shakespeare and the Culture of Paradox*, p. 21.

  – **misinterpretation of the work** Cited in Platt, *Shakespeare and the Culture of Paradox*, p. 24.

  – **Oftentimes** Puttenham, *The Art of English Poesy*, p. 311.

131 **a vile man** ibid., introduction passim.
  - **wash made of cabbage stalks** J. L. Heilbron, *Galileo* (2012), p. 86.
  - **Foulness is loathsome** John Donne, *Selected Prose*, ed. Neil Rhodes (1987), p. 38.
132 **That women are inconstant** ibid., p. 48.
  - **Women are like flies** ibid., p. 49.
133 **so many advantages** ibid., p. 53.
  - **we deny souls** ibid.
  - **Valens Acidalius** Michael Nolan, 'The Mysterious Affair at Mâcon: The Bishops and the Souls of Women', *New Blackfriars* 74:876 (November 1993), pp. 501–7.
  - **Perchance because the Devil** *Selected Prose*, p. 54.
134 **Some men** *Sermons*, Vol. I, p. 448.
  - **No author of gravity** ibid.
  - **He chose to level** Meg Lota Brown, *Donne and the Politics of Conscience in Early Modern England* (1994), p. 70.
  - **in a letter** Simpson, *A Study of the Prose Works*, p. 216.

Anne

137 **that fair and learned hand** This is still much debated: Janet E. Halley, 'Textual Intercourse: Anne Donne, John Donne, and the Sexual Poetics of Textual Exchange' in Sheila Fisher and Janet E. Halley (eds), *Seeking the Woman in Late Medieval and Renaissance Writings: Essays in Feminist Contextual Criticism* (1989), pp. 187–206, calls Anne 'functionally illiterate'. I believe Wotton's comment, along with George More's wealth and Donne's epitaph, are sufficient to think she was educated, but the point isn't universally agreed upon.
  - **passionate treatises** Lawrence Stone, *The Family, Sex and Marriage in England 1500–1800* (1977), p. 142.
  - **Do we not see** Richard Mulcaster, *Positions Wherein Those Primitive Circumstances Be Examined, Which Are Necessarie for the Training Up of Children, Either for Skill in their Booke, or Health in their Bodie* (1561), p. 168.

- **Women, in Castiglione's world** Stone, *The Family, Sex and Marriage in England*, p. 143.
138 **Plato in petticoats** ibid.
- **this humour in both sexes** ibid.
- **too quickly won** *Romeo and Juliet*, Act II, Scene 2, lines 96–7.
- **The richer you were** Stone, *The Family, Sex and Marriage in England*, p. 130.
- **beaten once in the week** ibid.

The Daring of the Lover, and the Imprisoned Groom

141 **Donne could be as metaphysical** Wayne K. Chapman, *Yeats and English Renaissance Literature* (1991), p. 144.
142 **Pierre de Ronsard** Hugh Richmond, *Puritans and Libertines: Anglo-French Literary Relationships in the Reformation* (1981), p. 246.
- **worst voluptuousness** *Letters*, p. 51.
- **the lazy seeds** Thomas Carew, 'An Elegy upon the Death of the Dean of Paul's, Dr John Donne', lines 26–8.
143 **about three weeks** Folger MS L.b. 526.
- **the Savoy** John Schofield, 'The Construction of Medieval and Tudor Houses in London', *Construction History* 7 (1991), pp. 3–28.
145 **I knew my present estate** Gosse, *Life and Letters*, Vol. I, p. 101.
146 **employed lawyers** Hester et al. (eds), *John Donne's Marriage Letters*, p. 16.
147 **that fault which was laid** Folger MS L.b.529.
- **it is not safe** *The Works of Francis Osborne* (1701), p. 66.
148 **disgusting and expensive** Walter Thornbury, 'The Fleet Prison', in *Old and New London: Volume 2* (1878), pp. 404–6.
149 **accusing the deputy warden** ibid., p. 406.
- **And though perchance** Gosse, *Life and Letters*, Vol. I, p. 104.
150 **all my endeavours** ibid., p. 106.
- **whom I leave no humble way** ibid.
- **be pleased to lessen** ibid.

151 **My conscience** ibid., p. 107.
- **neither gave rest** Walton, *Lives*, p. 20.
152 **and pardon me** Izaak Walton, *The Life of John Donne, with some original notes by an antiquary*, ed. T. E. Tomlins (1865), p. 29.
- **elegant irresistible art** Walton, *Lives*, p. 21.
- **I was four years** Gosse, *Life and Letters*, Vol. I, p. 114.
153 **To seek preferment** ibid.
- **unfeignedly sorry** Walton, *Lives*, p. 21.
- **unambiguous victory** Hester et al. (eds), *John Donne's Marriage Letters*, p. 18.
- **A true and pure marriage** ibid., p. 19.
154 **possible the pun was never Donne's** Ernest W. Sullivan, 'Donne's Epithalamium for Anne', in Hester (ed.), *John Donne's 'Desire of More'*, pp. 36–8.
- **Immediately after his dismission** Walton, *Lives*, pp. 17–18.
- **the remarkable error** ibid., p. 53.
- **In the time of Master Donne's** Sullivan, 'Donne's Epithalamium for Anne', p. 37.
155 **Doctor Donne after he was married** ibid.

The Anticlimactically Married Man

156 **adorned with paintings** Bald, *John Donne: A Life*, p. 140.
157 **George More had published** Bald first gestured to this link; *John Donne: A Life*, p. 129, which was also noted in Alistair Cameron Crombie and Michael Hoskin (eds), *History of Science* (1968), p. 35, but first rigorously expanded by John Stubbs in *Donne: The Reformed Soul*, p. 178.
- **England, my dear country** George More, *A Demonstration of God in His Workes* (1597), p. 1.
158 **We can die by it** 'The Canonisation', line 28.
- **I died at a blow** *Letters*, p. 51.
- **Your friends are sorry** Bald, *John Donne: A Life*, p. 144.
159 **When Octavio Baldi came** Walton, *The Life of Henry Wotton*, *Lives*, p. 26.

160 **he departed as true** ibid.

- **such a one as I** Cited in Bald, *John Donne: A Life*, p. 146.
- *For me*. This letter to Wotton, and the logistics of their friendship, are discussed in Bald, *John Donne: A Life*, p. 146.

162 **I accompany** *Letters*, p. 88.

163 **Sometimes when I find** ibid., p. 71.

The Ambivalent Father

164 **Gentlemen of thirty** John Aubrey, *Brief Lives: And Other Selected Writings*, ed. Anthony Powell (1949), p. 11.

165 **kneel to ask blessing** *Sermons*, Vol. IX, p. 59.

- **I have not been out** *Letters*, pp. 137–8.
- **When I must shipwreck** ibid., pp. 50–1.
- **I write not to you** ibid., p. 137.

166 **Thou hast delivered** John Donne, *Essays in Divinity: Being Several Disquisitions Interwoven with Meditations and Prayers*, ed. Anthony Raspa (2003), p. 83.

- **unlikely to lie** Carey, *John Donne: Life, Mind and Art*, p. 73.

167 **spectacularly off** This assessment – that the poem would fail as a piece of indirect compliment, and is more likely to have been a paradox composed by Donne to send among his male coterie – is indebted to Robin Robbins, *Poems*, p. 733.

- **a world alone** Walton, *Lives*, p. 101.

168 **the incommodity** Bald, *John Donne: A Life*, p. 158.

- **closer to London** ibid.
- **ordinary forges of letters** *Letters*, p. 137.

169 **Anne's sisters** Bald, *John Donne: A Life*, p. 158.

- **I am a Father** *Letters*, p. 119.
- **I must beg of you** ibid., p. 232.
- **The newest thing** ibid., p. 154.

170 **I stand like a tree** ibid., p. 233.

- **I have already lost** ibid., p. 153.
- **of one of which** ibid.

171 **Because I loved it** ibid., p. 273.

- **Infant mortality** A. Wrigley and R. S. Davies et al. (eds), *English Population History from Family Reconstitution 1580–1837* (1997), p. 207.
- **stone effigies** Stone, *The Crisis of the Aristocracy*, p. 595.

172 **Rest in soft peace** *The Cambridge Edition of the Works of Ben Jonson: 1601–1606*, ed. Ian Donaldson et al. (2012). 'On My First Son', lines 9–10.

- **the Lord hath taken** Raymond Anselment, *The Realms of Apollo: Literature and Healing in Seventeenth-century England* (1995), p. 82.
- **Dear infant** Pamela S. Hammons, *Despised Creatures: The Illusion of Maternal Self-Effacement in Seventeenth-Century Child Loss Poetry* (2002), 30.
- **Nor can I think** ibid., p. 29.
- **people of bygone ages** Marcel Proust, *In Search of Lost Time*, Vol. III, *The Guermantes Way*, trans. C. K. Scott Moncrieff, ed. William Carter (2018), p. 460.

173 **Two days after** Gosse, *Life and Letters*, Vol. I, p. 280.

174 **the same day** Bald, *John Donne: A Life*, p. 252.

How to Pretend to Have Read More than You Have

175 **Must!** J. R. Green, *A Short History of the English People* (1874), ch. 7.

- **children of the chapel** James Basire II after William Camden, *The funeral procession of Queen Elizabeth I on 27 numbered sheets* (1791).
- **In the death of that Queen** *Sermons*, Vol. I, p. 217.

176 **indeed made up of two** James Spedding, *Evenings with a Reviewer* (1848), p. 229.

- **The new king** *Calendar of State Papers (Venetian) 1603–1607*, p. 70, cited in Robbins, *The Complete Poems of John Donne*, p. 247.

177 **he was the most honest** Walton, *Lives*, *The Life of Sir Henry Wotton*, p. 113.

178 **satirical list of books** Daniel Starza Smith, Matthew Payne and Melanie Marshall, 'Rediscovering John Donne's *Catalogus librorum satyricus*', *Review of English Studies* 69:290 (June 2018), p. 455.

179 **Sir Edward Hoby's Afternoon Belchings** *The Courtier's Library*, ed. and trans. Simpson, p. 50.

– **What Not?** ibid., p. 52.

– **itself a joke** Starza Smith et al., 'Rediscovering John Donne's *Catalogus librorum satyricus*', p. 455.

180 **a Latin letter** The first ever English translation of this letter is offered by Melanie Marshall in Starza Smith et al., 'Rediscovering John Donne's *Catalogus librorum satyricus*', Appendix III

181 **Donne implied** This reading is wholly indebted to conversations with Daniel Starza Smith, and his blog with Melanie Marshall, 'John Donne and the Jacobean Fake Media', 15 August 2018, blogs.kcl.ac.uk/english/2018/08/15/john-donne-and-the-jacobean-fake-media.

– **jabs of disapprobation** ibid.

The Suicidal Man

183 **The pleasantness of the season** *Letters*, p. 78.

– **I have contracted** ibid., p. 32.

– **The day before** ibid., p. 34.

184 **conclude two things** John Donne, *Biathanatos* (1644), p. 183.

185 **Successful suicides** Carey, *John Donne: Life, Mind and Art*, p. 206.

– **And Nicephorus** *Biathanatos*, p. 186.

186 **many martyrs having hanged** ibid., p. 189.

– **other than His own will** ibid.

– **utterly defeated** Cited in Jeremy Bernstein, 'Heaven's Net: The Meeting of John Donne and Johannes Kepler', *The American Scholar* 66:2 (1997), pp. 175–195, 185.

– **because I had my first breeding** *Biathanatos*, p. 17.

187 **whensoever any affliction** ibid., p. 18.

- It was written by me *Letters*, p. 22.
188 a stomach colic ibid., p. 57.
- it hath pleased God ibid., p. 168.
- I have passed ten days ibid.
189 this advantage ibid., p. 242.
- I am not alive ibid., p. 317.
190 Anthony Tuckney Carey, *John Donne: Life, Mind and Art*, p. 209.
- Thomas Creech ibid.
- Charle Blount wrote approvingly Lucio Biasiori, 'The Exception as Norm: Casuistry of Suicide in John Donne's Biathanatos', in Carlo Ginzburg and Lucio Biasiori (eds), *A Historical Approach to Casuistry* (2020), p. 168.
191 found that self-preservation ibid.

The Flatterer

192 I may not accept Walton, *Lives*, p. 26.
193 your going away *Letters*, p. 1.
- they are disfigured Allen Barry Cameron, 'Donne's Deliberative Verse Epistles', *English Literary Renaissance* 6:3 (1976), pp. 369–403, 370.
- I am not come out *Letters*, p. 244.
197 that favour ibid., p. 104.
- I have learned Preparatory letter, 'Obsequies to the Lord Harington, Brother to the Countess of Bedford'.
198 I confess to you *Letters*, p. 219.
- tell you truly Peter Redford, *The Burley Manuscript* (2017), p. 210.
199 A man may flatter *Sermons*, Vol. V, p. 58.
200 The influence of those *Pseudo-Martyr*, dedicatory letter, 'To the high and mighty Prince James, by the Grace of God, King of Great Britain, France and Ireland, defender of the faith'.
201 who but a monomaniac Simpson, *A Study of the Prose Works*, p. 179.
- apprehending it Walton, *Lives*, p. 34.

- **Ignatius rushed out** John Donne, *Ignatius His Conclave*, ed. T. S. Healy (1969), p. 31.
- **whosoever flatters** ibid., p. 33.

202 **(at the best) instructs** ibid.
- **Whoe'er is raised** Jonson, 'To My Muse', Epigram 65.
- **not worth/The least** *Works of William Drummond of Hawthornden*, p. 225.

203 **had her ears boxed** Le Comte, *Grace to a Witty Sinner*, p. 129.

204 **descend[ed] to print** *Letters*, p. 74.
- **if he had written it** Ben Jonson, *Selected Works*, ed. Ian Donaldson (1985), p. 596.
- **if any of those ladies** *Letters*, p. 239.
- **For since I never saw** ibid.

205 **An exercise in testing** As argued by John Carey, *John Donne: Life, Mind and Art*, p. 103.

The Clergyman

207 **at every corner** Thomas Dekker, *The Seven Deadly Sins of London*, ed. H. F. B. Brett-Smith (1922), p. 37.
- **The inhabitants** Charles Dudley Warner, *The People for Whom Shakespeare Wrote* (2018), p. 41.

208 **they care little for foreigners** ibid.
- **give up his horse** Bald, *John Donne: A Life*, p. 280.
- **expectation of a state-employment** Walton, *Lives*, p. 25.

210 **still charm[ed]** A. J. Smith, *John Donne: The Critical Heritage*, Vol. II, p. 153.

211 **Donne had to fight** This reading is indebted to Jeanne Shami, 'Donne's Decision to Take Orders', in *The Oxford Handbook of John Donne*, who lays out the newest evidence for re-dating the Carr letters in a way that suggests Donne pushed for ordination for significantly more than a year, before he was able to take orders. The forthcoming *Oxford Edition of the Letters of John Donne*, ed. Daniel Starza Smith, Lara Crowley et al., will take the same stance.

- a new reading has emerged Most notably Jeanne Shami's reading.
- if any mischance Robert Chambers, *The Life of King James the First: In Two Volumes* (1830), Vol. II, p. 181.
212 *Rex fuit Elizabeth* John Lockman, *The History of England, by Question and Answer* (1811), p. 140.
- constantly leaneth Alan Stewart, *The Cradle King: A Life of James VI & I* (2011), p. 258.
213 that men had had David Lindley, *The Trials of Frances Howard: Fact and Fiction at the Court of King James* (2013), p. 97.
214 all the ladies about the Court ibid., p. 55.
- immoderately given up ibid.
- Carr was the route Daniel Starza Smith, *John Donne and the Conway Papers: Patronage and Manuscript Circulation in the Early Seventeenth Century* (2014), p. 258.
215 For, having obeyed Gosse, *Life and Letters*, Vol. II, p. 20.
- perchance this business *Letters*, p. 270.
216 by my troth ibid., p. 180. The Oxford *Letters*, the first modern edition of Donne's letters, will date this letter to 19 January: almost a full month after the wedding, Donne had not yet started the poem, though he dates it, once it is finally completed, 26 December. Starza Smith, *John Donne and the Conway Papers*, p. 258.
217 the implication in his letter Shami, 'Donne's Decision to Take Orders', p. 531.
- surprised that my ancestors John P. Kenyon, *The Stuarts: A Study in English Kingship* (1959), p. 56.
- pursue my first purpose Shami, 'Donne's Decision to Take Orders', p. 532.
218 a treason against myself ibid., p. 534, citing the Donne marriage letters, a collection of letters between Donne and his in-laws which were not available to earlier scholars.
- the handsomest-bodied man Angus Stroud, *Stuart England* (2002), p. 35.
- I desire only David Bergeron, *King James and Letters of Homoerotic Desire* (2002), p. 138.

219 **A page, a Knight** Lindley, *The Trials of Frances Howard*, p. 178.

– **as good allowance** Shami, 'Donne's Decision to Take Orders,' p. 535.

– **in the search of the Eastern tongues** Gosse, *Life and Letters*, Vol. II, p. 16.

220 **she had more suspicion** *Letters*, p. 218.

– **though better than any other** Bald, *John Donne: A Life*, p. 305:

221 **a sheaf of snakes** 'To Mr George Herbert with My Seal of the Anchor and Christ', lines 22–4 and 27–8.

– **now all his studies** Walton, *Lives*, p. 37.

– **I would fain do** *Letters*, p. 50.

222 **now, all his earthly affections** Walton, *Lives*, p. 37.

– **villagers of Shadwell** W. G. Hoskins, *Provincial England: Essays in Social and Economic History* (2015), p. 179.

– **somebody most beastly** Kevin Sharpe, *The Personal Rule of Charles I* (1992), p. 398.

223 **rest a little** Peter McCullough, 'Donne as Preacher', in Achsah Guibbory (ed.), *The Cambridge Companion to John Donne* (2006), p. 172.

224 **the preacher . . . standeth** Andreas Hyperius, *The Practise of Preaching*, trans. John Ludham (1577), p. 70, cited by McCullough, 'Donne as Preacher', p. 175.

– **a preacher in earnest** Walton, *Lives*, p. 38.

– **there shall be no cloud** *Sermons*, Vol. VIII, p. 19.

225 **he did preach there** Bald, *John Donne: A Life*, p. 426.

226 **I would gladly see** Cited ibid., p. 323.

The Widower

227 **my good is dead** 'Since She Whom I Loved', line 12.

– **the affections of his hearers** Walton, *Lives*, p. 42.

– **as common people are not** ibid.

228 **words for her that unfurl** M. Thomas Hester, 'Faeminae Lectissimae: Reading Anne Donne', in *John Donne's 'Desire of More'*, p. 18.

230 **shape of a cross** Loseley manuscript collection, Folger
Shakespeare Library, MS L.b.541.

- **well read, and read hungrily** Hester, 'Faeminae Lectissimae',
p. 23.

- **awkward and uneven** ibid.

- **Language, thou art** 'Elegy upon the Death of Mistress
Bulstrode', lines 1–2.

The (Unsuccessful) Diplomat

232 **to surprise his bride** John Carey, *The Unexpected Professor: An
Oxford Life in Books* (2014), p. 277.

233 **The vanity of the present King** Bernstein, 'Heaven's Net', p. 192.

234 **a great many noblemen's sons** Cited in Bald, *John Donne: A
Life*, p. 343.

- **I leave a scattered flock** *Letters*, p. 174.

235 **had to halt** Stubbs, *Donne: The Reformed Soul*, p. 343.

237 **decrees of condemnation** *Sermons*, Vol. VIII, p. 246.

238 **small, thin, swarthy** Rocky Kolb, *Blind Watchers of the Sky:
The People and Ideas That Shaped Our View of the Universe*
(1999), p. 44.

- **the spreading abroad** Cited in Marjorie Nicolson, 'Kepler, the
Somnium and John Donne', *Journal of the History of Ideas* 1
(1940), pp. 259–80, 268.

- **I suspect that the author** Cited ibid., p. 269.

- **too much credit** Johannes Kepler, *Kepler's Somnium: The
Dream or Posthumous Work on Lunar Astronomy*, trans. with
commentary by Edward Rosen (1967), pp. 212–13.

- **The actual reference to Kepler** ibid., p. 212.

239 **the inscrutable depths** Francis Nethersole, cited in Bald, *John
Donne: A Life*, p. 365.

240 **convey and commend** Bernstein, 'Heaven's Net', p. 192.

241 **a reference to the planet's quartet** David Levy, *The Starlight
Night: The Sky in the Writings of Shakespeare, Tennyson and
Hopkins* (2016), p. 73.

- And new Philosophy 'The First Anniversary', lines 205–13.
- loves not innovations *Sermons*, Vol. II, p. 305.
242 gave an affront *Ignatius*, p. 9.
- thereby almost a new Creator ibid., p. 15.
- In the beginning *Sermons*, Vol. IV, p. 136, cited in Achsah Guibbory, *Returning to John Donne* (2016), p. 25.
- For knowledge kindles 'To Sir Edward Herbert at Juliers', lines 43–4.

The Dean

243 refused to receive the consecration Bald, *John Donne: A Life*, p. 372.
244 When his Majesty sat down Walton, *Lives*, p. 46.
- His tongue It's a fact about James that's much loved by scholars: cited in Stubbs, *Donne: The Reformed Soul*, p. 368, and Derek Parker, *John Donne and His World* (1975), p. 82.
246 all that I mean Gosse, *Life and Letters*, Vol. II, p. 140.
- Portland stone Carey, *John Donne: Life, Mind and Art*, p. 90.
- Though be I not Dean *Letters*, p. 227: cited in Bald, *John Donne: A Life*, p. 381.
248 be no stranger there Bald, *John Donne: A Life*, p. 383.
249 though the poorness of my fortune Sir Tobie Matthew (ed.), *A Collection of Letters* (1660), p. 326.
250 the boys and maids *Calendar of State Papers, Domestic, 1631–1633*, cited in William Longman, *A History of the Three Cathedrals Dedicated to St Paul in London* (1873), p. 54.
- spur-money Roze Hentschell, '"Our Children Made Enterluders": Choristers, Actors, and Students in St Paul's Cathedral Precinct', *Early Theatre* 19:2 (2016), pp. 179–95, 184.
- all the diseased horses *The Non-Dramatic Works of Thomas Dekker: In Five Volumes*, ed. Fredson Bowers (1884), Vol. II, p. 234.
251 or, for want of a name ibid., p. 236.
- I have obeyed the forms *Letters*, p. 316.

- **choose your day** ibid.
252 **a re-enactment** John N. Wall., Principal Investigator, *Virtual Paul's Cross Project: A Digital Re-creation of John Donne's Gunpowder Day Sermon.*
255 **Donne loves best** *John Donne's Sermons on the Psalms and Gospels: With a Selection of Prayers and Meditations*, ed. Evelyn M. Simpson (2003), p. 11.
- **The whole frame of the poem** ibid., p. 4.
- **Lying at Aix** *Sermons*, Vol. I, p. 112.
256 **we rise poorer** ibid., Vol. VIII, p. 101.
257 **to hasten their end** *Biathanatos*, p. 137.
- **at the sacrament** *Sermons*, Vol. X, p. 18.
258 **I throw myself down** ibid., Vol. I, p. 95.
259 **We ask our daily bread** ibid., Vol. VI, p. 172.
260 **But how far** ibid., Vol. X, p. 216.
- **It is a dangerous weakness** ibid.
- **Our nature is meteoric** *Letters*, p. 46.
261 **Man would be the giant** *Devotions upon Emergent Occasions*, Meditation IV.

The Monied

262 **lay for their fees** Walton, *Lives*, p. 65.
- **a continual giver** ibid.
263 **there is a trade** *Sermons*, Vol. IV, p. 62.
- **I, when I value** 'Love's Progress', lines 11–16.
- **only the observation of others** *Letters*, p. 142.
264 **My daughters** ibid., p. 117.
265 **Tell both your daughters** ibid., p. 187.
266 **after dinner in your parlour** Some renderings of this letter have 'gave you not content', others 'gave content', as George Hosking, *The Life and Times of Edward Alleyn* (1970), p. 331. From the context, 'not' seems more likely.
- **I see he fears** Gosse, *Life and Letters*, Vol. II, p. 184.
- **barred of my ordinary diet** ibid., p. 208.

- though I have left my bed ibid., p. 189.
268 As sickness is the greatest *Devotions upon Emergent Occasions*, Meditation V.
- We study health ibid., Meditation I.
269 I am more than dust ibid., Expostulation I.
- a little nag Gosse, *Life and Letters*, Vol. II, p. 218.
270 unkind, unexpected and undeserved Bald, *John Donne: A Life*, pp. 464–5.
- a young maidservant Daniel Starza Smith, 'Busy Young Fool, Unruly Son? New Light on John Donne Junior', *Review of English Studies*, 62: 256 (2011), pp. 538–56, p. 540. Sara's employer Robert Bedingfield publicly accused John junior, who in turn sued Bedingfield for slander. John junior was acquitted, and the slander action successful, but the balance of evidence suggests John junior was fully guilty.
- His nature being vile Anthony à Wood, *Athenae Oxonienses*, ed. Philip Bliss (1813, repr. 1967), Vol. I, p. 503.
271 his annual income Bald, *John Donne: A Life*, p. 426.
- yearly wage bill Jane Whittle, 'Servants in Rural England 1560–1650: Kussmaul Revisited', Exeter University Working Paper (2015), p. 4.
272 at one after noon *Letters*, p. 311.
- William Cokayne Coburn Freer, 'John Donne and Elizabethan Economic Theory', *Criticism* 38:4 (1996), pp. 497–520.
273 The scheme went explosively badly ibid., p. 509.
274 did his part diligently *Sermons*, Vol. VII, p. 274.

Donne and Death

276 a pin, a comb *Devotions upon Emergent Occasions*, Meditation XII – as noted by Carey, *John Donne: Life, Mind and Art*, p. 203.
- the picture called The Skeleton Donne's Will and Testament, reprinted in Gosse, *Life and Letters*, Vol. II, p. 360.
- there were rumours N. E. Land, 'Michelangelo, Giotto, and

Murder', *Explorations in Renaissance Culture* 32:2 (2006), pp. 204–24.

277 **thrums with strange images** Carey, *John Donne: Life, Mind and Art*, p. 201.

– **Death! Be not proud** Holy Sonnet VI, lines 1–2.

278 **I would not that death** *Letters*, p. 50.

– **it hath been my desire** ibid., p. 209.

– **his other, permanent love** Holy Sonnet XI: 'Death be not proud'.

279 **If I had fixed** *Sermons*, Vol. VII, pp. 25–6, cited in Bald, *John Donne: A Life*, p. 491.

– **I shall have my dead** ibid.

280 **he floundered** This sense of Goodere's struggles with the evolving world of the court is wholly indebted to Starza Smith, *John Donne and the Conway Papers*, passim.

– **make . . . to yourself some mark** *Letters*, p. 52.

– **my desire is** Walton, *Lives*, p. 66.

281 **I have cribrated** Bald, *John Donne: A Life*, p. 493.

– **his Majesty King Charles** *The History of the Troubles and Trial of William Laud*, cited in Bald, *John Donne: A Life*, p. 494.

282 **I should be sorry** Cited in the introduction to *Sermons*, Vol. VIII, p. 25.

283 **A man would almost be content** *Letters*, p. 242.

– **he wanted to see in death** Carey, *John Donne: Life, Mind and Art*, p. 202.

– **whole Christian Churches** Ramie Targoff, *John Donne, Body and Soul* (2008), p. 26.

– **who can fear** *Sermons*, Vol. VII, p. 298.

– **In the agonies** ibid., pp. 70–1.

284 **list of paintings** Bald, *John Donne: A Life*, p. 523.

285 **that by cordials** Cited ibid., p. 526.

– **he would not drink** ibid., p. 526.

– **I am afraid** Gosse, *Life and Letters*, Vol. II, p. 269.

– **decayed body** Walton, *Lives*, p. 71.

– **saw his tears** ibid.

286 **Our very birth** John Donne, *Devotions upon Emergent Occasions and Death's Duel* (facsimile edition, 2010), p. 170.

– **a death united** Michel de Montaigne, *The Living Thoughts of Montaigne*, ed. André Gide, based on translation by John Florio (1946), p. 22.

287 **There we leave you** *Devotions upon Emergent Occasions and Death's Duel*, p. 189.

– **Who is that 'we'** This shift between I and we in Donne's final work is explored by Ramie Targoff, 'Facing Death', in *The Cambridge Companion to John Donne*, p. 230.

– **God hath made himself** *Sermons*, Vol. X, p. 117.

288 **It seems to breathe** Walton, *Lives*, p. 80.

– **His speech** ibid., p. 78.

290 **he closed his own eyes** ibid.

– **I were miserable** ibid.

Super-infinite

291 **since but thine own** Alison Shell, 'The Death of Donne', in *The Oxford Handbook of John Donne*, p. 651.

292 **a scattered limb** John Donne, *Poems* (1633), sig. A1r.

– **stole lines** Ernest W. Sullivan II, 'John Donne's Seventeenth Century Readers', in *The Oxford Handbook of John Donne*, p. 30.

– **doing it to Shakespeare** Lukas Erne, *Shakespeare and the Book Trade* (2013), p. xx.

293 **'Dun's Answer to a Lady'** Robert Chamberlain, *The Harmony of the Muses* (1654), p. 72.

– **'The Rapture'** ibid., 7.

295 **Now was there ever any man** *Sermons*, Vol. I, p. 197.

– **Attention** *Letters*, p. 94.

– **Our creatures** *Selected Prose*, p. 105.

296 **When one man dies** *Devotions upon Emergent Occasions*, Meditation XVII.

– **No man is an island** ibid.

PICTURE CREDITS

INDEX

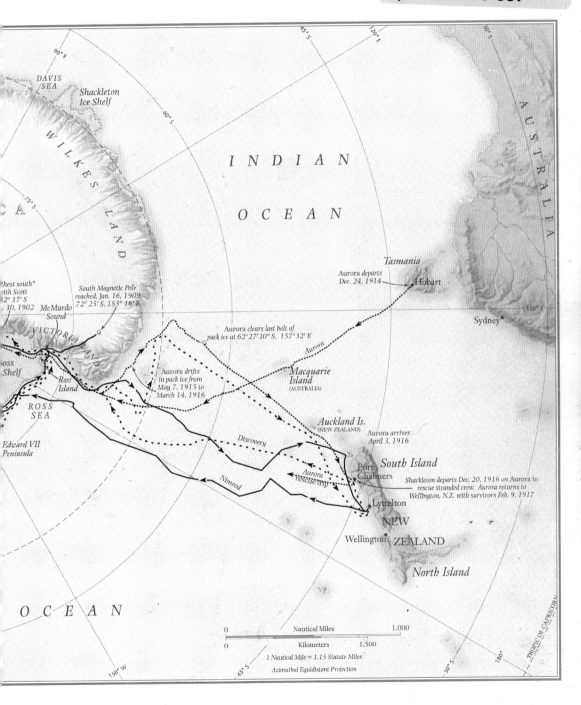

DAVIS
SEA

*Shackleton
Ice Shelf*

W I L K E S   L A N D

90° E

60° S

75° S

I N D I A N

O C E A N

45° S

120° E

30° S

A U S T R A L I A

Tasmania

Aurora departs
Dec. 24, 1914

Hobart

150° E

Sydney

*hest south"
ith Scott
2° 17' S
30, 1902*
McMurdo
Sound

*South Magnetic Pole
reached, Jan. 16, 1909,
72° 25' S, 155° 16' E.*

V I C T O R I A   L A N D

Aurora clears last belt of
pack ice at 62°27'30" S, 157°32' E

Aurora

*Macquarie
Island*
(AUSTRALIA)

oss
Shelf

Ross
Island

*Aurora drifts
in pack ice from
May 7, 1915 to
March 14, 1916*

ROSS
SEA

*Edward VII
Peninsula*

Nimrod

Discovery

Auckland Is.
(NEW ZEALAND)

Aurora arrives
April 3, 1916

Aurora
rescue trip

Port
Chalmers

South Island

Shackleton departs Dec. 20, 1916 on Aurora to
rescue stranded crew. Aurora returns to
Wellington, N.Z. with survivors Feb. 9, 1917

Lyttelton

N E W

Wellington

Z E A L A N D

North Island

O C E A N

150° W

45° S

30° S

180°

TROPIC OF CAPRICORN

0 ————— Nautical Miles ————— 1,000

0 ————— Kilometers ————— 1,500

1 Nautical Mile = 1.15 Statute Miles

Azimuthal Equidistant Projection

Shackleton

An Irishman in Antarctica

JONATHAN SHACKLETON

AND JOHN MacKENNA

THE LILLIPUT PRESS • DUBLIN

To Daphne, David, Jane and Hannah
for their support

For Eoin O'Flaithearta

© Jonathan Shackleton, John MacKenna and the Lilliput Press Ltd, 2002

First published 2002 by
THE LILLIPUT PRESS LTD
62-63 Sitric Road, Arbour Hill, Dublin 7, Ireland

A CIP record is available from the British Library.

ISBN 1 84351 009 x (cased)

Designed and typeset in Sabon by Anú Design, Tara
Printed in Dublin by βetaprint

Contents

Shackleton

An Irishman in Antarctica

SHACKLETON FAMILY TREE

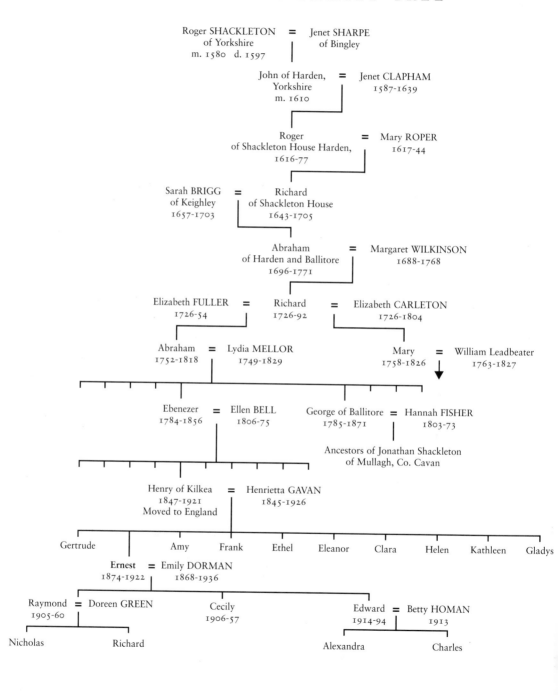

Roger SHACKLETON = Jenet SHARPE
of Yorkshire   of Bingley
m. 1580 d. 1597

John of Harden, = Jenet CLAPHAM
Yorkshire   1587-1639
m. 1610

Roger = Mary ROPER
of Shackleton House Harden,   1617-44
1616-77

Sarah BRIGG = Richard
of Keighley   of Shackleton House
1657-1703   1643-1705

Abraham = Margaret WILKINSON
of Harden and Ballitore   1688-1768
1696-1771

Elizabeth FULLER = Richard = Elizabeth CARLETON
1726-54   1726-92   1726-1804

Abraham = Lydia MELLOR   Mary = William Leadbeater
1752-1818   1749-1829   1758-1826   1763-1827

Ebenezer = Ellen BELL   George of Ballitore = Hannah FISHER
1784-1856   1806-75   1785-1871   1803-73

Ancestors of Jonathan Shackleton
of Mullagh, Co. Cavan

Henry of Kilkea = Henrietta GAVAN
1847-1921   1845-1926
Moved to England

Gertrude   Amy   Frank   Ethel   Eleanor   Clara   Helen   Kathleen   Gladys

Ernest = Emily DORMAN
1874-1922   1868-1936

Raymond = Doreen GREEN   Cecily   Edward = Betty HOMAN
1905-60   1906-57   1914-94   1913

Nicholas   Richard   Alexandra   Charles

1

Irish Family Background

◆

The man was standing at the foot of the long incline, watching seven figures on the horizon. The first was moving carefully, the other six fanning out behind across the white country-side. The group travelled in a line, edging down the side of the slope, bent low against the sun. Gradually, the last of the seven began to lose contact with the others, his pace slowing, dropping farther and farther behind, until, finally, he came to a halt and crouched in the blinding whiteness. The others went on, too intent on their own expedition to notice his loss. Only when they had reached the security of level ground at the foot of the hill did they stop to take stock. The leading figure, by far the tallest of the seven, glanced back along the track they had descended and saw the distant figure, all but lost in the whiteness of the landscape.

'Mr Lag!'

There was no response from the distant figure.

'Mr Lag!'

The voice was louder now.

The crouching figure looked up, disorientated and surprised at how far he had fallen behind his comrades. Rising slowly and taking his bearings, he trudged down the hill, the snow-white heads of cow parsley hanging across his path.

'We can't wait all day for you, kindly keep up with the rest.'

Kilkea House. Built in the early nineteenth century for the Duke of Leinster. Leased by Ernest's father Henry Shackleton c.1872-80; six of of his children were born there.

'Yes.'

'Now, on we go. Gertrude, you walk behind Ernest. That way we may keep from losing your brother. Again.'

And so the procession continued across the foot of Mullaghcreelan Hill. The nurse leading her charges through the long summer grasses, Amy and Frank and Ethel and Ernest and Gertrude Shackleton following in her footsteps.

The watching figure, Henry Shackleton, the children's father, turned back to examine his beloved roses, smiling at the picture of his eldest son, lost among the wild flowers, living in a world of his own.

The Shackleton children making that afternoon journey across the fields near Kilkea, in the south of Co. Kildare, were the descendants, on the one hand, of a family whose roots ran back to Quaker stock and who had arrived in the area two and a half centuries earlier. On the other, the family tree was grounded in the Fitzmaurices, a wild and adventurous Kerry family.

The Quakers, or Religious Society of Friends as they were more formally known, were founded by George Fox in the north of England in the mid-seventeenth century. The sect, like other similar groups of the time, was intent on moving away from the structured forms of the Church of England and the Catholic Church. William Edmundson had brought the ideals of the Quakers to Ireland, establishing the first Irish Quaker meeting in Lurgan in 1654.

What marked the early Quakers out from the plethora of other sects of their time was their belief in the Inward Light, a phrase they used for the direct link they believed themselves to have to the Holy Spirit. Not for them the notion of a clerical hierarchy of middlemen through whom God might be reached.

The Quakers, who earned their colloquial name from the custom of members quaking during meetings, were non-violent in creed and practice and brought a stringency of clothing, lifestyle and business to their daily lives.

Women and men were treated equally within their fellowship, and indeed women were among the earliest preachers of Quakerism in Ireland, though by 1700 their preaching was being discouraged by the Elders and their position eroded by the late seventeenth century influx of soldiery into the ranks of Irish Quakerism.

Not surprisingly, the Quakers in Ireland were to live paradoxical lives. Not only did they bring a new religious belief and practice into the country, they also laid the foundations for the development of a trader class that was, on the one hand, distinct from the Anglo-Irish Protestant landlords and, on the other, separate from the Irish Catholic peasant class. The more prominent early Irish Friends became known outside their own community through their involvement in business, and among the better known family names were Bewley, Jacob, Shackleton and Lamb. While both Protestant and Catholic ranks may have been envious of the newly emerging merchant group, their envy was tempered by the lack of ostentation shown by the Quakers. They had no desire to clamber into the world of the big house, nor to proselytize among their poorer Catholic neighbours.

Despite the attempts of the early Quakers to live quiet lives, they didn't always escape the often unwelcome attentions of their fellow citizens. Their dress, religious beliefs and refusal to swear oaths, use the names of days and months or the pronoun 'you' or even to have images on their chinaware, made them easy targets for vilification.

One of the earliest Quaker settlements in Ireland was at Ballitore in Co. Kildare, thirty miles south-west of Dublin. The first Quakers to arrive in the village had been John Barcroft and Abel Strettel, who bought lands there in the 1690s. They arrived into an already established but poverty-ridden community. The local land was poor and poorly cared for. Barcroft and Strettel set about changing that, planting trees, orchards and hedges, putting their own kind of order on the wilder landscape that had met them on arrival.

In 1708 a Meeting House was completed in the village, with others built in the nearby towns of Carlow in 1716 and Athy in 1780 (although the first Quaker meeting here was held in 1671).

Shackleton House, Harden, Yorkshire. The family owned the Harden property since the sixteenth century. The house was demolished in 1892, when the door and lintel stone were brought by the Shackletons to Lucan, County Dublin, and in 1983 given to the restored Quaker Meeting House in Ballitore, County Kildare.

While most early Quakers in Ballitore made their living from industry and farming, Abraham Shackleton chose to open a boarding school in the village in 1726, beginning the Shackleton connection with Quaker life in the area.

The Shackletons came from the village of Harden in West Yorkshire, England, and Abraham had been born in 1696. The studious youngster had lost both parents before his eighth birthday but he showed a tenacity that was to stand to him in establishing his school.

As a young man he became an assistant teacher in Skipton where he met his wife, Margaret Wilkinson. He came to Ireland as a tutor to the Quaker Cooper and Duckett families, who lived at Coopershill, near Carlow, and at Duckett's Grove, on the border of counties Carlow and Kildare, less than ten miles from Ballitore. Encouraged by these two families, Abraham established his school.

The initial roll for the school numbered thirty-eight pupils. Two years later the numbers had grown to sixty-three. The school became so successful in such a short time that its reputation drew students from as far afield as France, Norway and Jamaica. Many children, arriving in Ballitore at the age of four, were to remain there without seeing their parents again until they were eighteen. Some of the boys, falling prey to measles or smallpox, were never to return home, dying in the village to which they had come to be educated, far removed from parents and family. These tragedies, when they occurred through the years, cast shadows over Ballitore where everybody knew everybody else and many pupils lodged in local houses, integrating fully into village family life.

The curriculum in Ballitore School included the classics, history, maths, geography, English literature and writing and composition. Not all the teachers or pupils came from Quaker backgrounds and among early alumni were the statesman Edmund Burke (1729-97), the revolutionary Napper Tandy (1737-1803) and the future Cardinal Cullen (1803-78).

Above: Richard Shackleton (1726-1792) who succeeded his father as master of Ballitore School in 1756 until 1779, was a founding member of the Trinity College Debating Society, and a lifelong friend of Edmund Burke. (Courtesy Desna Greenhow)

Left: Abraham and Richard Shackleton. Abraham (1696 - 1771), born Harden, Yorkshire, where his father was the first of the family to be a Quaker, came to Ireland in 1720 and opened a school in Ballitore, County Kildare in 1726.

13

Shackleton School, Ballitore. Opened on the first of the third month 1726 by Abraham Shackleton and closed in 1836, having had over a thousand pupils. Building demolished c.1940.

When Richard Shackleton, Abraham's son, born in 1726, took over the running of the school thirty years later, he broadened the curriculum while introducing a more stringent regime, leaving little room for amusement. (His stringency led, on at least one occasion, in 1769, to the pupils locking the staff out of the school, demanding a summer holiday. Pacifist or not, the headmaster quickly broke down the school door and the boys were thrashed.) Richard had been a schoolmate and friend of Edmund Burke's in Ballitore and an observer of their student days commented that Shackleton was 'steadier and more settled than Burke was ever to become'.

Richard had received his first and second level education in Ballitore and had gone on to study languages at Trinity College in Dublin, the first Quaker to do so. He was an active member of the Historical Society and received a special dispensation to address the Society while wearing his hat – a Quaker practice based on the belief that all people were equal and

14

none in particular merited the doffing of a hat. The attractions of *the world* might have drawn another young man away from Ballitore and Quakerism but not Richard. He was single-minded in his commitment to his faith and his education.

Eighteenth-century Quakers were forbidden from taking degrees so Richard, having completed his studies in Trinity, returned to the quieter and more austere life of a school-master in Ballitore.

At the age of twenty-three he married Elizabeth Fuller, a granddaughter of John Barcroft, one of the original settlers at Ballitore. The couple had four children. Elizabeth died in 1754 and a year later Richard married Sarah Carleton. They had two surviving children – Elizabeth and Mary.

Mary was to leave a legacy of history, culture and literature through her poetry and prose. Richard had insisted his daughters receive as wide an education as his sons and in Mary's case he greatly encouraged her in her writing. When he travelled abroad, to London and Yorkshire, Mary travelled with him. While visiting

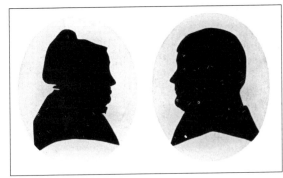

Mary and William Leadbeater. Mary (1758-1826), daughter of Richard Shackleton and his second wife Elizabeth, was a prolific poet, correspondent and diarist. William (1763-1827), Mary's husband, an orphan, attended Ballitore School. Their daughter Lydia Fisher was a secret love of Limerick-born novelist Gerald Griffin (1803-40). Plain silhouettes were the usual form of portrait for Quakers.

cousins in Selby in Yorkshire, they were invited to tea in house after house. Typically, Mary noted in her diaries that the silver coffee-pot from the local big house was there to greet them on each tea-table in turn.

Born in 1758, Mary had developed both an academic and a personal friendship with the other pupils in Ballitore School. One of her close school friends, William Leadbeater, was to return to Ballitore as a teacher and, at the age of thirty-three, Mary married him. All the while, Ballitore School was growing in size – as many as twenty-three new pupils enrolling in one year.

Richard Shackleton died of a sudden fever in 1792, on his way to a school board meeting in the town of Mountmellick. He was sixty-six. The running of the school was now taken over by his eldest son Abraham.

Abraham was to undo many of the changes his father had made. Where Richard had widened the curriculum, Abraham narrowed its focus. Where Richard had thrown open the school doors to a multitude of denominations, Abraham restricted entry to Quakers.

As the eighteenth century drew to a close, Abraham married Lydia Mellor and set about tracing the family history, bringing to light, among other things, the family crest and motto, *Fortitudine Vincimus – By Endurance We Conquer*.

Whether the changes introduced by Abraham would have led to the decline that followed in Ballitore School is impossible to tell, but the rebellion of 1798 brought an immediate dip in its fortunes. That the rebellion should occur in that year was hardly surprising.

Ireland in the 1790s was a country riven with dissension. It had a parliament established for its minority community, while its Catholic population was petitioning for King and Parliament to 'relieve them from their degraded situation and no longer suffer them to continue like strangers in their native land'.

In April 1790 a meeting was held in Belfast where those attending agreed to 'form ourselves into an association to unite all Irishmen to pledge themselves to our country'. Thus was the foundation laid for the founding of the revolutionary United Irishmen, whose first Secretary was Napper Tandy, former pupil of Ballitore. Through the 1790s the United Irishmen worked to establish their organization across the country. They drew inspiration and aid from revolutionary France and their ambition was a rebellion that would overthrow British dominance in Ireland and establish an independent state, unifying Catholic, Protestant and Dissenter against the imposition of rule, through a puppet parliament, from Britain. As the power of the United Irishmen grew, Parliamentary Acts were introduced in 1794 to outlaw their meetings, but the organization continued, underground, as a secret society. The following year a Catholic Relief Bill, designed to make daily life easier for the vast majority of the population, was defeated in Parliament.

Nor were the United Irishmen the only ones with an interest in Ireland's political future. In 1779 the first regular Volunteer Corps was founded in Belfast. The immediate objective of the Volunteers was to defend Ireland, in the absence of sufficient British troops, against invasion by French or American marauders. The incident, which sparked panic among the citizenry, was the capture of a ship in Belfast Lough by American privateer Captain Paul Jones.

Mary Leadbeater's house, Ballitore. From here Mary recorded many of the comings and goings in the village. Building recently restored and open to the public. (Photograph c.1890s)

Initially, the Volunteers were Protestant but they were armed, and an armed group of citizens was a frightening prospect for the government. And worse, as the Volunteers spread, Catholics were welcomed into their ranks and an organization that had started as a last line of defence quickly became a potential threat.

The drain of British soldiery from Ireland reached crisis point in the 1790s because of war with France. England's problem was seen, by the United Irishmen, as their opportunity to push for a full rebellion and by those loyal to the Crown as a chance to establish a Yeomanry force within the country.

Arrests of suspected United Irishmen continued through 1796 and 1797. In October of that year *habeas corpus* was suspended to deal with trouble from both the United Irishmen and the emerging loyalist Orange Order.

Early in 1798 the United Irishmen in Leinster resolved that they 'would not be diverted from their purpose by anything which could be done in parliament'. In May a rebellion organized by the United Irishmen broke out in many Leinster counties, including Kildare. Ballitore did not escape the bloodshed.

Parents, fearing for their children's welfare, in a village where violence, warfare and murder had become commonplace, removed them as quickly as possible. Despite the fall in numbers, the school struggled on until in 1801 Abraham decided to close it.

Several years earlier William Leadbeater had left teaching and gone into business and Mary had opened the first Post Office in Ballitore. This allowed her to continue her writing and kept her well informed about local comings and goings.

While her main concern was with local life, Mary also corresponded widely with people like Edmund Burke and the novelist Maria Edgeworth (1767-1849), as well as a wide circle of past pupils across the globe. While Burke had been an acquaintance at school, Maria Edgeworth became an epistolary friend. Their letters grew out of a shared interest in the improvement of the peasantry and in the education of women, a topic Edgeworth had used for her first publication, *Letters to Literary Ladies*, published in 1796.

It is Mary's insatiable appetite for gossip that makes her diaries so interesting. They were published long after her death as *The Annals of Ballitore* (1862), generally called *The Lead-beater Papers*, and deal with the period 1766 to 1824. They include one of the few impartial accounts of the 1798 rebellion, which began on 23 May and continued with sporadic fighting until mid-July.

At the end of 1798 Mary noted the constant presence of the reminders of loss in her own and others' lives.

'*Late one evening, as we leaned over the bridge, we saw a gentleman and a lady watering their horses at the river, attended by servants fully armed. They wore mourning habits, and though young and newly married, looked very serious and sorrowful. Their chastened appearance, their armed servants, the stillness of the air scarcely broken by a sound, rendered the scene very impressive ... Mourning was the language – mourning was the dress of the country.*'

Mary was also deeply involved in the movement to 'improve' the peasantry and to promote ideals of progress, abstinence, thrift and self-esteem. These were the principles evinced by her

BALLITORE SCHOOL,
(COUNTY OF KILDARE,)
CONDUCTED BY JAMES WHITE,
AND
THEODORE E. SULIOT, A.M.

Terms:

For board, washing, &c. and instruction in *English*, with *Arithmetic, Algebra*, and *Book-keeping—Geometry, Mensuration, &c. Geography, the Use of the Globes*, and the Elements of *Astronomy* and *Natural Philosophy*.

For Pupils under the age of eleven £34
.... from eleven to fifteen . . . . . . £38 per annum.
.... above fifteen £44
payable half yearly in advance.

For *Latin, Greek*, and *Hebrew*, an additional charge of £2 per annum. *French, Italian*, or *German*, each £2 per annum.

☞ A VACATION OF ABOUT A MONTH IN SUMMER.

A number of references, both in Ireland and Great Britain, can be furnished to inquirers, on application to JAMES WHITE, or THEODORE E. SULIOT, at the School, or to RICHARD D. WEBB, 10, *William-street, Dublin*.

Fifth Month 1st, 1832.

grandfather and father through Ballitore School, and she was anxious that they become part of the lives of those about her.

In 1806, five years after the school had closed its doors, Abraham Shackleton's son-in-law James White reopened them and with the return of peace to the countryside the classrooms quickly filled with students from Ireland and elsewhere.

Abraham, however, decided not to become reinvolved and turned, instead, to milling as a second profession, running the family mill at Ballitore and continuing to work there until his death in 1818.

Milling carried through to the next generation with Abraham and Lydia's son Ebenezer, who bought a mill in the village of Moone, a couple of miles along the road from Ballitore.

Ebenezer, born in 1784, had grown up in a Quaker family but from early adulthood questioned the direction Quakerism was taking in Ireland, believing the community was straying from its original ideals. He took this as his main reason for converting to the Church of Ireland and bringing his children up in that faith. One of those children was Henry Shackleton, father of the young walkers spread out across the sunlit fields on Mullaghcreelan Hill.

Left: James White (1778-1847), master at Ballitore School (1806-36), married the previous master Abraham Shackleton's daughter Lydia. Their daughter Hannah married a teacher at the school, Theodore Suliot and they emigrated to Ohio. After Lydia's death White married Mary Pike. (Ambrotype courtesy Jeremy White)

Above: Terms of enrolment of school in 1832.

19

Ebenezer Shackleton (1784-1856), married secondly Ellen Bell, grandparents of EHS. Ebenezer took on the Moone Mill in 1824 and lived at Moone Cottage (now demolished). (Courtesy the late Betty Chinn)

On the other side of the family, the children's mother Henrietta was the daughter of John Henry Gavan and Caroline Mary Fitzmaurice. Henrietta's mother was the daughter of John Fitzmaurice of Carlow, himself the great-grandson of William Fitzmaurice, the twentieth Baron of Kerry.

The Fitzmaurices, through marriage into the Petty family, had inherited large tracts of the Petty estate of 270,000 acres in Kerry. (William Petty (1623-87) had been Cromwell's physician-general and surveyor.) But their roots in the area went back much further, to Thomas Fitzmaurice who had arrived as part of the Norman force in Ireland in the thirteenth century. Fitzmaurice had been styled the First Lord of Kerry. The earldoms of Kerry and Shelbourne and the title of Marquess of Lansdowne were subsequently created for members of the Fitzmaurice family.

Not that the Fitzmaurices had escaped political and military troubles in the course of Irish history. In the Geraldine rebellion of 1579 the family had much of their lands seized and sold.

In July that year James Fitzmaurice had landed at Smerwick harbour in Co. Kerry and established a base at Dún an Oir with a force of Spanish and Italian soldiers. The Papal Legate, Nicholas Sanders, accompanied him, with letters from the Pope to the Irish Lords discharging them from allegiance to Queen Elizabeth of England and urging them to rebel in support of the Catholic faith. Two months later Fizmaurice was killed in a skirmish with the Burke clan in Co. Limerick.

In 1691 lands were again confiscated when James and Henry Fitzmaurice remained loyal to King James against King William. Later, the family returned to the safer confines of the establishment. The First Marquess was First Secretary and then Prime Minister in Britain from 1782 to 1783. The Third Marquess was Chancellor of the Exchequer from 1806 to 1807 and later Home Secretary. The Fifth Marquess was Viceroy of India from 1888 to 1894 and subsequently British Foreign Secretary.

On the Gavan side, Henrietta was descended from a family connected to church and state. Her father, Henry, had been involved, with his father Rev. John Gavan, rector of Wallstown, Doneraile, Co. Cork, in the battle of Wallstown, a tithe-assessing incident (whereby a tenth of annual produce was levied in support of the Anglican Church) which occurred in September 1832.

Rev. John Gavan was an unpopular man in the area. He and his son had gone, one afternoon, to mark tithes on a farm. Once there, an angry crowd surrounded them. The Gavans drew their pistols but were disarmed. The following day, with three magistrates and a number of policemen, they went to another farm. Some stoning of the police and magistrates, mostly by women and children, followed and, apparently, one of the magistrates, a man called Evans, panicked and ordered the soldiers to open fire on the crowd. Four of the tenants were killed, one a boy of fourteen, and many were injured.

A subsequent investigation suggested that the turning points that led to the heightening of tensions and the subsequent deaths were Henry Gavan's over-zealousness and Evans's panic.

Henry had originally studied medicine and qualified as a doctor but his interest lay in joining the Royal Irish Constabulary. Through the political influence of Lord Cornwallis, Henry obtained a commission in the RIC, and after his marriage in 1844, to Caroline Mary Fitzmaurice of Carlow, he was appointed Inspector General of Police in Ceylon.

Henry and Caroline sailed from Falmouth for Ceylon on the *Persia*. Shortly after its departure, the ship was forced to return to Falmouth after a ten day buffeting at sea. The Gavans refused to re-embark. Such was the ferocity of the experience, Henry never fully recovered and died two years later, leaving his wife and an infant daughter, Henrietta Letitia.

Henrietta's birth, on 28 September 1845, came just two weeks before the first reports of a widespread potato failure in Ireland. Over the following three years Ireland would go through the bleakest period of its history.

Failure of the staple diet crop of potatoes through 1845, '46, '47 and '48 was mirrored by trader speculation which saw the price of corn rise beyond the means of the destitute, and by government inaction. The relief measures introduced were often ill-conceived and badly organized.

Help did arrive from abroad, mainly from the United States, but distribution was haphazard. By 1848 more than a million people had died from starvation and malnutrition. Those who were healthy enough and could find the fare emigrated, leaving a devastated country.

For those who stayed, eviction was a constant threat. With crops continuing to fail and no money available for rents, the poorhouses and roadsides were thronged with evicted families. By 1 July 1848, almost 840,000 people were in receipt of relief.

The Great Famine, however, was not a matter of life and death for all classes in Ireland. Caroline Gavan had lost her husband but neither she nor her daughter was in any danger of falling victim to starvation or emigration. The effects of the famine did not impinge materially on the lifestyle of the Gavans or their class.

Brought up by her mother, Henrietta grew into a bright, vivacious and good-humoured young woman. On 28 February 1872 she married Henry Shackleton and moved with him to live at Kilkea House, a large square, comfortable farmhouse. To the side, as one entered, were solidly built, slated stone outhouses which enclosed a courtyard.

Everton, Crockaun, County Laois, a Fitzmaurice house outside Carlow from where EHS's parents were married. Kelvin Grove and Laurel Lodge were other Fitzmaurice houses in the Carlow area.

The house was surrounded by rolling grassland that rose along the flank of Mullaghcreelan Hill on one side, and fell to the banks of the river Griese on the other. It was rich land, good for tillage as well as cattle and sheep rearing.

Henrietta's verve and sheer good humour were to help her create – even in difficult times – a sense of order, enjoyment and support for her children at Kilkea.

Unusually in a Victorian family, both Henry and Henrietta were constantly available to their children, including them in virtually all family activities, listening and advising and, most of all, encouraging them to express themselves.

These two family lines – hardworking Quaker pacifists and hot-blooded adventurers – were to find a perfect point of fusion in Ernest.

Bent low between his rose bushes, Henry's thoughts had moved away from the sight of Ernest, lost in wonder among the cow parsley, to the more pressing business of money. He had hoped to make a living as a farmer and find time and opportunity to develop his interest in homoeopathy, but, confronted with falling prices and a downturn in the agricultural economy, he faced the possibility of a change of career. It wouldn't be his first.

Henry had been sent to school in Wellington College in England, carrying his mother's hopes of an army commission, but ill health had brought him back to Ireland and to Trinity College in Dublin, where he took an Arts degree in 1868.

Four years later, when he married Henrietta, they opted for a life of farming. Land was leased from the Duke of Leinster and the couple set up home at Kilkea House. The farm, set close to the hamlet of Kilkea – built to house workers on the estate of the Duke of Leinster – was equidistant from the market towns of Athy and Carlow and close to the village of Castledermot.

With family connections on both sides, they were five miles from Henry's birthplace and seven miles from Henrietta's mother's home in Carlow; there were numerous friends and relatives to visit in the area and they enjoyed the freedom that rural life allowed. Wandering the fields and the banks of the river Griese, which flowed through the farm, Henry could indulge his passion for collecting herbs. Henrietta travelled regularly to visit relatives in Carlow and the couple became part of the local social life.

Their time at Kilkea was to prove a fertile one, six of their ten children being born in the house over the following seven years. Their first, Gertrude, arrived at the end of 1872.

At five o'clock on the morning of 15 February 1874 Henrietta gave birth to the couple's second child, Ernest Henry. A year later Amy was born and a second son, Frank, was born in 1876. In 1878 the new arrival was Ethel and the last of the Kilkea children, Eleanor, was born in 1879.

With six children to raise, Henry and his wife had to face the fact that farming could no longer provide them with a livelihood.

While the famine days of the 1840s were past, there were still regular crop failures due to blight. More importantly, the whole question of land ownership and reform hung over the future of farming in Ireland, and the previous two decades witnessed the cumulative and spreading force of agrarian tension.

Land and its ownership had never been far removed from Irish politics, as the Gavan family would have known. By 1858 the introduction of the Landed Estates (Ireland) Act brought the question of land ownership and control back into the domestic limelight. The 1860 Land Improvements (Ireland) Act had made provision for loans to tenants for the erection of labourers' cottages but the issue of the ownership of land ran much deeper. The movement towards independence, which had grown out of the 1798 rebellion and the evictions following the Great Famine and led to the abortive Fenian rebellion of 1867, was inseparable from the land question.

The failure of the Fenian rising had done little to stem the tide of demands for reform and through the 1870s there were regular calls for action by the British government. In 1878 Michael Davitt – who would found the Land League in October 1879 – was demanding 'agrarian agitation'. His calls were met with support across the country and tenants were organising themselves in virtually every parish. This political uncertainty, coupled with a periodic downturn in agricultural prices, meant that farming looked less and less promising.

Henry was neither accountant nor politician and, despite the children's happiness at Kilkea, he and Henrietta concluded that they must move on and find an alternative way of making a living. Medicine seemed to offer the best hope.

The sound of the children's laughter caught Henry's attention and he stood to watch them troop across the yard. Again, Ernest was lagging behind, Mr Lag by nickname and Mr Lag by nature. And then, at the sound of passing carriages, the boy was gone, racing along the gravelled path, out through the gate and onto the lane that ran past the house. Henry hurried to follow his son.

'It's just a funeral, sir,' the nurse assured him.

Henry slowed his pace and walked to the gate where he stood watching Ernest. The young boy was trotting after the receding carriages, his short legs working to carry him closer to the hearse. At the end of the lane, where it met the main road between Castledermot and Athy, the funeral cortège picked up speed, leaving Ernest far behind. Only then did he stop running and turn again for home. His father smiled, seeing the boy idling slowly towards him, amused by his son's fascination with funerals.

Later, when the afternoon was at its hottest, Henry took the children swimming in the nearby river and they repeated the old family joke over and over, laughing boisterously, as they plunged into the clear water.

'You swim in the Griese and come out dripping!'

While Henry and Henrietta prepared to move to Dublin, life at Kilkea House continued as it had done. The children played in the garden, the scent of the climbing roses, which shadowed the walls of the house, blending with the perfume of the wild honeysuckle that threaded through the field hedges. Passing carts and carriages on the road between Athy and Castledermot drew them to the end of the field that fronted the house. This passing traffic and the occasional trips the family took to the surrounding towns broke the rhythm of their days at home.

On one such family visit, to their cousins at Browne's Hill in Carlow, Ernest saw, for the first time, a penguin skin. He was fascinated by the pelt, given as a gift to the Brownes. It was unlike anything he had ever seen. He was well used to the moth-eaten fox heads mounted on the walls of many of the houses he visited, and the stuffed remains of tigers and lions brought from India and Africa, while uncommon, were not extraordinary. But this penguin skin was different. Its shape and colour and texture intrigued the young boy and set his imagination racing. There were endless questions about its origins and its habitat. He conjured up stories about where it had come from and how it had reached his corner of the globe. It remained a source of curiosity for a long time and, on subsequent visits, it was the first thing he sought out in the house.

Henrietta Shackleton (1845-1926), née Gavan, married Henry 28 February 1872. (Athy Heritage Centre)

Henry Shackleton (1847-1921), fifth eldest son of Ebenezer and Ellen Shackleton's ten children, and father of EHS. His vigorous beard earned him the nickname 'Parnell' when he returned to Trinity College. Appropriately, he favoured Home Rule. (Athy Heritage Centre)

The last thing Ernest did at Kilkea House, before climbing into the carriage that would take him away from his birthplace, was to stand on the fallen tree trunk on the lawn. This had been his ship's cabin for as long as he could remember, the place where he played on summer afternoons and lay long into the evening, watching the stars appear over Mullaghcreelan Hill, singing his favourite song quietly to himself.

> *'Twinkle, twinkle, little star,*
> *how I wonder what you are,*
> *up above the world so high,*
> *like a diamond in the sky.'*

Only then did he join the others waiting to leave for a new life in Dublin, where his father would begin his medical studies in Trinity College.

The Shackleton family settled at 35 Marlborough Road in South Dublin and Ernest immediately requisitioned the garden frame as a replacement for the ship's cabin he had left behind on the lawn at Kilkea House. The house in Marlborough Road was a two-storey over basement, red-bricked dwelling, with gardens back and front, built a decade before the Shackletons moved there and part of the new development of lands close to the suburban village of Donnybrook.

35 Marlborough Road, Dublin, home 1880-84 to Henry and Henrietta, their six children and three more daughters born there. A commemorative plaque was unveiled by EHS's granddaughter, Alexandra Shackleton, in May 2000.

Life in Dublin offered fresh wonders to be explored. For the children, St Stephen's Green, recently opened to the public, was a place of excursion with their nurse, while the newly opened manual telephone exchange in Dame Street, with its five subscribers, was a topic for comment and discussion over the dining table.

But for Ernest Marlborough Road provided another diversion. A regular procession of passing funerals meant he could more easily indulge his passion for playing chief mourner, watching for the cortèges from the front window and racing down the granite steps to follow the processions.

While Henry pursued medicine at Trinity, the family expanded with the arrival of Clara in 1881, Helen in 1882 and Kathleen in 1884. For Ernest, these additions were little more than distractions, as he had other undertakings to pursue.

The first was the excavation of a large hole in the back garden, which, he told his father, would eventually take him to Australia. The second involved borrowing one of his mother's rings. Having liberated it from her room he buried it in the garden and arranged for his nurse to be present when he unearthed the unexpected treasure, glorying in her surprise and delight.

Evenings were spent reading and sketching. Ernest had had some lessons in sketching and, even as a child, was keen to develop this talent. The Jules Verne stories in the *Boys'*

Aberdeen House, 12 West Hill (now Westwood Road), Sydenham, where the Shackletons moved in June 1885, when Henry started his practice as a local doctor for the next thirty-two years.

EHS aged eleven, when he was a pupil at Fir Lodge Preparatory School, Sydenham, London.

Own Paper were Ernest's favourite reading material. Indeed, as a quiet child, he often seemed most happy with his own company, not that solitary moments were frequent in a house where there were now nine children.

As at Kilkea, mealtimes regularly found the family playing a favourite game of *capping* quotations, with Henry giving the children a fragment which they would try to complete. Ernest was particularly adept at this, Tennyson being his favourite source.

In 1884 Henry qualified, with distinction, taking an M.B. and M.D. from Trinity College. Again, it was decision time. Henry and his wife discussed the possibilities of establishing a practice in Dublin but opted for the greater opportunities offered by London.

In December 1884 Henry, Henrietta and their nine children sailed on the *Banshee* from Kingstown (now Dun Laoghaire) across the Irish Sea to Holyhead, and travelled from there to London.

The Shackleton's first home in London was in South Croydon. Despite Henry's best attempts, he found it impossible to establish a successful practice there and, the year after his arrival in England, he moved the family to Aberdeen House, 12 West Hill (now Westwood Road) in Sydenham. Two years later, in January 1887, Henrietta gave birth to the couple's tenth child, Gladys.

Life as a doctor was more rewarding for Henry in Sydenham. Henrietta, however, worn out by the birth of ten children, fell victim to a mysterious illness which left her without any energy. It was a sickness that Henry might have come across in Kilkea, where the locals would have described it as *the mionaerach*, a disease that wouldn't kill but debilitates the sufferer with little or no energy. Henrietta, so long the vital and good-humoured heart of the family, withdrew to her sick-room and rarely left it until her death in September 1926.

Despite their mother's illness, the children set about establishing new lives for themselves and were enrolled in schools in Sydenham. Ernest began attending Fir Lodge Preparatory School and rapidly acquired a new nickname, Micky, which also stuck at home. His new schoolmates found his Irish accent and manner an easy target for their sarcastic jibes. He had arrived a quiet and pacific boy but in his early days at the school he obviously decided it was time for a change. As a result he quickly acquired the reputation of 'a brave little fellow, ready to fight the universe and all therein'.

Among the friends he made at school the closest was Maurice Sale-Barker. They played football together and mercilessly taunted the younger Shackleton sisters.

Meanwhile, Henry was busy establishing his medical practice. The difficulty of bringing up a large family, pursuing a career in medicine and looking after an ailing wife did nothing to dent his enthusiasm for work.

Among his patients was Eleanor Marx, daughter of Karl Marx. Eleanor lived just around the corner from the Shackletons, in Jew's Walk, and it was to her house that Henry was called one afternoon in March 1898. Arriving quickly, he found that, as a reaction to the end of a love affair, she had taken an overdose of prussic acid and died before he could be of any help.

However, most of Henry's cases were more mundane. He was a hardworking man, popular with his patients and as a result he built up a thriving practice which was to continue in Sydenham for thirty-two years.

In 1887 Ernest was enrolled at Dulwich College as a day-boarder. The college had been founded in 1618 and, while not in the first rank of public schools, had a substantial reputation for producing businessmen and civil servants, the backbone of the middle class. It drew its boys from the locality and from families that were solvent rather than wealthy. In later years it would become known as the *alma mater* of P.G. Wodehouse and Raymond Chandler.

While Ernest was extremely accomplished at boxing and gym, and did well at cricket and football, his academic achievements at Dulwich were marked by a succession of reports through which ran the common thread that he could apply himself more, work much harder and do a great deal better. John Quiller Rowett (later the main sponsor of Shackleton's final *Quest* expedition) used to walk with him to school and wrote: 'He was always full of life and jokes, but was never very fond of lessons ... I had a friend who knew German very well, and I used to get hints from him which I passed on to Shackleton.'

Boredom rather than lack of ability was Ernest's chief problem. He excelled at the things he enjoyed and went to great lengths to collect foreign stamps, for instance. But he found little in the way of inspiration in the droning of his masters.

However his interest in the sea and all things maritime was growing. He regularly spent schooldays playing truant with friends near the local railway line. There the boys would cook over an open fire, smoke endless cigarettes and listen to Ernest reading stories of seafaring and adventure. Their campfire talk turned, time and again, to the exciting prospect of running away and joining a ship. Eventually, words led to action and the friends made the journey to London Bridge to enlist on a ship. They queued for an interview with the Chief Steward, who took one look at the motley crew and sent them packing.

Ernest wasn't in the slightest discouraged by this setback. The idea of a life before the mast grew and he never missed an opportunity to discuss it at home. The young Shackleton was insistent that he didn't want to continue in school and his obvious unhappiness was treated sympathetically. The openness and patience with which all of the children's problems had been entertained by their parents continued into their adolescence. While Ernest's father had hoped he might follow him into the medical profession, he never insisted on it as a career.

They promised, on condition his school performance improved, to try and get him onto a ship. The Royal Navy was ruled out. Money to put a son in the navy was simply not

available. Undaunted and encouraged by the possibility of escape, Ernest set his mind to his academic work and his school performance improved greatly.

Henry's cousin, Rev. G.W. Woosnam, a member of the Mersey Mission to Seamen, was called on for help, and he arranged for the boy to make a trial voyage on the *Hoghton Tower* out of Liverpool.

Easter 1890 brought freedom for Ernest as he said his farewell to Dulwich College, an institution to which he wouldn't return for nineteen years – as a lauded past-pupil presenting the school awards on prize-giving day.

Dulwich College., the secondary school in London attended by EHS as day pupil 1887-90 and by his brother Frank 1891-3. Home of the James Caird and venue for the biannual meetings of the James Caird Society.

2

Merchant Navy Years

1890–1901

◆

When Ernest Shackleton boarded the *Hoghton Tower* in Liverpool as a ship's boy on 30 April 1890, he was stepping back and stepping forward. Forward into a life on the high seas, backward onto a ship whose time had passed, a square rigger whose sails might be strikingly beautiful but whose demands were beyond anything experienced on the steamships that were changing the face of maritime history.

The Shackleton family might have harboured social aspirations in moving to London, but Ernest was well aware that in the Merchant Navy he was apprenticed into the poor man's Royal Navy.

Life on the *Hoghton Tower* was everything that life at home was not. The adoration of his sisters and the warm concern of his parents were replaced by the hardship of a life at sea, with men who had little regard for anything beyond the apprentice's ability to do his job.

Shackleton the teetotaller now came face to face with a life where alcohol was one of the few distractions available. His habit of quoting poetry was met with bemusement, though his fondness for reading his Bible proved more acceptable. 'The first night I took out my Bible to read,' he wrote to his parents, 'they all stopped talking and laughing, and now every one of them reads theirs excepting a Roman Catholic, and he reads his prayer book.'

Hoghton Tower, *a fully rigged 1600-ton clipper at Newcastle, New South Wales, Australia, in 1893 where they took on coal. EHS was an apprentice on this trip, his third voyage.*

Shackleton's first days on the *Hoghton Tower* were blessed with calm seas and a fair wind although that didn't prevent his suffering seasickness. Having found his sea legs and with good weather, he must have imagined life had little better to offer, but change was coming and harsher realities were just over the horizon.

Shackleton's maiden voyage took him to Valparaiso in Chile. His first experience of Cape Horn, like that of many other sailors, was an unhappy one. The *Hoghton Tower* reached the Cape in severe weather. Mountainous waves and gale-force winds pounded boat and crew, spars were damaged and several sailors were injured. The gales continued to pursue the old ship round the Horn. Shackleton was to learn that weather at sea bore no resemblance to weather on dry land. Romantic notions were blown away.

'It is pretty hard work and dirty work,' he wrote. 'You carry your life in your hand whenever you go aloft, in bad weather; how would you like to be 150 feet up in the air, hanging on with one hand to a rope while with the other you try to get the sail in.'

Despite the demands of work and weather, the young Shackleton was fortunate in that Captain Partridge was a kind man who had the interest of his crew at heart. Occasionally, he invited the apprentice to dine at his table. The youngster, for his part, was impetuous, adventurous and stubborn, having little or no time for red tape – the characteristics that made him resolute about his work and popular with his shipmates.

Valparaiso proved a welcome haven after the trauma of rounding the Horn. From there the *Hoghton Tower* sailed up the Chilean coast to Iquique, a port on the edge of the Atacama Desert, where she spent six weeks loading nitrates. The work was tedious, the port depressing, and Shackleton was learning another lesson about the hardships of a life at sea. Danger, boredom and demanding work were three of the greatest tests the novice would face.

The *Hoghton Tower* returned via Hamburg and Shackleton reached home on 22 April 1891. Captain Partridge spoke with Archdeacon Woosnam about Shackleton on his return, describing him as 'the most pig-headed obstinate boy I have ever come across but no real fault is found with him'. Partridge's willingness to take him aboard again, however, showed that pig-headedness and obstinacy could be a virtue.

Shackleton was greeted like a prodigal son by his parents and sisters but his stay with them was short. Nine weeks after his arrival, he was gone once more, to begin his full apprenticeship. Again, he sailed on the *Hoghton Tower*, leaving Cardiff on 25 June bound for Iquique. There was one major difference in this trip, however. Robert Robinson, a tough, no-nonsense man who cracked a harsh disciplinary whip, had replaced Partridge.

Robinson's autocratic attitude didn't help in settling the young man but there were other pressures. His unhappiness was compounded by extreme homesickness. He knew what lay ahead – good and bad – and the nine weeks he had spent with his family had left a residue of warm feeling that was at odds with the authoritarian manner of the new captain. On top of all this, there were the demands of his apprenticeship. His first voyage had been one of discovery, this was one of judgment.

To take his mind off his homesickness, Shackleton worked hard. During his leisure periods he wrote long letters, urging his sisters to write back and inventing games for them to play.

His three younger sisters would recall that he always arranged that there be three prizes for these contests, so that none would feel left out. When he wasn't writing, working or studying, Shackleton spent much of his time reading. Sometimes the sober words of the Bible, sometimes the lighter passages of *Vanity Fair*.

All his life Shackleton valued friendships and family. On January 1892 he wrote to a schoolfriend from Iquique, 'I am anxiously looking out for a letter from you but I suppose you have forgotten my existence altogether. Being away is I suppose "out of sight out of mind".'

Whatever about the toughness of Captain Robinson, the second mate on the ship was far more encouraging to the apprentice, urging him on in his studies and helping him learn the ropes of sailing. This was all the young man needed and he responded with enthusiasm. He might not always agree with his superiors but he was prepared to dedicate himself to those who showed any sign of believing in him.

Cape Horn proved no more hospitable the second time round. There were storms, high seas and injuries. Shackleton was extremely sick from lumbago for much of the journey. Reaching Chile he endured a bout of dysentery, which brought severe diarrhoea and bleeding.

The *Hoghton Tower* ploughed her way to Iquique, arriving there in October and then fought her way home, arriving in England on a warm day in May 1892. As he disembarked in London there seemed little reason to savour the idea of another trip on the *Hoghton Tower*.

If Shackleton had missed home on his second voyage, his sisters missed him even more, and they had the house decorated with flags and banners to welcome him back. He was deeply embarrassed by the ostentation and asked the girls not to repeat the display. They promised but the promise was forgotten and subsequent returns were greeted with the same excitement.

In the weeks that followed, Shackleton was faced with a decision. He was not enamoured at the prospect of another two years apprenticeship under Robinson's iron fist. Life at home was easy and there would have been no recriminations had he opted out of his apprenticeship.

But opting out wasn't something that ever had or ever would appeal to Shackleton. Despite his qualms, he refused to admit defeat and went aboard the *Hoghton Tower* again on 27 June, bound for India.

EHS aged sixteen in 1890. He left Dulwich this year and joined the North-Western Shipping Company.

This voyage, like the previous two, began in fine, calm summer weather. It wasn't until the ship rounded the Cape of Good Hope that she was hit by storms with a ferocity that Shackleton had not previously witnessed. He did his stint at the wheel of the ship during the worst of the gales, proving himself and rising in the estimation of his superiors.

As always, his shipmates were a mixed lot with backgrounds in farming and industry, many of them running from the past. One had fled America, having committed murder. Violence was never far away and there were regular fights and the occasional stabbing on board.

In India Shackleton's task was to work on cargo, a job he thoroughly disliked. Away from the romance of the open sea, he became morose and unhappy. His lowest point came in the Bay of Mauritius where days were spent loading bagged rice by hand. This was not a part of the dream. To make matters worse, he was laid low by a virulent bout of fever. Only when the ship reached Australia did his health and temperament began to improve.

Crossing the Pacific, bound for Chile, Shackleton continued his reading and developed a habit of hanging around the ship's galley, concocting various culinary oddities involving biscuits and beef, much to the annoyance of the cook.

On the return journey they stopped at Queenstown in Cork at the end of June, and he visited relations in Moone near his birthplace in County Kildare.

Back in England, he registered for the Board of Trade examinations and studied under Captain J. Jutsum at the London Nautical School. In October 1894 he passed his examination and became a second mate.

At the end of October an old school friend, Owen Burne, took Shackleton to see the manager of the Welsh Shire Line about a job as fourth mate on the *Monmouthshire*, a tramp steamer. Shackleton was so taken aback by the condition of the fourth mate's quarters that he turned down the job. He did, however, offer to sail as a third mate and the offer was accepted, the line manager commenting that he 'rather liked him'.

On 15 November Shackleton embarked, travelling through the Mediterranean, the Indian Seas and down to China. The voyage was more placid than his storm-tossed months on the *Hoghton Tower.*

Shackleton's major responsibility was the checking of cargo. While he tended to be busy in port, the job allowed him more time to himself at sea for reading and writing.

A product of that trip is his poem 'A Tale of the Sea'. Like Mary Leadbeater, poetry was not his forte. It is, however, interesting to look at the outpourings of the twenty-two year old as he journeyed from China to Europe.

> *I slept and dreamt of the ocean:*
> *Of tarry sailors joys:*
> *Of the tales which they loved to fashion*
> *Of days when they were boys:*
> *And I laughed aloud in my sleep:*
> *"In those days they said they were men:*
> *Is there one who has a record*
> *Of worth: for a poets pen?"*
>
> *Then I saw a great long line*
> *Of ghostly ships come from the North;*
> *Come churning the seas to foam*
> *Splashing their bows with froth.*
> *Dipping now into the hollows:*

Shackleton family group c. 1894

Standing, left to right: Clara (1881-1958), attended Sydenham Girls High School, sometime clerical officer in Customs and Excise. Ernest (1874-1922). Eleanor (1879-1960), attended Sydenham Girls High School; nursed in London, New York, Winnipeg, France during World War I and Canada, where she died.

Seated in dark dresses, left to right: Ethel (1878-1935), nurse, married Rev. Frank Ayers. Amy (1875-1953), lived with family, caring for her ailing parents despite poor health, moving to Chichester to run brother Frank's antiques business. Alice (1872-1938), lived with family.

Seated in light dresses: Kathleen (1884-1961), artist, attended Sydenham Girls High School; her friend George Marston was the official artist on her brother's Nimrod and Endurance expeditions; to Canada in 1912 as artist and editor on the Montreal Star; to London during the War specializing in portraits of celebrities, and to Ireland in 1925 sketching, among others, George Russell, W.B. Yeats, G.B. Shaw, Sean O'Casey, Douglas Hyde; back to Canada c.1929 to paint Canadian Pacific Railway personnel; finally lived with sister Gladys in Dulwich, London. Gladys (1887-1962), attended Sydenham Girls High School. Helen (1882-1962), attended Sydenham Girls High School; journalist with Montreal Star and married Edmund Brietzcke in 1912.

Seated on raccoon skin rug: Francis Richard, 'Frank' (1876-1941), Royal Irish Fusiliers, Boer War 1900-01; Dublin Herald 1905 until resignation in 1907 following disappearance of 'Irish Crown Jewels'; 1913 imprisoned 15 months for fraud, later assuming a family surname Mellor; in 1930s until death ran antique shop in Chichester, in whose cemetery his inscription reads 'He lived for others', though it might be said 'He lived off others'.

Now on the top they rise;
Pointing their booms to the oceans bed
And anon to the wind swept skies.

Like so many other things in his life, punctuation was not to be influenced by rules and regulations.

Returning in July 1895, Shackleton brought with him three baby alligators which he named Faith, Hope and Charity. These were kept in the garden pond at his parents' house until his father found a new home for them in London Zoo.

In August he was off east on the *Monmouthshire*. On this voyage he continued his paradoxical behaviour. On the one hand, he was an affable, sociable shipmate who charmed everyone on board, on the other he was studious and distant, spending long periods alone, lost in his books. He was the practical joker who, at the same time, made great efforts to persuade his companions to sign his abstinence book. He was the romantic who preferred to commune with the stars rather than visit the brothels of distant ports.

Back in London in April of 1896, he set about studying for his second-mate's examination. At the beginning of June, having passed, he immediately signed on as second mate on the *Flintshire* at a salary of £8 a month. He quickly became known on board by the nick-name 'Shacky'.

His first trip, under Captain Dwyer, was to Penang, Singapore, Hong Kong, Yokohama and San Francisco. The young dreamer had travelled a long way from the lawn of Kilkea House. This was the first of six voyages he was to make on the *Flintshire*.

On 29 June 1897 Shackleton came home for what was to prove a life-changing shore leave. He met Emily Dorman for the first time, a friend of his sister Ethel. She was twenty-nine and he was twenty-three, but the age difference didn't matter. Rather, they concentrated on the things they had in common. Both came from large families. Both shared a passion for poetry.

Emily also loved art, and as early as 1885 would write to her mother from school in Kent about her homesickness and her drawing. A letter from the same year betrays her romantic nature. Dated 14 February, it reads: 'My dearest mother ... you are the only nice person in the world to me ... I did so expect one Valentine at least. No one seems to know what it is to have just left home for a strict school ... With love to no-one but yourself.'

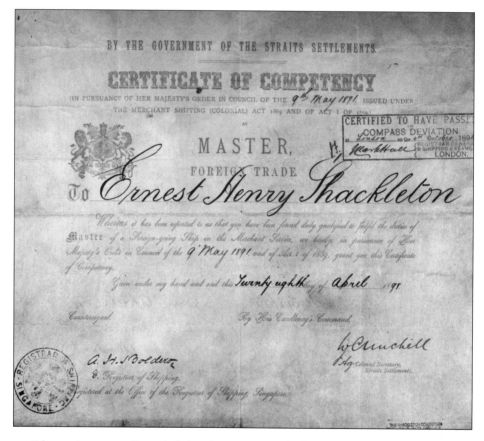

EHS Master's Certificate of Competency of Foreign Trade, Singapore 28 April 1898, signed by Acting Colonial Secretary W.S. Churchill. Date and place of birth 1874, Athy, County Kildare.

Of more interest to Ernest's father, however, was the fact that her father, Charles, who practised law, had a farm in Kent where he grew orchids, something that endeared him to Shackleton senior.

Charles Dorman was a successful solicitor, a partner in the firm Kingsford Dorman which had offices close to the Law Courts on the Strand in London. He was married to Jennie Swinford who had grown up in Kent in a well-to-do but sheltered family. The couple's six children had pursued a variety of careers. The older boys, Herbert and Frank, followed

40

their father into the law. Arthur had been ordained a Minister in the Church of England. Julia, the older of the three girls in the family, remained unmarried until she reached her forties but she was greatly taken up with the endless intrigues of her two younger sisters, Emily and Daisy, who were forever falling in and out of love.

As the nineteenth century drew to an end two things happened in the Dorman family symptomatic of middle-class life at the time. Firstly, they moved from Sydenham to the more exalted surroundings of Wetherby Gardens in South Kensington. Secondly, Charles Dorman became concerned about the state of the British empire. This concern was not unique to him, rather it was part of a wider questioning in middle England. A century of economic domination was ending and Charles Dorman suspected that the old order was changing and was anxious that his daughters should be well looked after. While he was fond of the personable Irish sailor who had befriended Emily, he was less than whelmed by the young man's prospects and by his apparent unconcern for earning a decent living.

He was also aware that Emily, while sociable and articulate, was neither as energetic nor as gregarious as the young man she was seeing. Charles Dorman was concerned about the future welfare of his daughter.

For her part, Emily appears to have seen Shackleton, initially, as a confidant rather than a prospective husband. She was coming to the end of an unhappy love affair and the seaman was prepared to listen and sympathize.

Whatever the possibilities of the relationship, they were abruptly postponed when Shackleton set sail, on 17 July, for Japan and Oregon. But now there was more on his mind than his books and his work and, when he returned to London in February 1898 for two weeks leave, he made contact with Emily and the pair visited the National Gallery and the British Museum.

Much of their time was spent discussing poets and poetry. Swinburne was then Shackleton's favourite poet and Browning was Emily's. She quickly converted him, so that, when he set off again on 11 March he took a copy of Browning's work with him.

Not that love or the prospect of love kept him from his studies. In Singapore, three days from the end of April, he was presented with his Master's Certificate in the Naval Court signed by the Colonial Secretary, Winston Churchill. By June he was home again, among his 'harem' of sisters as he called them, and close to Emily.

That shore leave was to be decisive in shaping the couple's future. While they both avoided the subject of a long-term relationship, there was almost an inevitability in its course. Emily was falling in love with Ernest but she found it difficult to say so in as many words. Even in her letters to him she constantly took one step forward and two back. Often, a letter from Emily, seeming to suggest a future for the pair, was followed immediately by another that, in trying to clarify the first, undermined whatever feeling had been expressed. Despite the obvious depth of feeling the pair had for each other, they were unable to openly declare their affection. Yet there was no question of the friendship ending.

On 27 July Ernest was off again, and the letters from Emily followed, filled with intimations of love and suggestions of doubt.

And the letters went back, from Ernest to Emily, filled with insecurity: '… I am: a man longing for the good of life which he sees shining ahead but unreachable, at least now: and the future is so uncertain that I dare hardly shape a hope.'

Back in England in the first week of December, Shackleton and Emily continued to meet. He was convinced that she was the woman for him and the Christmas season brought a new and deeper excitement than any he had experienced before. But the sailor's life was no respecter of season or sentiment and, on Christmas Day, he took ship as second mate on the *Flintshire* on a short voyage around Britain. The trip was to be even shorter than planned. The ship ran aground off Redcar on the night of 26 December. One of his shipmates, Third Engineer James Dunmore, remarked on Shackleton's interest in everything that happened that night and would later write: 'To see him once made an impression on one's mind, and my first impression was: That this man is made for something better than a captain of a small trading vessel. At that time a marked "standoffishness" existed between officers and engineers but Shackleton soon broke down the barrier which showed he was a man among men.'

As a result of the ship running aground Shackleton got leave to go home for his father's birthday. On his way he visited Emily and told her he loved her.

She wrote: 'I was deeply moved … he put his cigarette on the ledge of the big oak chimney piece and it burnt a deep dent which we tried to rub out … I let him out through the conservatory about 10.30 … and he kissed my hand.'

Emily, EHS and her sister Daisy (Daedels) photographed in 1900. Daisy was an affectionate admirer of her brother-in-law Ernest to whom she referred as Mike. She died suddenly in 1916.

A week later, Shackleton was discharged from the *Flintshire*.

With the possibility of marriage now in his mind, Shackleton recognized that a career as a second mate was not going to keep Emily in any kind of comfort. He would have to look for a more rewarding career in the Merchant Navy.

A week after his discharge Shackleton wrote to the Welsh Shire Line, resigning his position. Again, through his friendship with Owen Burne, he secured a job as Fourth Officer on the *Tantallon Castle*, sailing to Cape Town.

The *Tantallon Castle* was a 3000-ton passenger liner and Shackleton found the change to his liking. The ship was comfortable and he had the opportunity to mix with the passengers and make contacts. Between March and December he made three trips on the *Tantallon* before transferring to the *Tintagel Castle*, a troop ship sailing to and from South Africa. This move was a definite improvement. His salary went up to £7 per week and he was promoted to Third Officer.

Apart from the companionship of the troops on board, Shackleton thoroughly enjoyed organizing social events and himself published a souvenir booklet, *How 1200 Soldiers went to Table Bay.*

EHS on the Tantallon Castle, 30 March 1899.

Not everything on the *Tintagel Castle* was to Shackleton's liking. When a man fell overboard, a rescue boat was launched, manned by an officer and the ship's cook. Reaching the man, the cook dived into the sea to save him. As he did, the lifeboat became unsteady and the officer also fell into the sea. All three eventually made it safely back to the ship and the officer was presented with a medal for his bravery while the cook's action was ignored. Shackleton was angered and got his sister Kathleen, the artist in the family, to do a drawing of the event which he displayed in the officer's mess as his demonstration of disapproval.

In early October 1900 Shackleton joined the Union Castle liner *Gaika* as Third Officer, with an increased salary of £8 per week. He sailed to South Africa, this time returning to England a week before Christmas to see his family and Emily.

On 5 January 1901 he boarded the *Carisbrooke Castle* and set off for the Cape, returning in mid March. This was to be his last trip as a ship's officer. On 13 March he was discharged and paid an annuity of £1/16/3, the lowest pay-off of any of the men on board.

Shackleton had many reasons for leaving the Merchant Navy. He had been working as an apprentice, a mate and an officer for eleven years and he was ready for a change. And there was the boredom factor, which constantly shadowed him. He had done what he set out to do as a teenager and, while the ocean still offered challenges, the work no longer appealed. Most important was the question of his future with Emily. Ernest wanted to marry the love of his life. Her father might see him as a likeable but poor Irish ship's officer, but he resolved nothing would stand in his way when it came to finding personal happiness.

3

Antarctica and Polar Exploration

◆

Antarctica is not some quaint and distant piece of ice happening to house the South Pole, but the fifth largest continent on earth: 2800 miles wide and 5,500,000 square miles in area, its landmass is larger than the United States, Europe, Australia or Canada.

Unlike its northern twin, the Arctic, which is ice surrounded by a mass of land, the Antarctic is land surrounded by ice. Indeed, almost 98 per cent of the Antarctic is covered in ice. Seventy per cent of the earth's fresh water and 90 per cent of the earth's ice are locked in the frozen wastes that surround the South Pole. If all of the Antarctic's ice melted, world sea levels would rise by approximately 200 feet.

Each April, with the arrival of the southern winter, the Antarctic sea begins to freeze at a rate of up to three miles a day. By late September the continent has doubled in size, surrounded by an immense ring of sea ice, stretching from between 900 and 1000 miles in width.

The average summer temperature on the continent is 0 Celsius. In winter that temperature drops to an average of -45 Celsius. At the South Pole itself the average winter temperature is -60 Celsius. Add to this a climate that is constantly turbulent, with wind speeds of up to 180 miles an hour, and the bleakness and desolation are apparent.

There is remarkably little snowfall in the Antarctic, often as little as six inches in a year. As a result it has taken millions of years for the snowcap to reach its current state, with a depth of three miles in places and an average depth of almost a mile and a half. At 8000 feet, the average Antarctic elevation is almost three times higher than its nearest rival, Asia, and completes a landscape that is forbidding.

The very hopelessness of the continent was an essential part of its mystique. And, even if the lands offered no more than shifting, groaning ice and treacherous wind and snow storms, there was always the most basic and engaging of battles to be fought there, that between human will and the natural world.

If nothing else, Antarctica provided a place so distant from civilization that it was virtually impossible for adventurers not to be drawn into its great, white and empty heart.

For those who rose to the challenge there was further allure. The Antarctic continent wasn't entirely desolate. Life went on there, birds and fish and mammals survived. Wildlife was to be found in or close to the sea, as abundant in numbers as it was limited in diversity.

Twenty-two million penguins inhabit the Antarctic including seven of the seventeen known species, though only two – the Emperor and Adelie – are true Antarctic penguins.

The 5,000,000 Adelie penguins consume 9000 tons of shrimp per year and although they can neither fly nor sing they are ideally adapted to their environment. From the earliest landings in Antarctica, explorers have been fascinated by the behaviour of these penguins, despite their off-putting smell.

Antarctica is also home to six species of seal, among them the Fur seal, which is increasing at a rapid rate on the sub-Antarctic island of South Georgia. No longer hunted for its skin, it feeds largely on krill, which is widely available, ironically due to the virtual extinction of whales, the seals' main competitor for food in the area in the first half of the twentieth century.

Summer draws several types of whale to the Antarctic. Among them are the Fin-whale, weighing up to ninety tons; the Hump-back, weighing up to fifty tons; the Minke whale, weighing up to ten tons, and the Killer whale, which in fact is a type of dolphin.

The most impressive of the birds in the area is the albatross with its eleven-foot wingspan. Shackleton was to capture one of these on his 1907-09 *Nimrod* expedition and his crew blamed the bad weather, which dogged them, on its captivity.

Less impressive but more numerous are the petrels and other smaller birds which nest on the continent in summer.

The attraction of Antarctica for wildlife is due to the up-welling of nutrients along the Antarctic Convergence, where the warmer waters from the north meet the colder waters from the south. The edges of the continental islands and the waters off them provide homes in summer, in the months when the snow has melted and the ice is disintegrating.

Sperm Whale. Whaling in the Antarctic developed vigorously with the advent of explosive harpoon-heads in the 1840s. Larsen, a Norwegian, established the first whaling station in South Georgia in 1904; some 175,000 whales were killed between then and 1966.

For much of recorded history, Antarctica was simply unknown. By 150 AD, however, Ptolemy, in reaching the conclusion that the world was symmetrical, suggested the existence of a southern continent which he named *Terra Australis Incognita*. Not content with summoning this strange land from his imagination, he decreed that it was fertile and populated but cut off from the known world by a tropical zone.

In September 1578 Sir Francis Drake, aboard *The Golden Hind*, sailed through the Strait of Magellan, south of Cape Virgenes and north of Tierra del Fuego. In doing so, he proved that the Strait did not separate South America from *Terra Australis Incognita*. Rather he discovered islands to the south – among them Hoste and Los Estados. Farther south lay the ocean now known as the Drake Passage.

Thirty-eight years after Drake's voyage, in January 1616, a Dutchman, Willen Schouten, sailed around the southern tip of the islands Drake had seen. Schouten's journey from Europe had been made with a small fleet. In December 1615 one of his ships, the *Hoorn,* had been destroyed by fire while having her hull cleaned in Port Desire. Schouten decided to call the southern point of the islands after the lost ship and thus was Cape Horn named.

In 1739 a Frenchman named Bouvet thought he had located Antarctica. Given that he spent seventy days in fog and forty of those days among icebergs, with snow falling constantly, his claim is dubious.

Map of Antartica (French, c.1780). The earliest maps developed from the Egyptian geographer Ptolemy's idea of a Terra Australis Incognita. Eighteenth-century voyages by Bouvet de Lozier in the 1730s and Kerguelen in the 1770s signalled France's interest in the area. This map charts James Cook and Furneaux's voyages of the 1770s. Iles et Plaines de Glace seem predominant, and the prime meridian line passes through Paris.

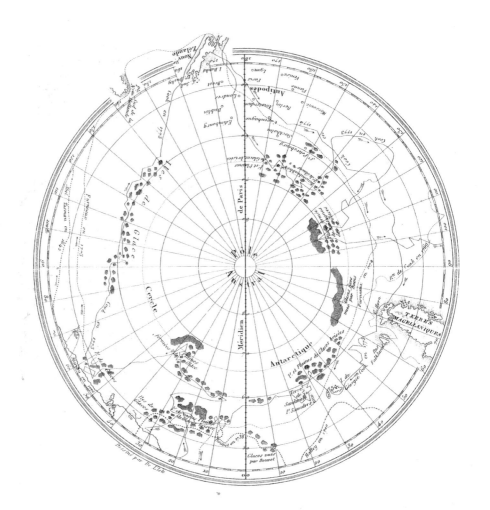

Thirty-three years later another Frenchman, Kerguelen, discovered a land he named *La France Australe*. The place was, according to Kerguelen, extremely habitable and ideal for colonization. In due course he returned with seven hundred men to colonize this new French domain. His fellow colonists, however, were less than impressed by the charms of the islands and the experiment didn't last.

48

Returning home, Kerguelen was rewarded for his misadventure with a twenty-year jail sentence.

In the same year that Kerguelen made his discovery, James Cook, a forty-four year old navigator, was setting sail from England, heading south for Antarctica.

Cook had been due to take the renowned botanist Joseph Banks with him but Banks had insisted on bringing a party of thirteen, including two French horn players. He had also insisted that Cook stop off in Madeira to pick up a third horn player, a woman.

Banks, President of the Royal Society for forty-one years, had accompanied Cook earlier on his voyage to the South Seas between 1768 and 1771. This time, however, his demands proved too much and he was left behind. His unfortunate female musician friend waited for three months in Madeira before discovering neither of them was travelling.

Captain James Cook (1728-79), a Yorkshireman, seaman and explorer, circumnavigated the world three times. First to cross the Antarctic Circle on 17 January 1773. His descriptions of large numbers of seals and whales brought the sealers south. Killed by Hawaians aged fifty.

In January 1773 Cook in HMS *Resolution* and Commander Furneaux in HMS *Adventure* took their ships across the Antarctic Circle, the first men recorded as having done so. Two years later, on 17 January 1775, Cook landed at Possession Bay in South Georgia, north of the Scotia Ridge, and claimed the island for King George III of England.

Cook was not impressed with South Georgia, describing it, with echoes of Cromwell's account of Connaught in the west of Ireland, as a 'savage and horrible country, not a tree to be seen nor a shrub even big enough to make a toothpick … doomed to perpetual frigidness' and claimed, furthermore, with all the certainty of the uninformed: 'I make bold that the world will derive no benefit from it.'

Cook never saw the southern continent but did note the large numbers of whales and seals, and his reports heralded a huge influx of British sealers and whalers into the region.

*Fabian Thaddeus
Bellingshausen (1787-
1834), born Estonia;
joined Russian Navy;
probably first to sight
the Antarctic continent
on 27 January 1820 in
ships* Vostok *and*
Mirnyi. *(Central Navy
Museum, Leningrad)*

The first British sealers to arrive in South Georgia came in 1786 and so began a trade that was to peak in the nineteenth century with over 1100 recorded sealing expeditions. Many other voyages were not recorded to keep them secret from competitors.

In the two-year period from 1800, Edmund Fanning, a New York sealer, took 57,000 fur seal-skins from South Georgia alone, bringing them directly to China, where they were sold at a huge profit for felt-making. Indeed in the early years of the nineteenth century millions of seals were slaughtered in the Antarctic.

On 27 January 1820 the Russian Fabian Thaddeus Bellingshausen unwittingly made the first sighting of Antarctica. Bellingshausen, an admirer of Cook, circumnavigated Antarctica and crossed the Antarctic Circle six times in his ships the *Vostok* and the *Mirnyi*.

Coincidentally, three days after Bellingshausen's sighting, Edward Bransfield, a Cork-born sailor who had been pressganged into the British Navy, also sighted the continent and charted the north-west end of the peninsula, naming it the Trinity Land.

Apart from his discovery work, Bellingshausen had advanced views on health and hygiene. All his crew-members had to be under thirty-five years of age and extremely fit. One of the ways in which he maintained the men's health and fitness was by organizing regular saunas for them, with steam-rooms heated by hot cannon balls.

On one trip he collected thirty penguins, some of which were eaten and the rest kept in chicken runs and bathtubs, being fed on pork before they died. The skins of the dead penguins were used to make caps and their fat was used for greasing boots.

Bellingshausen also met Nathaniel Palmer, a Connecticut-born sealer, in 1820 and, on 16 November of that year Palmer, and the crew of his ship, *Hero*, also sighted the Davis Coast of the Antarctic Peninsula. Bellingshausen's achievements were to go unpublicized, and a century was to pass before he received due recognition.

Insofar as it's possible to date the first landing on the Antarctic continent, and despite later well-publicized claims, the honour appears to go Captain John Davis, a sealer from the United States of America, who landed at Hughes Bay on the Antarctic Peninsula on 7 February 1821.

In 1823 James Weddell took his two ships, *Jane* and *Beaufoy*, on an expedition that married his sealing interest with exploration. Weddell was an inspired leader of men and committed to the latest and best in available scientific instrumentation. With the benefit of warm weather, Weddell pushed over two hundred miles farther south than Cook had done. Such was the regard in which Weddell was held that the sea into which he took his ships was later named for him.

Eight years later two British sailors, Biscoe and Avery, circumnavigated Antarctica. The pair worked for the Enderby Brothers as sealers but, like Weddell, they shared a keen interest in exploration and their work confirmed the status of Antarctica as a continent.

In 1838 the French made another investigative foray south. This voyage was led by Admiral Jules Dumont d'Urville, a native of Calvados. D'Urville was a gifted explorer who discovered the Venus de Milo on the island of Milos. In 1840 he planted the French flag on an island off the Antarctic coast, being unable to land on the mainland. He named the land for his wife, Terre Adelie. She had accompanied him and they celebrated the naming with a bottle of Bordeaux before almost losing their lives in a horrific storm. D'Urville also named the Adelie penguin for his wife.

As he made his way home he met the New York adventurer Charles Wilkes, in his ship *The Porpoise* heading south. Wilkes had a much tougher trip than d'Urville and he lost 119 of his crew of 342. Wilkes claimed the existence of land in areas James Clark Ross was later to sail over. On his return, he was welcomed with a court-martial. Apart from the magnitude of his imagination, Wilkes left one abiding contribution to the history of the exploration of the southern continent, naming it the Antarctic.

James Weddell (1787-1834), Scottish explorer and sealer, voyaged to Antarctica on the Jane and Beaufoy 1819-24. Sailed into the Weddell Sea, naming the South Orkney Islands; the Weddell seal was also named for him.

The next important expedition was led the following year, 1839, by Sir James Ross, a Scot who had joined the Royal Navy as a boy of twelve years. In 1831, sailing with his uncle, Sir John Ross, they had located the Magnetic North Pole.

Ross was charged with making measurements of the earth's magnetic field and his was the first expedition into waters that were to become known as the Ross Sea.

Ross set a new farthest South record of 78 degrees, a record that remained unbeaten until 1900.

Ross and his crew caught Emperor penguins and wrote the first biological account of the contents of the birds' stomachs. He went on to describe and name 500 miles of new coastline, discovering the Transantarctic Mountains, the Ross Ice Shelf, Ross Island and two volcanoes, which he named Erebus and Terror, after his ships.

The commander of the *Terror* was Francis Crozier, who was born in 1796 in Banbridge, Co. Down. Crozier died on board ship in 1848 when, as commander, he took part in Sir John Benjamin Franklin's expedition to discover the North-West Passage.

Erebus, *built 1826, captained by James Clark Ross, and* Terror, *built 1813, captained by Francis Crozier 1839-43. Engraving depicts near-disaster off Antactica on 13 March 1842.*

In 1874 the modern age of steam made its impact on the southern continent. *The Challenger*, a steamship and floating laboratory, crossed the Antarctic Circle that year. The earliest known photographs of icebergs were taken from its deck. Later the ship was involved in oceanographic work in the North Pacific, taking ocean soundings to a depth of 26,850 feet.

Francis Rawdon Moira Crozier (1796-1848), born Banbridge, Co. Down, Ireland. After his trip with Ross he went with Sir John Franklin's ill-fated expedition to find the North-West Passage. Both ships, Erebus and Terror, were lost and all 129 men died.

Left: Crozier Memorial, Bambridge, built in 1862 at a cost of £700.

Between 1893 and 1895 a Norwegian sealing and whaling expedition, led by Henrik Bull, who lived in Australia, reached the Ross Sea in its search for whales. On 24 January 1895 Captain Kristensen and Carsten Borchgrevink each claimed to be the first to land on the continent. Borchgrevink enhanced his claim by drawing a picture of the landing. The ship, *The Antarctic*, was subsequently crushed and sank off Paulet Island on the Nordenskjold expedition of 1903.

This regular but unco-ordinated succession of discoveries in the Antarctic meant little to most people. Even within geographic circles, the Antarctic was far from top of the agenda. All of that was to change, however.

The Sixth International Geographical Congress of 1895, held in London, revived interest in the exploration of Antarctica and signalled the beginning of what was to become known as the Heroic Age of Antarctic Exploration.

Between 1897 and 1899 a Belgian expedition, led by Adrien de Gerlache – who was later to act as an interpreter of Shackleton's lecture to the Royal Society of Brussels and also provided the *Endurance* for him in 1914 – explored the Antarctic Peninsula and when his ship became stuck in ice, he and his crew were forced to overwinter on the ice, south of the Antarctic Circle, the first men to do this. So desperate were conditions that the crewmen were forced to pile snow up and around the deck of the ship, forming a virtual igloo in order to maintain what little warmth there was.

Interestingly, among the international party on board the *Belgica* were Roald Amundsen *you dont that the was first??*

and Dr Frederick Cook. Amundsen discovered the North-West Passage in 1905 and led the first group to reach the South Pole in December 1911, while Cook was to claim to be the first man to reach the North Pole in 1908. Whatever about the veracity of Amundsen's claim, there were serious doubts cast over Cook's.

De Gerlache and his men achieved the recognition of scientists and geographers as the first group to spend the winter on their ice-bound ship. The achievement, however, also brought serious pressures. The isolation and the uncertainty got to some of De Gerlache's crew. One man climbed off the ship onto the ice and told his startled shipmates that he was off to Belgium.

Despite these personal traumas, the crew of the *Belgica* carried out numerous experiments from their winter quarters and took the earliest known photographs of the continent.

Carsten Borchgrevink returned to Antartica in 1898, this time aboard the *Southern Cross* and leading his own expedition. Borchgrevink's trip was largely sponsored by the British publisher Sir George Newnes, who made much of his money through his populist publications, including the sensationalist *Tit Bits* magazine. Not surprisingly Sir Clements Markham, President of the Royal Geographical Society, was unimpressed by Newnes donating money to an expedition led by a Norwegian, and it spurred him on in the planning of his own British Antarctic expedition.

Borchgrevink – an opportunist and an egoist – was especially unpopular on the *Southern Cross*. There were regular disagreements between him and his fellow expedition members.

54

At one point he dismissed William Colbeck, an extremely well-qualified navigator, and then asked him to stay on as a guest. Another crew member, Klovstad, was dismissed and reinstated a few days later. Bernacchi, who later travelled on the *Discovery* expedition, wrote of Borchgrevink that he grinned 'in an imbecilic manner ... [and] made use of some coarse, ill-bred remarks – language of the gutter'.

The biologist Hanson died in the course of the *Southern Cross* expedition. Hanson had become fascinated and enthralled by the behaviour of the penguins in Antarctica and had waited for their return to breed, before dying – with a penguin on his chest. Such were the conditions that his colleagues were forced to use dynamite to dig his grave.

Later, on his *Nimrod* expedition, Shackleton was to include nine dogs descended from the dogs used by Borchgrevink.

Much of the work done by the expeditions to the Antarctic was cartographic. As the expeditions pushed south, mapping was a regular part of the work undertaken, though it wasn't until the advent of Antarctic flight that the mapping could finally be completed.

The first man to fly by aeroplane above the Antarctic was Hubert Wilkins, a member of Shackleton's last *Quest* expedition. He did this in November 1928 and a month later flew over the Antarctic Peninsula, a journey of 1300 miles, which took eleven hours to complete. During the flight, Wilkins took a large number of photographs of the continent below him.

Eventually, in 1946, the United States organized Operation Highjump, using 4700 men and 13 ships, as well as aircraft, to take 3260 metres of cine-film of three-quarters of the perimeter of the continent. They also took 65,000 aerial photographs of Antarctica and finally put to rest the fanciful theory of the nineteenth-century American eccentric, John Symmes, that the earth was hollow and open at the poles.

4

South with Scott

1901–1903

◆

The dawn of the twentieth century was to prove momentous for Ernest Shackleton. He had reached a point in his life where decisions needed to be made. He was determined to marry Emily Dorman and felt she was of like mind, but he was also eager not to spend the rest of his working life in the Merchant Navy.

In the early summer of 1900, while Shackleton was on leave from his ship, he saw an article in the London *Times* about an Antarctic expedition being planned by Robert F. Scott. Shackleton's membership of the Royal Geographical Society allowed him to know that, while Scott might lead the expedition, the man behind the plan was Sir Clements Markham, President of the Royal Geographical Society.

Markham was adamant, in spite of government and Royal Navy disinterest, that Britain should remain to the fore in exploration. The idea that foreigners might lead the race to the South Pole incensed him and he saw the Royal Navy as the answer to Britain's problem.

Markham was well used to finding little sympathy in the upper echelons of the Royal Navy but, in 1898, the Royal Geographical Society had organized a meeting about Antarctica. Sir John Murray had suggested a number of areas, including meteorology, glacial studies, geology and coastal surveys, in which an expedition might prove worthwhile. The following year Markham announced plans for an expedition to Antarctica. A successful trip would, he was convinced, restore confidence in the Royal Navy and in Britain's reputation.

Not that Markham was alone in his view that Britain deserved better. Queen Victoria's reign was drawing to a close and her years on the throne had seen the British empire spread and consolidate. Yet there was a feeling, which Markham shared, that Britain was in danger of being left behind by other, more eager nations. The boundless optimism of the late nineteenth century was slowly being eroded by the Boer War. It was clear that Victoria could not reign forever and minds were already turning to life under Edward. Empire or not, Britain's glory was looking in need of a new burst of energy, enthusiasm and, above all, achievement. Markham's patriotic concerns were, however, constrained by snobbery. His initial insistence that the expedition be manned from the Royal Navy was based on a contempt for the Merchant Navy. However, without the support of the government and with only £5000 available through the RGS, he was forced to turn to private sponsorship and this was where Ernest Shackleton found his opening.

Sir Clements Markham (1830-1916), another Yorkshireman; President of the Royal Geographical Society 1893-1905; determined and obstinate instigator of Scott's Discovery *expedition; in later years went strongly against Shackleton. Related to the Irish Clements family.*

He already felt that life was passing him by. His brother Frank had enlisted in the Royal Irish Fusiliers and gone to South Africa. Exploration seemed to offer a means of finding the finances to impress Emily's father. A lecture in London by Borchgrevink in the summer of 1900 reinforced that sentiment. Finance and adventure, it appeared, lay to the south.

Among the passengers Shackleton befriended in his time sailing to South Africa was Cedric Longstaff, whose father Llewllyn emerged as one of the major sponsors of the planned Antarctic expedition. Through Cedric, Shackleton met Longstaff senior and impressed him with his friendliness and his energy. Longstaff got in touch with Markham and let it be known that he was anxious for Shackleton to join the expedition. Markham could hardly refuse – £25,000, a quarter of the estimated budget for a three-year expedition, depended on Longstaff's generosity.

Markham asked Albert Armitage, who was to be Scott's second-in-command, to make enquiries about Shackleton and this he did, to his own and Markham's satisfaction. In February he was appointed as a member of the expedition while away at sea on the *Carisbrook Castle*. In March he learned of his appointment and of his leave from the shipping line. Markham salved his own patriotic conscience by getting Shackleton a commission in the Royal Navy Reserve.

In the meantime Markham and Scott were forging ahead with plans. Scott had been chosen for his youth – he was thirty-two at the time – his commitment and, presumably, his inexperience, which allowed Markham to command the details of the expedition as he wished. He suggested the route *Discovery* might take and where she might berth for the winter. Scott would be Markham's proxy in Antarctica.

In Scott, Shackleton was meeting a man who was, in some ways, a reflection of himself, but also a man who was radically different. Each was ambitious and young, but where Scott was introvert, Shackleton was outgoing. And where Scott was a product of the Royal Navy and a protégé of the ostentatious and overbearing Markham, Shackleton was very much a Merchant Navy man and possessed of a strong Irish strain of independence and egalitarianism. One was a businessman, the other something of an idealist.

Scott was the son of an easy-going father and a deeply religious mother. As a child he had been a dreamer with twin aversions to the sight of blood and cruelty to animals. He made his first voyage in 1883, at the age of thirteen. His experience of life at sea had, like Shackleton's, shown him that while a young boy's dreams might be of adventure, the reality was a life of hard work and danger. In 1891 he began training on HMS *Vernon*, a torpedo ship. Three years later his father went bankrupt and was forced to find a job as a brewery manager. By 1897 he was dead, leaving his two sons to support the rest of the family.

Poverty set Scott aside from his friends and was responsible for a secretive nature that was to be an integral part of his character.

In 1898 Scott lost his brother Archie to typhoid fever. The responsibility for keeping the family solvent now lay on his shoulders alone.

A year later he met Markham, learned of the forthcoming Antarctic expedition and applied for a place on it. He had, according to himself, 'no urge towards snow or ice' but he did want 'freedom to develop more widely'. Markham put forward the names of three men as possible leaders, Commander John de Robeck, Charles Royds and Scott. Scott and Royds were released by the Navy and, following what some members of the selection

The Discovery, *over wintering in McMurdo Sound. The classic Antarctic ship, purpose-built in Dundee, Scotland, at a cost of £34,050, for Scott's 1901-04* Discovery *expedition. Later used in the Arctic and for scientific research work. Now open to the public in Dundee.*

59

committee saw as Markham's high-handedness, Scott was appointed leader. Markham believed he had found the man to direct the expedition, a man who possessed 'the very same qualities that are needed in the stress of battle'. Only later was his suitability as a leader called into question.

Whatever unease Shackleton may have felt at encountering the expedition leader soon disappeared. He wanted to make the best of the opportunity Longstaff had procured for him, and he quickly settled into the offices of the expedition in Burlington Gardens in London.

Being on land also meant he could see Emily regularly. Now that he had a career, he felt that his chances of impressing her and her father were greatly enhanced.

Markham was struck by Shackleton's manner and ability and welcomed him as a regular guest at his home in Eccleston Square. Shackleton, on his part, avoided the infighting that went on between the Royal Geographical Society, the Navy, the Royal Society and the government, which had now come in with a grant of £45,000.

The vessel built to carry the expeditionary group was the *Discovery*, a 172-foot, 1620-ton, steel-plated, coal- and sail-powered ship. She had been launched in Dundee on 21 March and now, as the summer arrived, Shackleton was sent to her trials off the Scottish coast in the Firth of Tay.

Back in London, Shackleton realized that while the plans for the expedition might be advanced, much practical work had been left undone. Markham was impressed by his attention to detail. Nothing was too banal. He organized a collection of wigs and dresses – for the theatricals that were to be part of the long winter nights in Antarctica – and ensured there was a typewriter for the typing of an on-board newspaper.

In June *Discovery* arrived in London and the level of excitement in the expedition offices began to rise. Shackleton was appointed third mate and given responsibility for stowing the ship. When the final list of officers and crew of the *Discovery* was drawn up, Shackleton's biography appeared as follows, including a mistaken birth date:

'5. Third Lieutenant – ERNEST SHACKLETON, born 4 November 1874. He entered the Merchant Service in 1890, and served in sailing ships in the Pacific, afterwards in the *Castle* line. *Sub-Lieut.*, R.N.R. F.R.G.S. In charge of sea-water analysis. Ward room caterer. In charge of the holds, stores, and provisions, and arranges and serves out provisions. He also arranges the entertainments.'

As departure day drew nearer, Shackleton was sent for a short training-course in balloon-ing at Aldershot and on a detonation course on the Thames estuary. The detonation was for the practical purpose of learning how to free the ship from ice and the ballooning was to prepare him for aerial photography.

Shackleton was initiated as a Freemason on 9 July 1901 in the Navy Lodge No. 2612, London. On 30 May 1913 he was raised in the Guild of Freemen, Lodge No. 3535. He was a member of both lodges until his death. He probably viewed this as another step up in society and might well have argued that it was a harmless one, but it sits uneasily with the image of the laughing, carefree Irishman he promoted. The Freemasons were a secret society who portrayed themselves – when they admitted to membership at all – as a charitable and positive organization. Their exclusivity was at odds with the idea of a man like Shackleton, supposedly at one with the world.

About this time, Emily informed Shackleton that she was in love with another, unnamed young man. Rather than run from this news, he appears to have decided to spread his dreams before her and risk rejection in vying for her affection.

'I said it in the old days "Love me a little only a little",' he wrote. '... as I grow older I am saying "Love me altogether and only me" ... I have nothing to offer you: I am poor: I am not clever, it is wicked of me to want you to keep caring for me ... Why did you not tremble to my touch first of all the men in this world.'

Whether Shackleton moved Emily with his words, or whether she had already grown tired of the other love in her life, by the time *Discovery* sailed in July 1901 he was convinced that she would marry him.

He had asked that the family not come to see him off. Instead, three of his sisters – Helen, Kathleen and Gladys – were at the Albert Docks and he signalled his farewell to them using semaphore flags.

The crew of *Discovery* were leaving behind a country supportive of their endeavours, but not overly so. The British newspapers wrote positively of the expedition, the govern-ment had come up with some money, and most people wished the expedition well, but there was little of the flag-waving that might have been expected.

Shackleton – once safely on board – wrote to Emily's father, asking for her hand in marriage. The letter is a mixture of hope and ambition.

My dear Mr Dorman,

I must thank you very much for all your good wishes for the coming voyage. I would like to tell you in this letter that it is mainly for one reason that I am going is to get on so that when I come back or later when I have made money I might with your permission marry Emily if she still cares for me then as I feel she does now; it is needless to say that I care for her more than anyone else in the world but I fully see the difficulties in the way as regards my not having money but time will overcome that and you will not object if I have sufficient and keep her as you would wish. I can see well how you must look at my wanting always to be with Emmie knowing that my circumstances are not rosey and I can only thank you for your goodness in allowing me to see so much of her. If she cares for me later and you can see that I may honestly marry her I would be ever happy. I have of course spoken to her all these years but only lately has she I think really cared altogether for me. However she will talk to you ... for me my future is all to make but I intend making it quickly. I would have spoken to you myself before only Emily had not given me a full answer. Now I feel it is all right so am asking you not now but when I make money or position and money to marry her.

Yours sincerely,
Ernest H Shackleton.

It says much of his character that he was prepared to wait for word until such time as a reply caught up with him. It also suggests that he was less than optimistic and that a rejection on the page might be more bearable than one coming face to face.

After King Edward VII had come aboard and wished the crew well, *Discovery* set off. Shackleton quickly made friends with Hugh Robert Mill, brought along at the last minute to put some order on the ship's library between England and Madeira, where he would leave and return home. Mill also taught him how to determine the density and salinity of seawater. Years later he would note that Shackleton found this work 'rather irksome, and was long in grasping the importance of writing down one reading of an instrument before making the next'.

As the voyage progressed, it became apparent that *Discovery* was slow and not totally suited to the trip in hand. She leaked in several places, creating problems for Shackleton as he was responsible for the stowing of supplies. But there were greater problems with Scott who seemed unable to relate to his men and alienated many of the crew, particularly those used to the more relaxed ways of the Merchant Navy.

After *Discovery* left Madeira, Shackleton became a close friend of Edward Wilson, the junior surgeon. Wilson was a good listener and Shackleton a good talker, and the pair enjoyed each other's company. Shackleton thought Wilson needed looking after and bought him matting to lie on in the tropical heat.

'He has quite taken me in charge,' Wilson noted. For his part, Wilson curbed Shackleton's wilder excesses and kept him out of trouble. Often, the pair sat on deck, in the afternoon sun, reading poetry and talking. When it came to work, Shackleton regularly helped Wilson with his notation of birds.

While he kept himself busy with work, Emily was constantly in Shackleton's thoughts and her father's reaction to his request for her hand hung uncertainly over him. Eventually, the long-awaited letter arrived.

My dear Ernest,

I have received your letter of the 3rd. I quite appreciate all you say and was not the least surprised to read it. I sincerely and heartily wish you a safe voyage and a happy return some 2 or 3 years hence having accomplished the arduous task before you and that you will be able to tell us what the Antarctic really is. I can only say now that if & whenever the time comes when you are in the pecuniary position you long for & that if you & Emmy are still of the same mind my consent to your union will not be wanting – with all good wishes.

I am yours sincerely,
Chas Dorman.

Ironically, by the time the *Discovery* docked in New Zealand and Shackleton received the letter, Charles Dorman was dead.

New Zealand offered a chance for the scientific staff on the expedition to get away from the ship but, for Shackleton and his fellow sailors there was work to be done on board, stowing supplies and settling the pack of dogs Scott had agreed to take. Shackleton was also given responsibility for forty-five sheep donated by New Zealand farmers.

On 24 December 1901 the *Discovery* left Lyttelton on the final and most important leg of its journey south. Three days later, on Christmas Eve, New Zealand faded from sight.

The early days of the New Year saw *Discovery* sailing calmly through quiet waters, the weather settled, and then the crew saw their first icebergs. Louis Bernacchi, one of the scientists on the ship, described the men's reaction to their first sight of Antarctica: 'It was a scene of fantastic and unimagined beauty and we remained on deck till morning.'

For Shackleton and others who had never before had this experience, there was an intense feeling of exhilaration. This was a new seascape. First came the strange glow in the sky, the reflected light bouncing off ice and snow. Then the sight of the ice floes themselves, huge mountains of white that radiated greens and blues as they glided by. And, finally, the sound of the grinding of ice as berg pushed against berg. And then another sound, like waves on shingle, of water breaking on pack ice. Everything was new, everything was fresh and sharp and promising. There was a sense that a step had been taken and nothing could ever be the same about life again, as the men stayed on deck to see and hear and wonder at the new continent.

Discovery made good time, even through the pack ice facing her at the Ross Sea. Apart from the dogs taken to draw sledges, the expedition had also been equipped with skis, though no one knew how to use them properly. Scott devised a system of learning as they went. Men would leave the ship and step onto the ice floes to practice skiing, something Shackleton never mastered.

On 9 January Shackleton was among the first party to land at Cape Adare. An ambition had been achieved. The party left a note for any relief ship that might follow, deposited, as arranged, in a hut built by Borchgrevink's party two years earlier.

From this point, *Discovery* sailed along the coast, through the muttering icebergs, reaching

Wood Bay – Markham's suggested landing-point, only to find it frozen over. Two days later Shackleton led a geological party onto the ice and, to their great excitement, discovered moss, the farthest south any moss had then been found.

At the end of the month *Discovery* came within sight of Mount Erebus and continued east along the Great Ice Barrier. By the second last day of January they were in territory unseen by previous explorers. They discovered and named King Edward VII Land for the new king.

It was, as Shackleton noted, a 'unique sort of feeling'. Hopes were high.

On 31 January *Discovery* sailed into a snare of icebergs. By evening the ship was completely trapped. It was to be almost twelve hours before she broke free.

Scott's handling of the crisis impressed few of the men. It seemed to many that he had panicked in the face of danger.

Immediately after their escape, Scott called the crew together and informed them they would winter in the Antarctic. Shackleton was overjoyed. He had feared that *Discovery* might be turned north and the expedition curtailed.

Before finding a winter home, Scott took *Discovery* into an inlet in the Barrier and arranged for ballooning trips. Scott, despite the fact that he had no training, was first to ascend in the balloon, nicknamed *Eva*, followed by Shackleton who, to his delight went higher than the Captain, reaching an altitude of 800 feet and taking the first aerial photographs on the continent, achievements that were medal ribbons to his mind.

Moving on, Scott brought the ship close to Mount Erebus on Ross Island and decided this was where they would winter. The plan was for the ship to be frozen in, making her stable until spring. This took longer than anticipated. Storms constantly broke the surrounding ice and it was some time before *Discovery* was finally part of the continent to which she had delivered her crew.

Shackleton remained busy, overseeing stores, continuing his water-testing duties, arranging for the slaughter of the sheep which were then hung up to be frozen. The state of the stores concerned him: 'I am rather worried about some of our food for instead of being in good condition for the winter the vegetables got from Germany have turned out to be in a wretched state … We will have the mutton … every Sunday. And seal for all hands every second day. So there ought to be no chance of scurvy.'

The men settled quickly into the routine of being at sea but being on land. *Discovery* became their home but they could spend much of their time on the frozen continent. Scientific experiments continued and the men continued their skiing practice – in Shackleton's case without any noticeable improvement. He was also charged with training the dogs, at which he was equally unsuccessful.

In mid-February he was chosen, with Wilson and the Dublin-born geologist Ferrar, to make the first exploratory steps towards the Pole, in a trial expedition to White Island.

Unable to control the dogs or to ski properly, the three men set off walking, flags flying from their sledge. While the dogs stayed behind the three men trudged through the snow, expending energy on pulling a sledge which might have been pulled by the animals, walking when they might have skied much more easily.

Having a flag with the family motto, *Fortitudine Vincimus*, was more important, at least in Markham's mind when he planned the expedition, than having dogs which obeyed their masters, or sleeping-bags that kept out the cold. Shackleton might set off in the spirit which Markham had fostered, but he would quickly learn that practicality was more important to survival than the symbolic needs of a distant overseer.

Shackleton and his comrades learned that distances can be deceiving in a polar desert. Heading south-east and into the face of snowstorms, they soon suffered from frostbite.

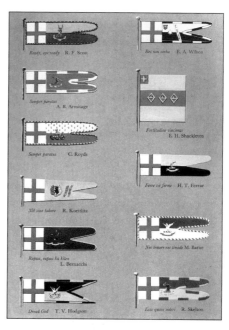

Left: Sledging flags for the Discovery expedition. Despite the design being clearly specified by Markham, the square Shackleton flag stood out defiant and conspicuous in its difference.

Opposite: Balloon trip; on 4 February 1902, on the ice edge at the Bay of Whales, nineteen cylinders of gas were used to inflate the balloon Eva. Scott went up first followed by Shackleton to a height of 800 feet to take the first Antarctic aerial photographs. Ted Wilson thoroughly disapproved, writing in his diary: ' ... if some of these experts don't come to grief over it out here it will only be because God has pity on the foolish.'

Twelve-hour marches with little or no food, time spent in a tent with no sleeping-bags and insufficient rations, were salutary lessons in the realities of exploration.

And there were other lessons. Socks soaked in sweat froze to boots. Tiredness meant that risks were taken. The three climbed, without being roped, to the top of the mountain they had set out to climb. There were falls into crevasses that might, but for luck, have ended in death or serious injury. Had not the dangers been so real, the whole thing might have been farcical.

The return journey took just eleven hours and Shackleton, when he reached *Discovery*, could not be kept from telling and re-telling every detail of the march. It wasn't long before his shipmates grew tired of his tales.

If that expedition had been blessed, another, which set out on 4 March, did not end so fortunately. A group led by Lieutenant Michael Barne became lost in fog and one of its members, a sailor named George Vince, slid to his death over a cliff.

'The South Polar
Times' title-page.

Deep winter was now drawing in as the men settled into their quarters. A hut was erected on the ice giving the place its name, Hut Point. The intention had been that, should the ship move back north for the winter, some men might live in this but, with the crew settled on board ship, the hut was used as a store.

Shackleton spent many of the dark days editing five issues of the ship's paper, *The South Polar Times*. The first issue was 'published' on 23 April 1902. For others, only work and occasional recreation, mainly draughts and shove-ha'penny, broke the long dreary winter. The scientists among the crew continued their studies, but the pressure of living together led to regular squabbles. Wilson, who had recovered from tuberculosis, insisted on taking a daily walk and Shackleton, generally, accompanied him, thus escaping much on-ship bickering.

Royal Navy men and Merchant Navy men were not particularly comfortable with each other and Scott's strong disciplinarian streak continued to irk his more easy-going colleagues. Shackleton, on the other hand, could be found in conversation in all quarters, with all of the crew.

In spite of the conflict and class division, four months of darkness passed without major incident. Shackleton's main concern was whether he would be chosen for the party heading south when the weather improved. He recognized that some of his colleagues might see this as arrogance, but he resolved to be in the group.

Initially, Scott had decided that two men would make the journey, but Wilson had persuaded him, sensibly, that a third was necessary. Should one become ill or be injured, a third person would give the party a greater chance of getting back safely. Finally, on 13 June, Scott informed the crew that the southern party would consist of three men – Wilson, Shackleton and himself.

It is not surprising that the final preparations for the push south were as ineffectual as most of what had gone before. Whether Scott believed luck and providence would take the party safely to the Pole and back is unclear. Wilson seems to have been the only one fully alive to the dangers that lay ahead.

Scientific experiments continued around *Discovery* in the days before their departure, yet the more important preparations were never made. None of the three men had mastered the dogs, so Shackleton was delegated to work with them but had neither the patience nor understanding to win their respect. Indeed, he spent much of his time perfecting a go-cart, a sledge on wheels driven by a sail, which proved impractical in the soft snow.

A trial run with the dogs earlier in September proved useless. The animals refused to pull the sledges and, to all intents and purposes, went their own way. Even then, no one faced the fact that the dog training was a necessity.

On another run, men, sledges and dogs constantly fell into crevasses. Again, the chaos was ignored and Scott returned to the ship ahead of the training party. The men were unimpressed by the notion of a captain abandoning men in trouble.

Scott, meanwhile, had other problems to deal with. Albert Armitage, his second-in-command, was bitterly disappointed at not being included in the expeditionary party. He'd accompanied Scott on the understanding that he would be one of the south party and now felt betrayed. The atmosphere between the captain and his deputy was tense.

To add to their troubles, Shackleton, among others, appeared to be suffering from a mild dose of scurvy. Scurvy had long been the curse of sailors. We now know it owes its origins to a lack of Vitamin C but, at the beginning of the twentieth century vitamins were unknown and the treatment for the disease altogether more uncertain. What were clear were the symptoms – swollen gums, the passing of blood and general debility. The absence of fresh vegetables and a diet limited to salted meat were among the main causes of scurvy and, while most sailors overcame the disease, they knew it could be a killer. Like so many other issues, this problem was not faced and it was presumed that everything would turn out all right.

Scott was so secretive about the expedition south that Wilson and Shackleton were informed of the date of leaving a week before departure. This led to a rush to finalize arrangements. Stores and sledges were prepared, and a last effort was made to get the dogs under

On 2 November 1902, left to right, Shackleton, Scott and Wilson before they set out on their southern journey.

control, but Shackleton abandoned this to complete the latest issue of the *South Polar Times* and to try to learn to use a theodolite, a skill Scott had forgotten to tell him he needed. Clothing was sorted and letters written to loved ones in the knowledge that the journey about to be undertaken could be the last the three men would make. With their lack of experience and the fact that they were facing the unknown, the shadow of possible death hung over them. Only their ignorance and bravado threw light on their situation.

The day before he left, Shackleton wrote a letter to Emily, intended to be read only in the event of his death.

Beloved I hope you may never have to read this, but darling loved one it comes to you. You will know that your lover left this world with all his hearts yours his last thoughts will be of you my own dear Heart, Child I am carrying your little photo with me South and so your face will be with me to the last: Child remember that I am your true lover, that you and you alone have been in my heart and mind all this time. Beloved do not grieve for me for it has been a man's work and I have helped my little mite towards the increase of knowledge: Child there are millions in this world who have not had this chance. You will always remember me my own true woman and little girl. I cannot say more my heart is so full of love and longing for you and words will not avail, they are so poor in such a case. Child we may meet again in another world, and I believe in God, that is all I can say, but it covers all things: I have tried to do my best as a man the rest I leave to Him. And if there is another world and he wills it we shall find each other. I feel that there must be. This cannot be the end, but I do not know, I only believe from something in me. Yet again I cannot tell if there is, I hope. Child you will comfort those at home. Know once more that I love you truly and purely and as dearly as a woman can be loved. And now my true love goodnight. Your lover, ERNEST.

Child take the little things I send you and take what you want from home. God bless you and keep you safe forever.

The following morning, Sunday 2 November, Scott, Wilson and Shackleton posed for photographs before setting off. The triangular pennants designed by Markham fluttered from the sledges – except in Shackleton's case. He had designed his own rectangular flag, which showed up much better in photographs.

The plan – according to Scott – was to make a thirteen-week journey. For the first week a back-up party would accompany them. After that the three would go on alone.

Initially there were fewer problems than might have been expected. Amazingly, the dogs who had refused to work earlier were now reasonably well behaved. Progress in the first week went well, men and animals were acclimatizing themselves to the snow. The only real problem seemed to be a cough which Shackleton had suddenly developed.

The departure of the back-up party coincided with a blizzard, leaving the men temporarily snowed in. When the weather cleared and the three pushed on, the dogs became impossible to handle, hardly surprising on starvation rations. To make matters worse, they were harnessed together and pulling all the sledges, in a train, a weight of one and a half tons. Only by pulling with them – a cardinal error in controlling a dog team – could the three

*Ted and Oriana
Wilson. The Wilson
family were friends
of Dr William
Shackleton in Bushey,
Hertfordshire. When
Dr Shackleton met
Captain Scott on a
visit to the Terra Nova,
Wilson smoothed this
awkward encounter.
(Peggy Larken, who
met Shackleton
aged five in 1913)*

make any progress. Very quickly, given the weight of the sledges, it became necessary to relay the loads. This meant taking some of the sledges to a point and then returning for the remainder, so that every mile forward involved three miles of walking. The men's progress dropped at times to as little as two and a half miles a day.

To add to difficulties none of the three had properly mastered skiing and their skis sat, virtually useless, on the sledges. They made efforts to learn as they went but, like so much about the expedition, it was all too little and too late.

Nor were these practicalities the most serious of their troubles. Wilson noticed that Scott and Shackleton shared a deep distrust of each other. Shackleton was unimpressed by his leader, Scott was threatened by his companion. The irritation finally sparked one night while Shackleton was preparing a meal in their tent. He accidentally overturned the stove, spilling the food and burning a hole in the groundsheet. Scott was apoplectic and the emotions which both had kept under control were immediately out in the open, angry voices echoing across the frozen emptiness. Wilson eventually placated the pair and an uneasy truce was called.

When Shackleton and Scott weren't squabbling or pulling the sledges across the wilderness or sleeping, they read aloud, in turns, in their tent. Their moods ebbed and flowed and only Wilson's patience kept the peace. At one point Scott, faced with physical and emotional fatigue, suggested turning back. Wilson dissuaded him.

As they moved on, Wilson developed other concerns about his companions. He was worried about their health. Shackleton had been coughing continuously through the first month of the expedition, keeping the others awake at night. By December he seemed to be losing energy and showed signs of scurvy. Scott, while not as ill, was also showing signs of the disease. Still living on minimum rations, men and dogs were already severely malnourished. In a month they had covered just over a hundred miles. It was a time for hard decisions.

Scott concluded that they must leave as much of the food as possible at a depot, marked with a flag so that they could collect the supplies on the return.

Given that the dogs were still proving of little use in pulling the sledges, he further decided that they would kill them as supplies grew lighter. The dead dogs would then be used as food for the surviving animals.

By mid December loneliness, boredom and fatigue followed them like Magi across the ice fields. Days were spent hauling sledges, digging themselves out of crevasses and constantly shouting at the dogs to keep them moving. Nights were spent in cooking, reading and sleeping.

They celebrated Christmas in a wilderness that was unending. Shackleton noted in his diary that it was a day of blinding sunshine. He produced a Christmas pudding which he had been carrying in a spare sock, and it was served hot with cocoa.

His diary for the day gave priority to food, then marching, then health and then thoughts of home.

'The warmest day we have yet had. Yet we made our best march doing over ten miles. Though we did all the pulling practically for the dogs were done up with the heat. Got up at 8.30 a.m. and B was cook. Breakfast a panikin of seal's liver and bacon with biscuit topped up with a spoonful of blackberry jam each. Then I set camera and took 2 photos of party connecting piece of rope to camera lever. Then did 4 hours march. lunch I cook. Bov Choc Plasmon biscuit 2 spoons jam each. very good. hot lunch. then two and a half hour march camp for night. I cook and in 35 min. cooked 6 pan of N.A.O.R. & biscuit for Hoosh. Boiled plum pudding and made cocoa. then we had jam to finish up so were really full for once. It is settled for our furthest South to be on 28th then we go into the land. Medical examtn. Shews Capt & I to be inclined to scurvy so will not be going on further as we are far from our base. We hope to cross 82 degrees S in 2 days anyhow. What a Christmas baking hot. It must have been so different at home.'

73

The men also took the opportunity to name a nearby peak Christmas Mountain, in honour of the day.

Wilson was now hoping that Scott might decide to turn for home. Scott, on the other hand, felt that the very least they must do was to reach 82 degrees south. On 28 December they achieved this goal with Shackleton, out in front, pulling the sledges in the same committed, almost manic way he had been doing for weeks. His head was constantly bent low, straining in the traces, his boots feathered in snow and ice. It was a source of pride and accomplishment to him that he was the first to cross the line, another small victory over Scott. And, yet, his overpowering emotion was one of disappointment.

All along, Shackleton had seen this expedition as an attack on the Pole. The scientific experiments and the farthest south achievements were not the object of the exercise. Neither glorious failure nor the humiliation of a badly organized fiasco held any appeal. He had wanted, more than anything, to be part of the campaign. The personal friction between Scott and himself was an element of the price to be paid for that privilege, but the fact that they might not make a serious attempt on the Pole had never been a real consideration. Now, as the pace slowed and the reality of the party's desperation set in, he knew that this was a journey that would end in defeat.

Wilson's worry, meanwhile, deepened. All three men were showing definite and recurring signs of scurvy. Wilson was anxious to turn for *Discovery*. The notion of defeat, however, was also weighing on Scott. He had come south with the hopes of Britain on his shoulders. The achievement of the South Pole was no longer a real possibility but that of getting farthest south was, and he determined to continue until that goal had been achieved.

On 30 December this objective was attained when the three reached 82 degrees 15' – they had become the first men to travel this far south. That afternoon, leaving Shackleton to guard the camp – against what no one knew – Scott and Wilson pushed on to 82 degrees 17'. Whether Scott's decision to leave Shackleton behind was one of mercy – allowing him to rest – or one of jealousy – not wanting him to be part of the farthest south achievement – remains uncertain. What Scott and Wilson did do was to name an inlet at the new farthest south point after Shackleton. But all of this, naming new points, travelling two hundred miles farther than any previous explorers, prospecting new coastline, was hollow stuff. The South Pole remained as elusive as it had done when they left England.

The three turned north as the New Year broke, with just over two weeks to reach the nearest food depot, still a hundred miles away. The remaining dogs were becoming less and less useful, and the burden of responsibility and disappointment was weighing more heavily on Scott.

Now only five of the nineteen dogs remained and the men were doing all of the work in pulling the sledges. If science was important to the captain, getting back safely to *Discovery* was uppermost in Wilson and Shackleton's minds.

As they trudged northward, Wilson noticed that Shackleton was constantly short of breath and they were forced to allow for extra stops. When he was capable of walking, his pace had slowed considerably. Again, Scott was forced to make an important decision. Rations, which were rapidly running out, would be cut again, otherwise the reduced pace might see them short of the food depot without supplies.

The depot flag, when they saw it, was glimpsed by accident. Nevertheless, the fresh supplies allowed them their first decent meals in many days. Even this improvement in diet didn't seem to help Shackleton. His cough had worsened and he was hacking blood. Scott forbade him to pull the sledges. The man who had previously been the mainstay of this work was forced to walk behind, still wearing his harness, while his companions laboured through the snow. On 18 January he collapsed with chest pains.

While the collapse itself was unexpected, Shackleton's health had been a constant source of worry to Wilson. He had not undergone any serious medical examination before joining the expedition and, since their arrival in Antarctica he'd had a series of illnesses. During the early training expeditions, he had suffered from stiffness and then a worrying cough, that had reappeared as soon as the push south had begun. It was clear that Shackleton was not a well man.

Scott and Wilson knew they couldn't carry Shackleton. There were only two dogs remaining, neither of them properly trained. There was nothing for it but to continue walking.

Again, Shackleton tried to ski but was hardly likely, in bad health, to master a skill he'd failed to learn in good health. When he used them, they were little more than large shoes.

The men came up with another device, which did help. They made a sail and mounted it on the front sledge, the wind catching it and moving the sledge, and the following sledges, along. But the sledges were now moving too fast for the men to keep up. Shackleton was put on the end sledge and given the job of using the brake to slow the train's progress. In his condition, however, he was too weak to do even this and, instead, Scott and Wilson travelled alongside the sledges, keeping them in check, while Shackleton walked behind, alone and at his own pace.

Shackleton's ill-health became a flashpoint between Scott and Wilson. Scott regularly referred to Shackleton as a 'lame duck' and an 'invalid'. This greatly angered Wilson who, when Shackleton was out of hearing, berated Scott for his insensitivity.

As January ebbed Wilson became concerned that Shackleton was more seriously ill than he had thought. On the night of 29 January a feverish Shackleton overheard Wilson tell Scott that he didn't expect him to survive until morning. Whether the thought of death galvanized him towards recovery or whether the worst of the sickness had passed, Shackleton was able to leave the tent the following day with the help of the other two. For a time he

On 3 February 1903, left to right, Shackleton, Scott and Wilson – after the southern journey.

laboured along on his skis but after a couple of hours even this proved impossible and he was put sitting in one of the sledges. By mid-afternoon he felt well enough to get back on the skis. Scott found it difficult to contain his annoyance. Energy that might have gone into sketching and notation was being used in looking after Shackleton.

Fortunately, on 3 February, six miles from *Discovery*, the three were met by Louis Bernacchi and Reginald Skelton, who took over the pulling of the sledges. At the ship there was flag-waving, cheering, songs and the warmest of welcomes. For Shackleton there must have been echoes of the welcomes his sisters had organized for him in London. This time, however, he had neither the strength nor inclination to object or enjoy. While the music and drinking went on into the small hours, he had a bath and retired to his bunk.

As Scott, Wilson and Shackleton were making their way back to the ship, the relief vessel *Morning* arrived. With *Discovery* due to spend another year in Antarctica, *Morning* had been sent to renew supplies and take home those who were not staying for another winter.

Scott asked Dr Reginald Koettlitz, senior surgeon on *Discovery*, to examine Shackleton. Koettlitz informed Scott that Shackleton had almost completely recovered from the effects of the trip. Scott wasn't convinced. He believed Shackleton had hidden the signs of illness before setting out on the expedition and that he was not sufficiently well to warrant his continuing on the *Discovery*. He informed Shackleton that he was being invalided home.

On the last evening of February 1903 Shackleton's companions sent him on his way with a dinner. The following day, carrying his luggage, he walked across the ice to the waiting relief ship. That night he wrote in his diary:

'*A beautiful day, but a sad one indeed for me: for today I left my home and all those who are chums as much as I ever will have any one for chums. I cannot write about it but it touched me more than I can say when the men came up on deck and gave me 3 parting cheers. Ah. It was hard to have to leave before the work is over and especially to leave those who will have to stay down here in the cold dark days for there seems to my mind but little chance of the old ship going out: Michael Ferrar came along with me and I went slowly for I had only been twice out of the ship since I came back from the southern journey. We had a very pleasant evening on "Morning" and with songs and one thing and another it was 3 am before we went to bed.*'

As *Morning* set sail, snow was falling and then the sun came out and Shackleton stood on deck, watching his hopes and aspirations fade behind him. When, finally, he went to his cabin he tried to read but, as he wrote, his thoughts went back: 'I took the photos of all our chaps before starting so that our people at home may have the last glimpse of their faces should we not succeed in getting out or they not succeed, I mean.'

Among the men to whom he refers were Wilson, his good friend, and Scott, the man who would become his arch-rival, though this was a rivalry that lay ahead. For now there was disappointment but also the novelty of being the first to return with an account of the adventure.

In Christchurch Shackleton awaited a passage home, and organized stores for *Morning*, which was to return as a relief ship to *Discovery*. Finally, on 9 May, he left New Zealand and sailed via San Francisco and New York on the *Orotava*. As he wrote in his diary, he was 'really going home'. He also made some caustic notes on his travelling companions:

'*There are a fair number of passengers on board but they seem to be a pretty dull and uninteresting crowd. There is one individual or rather two that I have made up my mind not to sit near for coming up in the train they did nothing but growl and talk about their aches "More!! More!! About yourself!!!" You know the type and very fussy reddish grey beard man and a fat and unwieldy woman they instinctively repel one even before you say a word to them and I do not intend to ...*'

On the homeward journey he had plenty of time to sieve through the memories and experiences of Antarctica. By the time he reached London, on 15 June, he resolved to return to the southern continent, but this time as leader of his own expedition.

5

Shackleton at Home

1903–1907

Shackleton's return to England was brightened by the prospect of seeing Emily again. Their meeting, on 12 June, was emotional. She had received letters from Shackleton, telling her he was recovered from the ordeal of 'breaking down', but she can hardly have expected to meet a man who was rested, sun-tanned and, apparently, in fine physical health.

Shackleton was disappointed not to have completed the Antarctic expedition. But he was heartened by the warm welcome from Sir Clements Markham, who wrote: 'I admire your pluck and the way you held out, and everyone speaks with admiration of it and of their sincere friendship for you.' Better still, Shackleton embarked on a round of lectures aimed at finding extra funds for the expedition. Most importantly, being the first man back, he enjoyed the kudos of telling the story of the expedition to date.

But Markham had other reasons for wanting Shackleton on side. There was much unhappiness in British geographical circles about *Discovery* spending an unanticipated second winter in the Antarctic. Markham, the target of criticism for what was now a financial disaster, met Shackleton the morning after his arrival in London, who agreed to do what he could to ease the situation.

In practical ways he was also able to help his colleagues still in Antarctica. Firstly, he advised on the equipping of the *Terra Nova*, a relief ship being fitted out by the Royal Navy to assist the *Discovery*. Secondly, he was asked to help fit out the *Uruguay*, a relief ship organized by the Argentinian government to rescue Nordenskjold's Swedish expedition, after the loss of their ship the *Antartctic* in the Weddell Sea area. He was also invited to serve as an officer on the *Terra Nova*, an invitation he declined.

In June Shackleton wrote articles for supplements in the *Illustrated London News*, giving his account of the first year of the expedition. In the articles, he referred to the fact that he 'broke down owing to overstrain ... I was, however, able to march the nine or ten miles a day that the party made ... Captain Scott and Dr Wilson could not have done more for me than they did. They were bearing the brunt of the work.'

The following month, he applied for a position as supplementary Lieutenant in the Royal Navy. The main reason for his application was to give him a steady income which would allow him to marry Emily. While she had an allowance of £700 a year for life, from her father's will, Shackleton was adamant that he must provide for her himself.

Markham, on behalf of the Royal Geographical Society and its President, William Huggins, recommended Shackleton for the position but the naval list was closed and the application was unsuccessful – which left Shackleton with the problem of no job, no income and no immediate prospects of marriage.

Meanwhile, fundraising and publicity for the *Discovery* expedition continued. In September he gave a slide lecture at a British Association meeting in Southport, earning praise for intriguing the audience without stealing Scott's thunder before his return.

Autumn saw Shackleton take a job as a sub-editor on the *Royal Magazine*. His experience on various naval and expeditionary magazines and papers had given him the idea that journalism might be for him. He was hardly qualified, however, and ended up enquiring of the editor how to correct a proof. Untroubled by his ignorance, he simply got on with entertaining office colleagues with tales of his Antarctic adventure.

In November he was invited to lecture to the Royal Scottish Geographical Society, speaking in Edinburgh on the 11th, Glasgow on the 14th and Aberdeen on the 15th. While there, he discovered that the position of secretary to the RSGS was about to become vacant and that it carried a salary. His pending marriage to Emily – fixed for the following spring – made the position all the more attractive. On 4 December he applied for the job with the backing of several notable members of the Geographical Society in England and the commendations of Markham and Huggins.

Huggins praised Shackleton's 'enthusiasm for geographical exploration'; Markham wrote that he believed he would be 'invaluable in the work of increasing the number of members' and Hugh Robert Mill described him as a man 'keen in taking up a new train of thought or line of work, and persevering'.

J. Scott Keltie, Secretary of the Royal Geographical Society wrote that he thought 'the Society would be fortunate in obtaining [Shackleton's] services'.

Shackleton felt confident about his chances but reckoned without the entrenched ideas of the Society committee, who noted two grammatical errors in his letter of application. He also heard that there were 'many men with splendid qualifications against me'.

14 South Learmonth Gardens, Edinburgh, Scotland. Shackleton and Emily lived here from April 1904 to 1907, paying £125 a year rent whilst he worked for the Scottish RGS. Now part of Channings Hotel.

Mill was quick to reassure him, writing: '... if you are not appointed Secretary of the R.S.G.S. I will resign my membership of that Society and take no more interest in its affairs to the end of time ... I know you are the best man for the job and a great deal too good for it too.'

On Christmas Eve a meeting of the Society failed to reach a decision, with members split between Shackleton and a candidate called Johnstone. Fortunately for Shackleton, one of his advocates, J.G. Bartholomew, had the vote postponed.

On 11 January, with Shackleton's supporters returned from their Christmas holidays, he was unanimously elected.

With a job that offered a regular income, Shackleton and Emily could now concentrate on their wedding. It would be necessary for Emily to move to Scotland and Shackleton, who intially stayed with the Beardmore family, set about finding a house. This he did, at 14

Emily Mary Shackleton, née Dorman (1868-1936), daughter of Charles Dorman and Jane née Swinford. Emily married Shackleton at Christ Church Westminster on 9 April 1904.

South Learmonth Gardens, on the edge of Edinburgh. The house was small but sufficient and approved by Emily.

Shackleton believed the honeymoon should be postponed until he was well settled in his new job. He wrote to Emily, using his most persuasive tone: 'I think we would be happier in our own little home … there is sunshine here too and there will be sunshine in our lives … It would be such a rush … and here we would be so quiet and I could take you away for a month in Sept or August or whenever you like.'

Emily, not for the last time, conceded to his wish.

Shackleton threw himself into the new job, reorganizing the office, setting up a series of lectures and delivering one himself on the subject of the farthest south. His warm attitude and his willingness to, mostly, humour those whom he felt were talking 'drivel' saw membership of the Society grow from 1430 to 1832, while the attendance at lectures leapt from just over two hundred to well over sixteen hundred. Most importantly, the Society's bank balance increased from £50 to almost £350.

On 9 April 1904 Shackleton and Emily were married at Christ Church, Westminister. Cyril Longhurst was his best man. The wedding breakfast was eaten in Sir Clements Markham's home in Eccleston Square. Markham had been invited to the wedding but was too ill to attend so breakfasting with him was, in Shackleton's eyes, a sign of friendship and loyalty. Immediately afterwards, the newly weds returned to Edinburgh and work with renewed energy. Without doubt Shackleton was happy with his new bride. She was the beautiful older woman he had been chasing for years. Emily, for her part, made every effort to immerse herself in the Edinburgh social circle.

A letter, sent to Emily with roses on her birthday, 15 May, is full of love and passion from the absent Shackleton who was away on business:

My darling Sweeteyes and wife.

Just a bunch of roses from your husband and lover forever and ever. I can see you darling reading this in bed today and am longing to be beside you in my own place. I am coming back quickly to you dear heart so do not be sad. I will be wanting you sorely today dearest. I hope the roses will be sweet.

The lovingliest birthday wishes to my darling from her husband.

Shackleton thrived in this new milieu, making himself a sought-after guest, renowned for his stories, wit and charm. He and Emily entertained regularly and quickly made many new friends, among them the statesman, Lord Rosebery, the scientist, Professor Crum Brown, and the captain of industry, William Beardmore.

Shackleton frequently travelled to London on Society business and it was there, in the summer of 1904, that he read the letters, from *Discovery*, by then in New Zealand, announcing that Scott and his colleagues would soon be back in England. Shackleton would have to make way, in the public imagination, for his Captain.

In the meantime, he and Emily took their postponed honeymoon in Dornoch, where they had a golfing holiday.

On 16 September he was back in London for lunch on the deck of the *Discovery*, which had berthed at the East India Dock. In early November he attended a formal dinner of welcome at the Savage Club and received the Polar Medal, the king's award for polar exploration, and a silver medal from the Royal Geographical Society. Scott received a gold medal.

Shackleton and Emily both enjoyed golf, which they played in Dornoch during a delayed honeymoon in summer 1904. Emily was the better player. (Courtesy Rhod McEwan)

Shackleton arranged for Scott to deliver lectures to RSGS members in Edinburgh, Dundee and Glasgow, and told him that he had given up the notion of another expedition. 'There seems to be no money about and besides I am settled down now and have to make money it would only break up my life, if I could stand it which Wilson thinks I could not.'

The return of Scott and his promotion to the rank of naval captain, the public interest in him and his achievements, all cast a deep gloom over Shackleton and it was obvious that he was finding life in Scott's shadow trying.

On 12 November Scott was guest of honour at the Scottish Society banquet and Markham travelled north for the occasion. During the visit he warned Emily that Shackleton was 'doing much more than the work of one man'.

Shackleton, however, didn't consider himself overburdened. On a visit to London in November he called to the Liberal Unionist Council and met Sir John Boraston, the chief Liberal Unionist agent, who suggested he might consider standing as a candidate in Dundee.

The Liberal Unionists were a breakaway group, having split from the Liberal Party in 1886, when the latter espoused Home Rule for Ireland. The dissenters, led by Joseph Chamberlain, established the new party and allied themselves with the Conservative Party.

It was ironic that they should be pursuing an Irishman as their candidate for Dundee, and even more so that the young boy with the strong Irish accent should now be a man willing to stand against Home Rule for his own country.

There are two aspects to this, neither of which reflects well on Shackleton. On the one hand, he may have felt that Ireland did not merit self-rule. If so, he showed little faith in his fellow countrymen – nor, by extension, in the people of Scotland. If, on the other hand, the candidacy was simply a step up a personal social ladder, it was an unconsidered one, dismissing the genuine aspirations of a people for personal gain. As with his decision to become a Freemason, there was no question which side of his family history was the more influential.

The Liberals had a reasonably safe seat in Dundee but the Liberal Unionists persuaded Shackleton that he had a fighting chance of taking it for them and this was enough to win his agreement. The Dundee Liberal Unionist committee, in its haste to parade the new boy, announced his candidacy before he had been approved by the general committee of the party and before he had time to tell his employers at the RSGS. Mundane as his work had become, he hadn't been prepared to step down as Secretary without alternative employment in sight. Now, it appeared, his new-found friends in the Liberal Unionist Party had fouled him up on two fronts.

Hugh Robert Mill was highly critical of Shackleton, on political and personal grounds, and Shackleton found himself defending his decision.

'I am perfectly honest,' he wrote to Mill, 'and it is not from any idea of newspaper publicity I became connected with politics, but as the result of careful thought on my part and a conviction that what I uphold is right.'

His claims to probity don't quite ring true. Shackleton wasn't particularly political and his knowledge of national and international affairs was no deeper than average. Protest as he might, his candidacy lacked conviction.

In early January 1905 he offered his resignation as Secretary of the RSGS. Two months later the Society, while 'deeply regretting' his candidacy for parliament, postponed its acceptance of his resignation. Shackleton, however, insisted that he was leaving. July was agreed as a parting date.

This left Shackleton with the recurring problem of finding a job. He talked to William Beardmore, a businessman with a shipbuilding firm on the Clyde, who promised to find him work. The birth of the Shackletons' first child, Raymond, on 2 February, came as a reminder that a career and a steady income were part and parcel of being a family man.

In April Shackleton travelled to Glasgow and had further discussions with Beardmore. He wrote, optimistic as ever, to Emily telling her there were 'four separate things that I can go into ... He [Beardmore] tells me that I can only begin at £300 but that the beginning is nothing if I do what he wishes and show I can work ... He is the sort of man who would raise me another £300 if he thinks I am doing well.'

Apart from shipbuilding, Beardmore had just bought out the Arrol-Johnston Motor Works and thought Shackleton would be useful in this company. Beardmore's wife Elspeth, whose interest in Shackleton was as much personal as professional, believed he could become an assistant to her husband. As was so often the case in Shackleton's career, nothing specific was decided beyond the promise of a job, should Shackleton fail to be elected.

Shackleton made other plans for garnering money. One was the opening of a shop and office to promote Tabard cigarettes. Several of his friends invested in the project, which was moderately successful but never likely to make his fortune.

That summer Shackleton, in company with Dr Charles Sarolea, the fiancé of Emily's sister Julia, visited the continent. The pair had hit on the idea of establishing an international news agency. Shackleton sank £500 into the venture and there was talk of introductions to royal circles in Belgium. The news agency was to be called Potentia. It may have been optimistically named but it proved even less successful than the cigarette company and, despite much talk, never got off the ground.

As the summer ended Shackleton's mind turned more and more to the notion of raising funds for another Antarctic expedition. This had been in his head since his return from the *Discovery* trip but now, with his boredom threshold falling, he became more convinced that it was something he must do. Scott's high profile in the public mind was a reminder of his own apparent failure. Most tellingly, in a lecture given by Scott in November – and widely reported in the newspapers – he had mentioned that he and Wilson had had to 'draw the sledge with their comrade who had become ill'. He felt humiliated at the thought of people knowing he had been unable to walk all the way, and Scott's reference to the fact angered him greatly. This, combined with Scott's less than flattering account of Shackleton's break-down in his newly published *The Voyage of the 'Discovery'* seem to have been the spark that rekindled his commitment to going south again and proving he was every bit the man Scott was.

What angered Shackleton most was Scott's failure to mention his steering the sledge while riding on it. Furthermore, in describing the condition of each of the three after their return to *Discovery* Scott claimed that he was by far the fittest, and that Shackleton 'would creep into his cabin and … rest until the exertion had worn off'.

That so much rested on so little says much about the competition between the pair. Scott had his doubts about Shackleton and felt the merchant seaman didn't respect him as he might have done. Shackleton was more convinced than ever that the Royal Navy man was jealous and would do him down at every opportunity.

The calling of an election in December turned Shackleton's attention temporarily to the im-minent campaign. As with all things bright and new, he immersed himself in the business of politics, addressing up to six meetings each day and mingling freely with the electorate. He promoted himself as a working man who had earned his living with his hands, and he throve on the rough and tumble of the hustings. Such was the warmth of the welcome he received in some parts of Dundee that he believed himself to have 'a good chance' of being elected. He also argued that, in standing against Home Rule for Ireland, he was a 'true patriot' who believed in King and Empire, an unwelcome line of reasoning in some parts of the city where the bulk of the population comprised Irish emigrants.

In working-class areas he played the anti-German card, blaming Britain's industrial troubles on German government subsidies for their manufacturers. In other company he pushed the idea of a stronger British empire through reinforced links between Britain and Ireland. When the election was held on 16 January 1906, Shackleton finished fourth of five in the poll. He may have got the cheers but the votes were another matter and the seats went to a Liberal and a Labour Party candidate. Times were changing and the Labour movement was on the rise.

No sooner was the election over, however, than Shackleton was in London involved in another money-making venture to ship Russian troops back home from the Far East.

Shackleton.

Frank, Ernest's younger brother, Dublin Herald at the Office of Arms, who resigned in November 1907 following the disappearance in July of the insignia of the Grand Master and five gold collars of the Order of St Patrick.

Right: Shackleton coat of arms. In 1898 Sir Arthur Vicars, Ulster King of Arms, confirmed the use of arms to Joseph Fisher Shackleton of Lucan, County Dublin, and his grandfather Abraham of Ballitore and their descendants. Frank had printed a family tree to show his family's descent from Louis VIII King of France and King John of England and, through the Fitzmaurices, to the barons of Kerry, the earls of Ormonde and King Edward I of England among others.

According to a letter sent to Emily, the Russians were going to pay '£12 per head for the soldiers and £40 for each officer ... and we could clear £100,000 but I cannot go into details now: and I don't want to raise hopes'. And rightly so. On 9 February he wrote that 'things will be alright'. By 14 February '6500 troops have been signed for by contract which will receive official rectification tomorrow'.

But another great plan disappeared, the contract didn't come through, and the project was abandoned. Shackleton returned to Scotland and a job with Beardmore's company.

Again, he was optimistic. He wrote to Emily: 'Will has given me a room right opposite his own so I am to be in close touch with him ... I mean to do my very best in this matter as he says his trouble is with me not having initiative enough.'

Nothing less than a directorship in his new employer's company was in his sights. The fact that his younger brother, Frank, was progressing in society was another reminder that he was not making headway as quickly as he might have imagined.

In 1899 Frank had found a job, through friends, with the Office of Arms in Dublin. After a sojourn in the army during the Boer War, he returned to Dublin and by 1903 was a Gold Staff Officer in the Heraldry Office in Dublin Castle. By 1905 he had advanced to the position of Dublin Herald. He had also managed to find himself three homes, in London, Devon and Dublin.

Ernest, meanwhile, was commuting daily from Edinburgh to Glasgow. Beardmore appointed him as secretary to a committee established to investigate the design of a new gas engine. Shackleton was note-taker to a panel of gas experts. Afterwards, he rewrote the notes and sent them for typing. He also travelled regularly to London on company business, interviewing prospective clients.

While in London he pursued a friendship with an American living there, a Miss Havemeyer. Whether this was a sexual relationship is unclear but Emily found the business of pregnancy 'distasteful' and Shackleton was said to have been 'virtually driven' to find sexual satisfaction outside his marriage. What is clear is that the time spent there was more interesting than the time spent in William Beardmore's office. The jobs given to Shackleton were time-consuming but boredom was setting in again. Closer to home, his friendship with Elspeth Beardmore too was deepening, and he claimed he always felt the more cheerful for meeting her.

Other problems were a constant drain on his financial and mental resources. His father was no longer practising full-time and needed money. His sisters also needed regular support and, in his own home, Raymond was ill and Emily was finding her second pregnancy no easier than her first. Elspeth Beardmore, at least, was not only sympathetic but encouraging as Shackleton became increasingly convinced that his best chance of security lay to the south.

The South Pole still awaited its first visitors and the call was growing louder. The Antarctic was a place he knew, where he could be his own man. It was also a potential gold-mine, if only he could find the initial capital to exploit it.

In searching for financial backers Shackleton put together a proposal for another expedition. This included the use of dogs, sledges and a 'specially designed motor car'.

Furthermore, he wrote, 'with sixty dogs and a couple of ponies, I am quite certain that the South Pole could be reached'.

Part of the plan was to have the car pull ten sledges, one of which would be dropped every hundred miles as a depot. Not only that but, travelling fifty miles a day in the car he believed he might be able to go 'beyond the South Pole and branch off East and West'. A second party would travel to the magnetic pole, without the assistance of the car. The expeditionary force would make use of the hut left by the crew of the *Discovery*. He estimated the cost of this expedition at £17,000.

Two days before Christmas Shackleton's plans were put on hold by the birth of his first daughter, Cecily. Over the Christmas holiday, while his wife recovered, Shackleton refocused on his expedition.

What he didn't explain were his reasons for wanting to go. There were many. He needed to prove himself to himself following his illness on the Scott expedition; he wished to prove himself to his wife; he wanted to make money; he needed excitement; he wanted fame and he was committed to geographical and scientific exploration and achievement. Reaching the South Pole would resolve everything.

To add to his worries, there were rumours that the Frenchman Charcot and the Belgian Arctowski were planning an expedition to the Antarctic. Shackleton redoubled his efforts and got some promises of money. Elizabeth Dawson-Lambton donated £1000 which Ernest passed to his brother Frank to invest while the expedition plans were developed. Frank's notion of investment was to use the money to bail out one of his own companies.

Travelling to London when he could, Shackleton continued his fundraising drive. Douglas Spens Steuart, a mining engineer who had just established a company called Celtic Investment Trust, agreed to allow 10,000 shares in the company to be used as backing for the expedition. The dream seemed achievable.

On a more practical level, Shackleton was faced with the problem of telling William Beardmore that he wanted leave to travel to the Antarctic again, having assured Beardmore only a year before that he had given up all ideas of another expedition. To Shackleton's delight, not only did Beardmore agree to let him go, he also agreed to go guarantor for some of the finances for the trip.

On 11 February, at a dinner hosted by the Royal Geographical Society in London, both Shackleton and Arctowski formally outlined their plans for expeditions to the South Pole. The following day's newspapers brought the news to the public. A month later, Shackleton published a detailed account: 'I do not intend to sacrifice the scientific utility of the expedition,' he wrote, 'to a mere record-breaking journey, but say frankly, all the same, that one of my great efforts will be to reach the southern geographical pole.'

There were other changes from the plans of the year before. The expedition party would be larger; the ship to take them south would be bought rather than specifically built; she would drop the expeditionary force and then journey back to New Zealand, returning the following year as a relief vessel. The party heading for the magnetic pole would be landed separately, ideally in Victoria Land, close to their course southward.

Shackleton concluded his proposal with a résumé of the aims: 'By the southern and eastern sledge journey we may possibly solve the problem of the great ice-barrier ... by the charting of new mountains and discovery of new lands in the far south we aid geographical science; by the magnetic work we help not only the academic side of magnetic science, but we may help the mercantile community in the way of better ... charts.'

The ultimate financing of the trip was to be made by selling shares from Celtic Investment to anyone willing to buy them. In turn, when he got back, he would repay his debts by writing a book, lecturing and writing for newspapers. Not only did he believe he could repay these debts, he believed that long sought-after fortune lay at the end of this particular expedition.

He wrote to Emily: 'the book ... means £10,000 if we are successful and that is quite apart from all newspaper news ... so it will leave me all the lectures etc free and the book can pay off the guarantees if people really want them ... I think it will be worth about £30,000 in the way of lectures alone ... Then Sweetheart we will settle down to a quiet life.'

With finances potentially under control, Shackleton set about organizing a crew. Among those he contacted was George Mulock – the man who had replaced him on the *Discovery*. He was shocked to learn, when Mulock replied, that he had committed himself to travelling south on another expedition, one about which Shackleton knew nothing, led by Scott.

6

The Nimrod

1907–1909

◆

Shackleton wrote, in the opening chapter of *The Heart of the Antarctic*, his memoir of the 1907-1909 British expedition: 'Men go into the void spaces of the world for various reasons. Some are actuated simply by a love of adventure, some have the keen thirst for scientific knowledge, and others again are drawn away from the trodden paths by "the lure of little voices," the mysterious fascination of the unknown. I think that in my own case it was a combination of these factors that determined me to try my fortune once again in the frozen south.'

What he didn't say was that failure was a sharp spur. Combining with his passionate desire to be back on the Antarctic ice, it drove him to organize the *Nimrod* expedition.

He also had an urge to explain the lure of the wild: 'The stark polar lands grip the hearts of the men who have lived on them in a manner that can hardly be understood by the people who have never got outside the pale of civilization.'

The Antarctic offered Shackleton a second chance to prove himself. Civilization stood for the warmth of home, of his wife and children, but it also signified the constraints of a society that knew nothing of the stimulation that danger and comradeship offered. Civilization meant making a living and supporting an extended family. Life in the civilized world was several vital steps removed from life in the wasteland.

The Antarctic held its own kinds of tensions, life lived literally on the edge; but it offered the imperative of dealing with those tensions in an immediate and physical way. When problems occurred, solutions had to be found. You solved or you died.

Returning from the *Discovery* expedition, Shackleton recognized something important had gone out of his life. This, and the gnawing suspicion that things might have gone otherwise had he not been with Scott, was the source of a deep and troubling frustration.

Later, he would tell his sister Kathleen: 'I don't want to race anyone but you can't think what it is like to walk over places where no one has ever been before.'

Raymond and Cecily, EHS's children, at Torquay, August 1907. Raymond is wrapped in the Union flag presented to EHS by Queen Alexendra.

The very people at the warm heart of Shackleton's *civilized* life, his wife, his young children, his extended family, were those who had to be considered when it came to deciding on another expedition. His elderly father and impecunious sisters; his two children under the age of two: it was hardly the best time to consider a long period of separation. However, Ernest argued that a successful journey to the South Pole would bring in enough money to make them comfortable.

At the same time, Shackleton's relationship with Elspeth Beardmore was a talking-point to many who knew them. He would write to her about his financial and family problems and then finish a letter with, 'You looked so beautiful the other night.' In his search for backing for his planned trip, she was on his mind: 'I have been hoping for a line from you.' Many, including her husband's work colleagues, suspected she was Shackleton's mistress.

Whatever the relationship, it was Elspeth who encouraged him to fulfill his dream.

Emily, suffering from post-natal depression, was less enthusiastic but recognized her husband's frustration. Ernest's going meant an absence of three years. More importantly, she would be raising the children, running their home, dealing with the demands of day-to-day survival and coming to terms with the emotional stress of parting from her husband. When finally she agreed, it was without eagerness, but once the decision was made she was committed in her support.

A letter from her sister Daisy, dated 14 February 1907, is full of sympathy and encouragement: 'I do think you are being most awfully good and brave over it all but after all it is a splendid thing to do and I think dear old Mike [Shackleton] would always have felt his life's work had been left undone if he had failed after all his trouble. I am glad for his sake he has got the money … I wondered … how you were feeling and if you were awake with a horrid sinking in your heart. I can't bear to think of Mike's going away, he is so bright and cheerie and we shall all miss him so but I cannot help thinking he has to be confident of success or he would not attempt it.'

In February 1907 Shackleton made public his expedition plans. Some queried his suitability, raising the issue of his ill health on the *Discovery* trip. Scott saw Shackleton's proposal as being in direct competition with his own long-term plan. And some, unsurprisingly, were shocked that a mere Merchant Navy upstart would dare undertake an expedition that was above his station. But such opposition and the practicalities of a lack of money were not to stand in Shackleton's way. He was committed to the expedition and to doing things on his own terms.

'*I decided I would have no committee* [he wrote] *as the expedition was entirely my own venture. I was fortunate in not being hampered by committees of any sort. I kept the control of all the arrangements in my own hands and this avoided the delays that are inevitable when a group of men have to arrive at a discussion on points of detail.*'

Shackleton approached the Royal Geographical Society for backing but he was also busy elsewhere trying to raise the necessary funds. He had already persuaded the Scottish businessman Douglas Spens Steuart, a mining engineer and partner in a firm of consultants, to back his proposal. Elspeth Beardmore helped to win financial support from her husband William, who agreed to guarantee a bank loan of £7000, on the condition that the first profitable returns from the expedition would go towards its repayment. He also insisted that the expedition ship would be his property, on loan to Shackleton for the duration of the voyage.

Beardmore was not alone in believing that Shackleton and Elspeth were involved in a long-running affair and, with Shackleton in the Antarctic, the relationship would, at the very least, be put on ice for three years.

With the promise of finance, Shackleton went to Norway to order sledges, boots, mits, sleeping-bags and skis. While there, he visited Sandefjord in the hope of agreeing a price for the 700-tonne *Bjorn*, a ship built in Dundee in Scotland specifically for polar work. The *Bjorn*, with triple-expansion engines, was ideal for the trip but its price was out of Shackleton's reach. Instead, on his return to London, he bought the *Nimrod*.

The *Nimrod*, at that time, was on a sealing expedition and was inspected on Shackleton's behalf. In mid-June she arrived on the Thames and he went to survey her. He came away from the inspection greatly disturbed.

Part of a letter from EHS to Elspeth Beardmore, wife of William Beardmore (later Lord Invernairn), an old Dulwich boy, whom Shackleton worked for in 1906 at his Parkhead Works in Glasgow. Beardmore became a major sponsor of the Nimrod expedition whilst Shackleton became very close friends with his wife.

'*She was much dilapidated and smelt strongly of seal-oil, and an inspection in dock showed that she required caulking and that her masts would have to be renewed. She was rigged only as a schooner and her masts were decayed, and I wanted to be able to sail her in the event of the engine breaking down or the supply of coal running short.*'

He handed the ship to R. & H. Green of Blackhall for overhaul and, as he was later to admit, 'I had not then become acquainted with the many good qualities of the *Nimrod* and my first impression hardly did justice to the plucky old ship.'

While the vessel was being renovated, Shackleton was in negotiation with the Royal Geographical Society and Scott – often through intermediaries, notably Edward Wilson.

At the same time he pursued further patronage. The agreement of the Marquis of Graham to become a backer proved an enormous boost. With Steuart, Beardmore and Graham behind him, the way was clearing.

However, Scott was now making demands on Shackleton about where he might land and where he might travel. Scott the explorer had suddenly become Scott the dog in the Antarctic manger.

Shackleton wasn't the only one receiving this treatment from the British geographic establishment at the time. The Polish scientist and explorer Henryk Arctowski was treated with imperial disdain by Sir Clements Markham. Arctowski's plan was similar to Shackleton's and the object of even greater arrogance. 'I certainly should have been much annoyed', Markham wrote, 'if that fellow Arctowski had gone poaching down in our preserves; but I believe he has not got any funds. Foreigners never get much beyond the Antarctic circle.'

Shackleton's initial reaction to Scott was to compromise. In spite of their differences, he didn't believe he should offend the man with whom he had sailed. But as the demands grew more specific, Shackleton reached a point of barely concealed exasperation in a letter to Scott in March 1907:

'I have been ready, as you realize, to meet you as regards McMurdo Base. I realize myself what I have given up in regard to this matter. Concerning the 170 Meridian West as a line of demarcation [sic]*, this matter will have to be discussed. I must tell you quite frankly that my agreement to this proposition might perhaps make a position untenable to me on my Southward journey and that I do not see my way, at the present moment, to accede to this. I also consider that the unknown land or the disputed land of Wilkes is free to anybody who wishes to explore that part, and as you know, my programme originally included the exploration of this quarter.*

I am ready to discuss with you the whole matter but I want you to understand that I do not look upon either Wood Bay or the land to the West of Cape North as being within the Province of any particular previous expedition. As you write to me openly, I therefore answer you in the same manner.'

Letters continued to be exchanged until, in April, the two men met. Shackleton set out the specifics that had been agreed. The list was long, and detailed the areas Shackleton would and would not traverse.

In May Shackleton forwarded the plan to Scott, whose response was as amenable and businesslike as it had previously been parsimonious:

My dear Shackleton,

I return you this copy of your letter which is a very clear statement of the arrangement to which we came. If as you say you will rigidly adhere to it, I do not think our plans will clash and I shall feel on sure ground in developing my own.

Yours very sincerely R.F. Scott.

In spite of all the pressures, Shackleton continued to immerse himself in the preparations. The *Discovery* trip had taught him the importance of groundwork: 'The equipping of a Polar expedition is a task demanding experience as well as the greatest attention to points of detail. When the expedition has left civilization there is no opportunity to repair any omission or secure any article that may have been forgotten.'

Most important in the preparations was the listing of possible crew-members for the expedition. He was extremely anxious that Edward Wilson, one of the intermediaries between Scott and himself, should accompany him. Wilson was a doctor and Shackleton believed he'd be an invaluable asset, both as a medical practitioner and as a colleague. Wilson, however, caught between loyalty to Scott and Shackleton, used the fact that he was busy conducting a survey of grouse disease in Scotland as an excuse not to travel. Despite intense pressure, he flatly refused to join the expedition.

Meanwhile, equipment for the trip was being prepared. A typewriter, a sewing-machine, a gramophone, a printing-press, hockey sticks and a football were among the less obvious but important items for inclusion, but by far the most intriguing was a 15-horsepower Arrol-Johnston car. Shackleton explained his decision subsequently.

Shackleton's hut at Cape Royds, on Ross Island. Fifteen men overwintered in this. The hut is still there.

'*I decided to take a motor-car because I thought it possible, from my previous experience, that we might meet with a hard surface on the great ice Barrier, over which the first part, at any rate, on the journey towards the south would have to be performed. On a reasonably good surface the machine would be able to haul a heavy load at a rapid pace.*'

Taking the car on the trip was good for publicity but proved impractical, its two-ton weight quickly bogged down in the soft snow. Of far greater use were the ten Manchurian ponies which were to join the ship in New Zealand. These had been taken from a wild herd of over 2000 ponies in Tientsin. Also due for collection in New Zealand were nine Siberian dogs, veterans of a previous expedition.

In Norway Shackleton had ordered sledges, designed by the Norwegian explorer Fridtjof Nansen, and reindeer-skin sleeping-bags. He also bought eighty pairs of dog- and wolf-skin mits and eighty pairs of finnesko boots made from the skin of reindeer head. Fifty kilos of Sennegrass was brought to absorb the sweat from feet in the boots.

For shelter, a pre-fabricated hut made by Humphrey's of Knightsbridge, and measuring 33'x 19'x 8' was included with the equipment. The roof and walls of the hut were covered in felt and the walls were made of 1" boards with 4" cavities filled with granulated cork for insulation. The hut was divided into cubicles with two men sharing an area of 7'x 9'x 1'5". Acetylene gas was used for lighting and an anthracite stove for heating and cooking.

Food was an essential and Shackleton had strong ideas about what should and shouldn't be taken. He believed the food must be wholesome, varied, nourishing and light to carry, good for physical health and a morale booster for the men. The stores taken included treats such as fish-balls, roast reindeer and roast ptarmigan. Twenty-seven cases of Montserrat lime juice, essential against scurvy, were also included. Under the supervision of manager Alfred Reid, the stores for the trip were packed in 2500 Veneseta cases and loaded onto the *Nimrod*.

Having abandoned hope of persuading Wilson to come, Shackleton set about interviewing and selecting members of the expedition. He had definite ideas on the qualities required: 'The men selected must be qualified to work. They must be able to live together in harmony for a long period without outside communication, and it must be remembered that the men whose desires lead them to the untrodden paths of the world have generally marked individuality.'

Shackleton particularly wanted two surgeons, a biologist and a geologist in the group. From the more than 400 applicants he chose his shore party. Of those chosen, all but three were unknown to him.

Lieutenant Jameson Boyd Adams had begun his career in the Merchant, before moving to the Royal Navy. When Shackleton invited him to take a place on the expedition he had just been offered a permanent commission in the Royal Navy but he opted, instead, to travel on the *Nimrod*.

Sir Philip Brocklehurst, a nineteen-year old, shared Shackleton's passion for boxing, and spent some time studying geology and surveying to assure his place in the final party.

Raymond Priestley was a twenty-year-old geology student. His memories were that the interview with Shackleton was somewhat unusual: 'He asked me if I could sing and I said I couldn't; and he asked me if I would know gold if I saw it, and again I said No! He must have asked me other questions but I remember these because they were bizarre.'

George Marston was expedition artist and practical joker in the pack. Dr Eric Marshall was senior surgeon made responsible for photography. Alistair Forbes Mackay was second surgeon.

Bernard Day, who had worked with the Arrol-Johnston Motor-Car Company, was brought along as driver and mechanic, and hotel chef William Roberts joined as cook. Ernest Joyce was given responsibility for looking after dogs and sledges, and Bertram Armytage was to look after the ponies taken on the expedition. Frank Wild was in charge of provisions, while James Murray was principal biologist.

Later, from Australia, Professor T.W. Edgeworth David would travel as director of the scientific staff and Douglas Mawson would be taken on as a physicist.

Early in July an exhibition of some of the stores and provisions was held in a room in Regent Street. It proved to be a popular event attended by thousands of visitors coming to see the array of foodstuffs and equipment.

Finally, on 30 July 1907, the *Nimrod* left the East India docks on the first stage of her long journey to New Zealand.

On 4 August King Edward VII and Queen Alexandra visited the ship at Cowes on the Isle of Wight.

Emily recorded in her diary: 'I was greatly favoured by a special Royal permission to be on board ... The King greeted Ernest with a cheery "Ah, there you are – very pleased to see you again." It was so sweet of the Queen to give Ernest a flag ... Ernest looked his best and you would know how nice that is. I was very proud of him.'

On the same visit, Shackleton was conferred with the Victorian Order.

Three days later the *Nimrod* sailed from Torquay, arriving in New Zealand on 23 November after a 100-day voyage.

For Shackleton, the *Nimrod's* departure marked the end of his problems. He had opted to stay behind to raise further badly needed funds. His plan was to travel by train to the south of England, crossing the English Channel at Dover. From Calais he would take a train to Marseilles, where he would board the P&O liner *India* and journey, via the Suez Canal, to link up with the *Nimrod* in New Zealand.

In the last days left to him in England, Shackleton spent time with Emily and the children but even that brief interval was broken by an urgent message from Frank, Ernest's brother, saying he was under suspicion and facing possible arrest for the theft of the Irish 'Crown jewels'. In addition, he had debts of £1000.

What was stolen were the insignia (diamond star and badge) of the Grand Master of the Order of St Patrick (the Lord Lieutenant of Ireland) and five gold collars worn by the knights of the Order on ceremonial occasions. Otherwise, they were kept under lock and key in the tower in Dublin Castle. In the same tower Sir Arthur Vicars held his heraldic court. Among his friends and regular visitors was Frank Shackleton. Sometime between 11 June and 6 July 6 1907 the jewels were stolen and Frank Shackleton was among the chief suspects.

An inquiry was subsequently held and Frank was cleared, although rumours persisted of a whitewash, with stories that Frank was part of a homosexual ring involving members of the Dublin judiciary, which he was willing to reveal if things went against him.

While there was nothing he could do about his brother and the Crown jewels scandal, Ernest – as if there was nothing else to concern him on the eve of his departure – borrowed another £1000 from William Beardmore, to pay off Frank's debts.

Finally, on 31 October, Shackleton began his journey south. His departure from Charing Cross Station passed without attention. Emily travelled to Dover with him and the image of her as they parted was one that would haunt him on the expedition. He later wrote:

'*I can see you just as you stand on the wharf and are smiling at me, my heart was too full to speak and I felt that I wanted just to come ashore and clasp you in my arms and love and care for you ... If I failed to get to the pole and was within ten miles and had to turn back it would or will not mean so much sadness as was compressed in those few minutes (of parting) ... I promise you that I will take every care and run no risks ... I promise you darling that I will come back to you safe and well if God wishes it.*'

Arriving in Australia, Shackleton discovered that over £4000 promised by his cousin, William Bell, had not materialized and that he didn't have the necessary funds to pay the crew of the *Nimrod*. He had estimated the cost of the expedition at £17,000. In the end, it would reach £50,000.

Through the generosity of the governments of New Zealand and Australia and the support of Welsh-born Edgeworth David, Professor of Geology at Sydney University, the money was raised. In return for his financial assistance, David and his colleague Douglas Mawson were to travel on the *Nimrod*.

As Shackleton travelled farther from Emily, the letters expressed his love and heartache:

'*... never again for us to be separated ... One's life is so short yet we will have good times and happy times together again ... My feelings are all too deep for words ... You stand apart entirely from the rest of the world ...You came absolutely and perfectly to my ideal of the perfect woman, I love you wildly. I have and do love you passionately.*'

On New Year's Day 1908, the *Nimrod* left Lyttelton harbour under tow from the steel steamship *Koonya*. Ten days before departure, Shackleton had realized the already overloaded *Nimrod* couldn't take enough coal on board to get her to and from Antarctica. He appealed to the New Zealand government who agreed to pay half the cost of a tow-steamer. The *Koonya* was hired and the owners, as a gesture of goodwill, opted to waive the other half of the fees.

The *Nimrod* had just 3'6" of freeboard when she left Lyttelton harbour and conditions on board were extremely cramped. For more than 1500 miles she plunged and swung on the end of a 600-foot cable, an umbilical cord to the *Koonya*.

One of the training ponies on Quail Island, outside Lyttelton, New Zealand: left to right, Tubman the horse-breaker and Dr Mackay, December 1907.

Dogs in truck at Lyttelton after Joyce had fetched them from Stewart Island, south of South Island, New Zealand, descendants of those used on the Norwegian Borchgrevink's 1898-1900 Southern Cross expedition. Joyce left, Marston the artist, Scamp (the lead dog, front centre), and Gravy.

The weather on the early stages of the journey was rough and Shackleton and his crew were reduced to signalling the steamer by flag, at one point requesting the captain of the towboat to pour oil on the sea in an attempt to calm it.

The crew suffered from seasickness and winds buffeting, the animals on board were in a worse predicament. The ponies needed constant attention and calming and at the height of the storms two had to be shot. On the other hand one of the dogs on board gave birth to six pups.

By 14 January the weather had improved and the ships encountered their first icebergs. The same day, twenty sheep carried on the *Koonya* were slaughtered and their carcasses prepared for transfer to the *Nimrod*. However, in the course of the transfer, ten of them were lost in the sea.

In the moments between supervising work, Shackleton wrote to Emily: 'I am always thinking of you and wanting you so much my heart goes out to you and the children and I

am yearning to see you and have you in my arms again through long peaceful nights ... long kisses from me over the wash of uncharted seas.'

The following day, exactly two weeks after their departure, the *Nimrod* and the *Koonya* went their separate ways, the towboat heading back towards New Zealand and home, the *Nimrod* heading south into uncertain waters.

Nine days later Shackleton and his crew came in sight of the Great Ice Barrier, the Ross Ice Shelf. Shackleton's intention had been to land at King Edward Land but the large number of ice floes in the area made this scheme impossible.

'All my plans were upset by the demand of the situation,' he wrote to Emily and they were. He had no option but to land at McMurdo. Given his undertaking to Scott, he was unhappy about this but the constraints of time and pack ice which constantly thwarted any progress left him with no alternative.

Eric Marshall was unhappy with Shackleton's decision. He saw it as a direct betrayal of Scott.

'He [Shackleton] hasn't got the guts of a louse,' he wrote, 'in spite of what he may say to the world on his return.' Marshall's attitude to what he saw as Shackleton's unforgivable

Nimrod, a 136-foot long barquentine built by Alexander Stephens and Sons of Dundee, Scotland, in 1865. Used as a sealer before being bought in William Beardmore's name for the 1907 expedition.

behaviour was not shared on the *Nimrod*. To most crew-members it was obvious that the pressures of time and the need to pursue their goal were of much greater importance than some egotistical demand made by Scott.

But Marshall was not convinced and, later, while at Cape Royds, wrote that Shackleton was 'vacillating, erratic and a liar, easily scared, moody and surly, a boaster'.

What Marshall didn't know was that Shackleton was not only confronting difficult decisions but he was facing serious disagreements with Rupert England, captain of the *Nimrod*. England was not a man to take risks and his natural reaction was to prevaricate. This was a luxury Shackleton could not afford. At one point, Frank Wild concluded that England had completely lost his nerve and was, in fact 'off his rocker'.

Eventually Edgeworth David intervened and restored peace and Shackleton realized the captain's word could and did overrule that of the expedition leader. Later, England was to be replaced as captain of the *Nimrod* by F. P. Evans, former captain of the *Koonya*.

The clashes between Marshall and Shackleton on the one hand, and England and Shackleton on the other, showed the difficulties involved in maintaining calm on a long expedition where a crew lived in such close proximity.

Not everything, however, was negative. Other events drew people together. One such occurred on 31 January.

In an awful accident, Second Officer Aeneas Mackintosh was hooked in the eye as the crew of the *Nimrod* began moving cargo in preparation for unloading. Later that day Marshall operated, having knocked Macintosh out with chloroform. Using the only pair of curved scissors on board and improvising with retractor hooks made from rigging wire, he excised the eye.

On 3 February Cape Royds on Ross Island was chosen as the spot for base camp and the motor-car was landed under the supervision of driver and mechanic Bernard Day. Marshall filmed the event.

15 February was Shackleton's birthday, and Marshall gave him a letter which Emily had entrusted to him before he sailed from England. It read:

'*This letter is for your birthday 15th February to tell you I am thinking of you all day long as I always shall be while you are away ... They* [the children] *will always kiss your*

*photograph night and morning and Ray will pray
"God bless my daddy and bring him safe home to us."
... Oh darling it is hard to write cheerfully ... I shall
be wondering if you found a good landing place.'*

A week later, on 22 February, the *Nimrod* departed for New Zealand and Shackleton and his expeditionary force began their work in earnest. Again,
he wrote to Emily about the weather and his troubles with England, concluding: 'I am longing for the time when I can clasp you again to my arms darling and hold our children in my
arms again, that will be next year please God.'

Shackleton was back in the Antarctic, back where he had dreamed of being, back where the

106

nightmare of illness had previously robbed him of the chance to prove himself. All the obstacles of finance and organization and doubt were behind him. Now the mission was clear. Ahead lay the object of his ambition – the South Pole.

Eleven days after the ship's departure a party of six – David, Mackay, Mawson, Adams, Marshall and Brocklehurst – set off for Mount Erebus, an active volcano some 13,370 foot high. The party made it to the summit on 10 March, but Brocklehurst suffered badly frost-bitten feet. He celebrated his twenty-first birthday in a blizzard almost 9000 feet up the mountain, eating ship's biscuits and chocolate. As a result of the frostbite he would have one of his toes amputated a month later by Marshall. Apart from this mishap, the expedition was a success.

The party returned to camp on 11 March bringing information on the height of the mountain, the position and state of craters and its geological significance. More importantly, from Shackleton's point of view, the expedition proved the stamina of the men and their ability to work well together.

A young Irishman's journal of the Nimrod's voyage from London to McMurdo Sound and return to Lyttelton gives a personal account of Shackleton's first expedition to Antarctica . . .

Taking Shackleton to Antarctica in 1907 was no pleasure cruise

Felix Rooney on the Nimrod.

By ROSEMARY BRITTEN

Felix Rooney (1885-1965) was a young Irishman on the Nimrod. In his diary he described the journey as, 'so rough the ship would roll the milk out of your tea'.

When Shackleton had travelled on the *Discovery* he had taken a typewriter to produce the *South Polar Times*, a monthly expedition magazine.

This time, however, he was prepared for the production of a far more ambitious publication. *Aurora Australis* was to be the first book written, edited (by Shackleton), illustrated, printed and bound in the Antarctic. With this in mind, he'd sent Joyce and Wild on a three-week crash course in printing and typesetting with Sir Joseph Causton, who loaned a printing and etching press to the expedition, as well as supplying paper and ink. All of this equipment was kept in the hut at Cape Royds in Joyce and Wild's chaotic cubicle, known as 'The Rogues' Retreat'. With the press in place and the typecase laid out, there wasn't room to lift, much less to swing, a penguin.

Aurora Australis. First book printed and bound in Antarctica; the sheep-backed Venesta (packing-case) boards were bound by the mechanic Bernard Day. Apparently 100 copies were produced in the Hut at Cape Royds but only about 65 have been accounted for to date. This copy was presented by Shackleton to his daughter Cecily. Kidney soup stencil indicated the original contents of the case. They brought 2500 cases with stores on the trip. (Christies catalogue)

Not alone was space limited but the conditions in which they worked on the project were less than ideal. Often the ink had to be kept liquid by placing a candle under the ink-plate. Despite difficulty, confusion and clutter the pair produced, at the rate of two pages per day, *Aurora Australis*, with its proud declaration: 'Published at the winter quarters of the British Antarctic expedition, 1907, during the winter months of April, May, June, July, 1908. Illustrated with lithographs and etchings; by George Marston. Printed at the sign of 'The Penguins' by Joyce and Wild. Latitude 77 degrees 32' South Longitude 166 degrees 12' East Antarctica. (All rights reserved).'

The finished product was bound with boards from packing cases, backed with sheep-skin and sewn with green silk cord by the motor engineer Bernard Day. Individual copies were identified by the names on the particular packing cases. One volume might be the Irish Stew copy, another the Kidney Soup copy, and so on.

During those bitter winter months, three of the seven ponies died or had to be shot as a result of poisoning. Two had eaten volcanic sand and the third had eaten some shavings from one of the chemical cases. The remaining four were carefully watched and schooled. Joyce, meanwhile, took responsibility for training the dogs, which had become camp pets.

But there was other work to be done, too. Geological specimens were collected. Meteorological records were kept. The car was tested. In the darkness of the long nights the men took it in turns to cook and there was widespread use of the expedition library. The gramophone was played constantly and Marston was involved in organizing theatrical productions.

There were occasional outbursts, particularly from Shackleton, but they tended to end as quickly as they had begun and were more than compensated for by his genuine concern for each of the men who accompanied him.

The deaths of the three ponies were to be of greater consequence than might have first been imagined. Shackleton's intention had been to have a party of six on the Polar expedition. But with only four ponies surviving, he revised the figure down by two. As July wore on and the departure date approached, he chose the members of the party.

Shackleton recognized the scientific significance of the journey to the South Magnetic Pole. David and Mawson were the obvious choices for that and Mackay was chosen as the medical man on the trip.

Otherwise, there were specific people suited to specific tasks. Day was the mechanic and would be needed to drive the car when it was possible to use it. Priestley was to undertake long-term geological research in the western mountains. Murray was to be in command at the base camp. That left seven men in the running for the Polar attempt – Adams, Marshall, Brocklehurst, Joyce, Wild, Marston and Shackleton.

Following medical examinations, Marshall concluded that Brocklehurst, still recovering from the loss of his toe, and Joyce, who had a weak pulse and liver problems, were unfit for the full trip. He also noted that Shackleton had a murmur in his heart and watched him closely throughout the expedition.

While there were problems to be faced in Antarctica, other problems had been left by Shackleton for his brother-in-law, Herbert Dorman, to solve. On 12 June Herbert wrote to

Emily, bemoaning the fact that money was hard to come by: 'I heard from WB [William Beardmore] this morning. He does not see his way to assist further, and seems vexed with E(rnest) because he lent him £1000 shortly before he left which was to have been repaid in 3 weeks. It was not repaid and E never even wrote from New Zealand ... It is a great anxiety to me to feel that I am landed with the responsibility of finding the money for fitting out the *Nimrod* and bringing back the expedition. I want something like £7000 and heaven only knows where it is to come from.'

Herbert, more than anyone, was aware of the financial mess Shackleton left in his wake, and of the dire financial straits in which his sister found herself. In mid-July he wrote to her again: 'If you want £50 or £100 meantime you have only to let me know ... I think you had better *not* write to Mrs Beardmore at present.'

Later, he wrote cheering Emily up: 'Fortunately we Dormans stick together and we shall do the trick somehow. I am getting used to these financial anxieties about the expedition and happily each new worry wears off in a few hours.'

On 22 September, having spent the winter months preparing equipment and clothing, Adams, Marshall, Marston, Wild, Day and Shackleton set off with the motor car and sledges to lay Depot A, 120 miles south of the base. The car proved useful on part of the journey but the brunt of the hauling was borne by the men themselves.

Eleven days later, on 3 October, David, Mawson and Mackay set off to locate the South Magnetic Pole. Their expedition would last 122 days and set a sledging record distance of 1260 miles.

On 29 October the reduced party of four – Adams, Marshall, Wild and Shackleton – set off at 10 a.m. on the 800-mile journey to the South Pole accompanied by the four ponies, each of which hauled a sledge carrying 600 pounds of provisions, enough food to last four months. A support party accompanied them with another sledge as far as White Island.

Shackleton wrote of that morning: 'A glorious day for our start, brilliant sunshine and a cloudless sky, a fair wind from the north; in fact everything that could conduce to an auspicious beginning.'

But it was hardly to be. An hour out from base, one of the ponies went lame and the party was forced to reduce speed. Then another of the ponies kicked Adams, cutting his

knee through to the bone. At Glacier Tongue, the car stuck in the snow and had to be taken back to base. Shackleton noted: 'I pray that we may be successful for my Heart has been so much in this.'

On their second day out the men reached Hut Point and the old *Discovery* hut, which gave them a night's shelter. From there the expedition truly began. Over the following days the weather was fine and all boded well, but on 4 November the day was so dark that they were reduced to travelling by compass. Worse lay ahead. On 6 November a blizzard struck and the men were trapped in their tents for three days, cutting back on their rations and looking after the ponies, but otherwise left to their own devices. Shackleton read the comedies of Shakespeare. Marshall read the Bible.

Knowing that the men would share tents, two and two, Shackleton had decided, before they left base, that they would alternate partners on a weekly basis. He was well aware of the danger of the four splitting into two groups.

On 9 November the weather cleared and the expedition moved on uneventfully through crevasses. By 15 November they had reached Depot A. The following day, in clearer weather, they made a record journey of seventeen miles. The ponies were proving invaluable in pulling the sledges but within days, the snow crust began cutting into their fetlocks. Chinaman, the oldest of the animals, was suffering badly from fatigue and chafing and Shackleton decided he would have to be shot.

First car on Antarctica, 1 February 1908. Made at William Beardmore's Arroll-Johnston Motor Works, its 12-15 horse-power air-cooled engine was capable of up to 20 miles an hour in ideal conditions and could carry fuel for 300 miles. Bernard Day, who worked for Beardmore, was motor engineer, as he was later on Scott's Terra Nova expedition. The motor car proved to be of limited use for travelling on ice and snow, its moving parts causing a number of personal injuries.

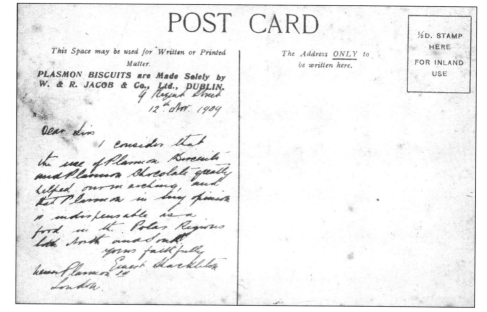

POST CARD

½D. STAMP
HERE
FOR INLAND
USE

This Space may be used for Written or Printed
Matter.

The Address ONLY to
be written here.

PLASMON BISCUITS are Made Solely by
W. & R. JACOB & Co., Ltd., DUBLIN.

*Nimrod postcard
extolling the merits of
the Plasmon Biscuits
made by W. and R.
Jacob, Dublin.*

*Below: first to the
South Magnetic Pole
16 January 1909: left
to right, Dr Mackay,
Professor David,
Douglas Mawson.*

Occasional blizzards slowed progress but, even in clear weather, the men were finding the vastness of the snowfields unsettling. They were constantly edgy and nervous, feeling lost in the tremendous but pallid landscape.

On 22 November the weather cleared again. The party had made Depot B and left stores and oil for the return journey. Despite the loss of Chinaman, shot the previous night, spirits were high. But, for Adams, it must have seemed that the opening of one door by the God of the Antarctic led to the closing of another. He developed a violent toothache and it took Marshall two attempts, without proper dental equipment, to remove the tooth.

The Polar party of
Adams, Marshall,
Shackleton and Wild,
heading into the
white unknown early
November1908.

Whatever the private flights of pleasure, imagination and achievement, Shackleton's
journal was as restrained as ever: 'It falls to the lot of few men to view land not previously
seen by human eyes and it was with feelings of curiosity, not unmingled with awe that we
watched the new mountains rise from the great unknown that lay ahead of us.'

There was still an expedition to complete and problems to surmount. Shackleton and Wild
were suffering greatly from snowblindness, the drops from their painfully watering eyes freezing on their beards. What little relief there was for the snowblindness came from the use of
cocaine ointment. On 26 November they celebrated reaching a new farthest point south with
a bottle of orange curacao which Emily Shackleton had presented to the expedition.

The following day, a second pony, Grisi, was no longer able to go on and was shot.

There were now just two ponies and four men pulling a weight of over 1200 pounds between them. The party had travelled more than 300 miles in less than a month but the remaining pair of ponies was weakening by the day. On 1 December Quan, Shackleton's favourite, refused to pull at all and that evening he too was shot and cut up for meat. The one remaining pony, Socks, was still able to work and, while the men pulled one sledge, he followed with the other.

All along Shackleton had been attempting to avoid the mountains, but with only one pony left and time and supplies limited, he realized they would have to cross higher ground. On 3 December the men left the pony with food for the day and set out to find what Shackleton described as a 'pioneer' way south.

That day's expedition was dangerous. The men, roped together, were in crevasse country but by early afternoon they reached the summit of the hill they would name Mount Hope. From there they saw what Marshall described as 'a glacier extended as far as the eye could reach, flanked on either side by rugged ice covered mountains'. This was their way forward.

Next day, beginning the most dangerous phase of their expedition, they knew that Socks would not manage the steep and crevassed countryside.

On 6 December the party left Depot D. On the 7th Socks fell into a crevasse, almost taking Wild and a sledge with him. The pony was killed instantly, losing them a valuable food source, and Wild, hanging over the chasm by his left hand, was fortunate to survive.

As the four travelled onwards, personality clashes emerged. The extra energy being used to pull the sledges ate into the reserves of mental strength of each. Wild became convinced that Marshall was, literally, not pulling his weight and wrote in his diary: 'I sincerely wish he would fall down a crevasse about a thousand feet deep.'

Shackleton, fighting his own battles with fatigue, was charged with keeping the group together and did. His belief that 'difficulties are just things to overcome after all' wasn't just a notion. It was something he practised. He encouraged the men in any way he could. Christmas became a topic of conversation and, then, an ambition and, finally, a target in time and space. The men put aside a little food each day towards a celebration.

The four celebrated Christmas, 9500 feet up the side of the Beardmore Glacier. Shackleton produced plum pudding, brandy, cocoa, cigars and Crème de Menthe from the stores. The food may have been good but for Frank Wild the surroundings and the 48 degrees of frost were anything but salubrious. He wrote: 'May none but my worst enemies spend their Christmas in such a dreary, godforsaken place as this.'

The contrasting feelings that Christmas brought – celebration and the awareness that, one way or another, the journey was far from over – were followed in late December and the early days of January by the full realization of the task that lay ahead. Each man was now pulling a 150-lb load and the course they were taking, upward through soft snow, was backbreaking. If they were going to make the Pole they were going to be short of food, so the decision was taken to make each week's food last for ten days.

Christmas Day 9500 feet up on the Polar plateau. Wild wrote: 'May none but my worst enemies spend their Christmas in such a dreary, godforsaken place as this.' Left to right, Adams, Marshall, Wild.

The men were suffering from low temperatures. Adams was particularly badly affected by the cold and Shackleton was enduring regular migraines and giddiness. All of the men were undergoing severe tiredness and breathing problems. They found it necessary, when a halt was called, to lie in the snow for three minutes to overcome their exhaustion. Marshall, noting that their body temperatures were now two degrees below normal, advised, as a priority, that they return to the fuller rations of the previous week.

By now both Wild and Marshall privately and separately began to doubt they would get to the Pole. Shackleton, despite constant altitude sickness, wanted to continue. He was, however, fully cognizant of the responsibility he bore. There was no one else to whom he could turn. This final group of four determined men had only one leader, only one man on whom the success and safety of the team depended. On 2 January 1909 he wrote: 'I cannot think of failure yet I must look at the matter sensibly and consider the lives of those who are with me.'

Success and safety had been the watchwords, but now it was dawning on Shackleton that he might be forced to choose between the two.

On 4 January the men discussed their position and decided to leave a sixth depot, Depot F, with only a small flag to mark it. It was a risk, another blizzard might obliterate the marker and leave them with a 150-mile walk to the next depot on the way back but it was impossible to carry enough supplies to cover all eventualities and still make good time. Once the depot had been made they set off with renewed vigour. Over the following two days, in the teeth of a headwind and drifting snow, they walked twenty-five miles.

Farthest South camp after a 60-hour blizzard 133 miles from the Pole on 8 January 1909; left to right, Adams, Wild, EHS.

On the night of 6 January Shackleton wrote in his journal: 'Tomorrow we march South with the flag.' It was not to be.

The following two days saw the men confined to their tent with gales of ninety miles an hour screaming around them. Shackleton read *The Merchant of Venice*. Snow drifted into the tent. The men suffered cramp but there was no talk of going back.

On 9 January the weather cleared enough to make a 'dash' possible. The four took what supplies they could, chocolate, biscuits and sugar, and began to run 'as hard as we could' over the snow. When they couldn't run they walked. They were less than 100 miles from the Pole.

The four figures were strung out across the landscape, sometimes one ran ahead, then another. Sometimes one lagged behind, but always they moved on, relentless, their eyes, hearts and minds set on that distant, untouched spot.

Shackleton's own account of that day, written in his diary, tells the tale with all the simplicity of great achievement and courageous failure.

'The wind eased down at 1 am. At 2 am we were up had breakfast. And shortly after 4 am started south with the Union Jacks and the brass Cylinder of Stamps. At 9 am hard quick marching we were in 88.23 and there hoisted H.M's flag took possession of the Plateau in the name of H.M. and called it K.E. Plat. Rushed back over a surface hardened somewhat by the recent wind and had lunch took photo of camp Furthest south and then got away marching till 5 pm dead tired Camped lovely night – 19. Homeward Bound. Whatever regrets may be we have done our best. Beaten the South record by 366 miles the North by 77 miles. Amen.'

And that was it. The diary entry says everything and tells little. It says where they were and what they achieved. It tells nothing of the enormous pride and the enormous sadness of those four figures on the vast, wasted, snow-blown face of the Antarctic. It tells nothing of the individual feelings of sorrow and relief in those four hearts.

Forty-seven years later Adams would say that he believed another hour's march towards the Pole would have been the death of all four. But, for Shackleton, coming so far and getting so close raised the possibility of going on, one more hour, one more day. It brought, too, the temptation to decide that reaching the Pole was worth everything including life. To be the first, even if that meant death, was something that could never be taken from them. As it was, there was no guarantee of a safe return. They were 97 miles from the Pole and 730 from base. Glory beckoned across the snows, even in death it must have shone with a particular and alluring radiance.

Shackleton, however, was not to be seduced. He considered the possibility of going on himself but that would simply put pressure on the other three. Even if they did allow him to go alone, they would have been burdened by a lifelong liability of doubt.

'Whatever our regrets we have done our best,' he wrote. The decision was made and there was no time for remorse. They were, as he wrote, homeward bound, and he was as determined to get himself, and his men, safely home as he had been to get them to the Pole. That, now, became the imperative.

Shackleton was determined to get his party back safely. Wild, always loyal, wrote in his diary: 'I don't know how S. stands it; both his heels are split in four or five places, his legs are bruised and chafed, and today he has a violent headache through falls, and yet he gets along as well as anyone.'

Both Adams and Marshall advised him to ease off. Shackleton had fallen several times descending walls of ice and worried that he was holding up the others. Yet the descent over the fretted ice needed to be slow if they were to avoid serious injury or death.

The remaining sledge had been damaged and was running on one blade, and food was getting low. On 26 January 1909 the men ate the last of their biscuits and cheese. They were still twelve miles short of Depot D. Lunch that day was a cup of tea and two ounces of chocolate. Their average walking speed had reduced to one mile per hour. Three miles from the depot they were so exhausted that they had to pitch a tent and sleep. The following morning they set off at 9 a.m. but Wild and Adams both collapsed. By 1 p.m. they were still a mile from the site of the depot. They had travelled two miles in four hours. Wild and Adams could no longer continue. Marshall volunteered to go alone and bring back food.

He returned with tea, sugar, horsemeat, biscuits and pemmican: a feast. They had gone forty hours and marched sixteen miles without a proper meal.

Shackleton wrote: 'These were the worst two days ever spent in our lives.'

29 January brought another blizzard and the men were snowed into their tent. While they able to move on the following morning, they were fighting against high winds. They were also faced with the worry of finding Depot C and the extra supplies they so badly needed. In drifting snow and bad conditions, it could easily be missed.

Again, Wild was struck down, this time with dysentery, and the medicine given him by Marshall made him drowsy. Unable to eat his horsemeat, Wild's strength was going and he found it almost impossible to walk. Biscuits were the only things he could digest but these were strictly rationed. Secretly, Shackleton insisted his companion eat a biscuit saved from his own meagre supply. Wild would later write: 'I do not suppose that anyone else in the world can thoroughly realize how much generosity and sympathy was shown by this; I DO and BY GOD I shall never forget it. Thousands of pounds would not have bought me that biscuit.'

Ninety years later a single biscuit from the expedition was sold to Sir Ranulph Fiennes at a Christie's Polar auction in London for several thousand pounds.

On 4 February Shackleton scribbled in his diary: 'Cannot write any more. All down with acute dysentery. Terrible day. No march possible. Our food lies ahead and death stalks us from behind.'

The combination of physical and mental exhaustion, starvation, illness and worry were unravelling him. The *Nimrod* would return as arranged to pick them up. She would not wait indefinitely. It was extremely likely that they would miss her and be left behind.

On 7 February the weather improved and the men began to track the snow mounds they had left on their outward journey. Their rate of walking increased but not dramatically. They were still exhausted and hungry and food was a constant subject of conversation. On 10 February they reached Depot B and feasted on the liver of Chinaman. Five days later, during the 85-mile trek to Depot A, Shackleton celebrated his thirty-fifth birthday. His three colleagues presented him with a cigarette made from shreds of loose tobacco they'd saved.

Amazingly, in the midst of all this uncertainty and misery, Shackleton asked Wild to accompany him on another trip south: even more amazingly, Wild agreed.

Shackleton also suggested that, should the *Nimrod* be gone, they consider the possibility of using a rowing boat to get back to New Zealand. Little did he know that an epic journey in a rowing boat would loom large in his future.

On 20 February the men sighted Depot A at midday and reached it at four that afternoon. The first thing they did was to

Chinaman, one of Shackleton's favourites, was nearly lost slipping in to the water on arrival in Antarctica. The oldest of the four ponies on the Polar journey, and the first to be shot on 21 November to provide meat for Depot B.

dig out the buried stores and cook themselves a decent meal. Marshall made 'the best pudding I ever tasted' – a mixture of broken biscuits and blackcurrant jam.

Three days later they reached a depot left by Joyce – accidentally seeing the flag that marked it well off their course – and had a supper of sausages and a breakfast the following morning of porridge and eggs. The dramatic change of diet brought on another severe attack of dysentery in Marshall, leaving him too ill to travel. Shackleton and Wild went forward to Hut Point to get help. The journey involved a detour of seven miles because of worsening weather and Shackleton suffered constant headaches. What awaited him was the last thing he needed.

A note had been left, telling the men the *Nimrod* would wait for them, at Glacier Tongue, until 26 February. It was now 28 February. What Shackleton couldn't know was whether the captain of the *Nimrod* was going to wait for another couple of days at Cape Royds or sail for New Zealand on the 26th. It was quite possible that they had been left behind to winter on the ice.

Wild and Shackleton spent the night in the *Discovery* hut and the following morning started signalling for the *Nimrod*. They set an outhouse on fire and, later, lit a carbide flare using their own urine, as there was no other liquid available.

On the *Nimrod*, Maxwell, peering through the blizzard a quarter of a mile off shore, saw the flare. The ship headed back immediately. By one in the morning Wild and Shackleton were clambering aboard to be greeted by the question everyone wanted to ask: 'Did you reach the Pole?'

They hadn't, but amazingly they'd all survived.

Having eaten and rested for a couple of hours, Shackleton led a party back to pick up Marshall and Adams. By 4 March all four men were safely aboard ship, though Marshall, absurdly wearing new finneskoes (reindeer-fur boots), slipped on ice and was almost killed.

By his own calculations, Shackleton's party had walked, including relay work, 1725 miles and 300 yards in 126 days. They had gone 366 miles farther south than anyone had previously done. And they had all returned safely.

Failure was hardly the word to describe what had been achieved and withstood.

What awaited them in England was a divided response. Shackleton and his team would be

The southern party rejoined the Nimrod on 3 March 1909; left to right, Wild, Shackleton, Marshall and Adams.

greeted as heroes by the populace but for individuals like Edward Wilson, his one-time friend, the news that Shackleton had 'trespassed' on Scott's territory meant only one thing: betrayal.

He wrote: 'As for Shackleton, I feel the less said the better – I am afraid he has become a regular wrong 'un, and I know too much of all that has gone on to speak about him with any pleasure at all. In fact I have broken with him completely and for good.'

Sir Clements Markham, President of the Royal Geographical Society, was another whose attitude to Shackleton hardened. At the time of the *Discovery* expedition he had written that Scott was 'fortunate in finding such an excellent and zealous officer as Ernest Shackleton'. After his return from the *Nimrod* expedition he altered his notes: 'He seemed a steady young man.'

Shackleton might have risked life and limb, he might have taken his men beyond the point where they could count on deliverance, and significantly beyond previous expeditions, but he had fallen foul of those whose main concern was that he had trodden, almost literally, on Scott's snowshoes. Never mind that Scott, in turn, would use Shackleton's route up the Beardmore Glacier and follow his example by using ponies. He might be the darling of the man and woman in the street; he might even be their hero; but according to Scott he was 'A professed liar and a plausible rogue.'

The geographic establishment would never forgive the upstart Irishman who hadn't played by their rules.

7

Knighthood and the Public Man

1909–1914

◆

When word reached Emily Shackleton that her husband had made the farthest journey south she told the *Daily Mirror* on 27 March 1909 that Ernest was 'a born organizer as all the world can see, and the love and admiration of his comrades prove his worth as a man'. The five years that followed that achievement, however, were, in differing ways, to be every bit as testing for the couple. Eleven weeks after she gave the interview, on 12 June, Shackleton arrived in England to a very public hero's welcome.

He had left New Zealand on 15 April, having earlier lectured in Wellington Town Hall, raising £300 that he immediately donated to local charities. After a formal farewell lunch given by the Prime Minister, Sir Joseph Ward, and his ministers, Shackleton gave a gracious, entertaining speech and extolled those New Zealanders who'd assisted him financially and through their goodwill and encouragement. He also noted, as he was to do time and again, that this had been a group effort of which he was only one member.

The following day he sailed on the *Riverina* with a Maori cry of farewell ringing in his ears. He left with unbridled elation, allowing him to write to Emily that he was coming home for good. 'I … want … to tell you how much I love you how much I have missed you all this time and how I long to see you and our little ones again. Never again my beloved will there be such a separation as this has been.'

The success of his New Zealand lecture, the promises made and the opportunities in the offing – the expectation of earning up to £10,000 from lecturing and £20,000 from the sale of commemorative stamps, plus the proceeds from the book he planned – were responsible for this surge of optimism. He was falling into the trap of believing most of what he was told and everything that he imagined. The faraway hills of England were green, just as the wildernesses of Antarctica would be when remembered from England.

In Australia, a series of successful lectures reinforced his sense that financial security lay at last in his own hands. Leaving on the *India*, he set about writing his book with the help of Edward Saunders.

Saunders had first seen Shackleton in 1901 when, as a young reporter of nineteen, he visited the *Discovery* in Lyttelton. Six years later, he interviewed Shackleton before the *Nimrod* left New Zealand. Now, two years on, Shackleton was back in Lyttelton and employing him as his confidential secretary for four months from 15 April, on a salary of £10 per week plus expenses and a return ticket to New Zealand. Beyond their working relationship, the two men became firm friends and they began the book which Saunders would shape from Shackleton's memories.

The journey from Australia to Port Said wasn't all work, and other passengers and crew-members regularly had to compete with raucous laughter in the dining-room. Shackleton, Armytage, Adams and Mackintosh made a drama of mealtimes with what one passenger described as Shackleton's 'Irish wit and inexhaustible supply of funny stories'.

Transferring to the mail boat *Isis* at Port Said in Egypt, Shackleton arrived in Dover on 12 June. The plan was for a quiet family reunion but what awaited was the first of many public receptions, this one led by the Mayor of Dover. Like it or not, Shackleton was now public property. His life was not to be his own for a very long time.

On 14 June he travelled by train to London. The reception was beyond even his vivid imagination. The station was packed and outside the scenes were chaotic. The top brass of the geographical world were there to meet their returning hero. Among the platform party were Scott, come to meet and laud the 'professed liar', and Markham, who suggested to Scott that Shackleton was suffering from 'a swollen head'.

Shackleton, as always, made a speech not about himself but about his men. The word *I* rarely featured in his lectures or speeches. Heroic he might seem to others, but he knew he was one of a tightly knit team and without it there could be no survival. It was a lesson Scott might have learned.

The official speeches over, Shackleton moved outside to meet the throng who had come to see this ordinary man who had done an extraordinary thing. In the public mind, heroic and human, he had organized his own expedition, come within miles of the South Pole and, in so doing, reached the farthest south by the greatest distance. He was a man they admired, loved, wanted to see and hear and touch. His arrival in London had echoes of Christ's entry into Jerusalem. It was reported that people took the horses out of the shafts of the coach in which their hero was travelling and pulled it by hand. Whether this is truth or rumour matters little. Shackleton was the people's hero. Nor did it occur to those who came to see him that knives were being unsheathed in the Royal Geographical Society or that Sir Clements Markham, who spoke with apparent sincerity of his long friendship with Shackleton, was already his chief critic. All the people saw was their champion, all they heard were his easy words and unceremonious introductions to his travelling companions.

While cliques within the RGS set about undermining him, praise poured in from fellow travellers, the Norwegians Nansen and Amunsden.

Nansen referred admiringly to Shackleton's 'remarkable deed, and important discoveries and the excellent way in which he led his men through all dangers'. Amunsden wrote: 'The English nation has by the deed of Shackleton won a victory which can never be surpassed.'

While the public clamour pleased Shackleton, praise of his peers was every bit as important. He was receiving recognition, from his equals, for the scientific work he had done in the Antarctic.

In one of the few quiet moments available to them, Shackleton and Emily discussed the expedition's failure. He asked her whether 'a live donkey is better than a dead lion?' and she replied: 'Yes, darling, as far as I'm concerned.' In her own words, she said: 'We left it at that.'

Much of the praise showered on Shackleton benefited the RGS by association. Markham strongly believed that Scott was England's man for the South Pole and that the Irishman was only queering the pitch for his candidate. He put Shackleton's efforts alongside those of the other 'foreigners' who were simply a nuisance, though he was not willing to say as much publicly. He knew that this was not the time to attempt to remove the halo.

J. Scott Keltie, Secretary of the RGS was to some extent Markham's stalking-horse. He was responsible for confirming Shackleton's claims about how far south he had travelled. He wrote to Shackleton: '[the] difficulty of taking any observations under the conditions must have been fearfully trying, but still, I have no doubt you established your latitude to your complete satisfaction.'

Meanwhile, Markham was writing to Major Leonard Darwin, President of the RGS, damaging Shackleton and laying claims not just for Scott but for himself: 'As I am responsible for having started all this Antarctic business, I think it right that I should send you a note ... Shackleton's failure to reach the South Pole when it could have been done by another, and is really a matter of calculation, rather aggravates me ... I cannot accept the latitudes ... I do not believe it.'

The man challenging Shackleton's claims and calling him a liar had sat safely in London, apart from holidaying in Portugal, through the whole affair.

Shackleton found himself replying in the *Geographical Journal*, to slurs as much as to direct accusations:

'The latitude observations ... were taken with the theodolite ... Variation was ascertained by means of a compass attached to the theodolite, and the steering compasses were checked accordingly ... The last latitude observation on the outward journey was taken in 87 degrees 22' S. and the remainder of the distance towards the south was calculated by sledge meter and dead reckoning.'

One wonders whether Scott would have faced the same innuendo.

Shackleton's Irishness, however, was viewed differently by Sir Arthur Conan Doyle who, according to *The Yorkshire Reporter*, referred to Shackleton as a 'fellow-Irishman' and urged people to 'think of what Ireland has done for the Empire ... think of that flag flapping down yonder on the snow field, planted there by an Irishman'.

In Dublin, at a time of resurgent national feeling, *The Weekly Freeman* writer was unequivocal: 'Let there be no mistake, the Shackletons are Irish,' he wrote. *The Dublin Express* referred to 'the qualities that were his heritage as an Irishman, the dash and buoyant enthusiasm, the cheerful unshakeable courage'.

At a ceremony in London's Albert Hall on 28 June, the Prince of Wales, representing the king who was unable to attend, gave Shackleton a gold medal 'in recognition of his great and unique achievement'.

The presentation itself had been the centre of continuing controversy. A letter on 19 April from the RGS to Cuthbert Bayes, who would strike the medal, had informed him that the Society did 'not propose to make the Medal so large as that which was awarded to Capt. Scott'. Three weeks later Bayes received another letter telling him that the Society were, in fact, going 'to let Mr Shackleton have a Medal of the same size'.

For this he and his comrades had tramped the wastes of Antarctica.

Shackleton in 1909, looking uncharactistically 'civilized'.

On the night of the presentation, Scott proposed the vote of honour to Shackleton and thanked him for the 'very substantial addition he had made to human knowledge, but most of all because he has shown us a glorious example of British pluck and courage'.

They made a striking pair on a public platform and while Scott's tribute was well received, neither man liked or trusted the other. For Scott, Shackleton was a threat, a man who had outdone him but had also failed to reach the Pole. Scott had access to money and support and, barring a disaster, would be back in the Antarctic before his rival.

The weeks that followed Shackleton's homecoming might have been intended as a quiet time in which to get to know his children but, instead, they became an endless social round. Lectures, dinners, meetings, a visit to his old school, a talk at the Authors' Club, the presentation of the freedom of the borough of Lewisham, were all part of what was expected of this very public man. The whirl culminated in a visit to Buckingham Palace where the king invested him as a Commander of the Royal Victorian Order. But the adventure was now over and had to be paid for.

Shackleton's book was due out in November and he was hopeful it would sell well. Between debts and money due for guarantees, the expedition was £20,000 short of funds. It had cost almost £45,000. Some of those who had acted as guarantors might not seek repayment but there still remained a small fortune to be found.

Herbert Dorman, Emily's brother, had done most of the financial drudgery for the expedition. While Shackleton was in the public eye, Herbert Dorman was in the firing line. Demands for money for the upkeep of the *Nimrod*, for men's wages – still, in many cases, unpaid – and for outstanding bills for equipment and provisions meant that the project was in severe financial trouble. Dorman even considered launching a public appeal through the *Daily Mail*. The Dorman family, particularly Daisy, gave unstintingly to help offset their brother-in-law's indebtedness.

To many of his crew, however, the public man being fêted in London was the same individual who owed them wages. They needed the money, and they too had families to support. Shackleton's habit of taking a taxi and keeping it on call for a day at a time, often with the meter literally running outside people's houses, did little to maintain his former crewmen's esteem for him.

Again, this is the paradox of Shackleton. He never had any intention of abandoning his men and the social round on which he found himself was necessary to build public support. At the same time he had the unhappy knack of forgetting that other people had troubles, too, and that good intentions make poor meals.

By August he found himself releasing a statement to the newspapers explaining his financial problems. On 19 August the Prime Minister, Asquith, wrote to Shackleton telling him that the government 'have decided to recommend Parliament to make a grant of £20,000 to meet portion of the expenditure'.

Immediately, Shackleton was out of the darkness and back in the sunlight of his own ambition. 'Isn't it splendid,' he wrote to Emily, '£20,000 will be paid in, in a few days … Just think of your Boy getting £20,000 from the country: What Oh!!'

On 27 August the *Nimrod* arrived in England and the following day she docked at London's Temple Pier and was opened to the public. Over the next eight weeks more than 30,000 people visited the ship and over £2000 was raised for charity. From late October, she toured various British ports raising funds for good causes.

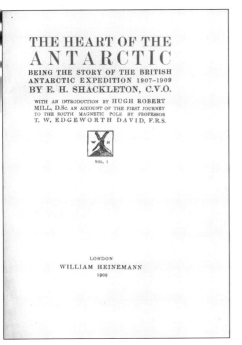

THE HEART OF THE
ANTARCTIC
BEING THE STORY OF THE BRITISH
ANTARCTIC EXPEDITION 1907-1909
BY E. H. SHACKLETON, C.V.O.

WITH AN INTRODUCTION BY HUGH ROBERT
MILL, D.Sc. AN ACCOUNT OF THE FIRST JOURNEY
TO THE SOUTH MAGNETIC POLE BY PROFESSOR
T. W. EDGEWORTH DAVID, F.R.S.

VOL. I

LONDON
WILLIAM HEINEMANN
1909

Title-page of The Heart of the Antarctic, *Shackleton's account of the* Nimrod *expedition. Shackleton dictated much of the book to Edward Saunders, a New Zealand reporter with the* Lyttelton Times *who travelled back with him to England during the summer of 1909. They worked well together; Saunders refused acknowledgment.*

In the last week of September Shackleton gave a lecture at Balmoral for the king. He was to be back in royal company eight weeks later but, in the meantime, he lectured in Copenhagen, Stockholm and Gothenburg before travelling to Brussels where his lecture was translated by De Gerlache.

The Heart of the Antarctic was published at the beginning of November, translated simultaneously in seven languages and in an American edition. It was well received, being both a good story well told and a scientific account accessible to the lay person. The one dissenting voice was that of J. Scott Keltie, who wrote: 'We may … cherish a hope that the Union Jack will be carried across the hundred miles or so which have been left untrodden by Shackleton … This we may be assured will be accomplished by Captain Scott in the next year or two.'

To crown the success of the book, Shackleton's name appeared in the king's birthday honours list – Ernest Shackleton, merchant seaman, was to become Sir Ernest. This honour, however, wouldn't pay the bills and he set off on a gruelling lecture tour that took him to all major British cities and to Paris over the following eight weeks. In the midst of this hectic schedule, on 14 December 1909, he received the first Antarctic knighthood to be bestowed since that of Sir James Ross in 1843.

Not that the knighthood made any difference, he was still Shackleton, man of the people and the people flocked to see him. The electricity of the Antarctic adventure was boosted by the charge of public acclaim. His lectures were never less than entertaining, whether relating the antics of penguins or the experiences of his comrades. His way with words and willingness to open himself to his listeners warmed his audiences.

After Christmas at home in Edinburgh, the early weeks of 1910 saw Emily and himself off again. They travelled to Rome and then Berlin and Vienna. In Germany and Austria he lectured in German, having learned his lecture off by heart. By the time he had reached Vienna, he felt comfortable enough with the language to answer questions in German.

The story is told that someone said of him that, if asked, he'd lecture in Chinese. To which he replied: 'But I *do* know some Chinese, I *could* lecture in it!'

Shackleton and Emily parted ways in Germany, she returning to the children, he going on to Budapest and St Petersburg. Wherever he went, rumours followed. He was going south again. He was joining a German expedition. He had every right to go at the same time as Scott. Some of these rumours must have reached Emily because he wrote to her, reassuring her that 'the main thing … is to see that we are all right financially before starting again'.

Back in Britain in February, the lecture tour continued and in mid-March he travelled, with Emily, on the *Lusitania* to New York. He left behind him a discussion on the relevance of the race for the South Pole. Geographers were adamant that research rather than competition was important. The South Pole of itself was of no value. Exploration and, as *The Times* put it, 'knowledge of the world's geography' were the important issues.

Arriving in New York in the last week of March he was entertained, in turn, by the British ambassador, the American President Taft and the American Geographical Society who awarded him their Gold Medal.

America, meanwhile, was taking to the Irishness in Shackleton. What they expected was a stuffy lecturer. What they got was a spontaneous, witty, engaging and dramatic talker who held them spellbound. Even the accent – once a problem for Shackleton – was received as a breath of fresh air. It was softer, less formal, than the British accents of the embassy staff. Knight and unionist he might be, but democratic America was impressed.

Not satisfied with lecturing, Shackleton had hoped to fit in a visit trip north to investigate the Alaskan landscape between the Mackenzie River and Point Barrow, but the trip fell through.

There were a few moments of unease. Shackleton's agent was charging people to attend his lectures while the American Geographical Society had a tradition of free admission. A compromise was reached and he lectured, for free, to the inner circle of the society, before going about the business of earning his living from the paying public. In May the news came

that the king had died. Shackleton, who'd had a good relationship with the monarch, was deeply upset.

The *New York Sun* correspondent, meanwhile, was impressed by the 'perils he and his party went through [which] were real and desperate ... He never missed a chance to say what fine fellows were [those] who toiled with him.'

In Canada the reception he received was every bit as warm. Attending a war veteran's dinner he talked of 'a body of men who have been tried and who know. I thank you for allowing me to talk to you.'

Back in the United States Shackleton's tour began to run out of steam. Poor advertising meant that the crowds in New England were small and by the time he returned to Britain

Sir Edmund Walker, EHS, Professor J.J. MacKenzie, on the front steps of Long Garth, 99 St George Street, Toronto, Canada, April 1910. (Courtesy Wentworth Walker)

131

in mid-June his thoughts were more of the possibilities of exploring in Alaska than they were of lecturing again.

The incessant talking of the previous eight months had made some money but not a fortune. Wherever he went, reporters questioned him on the possibilities of a new expedition. They were preaching to the converted.

There were more pressing and domestic matters at hand. In July the Shackleton family left Edinburgh and moved to Sheringham in Norfolk. That same month he went to see Scott off at Waterloo Station. While Scott was polite, his wife, Kathleen, was cold towards Shackleton.

A month later he was back on the lecture circuit, moving up the east coat of England into Scotland and back into northern England, to the news that Amunsden, on board the *Fram,* was also going south with the intention of reaching the Pole. With this in mind Shackleton headed for Germany in November.

On one of these trips he wrote to Emily telling her he was 'never again going south'.

If he meant what he said, it was undoubtedly brought on by the frustration of the lecture circuit. The depots were replaced by hotel rooms, the wilderness by a sea of faces on another unending journey in search of financial security.

The Germany Shackleton reached in November 1910 was not the same country he had visited earlier that year. The shadow of imminent war was stretching across Europe. From Cologne, he wrote to Emily: 'I can see a strong anti-English feeling in Germany … when the picture of the Queen's flag is shown there is stony silence … If things do not go better soon I will think very seriously of chucking the whole thing.'

From Germany Shackleton travelled to Poland and Switzerland. Apart from his lecturing he was still trying make money and the opportunity to invest in mining in Hungary was the latest solution to his ever-present problem. He was also promoting his Tabard cigarettes and an investment he had made in a taxi company in England was giving him a reasonable return, but none of these enterprises was going to keep Emily and himself and their children in any kind of comfort. This, however, didn't stem another of his rushes of optimism. A letter to Emily from Stuttgart, on a day when he had received an order for 20,000 Tabard cigarettes, was full of good tidings: '… that means £17 profit. If I can devote more time I will get much more like this.' On 14 December he was in Dublin, lecturing in Earlsfort Terrace less than

Lady DUDLEY'S SCHEME

FOR THE

Establishment of District Nurses in the Poorest Parts of Ireland.

ON BEHALF OF THE ABOVE,

Sir Ernest Shackleton

Will give his Illustrated Lecture on

'Nearest the South Pole'

In the

UNIVERSITY BUILDINGS, EARLSFORT TERRACE,

TUESDAY, Dec. 14th, at 8.0.

The Chair will be taken by

His Excellency The LORD LIEUTENANT.

SEATS, £1 1s. 10/6 7/6 5/-   UNRESERVED, 2/6

Doors open at 7.15.   Carriages at 10.
Plan and Tickets at Offices L.D.N.S., 30, Molesworth Street ; and Messrs. Cramer, Wood & Co.

The Lecture will be fully illustrated by

Kinematograph Pictures

And Photographs taken during the Expedition.

Shackleton gave a lecture at Earlsfort Terrace, Dublin in 1910.

two miles from the house in Donnybrook where he had spent the last years of his Irish childhood. Before the lecture, he was guest of honour at a dinner in the Gresham Hotel in Sackville Street. The people of Dublin, as elsewhere in the country, greeted and fêted him as an Irishman and he responded by telling them that he had been born Irish and he was still Irish.

The trip to Ireland, which also took in Belfast and Cork, brought to an end a year in which he had given 123 lectures, 50 of those in November and December alone. It was a year in which he had travelled over 20,000 miles and addressed more than a 250,000 people.

Making money was a difficulty for Shackleton, but staying at home, making ends meet, never being sure of where the next wild idea or uncertain income lay, was every bit as difficult for Emily. When her husband was in Antarctica she had a settled if empty life. Now that he was back in Europe things were little better. To add to her depression, early in 1911 she discovered she was pregnant again.

When he was in England, business seemed to take Shackleton more and more to London, leaving Emily with the children in Norfolk. This isolation and her pregnancy were a recipe for deep unhappiness. She and her husband had come from warm, happy families and he, when about, was generally an entertaining father. But his absence far outweighed his presence.

Sometimes, as on the occasion when he arrived disguised as an old man and convinced her and the children that he was his own long-lost Irish uncle, the possibilities of happiness opened before her. But there were other, longer, darker times when his life seemed much the better of the two.

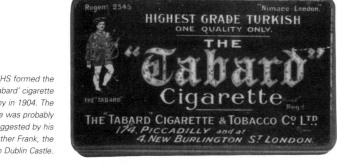

EHS formed the 'Tabard' cigarette company in 1904. The name was probably suggested by his brother Frank, the herald in Dublin Castle.

There was something of the manic-depressive in Shackleton. When life was good he was wonderful, but when boredom set in he could be unbearable. He might talk of spending more time at home but only did this when he was away, when the weight of his own guilt lay heavily on his shoulders. Back in Edinburgh or Norfolk, the trivialities of day-to-day life and the perceived demands of a wife and children were every bit as burdensome as the lack of finance. He loved his wife and children, but found living with them a challenge. He could entertain, he could swoop in and charm, but he needed to be away again, chasing money or security or achievement. She might be the base camp to which he returned, but she recognized that adventure was elsewhere.

In March 1911 Shackleton returned to Hungary, pursuing the elusive dream of a business that would bring in a lot of money. He told Emily that he wanted to 'feel I am clear of the Expedition and I have a straight road in front of me: If we live quietly for 2 or 3 years we can then do more … I want to consolidate our world.'

If those words put Emily's mind at rest, these must have raised the snowy ghosts again: 'I feel that another Expedition unless it crosses the Continent is not much.' By May, after attending at a meeting of the Aerial League of the British Empire in London, his thoughts turned to taking an aeroplane to the Antarctic.

The same month saw moves of a more practical nature, however. Emily, having enough of living in Sheringham, insisted that they move to London, where they took a house at 7 Heathview Gardens, Putney Heath. The latest move, like the initial move to Edinburgh, engaged his energy and preoccupied him for a short time. Carpets, wallpaper, even stair-rods, became the objects of his attention. For Emily, the house was something much more important, a move back to a world where she felt at home and in touch with the people she knew.

Two months later, Edward Arthur Alexander was born, on 15 July. A glorious summer of blue skies and soaring temperatures stretched ahead. But for Shackleton there was only frustration and a rising aggressiveness. Scott and Amunsden were gone south, he was stuck in London. The South Pole was, again, an object of contention but not for him.

It was also a summer when he had recurring chest pains. Nor were things at all well at home. Emily suffered from depression following Edward's birth and, more and more, Shackleton could be found visiting friends alone.

The end of the summer, and the shortening days, brought further bad news. His brother Frank, long under the shadow of suspicion for theft, was now being examined for bankruptcy. It transpired that he had debts in the region of £85,000 and had defrauded a number of people, among them Lord Ronald Sutherland-Gower and his adopted son, Frank Hird. Hird wrote to Ernest Shackleton, accusing him of being party to the fraud. Shackleton sued him for libel. Hird, however, withdrew his allegations before the case came to court.

Meanwhile Shackleton went back to things spiritual and resumed his association with Freemasonry, becoming inducted as a Second Degree Freemason in November.

The days leading up to Christmas were less than festive. A year had passed in which he had travelled and lectured, yet money was no more plentiful, business no more successful, his personal life no happier. The hankering to 'be away' was as strong as ever. There was hardship in the Antarctic, but it was a kind of hardship he could manage.

Worse was to come. On 14 December 1911, as far south as it was possible to go, his great dream came to an end.

The New Year of 1912 found Shackleton thinking actively about the possibilities of a new expedition, yet the intimations of his own eclipse were everywhere. Scott and Amundsen were moving towards the Pole, might even have reached it, for all he knew. It could only be a matter of weeks before word came of one or other having been successful.

But first there was other, more tragic news. On 15 April the *Titanic* sank in the North Atlantic with the loss of 1513 lives, having collided with an iceberg. This event, too, was to have repercussions for Shackleton.

A month later, on 17 May, the news he dreaded finally came. Amundsen had reached the South Pole. Shackleton, despite the sense of defeat, was fulsome in his praise for the new hero. He wired Amundsen, sending 'Heartiest congratulations' and wrote in the newspapers that the British people ought to acknowledge Amunsden's achievement in the same way that the Norwegian people would if Scott had reached the Pole first. He further described him as 'perhaps the greatest Polar explorer of today' and noted that (unlike Scott, who had followed his route) Amundsen 'made for himself an entirely new route'.

Kathleen Scott was not amused by Shackleton's graciousness and saw in it an attempt to denigrate her husband. She would, she said, 'willingly assist in that man's assassination,' as Roland Huntford reported in his book *Scott and Amunsden*.

Sir Clements Markham, as ever, had to have the last word and noted that Scott and his team would reach the Pole on foot, pulling their sledges, in 'the true British way'.

Amundsen, in his autobiography *My Life as an Explorer* (1928), described how after a lecture given by him in 1912 at an RGS dinner in London, its president Lord Curzon 'ended with the phrase "I therefore propose three cheers for the dogs" clearly indicating the next moment his satirical and derogatory intention by turning to me with an unnecessary calming gesture'. The insulted Amundsen called it a 'flagrant and insulting incident' and resigned his honorary fellowship of the society forthwith.

Shackleton's next engagement was the hearing into the sinking of the *Titanic*. He was called as a witness on 18 June as someone who had experience of navigation in ice. Almost immediately he and his interrogators, Sir Rufus Isaacs and Sir Robert Finlay, were at loggerheads. Suggestions were made that Shackleton's experience of ice in the northern hemisphere was limited but Shackleton stuck rigidly to his assertion that a captain on any vessel, even one travelling at six knots per hour, should be prepared to reduce speed in waters where there was a danger of icebergs. Sparks flew again when Shackleton suggested the captain of the *Titanic*, Edward John Smith, might have been under orders from the owners to maintain his speed. The sixty-two year old Smith, like Shackleton, had worked his way up through the ranks, in his case of the White Star Line, taking his first captaincy in 1887.

Ironically, when a statue of Smith was erected in Lichfield in 1914, its sculptor was Kathleen Scott.

The hearing, as so often, was a temporarily consuming issue for Shackleton. When his evidence was complete he was back to the mediocrity of real life. Even an invitation from the

Liberal Unionists to consider another attempt at a seat in Parliament held no attraction for him.

In November he was on the platform to greet Amundsen in London, one of the few senior figures in England to accord him that respect.

December saw him returning to New York, promoting his tobacco business yet still harking after a different lifestyle.

In the early months of 1913 Scott was back in the news. In February the *Terra Nova* arrived in England, bringing with it the ghosts of Scott and the men who had perished with him. The long wait was finally over. The sight of the ship docking confirmed the awful outcome of Scott's last expedition. It heralded, too, a not unsurprising upsurge in feeling for the dead explorer.

Shackleton's thoughts, however, were with the living rather than the dead, and more anxious than ever to be away from London. Frank was back in court, facing charges of fraudulently cashing a cheque.

With the Pole conquered, crossing the Antarctic continent was now the attraction. This had originally been mooted by the Scottish explorer William Bruce in 1908. His hope was that one person might put up the money for the trip in return for rights to the film footage he would take and the book and newspaper rights that could be agreed. He wrote and had printed a prospectus which summed up the objective of the expedition: 'To cross the South Polar Continent from sea to sea – from the Weddell Sea to the Ross Sea.' This was, he said, 'the last great Polar journey that can be made'.

For Emily the possibility of his being away, consumed by another great adventure, must have held some appeal for a woman who had seen her husband become morose and unsettled.

On 29 December 1913 Shackleton made his intentions public in a letter to *The Times*.

Sir,
It has been an open secret for some time past that I have been desirous of leading another expedition to the South Polar regions.

I am glad now to be able to state that, through the generosity of a friend, I can announce that an expedition will start next year with the object of crossing the South Polar continent from sea to sea.

I have taken the liberty of calling the expedition 'The Imperial Trans-

Antarctic Expedition', because I feel not only the people of these islands, but our kinsmen in all the lands under the Union Jack will be willing to assist towards the carrying out of the full programme of exploration to which my comrades and myself are pledged.

The announcement brought immediate protests from the Austrian, Felix König, who was planning an expedition into Antarctica from the Weddell Sea. Shackleton dismissed his protests, claiming the transcontinental crossing was much more important. Relations between Britain and the Germanic peoples were deteriorating at a rapid rate and Shackleton's stand was lauded as a patriotic one.

Interestingly, despite the wave of patriotism sweeping Britain, the Royal Geographical Society came down on König's side, although Shackleton was voted a grant of £1000 by the Society. More surprisingly, his long-time admirer, H.R. Mill, refused to support the idea on the basis that it was too dangerous.

The most venomous opposition came from Sir Clements Markham, who wrote to J. Scott Keltie, secretary of the RGS, on 14 January: 'I have been astounded at the absurdity of Shackleton's plan, alike useless and expensive and designed solely for self-advertisement.' In a 14-page report to the RGS Council three days later he questioned his qualifications: 'Shackleton's great grandfather had a pupil another great man, Edmund Burke, who habitually tinged facts with the colours of his own wishes or imagination. This may be a desireable habit for an orator or a journalist but not for an explorer.'

Shackleton was determined. He argued that much scientific research could be done on the journey and he gave details of his plans. There were to be two ships. He would take 120 trained dogs. The main mode of transporting supplies would be two large sledges with aeroplane engines and propellers.

In February he met with the RGS and told them that 'no expedition should set forth without the one object of being purely scientific ... My desire is to cross the Antarctic continent ... the members of it [the expedition] are the agents of the British nation. If I said differently I would be untrue to my conviction.'

In spite of scientific and patriotic cards, there were many sceptical voices in the RGS. Asked about the use of radios on the expedition, for example, Shackleton accepted that radios would be helpful: 'if I had the money,' he added, he would not 'want to communicate with England at all'.

This was his expedition and, while he might ask for support, he was not about to alter his plans for anyone. The very spirit which made him a hero of the people was the trait that annoyed the RGS members.

While few were willing to put money into the expedition, five thousand applied to join the enterprise. Among the applications was one from 'three sporty girls ... [who are] willing to undergo any hardships ... If our feminine garb is inconvenient, we should just love to don masculine attire ... we do not see why men should have all the glory.' Tempted or not, Shackleton politely declined their offer.

In October another fraud case involving Frank came to a head at the Old Bailey and he was sentenced to fifteen months hard labour for defrauding Mary Browne, an elderly lady, of £1000. More than ever, Shackleton wished to be away from the trouble his brother hauled in his wake. The publication of Scott's diaries the following month brought further pressures. References to Shackleton were mischievous, blaming him for miscalculations that had, supposedly, thrown Scott's progress into turmoil. The public were unaware that the diaries had been altered by Kathleen Scott, Sir Clements Markham and their publisher Reginald Smith before publication, to copper-fasten Scott's courageous image in the public eye.

One of the people who refused to accept the story as told in the diary was Caroline Oates, mother of Captain Oates who had died on the Scott expedition. Using her son's letters as a reference point, she was convinced that Scott's version did not tally with the version her son suggested. Little by little, through interviews with the survivors of the expedition, she elicited a story that convinced her that her son and the others who died had been needlessly sacrificed.

Not alone did she question the legend being built around Scott, but she was driven towards Shackleton and the things he stood for and, in time, she became friendly with Emily.

December brought a change of fortune for Shackleton with the government agreeing to give £10,000 towards his expedition; the rest he would have to find himself. Despite appeals to friends and business people, money was slow in coming. Shackleton, however, went ahead and bought a 350-ton wooden Norwegian ship, the *Polaris*, for £14,000.

The *Polaris* had been built in 1913 specifically to work in the ice but her prospective

The Shackleton family at Eddie's christening, Eastbourne, 19 September 1911.

Standing, left to right: Emily, Daisy Dorman (Emily's sister), Rev. Frank Ayers, EHS, Frank Dorman. Seated, left to right: Ethel Ayers (EHS's sister) with her daughter Joyce, nurse holding Eddie, Elizabeth Dawson-Lambton, Raymond and, front left, Cecily.

owners, Lars Christensen and Adrien de Gerlache, had been unable to find the money to pay for her and she was put up for sale. She sat, unwanted for over a year before Shackleton bought her and immediately renamed her the *Endurance*, after the family motto.

Finding large donations hard to come by, Shackleton changed his approach and asked several hundred wealthy people to contribute £50 each. Lord Rosebery sent a note with his £50, telling Shackleton that 'by the time you return … you will not find anyone in England with £50 left'. Markham, as usual, was quick to denigrate Shackleton's idea, describing him as 'worn out'.

Two people of very differing backgrounds suddenly came to Shackleton's rescue. Sir James Caird, the jute magnate who lived in Dundee, agreed to give £24,000, and Janet Stancomb-Wills also offered Shackleton substantial financial support.

Janet Stancomb-Wills had been adopted as a child by Sir W.H. Wills, the tobacco tycoon. She was a town councillor in Ramsgate and unmarried. While her initial interest in Shackleton was altruistic, in time she became a close friend and confidante. She was also to act as a benefactor to the Shackleton family, helping out with the children's school fees and acting as a sympathetic listener to Emily's woes.

Even though finances weren't fully in place, Caird and Stancomb-Wills' monies ensured that there was enough to make the expedition possible. In a moment of depression, he had said, 'I suppose I am really no good for anything but the Antarctic.' What he was good at was again within his sights. He was back in the business he loved more than anything: going south, adventuring.

8

The Endurance and Aurora

1914–1917

◆

Initially the Imperial Trans-Antarctic Expedition seemed to provide a remedy that would offer Shackleton redemption. The race to the South Pole was over. The deaths of Scott and his colleagues had, in some strange and tragic way, wiped that slate clean. The expedition across the continent was something fresh, free of politics and insecurities.

The proposal that there should be two ships on this expedition led immediately to problems of manning. Thanks to Shackleton's name and profile, there were some 5000 volunteers, including the 'three sporty girls' who failed to see why 'men should have all the glory'.

In February 1914, with war daily more imminent, he contacted the Admiralty about the possibility of having one vessel manned from the Royal Navy. This ship would sail to the Ross Sea and land a party to establish relay stations for the transcontinental group.

'For this purpose,' he wrote, 'I would ask for the loan of three executive officers and 15 to 20 men. The ship will not be wintering in the Antarctic and therefore in the event of war these men would not be far away from touch with civilisation for more than three months and could immediately return to their duties if necessary.'

The Admiralty was unhelpful. Another trip south was not high on their list of priorities. Eventually they allowed one man, Captain T. Orde-Lees, to join the expedition. This decision undermined Shackleton's plan. He'd hoped that the Royal Navy would help remove the financial onus from him. Obviously, this was not going to happen.

While negotiations went on with the Admiralty, Shackleton chose a New Zealander, Frank Worsley, as captain of his own ship, the *Endurance*. Like Shackleton, Worsley had worked his way through the ranks and was to become a close friend.

In choosing his second and third mates, Shackleton opted for the Irishman Tom Crean and Alfred Cheetham, men who already knew the Antarctic and the demands of life there. Cheetham had already served on the *Morning* (the ship sent in support of the *Discovery*), the *Nimrod* and the *Terra Nova*. Crean, an able seaman in the Royal Navy from Annascaul, County Kerry, had been on the *Discovery* and *Terra Nova* expeditions with Scott.

Tom Crean and Alf Cheetham (below). Tom Crean (1877-1938) later opened The South Pole Inn in Anascaul, County Kerry, Ireland. He is buried in a family tomb he built himself at Ballynacourty. Alf Cheetham served on four expeditions to the Antarctic. He was torpedoed and drowned off the Humber estuary in 1918.

The threat of war meant that many of the men Shackleton might have hoped to recruit were unavailable. The bulk of his crew was drawn from former merchant seamen now working on trawlers. Lionel Greenstreet, the navigating officer, was called in as a late replacement, getting the news the day before the *Endurance* sailed.

When it came to the shore party, the men with whom he would share the rigours of the expedition, Shackleton had already recruited Frank Wild, and together they discussed who they would take.

From Cambridge, Shackleton recruited the geologist James Wordie. George Marston was employed as expedition artist. Another Cambridge man was the physicist Reginald James.

James experienced one of those inimitable Shackleton interviews:

'I … was appointed after an interview of about ten minutes at the outside, probably more nearly five … he asked if my teeth were good, if I suffered from varicose veins, if I had a good temper, and if I could sing … he said: "O, I don't mean any Caruso stuff; but I suppose you can shout a bit with the boys?" He then asked if my circulation was good. I said it was except for one finger, which frequently went dead in cold weather. He asked me if I would seriously mind losing it. I said I would risk that. He did not ask me about my physics … After this he put out his hand and said: "Very well, I'll take you." '

Leonard Hussey, an anthropologist, physicist and meteorologist, was told to bring his banjo; Shackleton confided to him that he had chosen him because he thought he 'looked funny'.

Another example of a what made Shackleton select a man occurred when he was interviewing a surgeon, Alexander Macklin. Noticing that Macklin wore spectacles, Shackleton asked why. Macklin's reply, 'Many a wise face would look foolish without spectacles', caught Shackleton's fancy and he took him on.

It might seem that Shackleton was flippant, careless even, in choosing his comrades, but this hail-fellow-well-met attitude was simply a camouflage. Long before the pleasantries, he had done his research on the men's expertise. The final interviews provided a check on their social skills, their ease in getting on with others, the talents they might bring in music or entertainment or sheer good humour, qualities not to be underestimated on an expedition. Faith in a man was something Shackleton valued. He expected loyalty, but also believed in giving it. More than most, he knew what exactly was important in Antarctica.

Frank Hurley, the expedition photographer, had just returned from the Antarctic with Douglas Mawson, Australia's greatest polar explorer. Shackleton wanted him on the trip and wired him in Australia, inviting him to join the ship. Hurley immediately agreed.

Thus, man by man, the *Endurance* team was drawn together.

In the early summer of 1914 Shackleton left crewing concerns behind and travelled to Norway to test the propeller-powered sledge that he hoped would make life easier on the ice. Eight of the *Endurance* party went with him and they treated the trip as a dress rehearsal for the southern adventure. The all-important sledges worked, though Shackleton thought the engines needed to be stronger to pull the weights expected.

Frank Hurley (1885-1962), a professional and determined Australian photographer who accompanied the Endurance expedition, his second trip to the Antarctic; he took at least eight cameras including two cinecameras. His father advised him as a young boy, 'Find a way or make one for yourself.'

During the Norwegian stay, the team also tested the rations they would take. Shackleton was conscious as ever of the need for food that gave sustenance, and got the advice of the nutritionist Wilfred Beveridge. He also believed that a mixed diet of fresh meat where possible and tinned food where necessary would keep scurvy at bay. Charles Green, the cook who travelled on the *Endurance*, was to prove more than capable of looking after the dietary needs of the men.

Back in London preparations continued. Interestingly the *Endurance* was one of the first expedition vessels to be insured for her time in the ice floes. Until then ships were only insured to their last port of call before entering the ice. The hull and machinery were insured for £10,000. The premium was £665. An article in *The Times* noted that 'recent records of Antarctic navigation contain no instance of disaster that could be covered by insurance'.

Meanwhile, visitors to the ship, then on the Thames, were many and varied. Some paid for the pleasure, the money going towards the expedition. Others, like Queen Alexandra and Empress Marie of Russia, attended in their official capacities. During her visit on 16 July, the queen presented Shackleton with two Bibles, a Union Jack and a silk replica of her personal Royal Standard.

By the time the *Endurance* left London, on 1 August, war was no longer just a possibility. Two days later there was a general mobilization and Shackleton immediately offered the services of the *Endurance* to the Admiralty. When this was turned down, on the basis that the expedition was so far advanced that the money committed would be wasted, he offered his own services to the king, who advised him to continue. Even then, he was loath to opt out of the coming fight and, after the *Endurance* had sailed, continued to seek reassurance that he should follow her. Only at the end of August did he convince himself to go south and accepted that, while men aplenty were available to fight, few could do his job.

Three weeks later, on 27 September, he travelled to Buenos Aires to join the *Endurance*. Even then he was troubled, not by the war he was leaving but by unresolved financial and personal problems. As ever, there was enough money to get on with the current plan but the inevitability of a shortfall to come.

Endurance leaving Buenos Aires 26 October 1914. There were three new crew on board, Charlie Green the cook, Wiliam Bakewell, an American pretending to be a Canadian, and a ninteen-year-old stowaway, Perce Blackborow.

On a personal level Shackleton was haunted by the might-have-beens of life. He wrote to Emily bemoaning their parting: 'I don't want to go away into the South with any mis-understanding between us: I know that if you were married to a more domesticated man you would have been much happier and I also suppose I am just obsessed with my work ... just now my nerves are all on edge ... I could hardly have pulled through those last two months without a breakdown.'

The co-dependence between Emily and Shackleton surfaces in the letter. He wanted to travel but could only go with her support, and the unhappiness between them was now causing discomfort. He needed to be away, but needed her benediction.

Later, he would write to her pointing out he loved 'the fight and when things [are] easy I hate it ... I don't think I will ever go on a long expedition again.'

He was also aware of the constant financial pressure he was putting them under: 'Money is the most useful thing,' he wrote. For years he had been struggling to find money, believing that being best would bring the reward of security. Yet there were no firsts or bests to show for his work, nothing that would guarantee his place or his income.

Travelling south, with time on his hands, guilt preyed constantly on his mind. Once he joined the *Endurance*, work and the pressures he enjoyed, the physical and mental challenges of the expedition, took over. On 16 October the *Endurance* sailed from Buenos Aires and the expedition was officially underway.

A few days out from port, a young stowaway called Perce Blackborow was discovered and taken to Shackleton. Blackborow had tried to join the *Endurance* and, being told she

Perce Blackborow, discovered stowed away after leaving Buenos Aires, he was made a steward. On 16 June 1916 the toes of his left foot were amputated on Elephant Island. After the war he worked with his father in Newport docks in Wales. Died 1949. Mrs Chippy, expedition carpenter Henry McNeish's cat, a champion mouser who 'routinely monitored the ship's furnaces and stores'.

was sufficiently crewed, had decided to take his fate into his hands. Shackleton gave him a dressing down before signing him on, telling the nineteen-year-old: 'And if anyone has to be eaten, you will be the first.' At South Georgia, which the *Endurance* reached in early November, supplies and coal were taken on. During this period he made two decisions – one practical, the other a characteristic flight of money-making fancy. The first was that he would over-winter the *Endurance* and make his attempt at crossing the continent the following summer. The other was to establish a whaling company when he got back to England. He reckoned the profits could run to as much as £50,000 a year.

Within a few days of leaving South Georgia, the first of the troubles the *Endurance* was to face began. The Norwegian whaling men had warned Shackleton that conditions in the Weddell Sea were particularly bad that season. As Blackborow recounted in a lecture many years later: 'Actually, we met the pack on our second day out. This was very disturbing for our leader, for although he had been warned by the whalers of bad ice conditions he had expected a little better than this.' Shackleton himself described this as a 'gigantic jigsaw' of solid ice and open water that froze and smoked. At times the ice could be rammed but at other times the blocks were such that ramming was dangerous. It was more a question of the ship chasing her tail, winding through the pack-ice and moving slowly when she moved at all. The longer the time, the greater the concern about the coal supplies being eaten up by ice-floe delays where open water might have been expected.

Christmas Day, like the days before, was one of slow progress. Shackleton, as ever, ensured it was celebrated, with presents for the men and, as Worsley described it, a fine dinner of 'turtle soup, whitebait, jugged hare, Xmas puddg. Fired with brandy in approved style, mince pies, dates, figs, crystallised fruit &c. rum and stout for drinks … Party and singsong in evening.'

The cat-and-mouse chase between ship and ice continued over the following five days until the *Endurance* crossed the Antarctic Circle on the second-last day of the year.

Twenty-four hours later she was firmly wedged between two floes and pushed six degrees over. Only by anchoring and pulling on chains was the crew able to free her from this trap.

In the first week of January 1915 the crew took the opportunity to bring the dogs out on the ice floe for exercise while the men played football. At the end of the week, a break in the ice allowed the ship to make a hundred miles in open water and, by 15 January she was in a bay that seemed to offer shelter for the winter. Shackleton, however, decided to push farther south. It was to be a decision of enormous consequence, and one he would regret.

By the end of the third week in January the ship was again caught in ice and, to save coal, Shackleton ordered that the boilers be let go out. For a week he lived in the faint hope that the *Endurance* might float out of trouble.

Echoes of a previous experience in Antarctica were beginning to haunt him. The ship was jammed twenty-five miles short of his chosen landing-site and it looked as though she wouldn't get any closer before the following spring. Finally, on 24 February, Shackleton told the crewmen that the current position would be their wintering station. He had little choice.

With the boilers no longer working, there was no heat and less comfort on the ship. The cabins were bitterly cold, so new quarters were built by the carpenter, and the men moved into more bearable surroundings.

Once the wintering regime was established, the transcontinental group began working with the dogs. Each of the six men chosen – Shackleton, Crean, Wild, Hurley, Macklin and Marston – would have a team of seven dogs at his disposal. There would be no repetition of previous experiences; the dogs and their drivers would be well prepared.

Even though it seemed likely that the *Endurance* would return to South Georgia for a spring refit, before making another attempt at the crossing, Shackleton was adamant that the time on the ice was used to good effect. The ship might be frozen in but work must go on.

Apart from work, there was the usual winter entertainment and amusements. Books were available from the ship's library. Singing contests gave way to a bad singing contest, and Shackleton was voted a clear winner. In a mass haircutting all the men had their heads

Endurance fast in sea ice, February 1915.

shaved to the bone. Discussions and debates were constants, and slide-shows and mock trials proved very popular.

As on previous expeditions, Shackleton encouraged the men to take exercise and keep fit. Hurley erected electric lights on and around the ship so that they could walk safely on the floe.

The unchanging soundtrack for the *Endurance* crew through that winter was the noise of

Some hope. EHS inspecting lead in ice, October 1915, shortly before they had to abandon ship.

On deck of Endurance, end of winter 1915, showing dog kennels made from boxes.

the ice shifting and sighing. The ship, however, seemed safe enough and, on midwinter's day, 22 June, the crew organized a celebration which involved three full and appetizing meals followed by speeches, songs and sketches.

As the weeks passed, the ice tightened around the ship but nothing suggested that she wouldn't be free come spring.

October, however, brought a build in the ice pressure and by the 18th of the month the ship had tilted at an angle of thirty degrees. Added to the constant creaking of the ice and groaning of the ship's timbers was the sound of the terrified dogs howling. A week later the *Endurance* was leaking and Shackleton gave orders that provisions and equipment be moved onto the floe. Taking what they could, the men descended onto the ice, to be greeted by a chorus of eight Emperor penguins, which sang what sounded like a lament.

On 27 October Hurley recorded in his diary: 'Closer and closer the ice wave approaches ... Now it is within a few yards of the vessel ... We ... can only look impotently on ... All hands are ordered to stand by to discharge equipment and stores onto the ice ... The ship is doomed.'

And doomed she was. That night the men tried to sleep on the floe but sleep was impossible. Perce Blackborow would recall that 'our little ship was finally overwhelmed and

Endurance
in ice, 1915.

crushed … we camped on the ice with the nearest land 350 miles away. The "Boss" called us all together and told us our true position and his intention.'

The practicalities of organizing his men quickly took over from any feelings of loss Shackleton might have had. Looking back was not going to solve the problems of the present or the challenge of the immediate future. As ever in such circumstances, Shackleton was at his best.

The initial camp, about a hundred yards from the ship, had to be moved when the floe began to shatter. Once a new campsite had been chosen and the tents pitched, Shackleton called a meeting of the twenty-seven men and outlined his plan to walk to Paulet Island. Having thanked them for their calmness, he suggested they try to get some sleep. He kept watch through the night and raised the alarm around midnight as the floe began to crack again. Once more, the tents were moved to a safer place.

At dawn, Shackleton, Wild and Hurley went aboard and took petrol from the *Endurance*. They then boiled milk and brought it round to their comrades, some of whom were unimpressed, it seems, by the work that had gone into preparing the hot drink. Wild, annoyed at the nonchalance with which the gesture was received, commented wryly to some of the men: 'If any of you gentlemen would like your boots cleaned just put them outside!'

Much of that morning was spent taking what might be useful from the fractured ship. Three boats were loaded on sledges and the men packed personal belongings, being allowed no more than two pounds weight each. Shackleton took some pages from the ship's Bible but left his gold watch and several sovereigns behind. He did, however, insist that Hussey take his banjo.

On 30 October the party began its slow journey away from the *Endurance*. Given the dangerous state of the floe, Shackleton insisted the men stay together and move with as much care as possible. Heavy snow kept them on the floe in what they named Ocean Camp.

Again, Perce Blackborow remembered the men were on 'about 9 ozs food daily ration. I like to think of our leader as I recall him at this time. His hopes & ambitions had all been shattered – yet he was cheerful & went out of his way to impart some of his cheerfulness to others. He had a genius for keeping his men in good spirits, & need I say more, we loved him like a father.'

Day after day, parties went back to the ship. Nails were taken from planks and saved for future carpentry needs. Hurley and Shackleton spent hours sorting through the photographic plates, limiting what could be taken to the contents of one tin. The other plates were smashed. This was a brutal but final way of limiting the choice and avoiding second thoughts.

Life on the floe went on. Once the essentials had been established – safety and the building of a proper kitchen – the men settled into a routine. The future, whatever it might bring, was not yet an issue. Patience was the watchword.

On 21 November the packed ice temporarily broke and the men watched the *Endurance* slip to her end. Worsley wrote that she 'put up the bravest fight that ever ship had fought before yielding ... Nothing is now visible of her but 20 feet of her stern pointing pitifully up to Heaven. She remains like this a few minutes & then slowly slips down beneath her icy shroud & is seen no more ... .At 5 p.m. we saw her end.'

The break-up of the ice, which had swallowed the *Endurance*, also allowed for a possible escape from the floe. Knowing that it was time to move, Shackleton decided the team would celebrate Christmas Day on 22 December. A dinner of ham, hare, parsnips, baked beans, peaches, biscuits, jam and coffee or cocoa was followed by the striking of camp.

Next day Shackleton and Wild moved ahead to review the lie of the land. Worsley was left in charge. In Shackleton's absence, words passed between Worsley and Harry McNeish, the carpenter. The main party came to a halt, spectators to the stand-off. On his return, Shackleton found McNeish maintaining that the march across the ice was madness. Shackleton quickly reminded all of the men that they were still in his employ and that orders must be obeyed. In particular, he would not stand for anyone disobeying the order of an officer.

The falling-out came at a bad time. Progress was slow and Shackleton was under extreme pressure. His diary entry about McNeish was short and to the point: 'Everyone working well except the carpenter: I shall never forget him in this time of strain and stress.' Nor did he, refusing to recommend him for a Polar Medal when the expedition ended.

The initial hopes of the men – that they might make progress towards rescue – were to be stymied by the breaking ice and unstable conditions. Instead of going forward they were forced to retreat to a solid floe.

On New Year's Eve Shackleton wrote in his diary: 'May the new one bring us good fortune ... Ice seems to be rotting away ... I long for some rest free from thought.'

Two weeks later, knowing the boats were their only hope and that food supplies were dwindling, Shackleton ordered more of the dogs shot. Another week passed and the floe drifted back across the Antarctic Circle. Another small milestone had been reached.

Shackleton had taken two boats with him onto the floe but in early February he agreed to send a party back to bring the third boat to the camp. Until the men reappeared, he was ill at ease. Their safety was paramount to him. Sometimes, in the grip of a nightmare, his voice could be heard across the icy wilderness and, when he woke, he inevitably recounted some dream of losing men. In a strange way, his care for his men, always a priority, seemed regularly to be haunted by the ghost of his dead rival and the possibility that, but for the grace of God, he might find himself in a similar position.

Months drifted by on the ice, February moving into March without any change in the patterns of the men's lives. Late in the month their floe began to melt and to pick up speed. They sat on the ice, powerless to do anything to alter their course. On 7 April they came in sight of Clarence Island, next door to Elephant Island on which they were to land. With the sighting came the reminder that missing the island would send them out into the open ocean and God alone knew what fate. Then nature took a hand. The floe split through their camp and the following day the three boats were launched and the men began to row.

The fall of night saw them camp on another floe. During the night this floe cracked, throwing Holness into the sea. For the rest of the night, he was kept moving because there was no dry clothing for him. Walter How recalled how 'every movement he made with his legs and arms, there was a crackle of icy clothes'.

The days that followed, spent in the open boats, were terrifying. The ice floes were too dangerous to trust for camps and the boats provided little shelter. With no way of cooking, the men were reduced to eating dry dog food which brought on bouts of diarrhoea. Constantly wet from the breaking waves, constantly sick from the rough seas, the men finally got ashore on 15 April at Cape Valentine at the east end of Elephant Island.

Shackleton made an occasion of the landing, suggesting the stowaway, Blackborow, as the youngest, be first ashore. The young man, however, was badly frostbitten and, as soon as he set foot in the water at the shore, he collapsed into the waves. The men laughed emotionally, rushing to follow him, setting their feet on solid land for the first time in more than sixteen months.

Blackborow wrote of the day: 'Sir E.S. gave me the great honour of being the first man to land ... All the company had suffered severely from exposure & frostbite, several being in a very bad way.'

Two days later they were on the sea again, moving camp to a safer and more hospitable point up the coast to a beach they named Cape Wild.

Elephant Island measures 23 miles by 13 (at its widest point) and, while it offered fresh food in the form of penguins, birds and sea elephants, it was not a welcoming haven. Constant rain and snow and gale force winds meant that life there was extremely harsh. Worse still, the island was not on the regular whaling routes and the chances of their being found were slim. Shackleton decided there was only one choice in the circumstances. A boat would go for help, 800 miles to South Georgia. Wild was to take charge of the men on the island, while he led the rescue party.

McNeish set to work on the chosen boat, the *James Caird*, making a shelter and deck at the forward end of the craft. The six men chosen to crew the *James Caird* were Crean, McCarthy and Shackleton, all Irishmen, McNeish, Vincent and Worsley. On 24 April they left Elephant Island and the twenty-two men whose lives were to depend on their reaching land safely.

As Blackborow recalled, Shackleton and his crew set off on a 'desperate venture ... in a small lifeboat in an attempt to reach S. Georgia, over 800 miles away across the most tempestuous seas in the world'. By the next day, the pack ice closed in and their departure would have been impossible.

Life on the *James Caird* was precarious. Three man watches of four hours, during which each had a job – one on the tiller, one bailing, one attending to the sails - were followed by four hours off watch, when the men tried to sleep in the narrow and constantly wet confines of the boat. Cooking on board was limited to what could be done with a primus stove jammed between the feet of two men, one leaning against each side of the boat. Tom Crean was the primus expert and chef. Shackleton insisted that breakfast, lunch and an evening

James Caird departing Point Wild on Elephant Island, 24 April 1916. The next day the bay filled with pack ice, blocking it for weeks. The James Caird was a 22 feet 6 inches long, double-ended, carvel-built ship's boat now on display at Shackleton's old school, Dulwich College, London.

meal be taken at set times, the routine helping to maintain the generally high spirits of the men. Worsley described Shackleton's concern for his comrades as having 'a touch of woman'.

Each individual drew strength from the reliability of his comrades. Shackleton wrote that Crean's singing reminded him of 'the chanting of a Buddhist monk ... In moments of inspiration Crean would attempt "The Wearing of the Green".'

Icing on the boat and choppy seas made the first week and a half of the journey a trial but on 5 May difficulty gave way to danger when the boat was hit by a gale. Shackleton saw what he thought was a break in the cloud only to realize immediately that what he had imagined to be light was, in fact, the crest of a wave 'so gigantic ... a thing quite apart from the ... seas that had been our tireless enemies for many days. I shouted: "For God's sake, hold on! It's got us!" Then came a moment of suspense that seemed drawn out into hours ... We felt our boat lifted and flung forward like a cork in breaking surf ... but somehow the boat lived through it, half-full of water, sagging to the dead weight ... We baled with the energy of men fighting for life … and after ten minutes of uncertainty we felt the boat renew her life beneath us.'

The following day the sun put in a brief appearance, as though to check they were still afloat and alive. During the voyage, Worsley's four readings using sextant and sun were vital for keeping them on the right course for South Georgia.

The next problem was a shortage of water. One of the containers had been damaged and contaminated with seawater. Rations were cut to a half-pint per man per day.

8 May, however, brought a sight that lifted their spirits and gave them new energy. Just after midday McCarthy sighted a cliff face, and they realized that they were close to South Georgia.

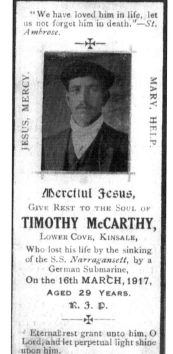

Tim McCarthy's Mass card. Born Kinsale, County Cork, Ireland, where there are now memorials to him and his brother Mortimer. Chosen for the James Caird boat journey, he was highly thought of by Shackleton and Worsley for his great cheerfulness and optimism. Died 1917 when his ship was torpedoed in the English Channel. (Courtesy Terry Connolly)

"We have loved him in life, let us not forget him in death."—*St. Ambrose.*

✠

Merciful Jesus,

GIVE REST TO THE SOUL OF

TIMOTHY McCARTHY,

LOWER COVE, KINSALE,

Who lost his life by the sinking of the S.S. *Narragansett*, by a German Submarine,

On the 16th MARCH, 1917,

AGED 29 YEARS.

R. 3. P.

✠

Eternal rest grant unto him, O Lord, and let perpetual light shine upon him.

The following day, in the teeth of a gale, they worked their way clear of rocks and on 10 May finally got ashore, landing by chance at the mouth of a freshwater stream. A stew of young albatross and Bovril formed their first hot and sustaining meal in over two weeks.

Shackleton planned to take the boat farther up the coast to find a better site for a camp and then set off on foot across the island for help. There was one problem: the rudder of the *James Caird* had been lost in the rough seas that took them in. Miraculously it seemed, on 13 May the rudder was washed up at the exact spot where they were camped. Repairs were made and two days later they were back at sea, working along the difficult coast until they found a safer place to land and a point from which Crean, Shackleton and Worsley would walk to Stromness in search of help. McCarthy was to look after McNeish and Vincent who were suffering from exposure.

At 3 a.m. on 19 May the three set off, ill clothed and ill equipped for the journey ahead, forced to use an adze as an ice-pick, carrying their equipment in bundles like schoolboys. Climbing to find their bearings, they discovered that their chart, no more than an outline of the island, was less than accurate. Time after time, they climbed only to be met by cliffs and forced back down again. The most immediate danger was the prospect of being caught at altitude without sleeping-bags or any proper protection from the bitter cold.

As darkness fell, the men cut ice-steps down the side of one cliff and then, peering through the darkness, they imagined the ground sloped away more gently. But between fog and blackness they couldn't be sure. Shackleton made a decision to risk sledging down, using their rope as a protection from snow burn.

Sitting one behind the other on the coiled rope, Shackleton then Worsley then Crean, the three pushed themselves forward, not knowing where they were going or what lay ahead.

Worsley described the sensation: 'I was never more scared in my life than for the first thirty seconds. The speed was terrific. I think we all gasped at the hair-raising shoot into the darkness … Then, to our joy, the slope curved out and we shot into a bank of soft snow. We estimated we had shot down a mile in two or three minutes and had lowered our altitude by two or three thousand feet. We stood up and shook hands.'

To Shackleton's amusement, Worsley had lost most of the backside of his trousers in their trip down the mountain. Turning around, however, he discovered that he was in a similar state himself.

Pushing on, dehydrated and exhausted, they were forced to stop for rest and sleep. The three huddled together for whatever passed for warmth, and Worsley and Crean slept. Fearing hypothermia and death, Shackleton stayed awake. He allowed the pair to sleep for what he said was half an hour. Afterwards, he would admit he had only let them sleep for five minutes before waking them and moving on.

Walking across the bleak island, under an intense full moon, the men walked down until, on the morning of 20 May they saw the sight they hardly dared imagine, the glimmering waters of Stromness Bay. Behind them lay months of pain and hunger and doubt, ahead lay twelve miles of difficult terrain but only twelve miles. Their hearts soared and their energy seemed suddenly restored.

As they made breakfast, Shackleton heard a steam-whistle cutting the white silence of the landscape. 'Never had any of us heard sweeter music,' he wrote. 'It was the first sound created by outside human agency that had come to our ears since we left Stromness Bay in December 1914.'

It was half-past one that afternoon when the three figures stumbled over the crest of a ridge and saw below them men and ships, life and hope. Again, they shook hands and moved down towards the harbour.

The full realization of how they looked hit home in the late afternoon when, as they reached the outskirts of the whaling station, two small boys ran away terrified at the sight. An old man directed them to the station manager's office.

A man named Mansell watched as the three came in. Later, he would describe the scene.

'Everybody at Stromness knew Shackleton well, and we very sorry he is lost in ice with all hands. But we do not know three terrible-looking bearded men who walk into the office off the mountainside ... Manager say: "Who the hell are you" and terrible bearded man in the centre of the three say very quietly: "My name is Shackleton." Me – I turn away and weep. I think manager weep too.'

Later, Shackleton would look back on the journey and write: 'We had "suffered, starved and triumphed, grovelled down yet grasped at glory, grown bigger in the bigness of the

Whaling manager's house, Stromness, South Georgia. Shackleton, Crean and Worsley arrived there 20 May 1916 after crossing South Georgia. They were welcomed by the amazed manager, Thoraff Sorlle, and that evening had their first baths for six months. This historic building still stands.

whole". We had seen God in his splendours, heard the text that Nature renders. We had reached the naked soul of man.'

His use of strong spiritual language in recounting how the journey across South Georgia affected him is hardly surprising. In time, Worsley and Crean and he would all refer to the fact that, as they crossed the high whiteness, they felt, constantly, that there was a fourth person present. None spoke of the feeling to the others. Shackleton recounts in his book *South* how Worsley said to him: '"Boss. I had a curious feeling on the march that there was another person with us." ' Crean confessed to the same idea. One feels ' "the dearth of human words, the roughness of mortal speech" in trying to describe things intangible'.

The echoes of Luke 24:13–16 are unmistakable. 'And, behold, two of them went that same day to a village called Emmaus … And it came to pass, that, while they communed together and reasoned, Jesus himself drew near, and went with them. But their eyes were holden that they should not know him.'

Whatever happened on that journey, collectively and individually, none of the three would ever forget the sensation of the other, the absent friend who was with them to the end and only left when they were safely delivered.

As soon as Shackleton had organized for a whaler, the *Samson*, Worsley boarded it and travelled back to pick up the three men on the other side of the island. Shackleton and Crean went on to Husvik and arranged that the *Southern Sky* be pressed into service to try to reach Elephant Island. Ingvar Thom, an old acquaintance of Shackleton's, agreed to captain her. He also arranged a get-together on his ship, the *Orwell*, where a large gathering of sailors and whaling men met to honour Shackleton and his comrades. Worsley described the scene: 'One spoke in Norse, and the manager translated. He said he had been at sea over forty years; that he knew this stormy Southern Ocean intimately … and that never had he heard of such a wonderful feat of daring seamanship as bringing the 22-ft open boat from Elephant Island to South Georgia, and then, to crown it, tramping across the ice and snow and rocky heights of the interior, and that he felt it an honour to meet and shake hands with Sir Ernest and his comrades. He finished with the dramatic words: "These are men!"'

The *Southern Sky* left for Elephant Island on 23 May but she was only three days out when they met ice and, though she got within seventy miles of the island, there was no way through. Instead, Shackleton took her on to the Falklands, to get word of their plight to the wider world and to send news of his survival to Emily.

'It was Nature against us the whole time' was his succinct way of describing what the men had been through and what those on Elephant Island were still enduring.

His wired appeals for help to the Admiralty and to South American countries brought a first response from the Uruguayans who offered a trawler. Shackleton, whom the Uraguayans dubbed 'el héroe irlandés', accepted immediately and on 10 June he set off on the boat, the *Instituto de Pesca No. 1*, and three days later came in sight of Elephant Island but was driven back by the ice.

Forced to return to the Falklands, Shackleton, Crean and Worsley then travelled on to Chile and secured the use of a wooden schooner, the *Emma*, and a small steel steam tug, the *Yelcho*. On 12 July they set out again but bad weather drove them back. Typically, he wrote home frequently to his family. On 1 August he told his elder son Raymond, 'I am writing this on the way up from the ice, we have just made another attempt to rescue the men on Elephant Island but our little schooner was not strong enough ... I know you will be a great help and comfort to Mummy by working well at school and looking after her when at home, she is a mother in a million as I know you must already realize and she has not had an easy time of it and there has been much sadness. God Bless you. Your loving, wandering father.'

Stranded in Port Stanley on 8 August, Shackleton waited for word from the Admiralty. Despite his impatience, he realized that war and distance were impediments to help from Britain. Wires from London informed him that the *Discovery* would be sent when she had finished being repaired and that he should rest up in Port Stanley. This was not what he wanted to hear. Again, the Chilean government came to his assistance. Taking the *Yelcho* alone, and promising not to risk her in the ice, he left Punta Arenas on 25 August and reached Elephant Island five days later.

At first, the men on the island feared the ship was passing them by. They had no way of knowing Shackleton was aboard. A fire was lit but by then the ship was making for them. Soon, a rowing boat was seen on the waves, Shackleton standing in it, enquiring across the water if they were all well. The twenty-two men could only stare.

Shackleton was greeted by a crew who had always tried to believe he would return for them. They were also men who had been pushed to the limits of their physical and psychological being, living under the two remaining upturned ship's boats. They were hungry and exhausted, in some instances living on the brink of madness. Frank Wild's calm leadership has seen them through. Shackleton he had done what he promised: he had come back for his comrades, and taken them to safety.

In October 1916 Shackleton wrote a letter to his agent Ernest Perris explaining he was 'dead tired and very lonely'. However, he went on to pen short, candid reports on each of the crew members: 'I know these men's hearts,' he wrote, and he did.

Back in Punta Arenas, Shackleton wrote in the visitors' book of the Spanish Consul lines by St John Lucas. They said more than he might ever have managed or dared to say about those he despised, those he respected, those he loved, and about himself:

> 'We were the fools who could not rest
> In the dull earth we left behind,
> And burned with passion for the south
> And drank strange frenzy from its wind.
> The world where wise men sit at ease
> Fades from our unregretful eyes,
> And thus across uncharted seas,
> We stagger on our enterprise.'

While this drama of survival had been played out on one side of Antartica, another was being played out on the other. The *Aurora* crew, charged with laying supplies on the Ross Ice Shelf for the transcontinental team, had, after financial problems kept them in Australia six weeks longer than intendeded, gone about their work. Again, not all went as planned.

Having landed shore crews and been anchored as a winter base, the ship was torn from her moorings in early May 1915 and left drifting with the ice, unable to make contact with either the ten men who had been stranded or with potential rescuers.

By 2 June the two parties left on the ice – one laying depots, the other engaged in scientific work – had reconnoitred at Cape Evans and prepared for the winter. Available supplies, while not what they would have chosen, ensured no one would starve.

The major problem was the surfeit of chiefs in the party. Aeneas Mackintosh was in

charge, theoretically, but neither Ernest Joyce nor Fred Stevens, the chief scientist, had much faith in Mackintosh, blaming him for the fact that men had been allowed to come ashore without adequate supplies in the event of an emergency. Furthermore, they blamed him for the positioning of the ship which, they believed, had led to her being blown out of reach by the storms. Their views on Shackleton also differed. Joyce was blindly loyal, Stevens was unimpressed by the planning – or lack of it – that Shackleton had put into the *Aurora*. The forced companionship of the moment was unavoidable, but it did nothing to ease the tensions between the men.

At the beginning of September, three ill-equipped parties of three set off to lay further depots, leaving Stevens to continue his scientific research alone at Cape Evans. Initially, and through the sheer hard work of the men, the depot laying went well. As there were few dogs left, the men were forced to pull loads of between 150 and 200 pounds each. Such was their determination to keep their promise to Shackleton, they worked willingly despite the continuing bickering of Mackintosh and Joyce. The arguments often revolved around the benefits of using dogs rather than man-hauling. Joyce had a way with dogs, Macintosh had little time for them. The root of the problem lay in the fact that neither Joyce nor Mackintosh regarded the other as a suitable leader.

On 3 January 1916, with one of the primus stoves no longer working, three of the men on the depot-laying trek were sent back to Cape Evans. A week later Mackintosh swallowed his pride and asked Joyce to take over as leader of a joint party. There were now six men left on the journey – Joyce, Mackintosh, Hayward, Richards, Spencer-Smith and Wild.

In the days that followed both Mackintosh and Spencer-Smith became ill and, although Joyce suggested turning back, Mackintosh emphatically refused. Whether his refusal was a sign of his intention to complete the job he had told Shackleton he would do or whether, having given up on the leadership, he was now refusing to bend to Joyce's control a second time is a moot point.

On 22 January Spencer-Smith was left behind with a fortnight's supplies, while the other five went on. Finally, on 26 January a depot was laid at the Beardmore Glacier. They had achieved what they set out to do.

Turning for base that day, the men recognized the dangers that lay ahead. Mackintosh's knee was severely swollen, Joyce was partially snow-blind, and all five were suffering from scurvy.

On 29 January they reached Spencer-Smith to find him too ill to walk. Putting him on a sledge they moved on again. Mackintosh's knee was now so badly swollen that he could barely walk but he refused to be put on a sledge and so the ragged band continued, moving painfully slowly through the snow, undernourished and suffering from exposure.

By 23 February the men were so weak that they could no longer pull Spencer-Smith on the sledge and he and Mackintosh were left behind with Wild to look after them. So weak

Mackintosh and Rev. Spencer-Smith on sledge, February–March 1916. Spencer-Smith, who knew Charlie Green, met Shackleton in Buenos Aires and was taken on as photographer on the Ross Sea party. The first cleric in Antarctica, Spencer-Smith died 9 March 1916. Mackintosh was last seen setting out over sea ice to the hut at Cape Evans with Hayward on 8 May.

165

was Spencer-Smith that he couldn't leave his sleeping-bag and Wild had the unenviable task of looking after his hygiene.

Joyce, Richards and Hayward went on. A blizzard forced them to camp, even though they were out of food and reduced to eating dog food and letting the dogs go without. The shadow of Scott fell over Joyce. Constantly mindful of what had happened to Scott and his men, he was determined he and his comrades would not suffer a similar fate. Somehow the three moved on, taking two hours to cover a distance of three-quarters of a mile, and finally reached the depot on 26 February. They were exhausted, ill and starving, faint mirror images of the trio who would later stagger into a whaling station on South Georgia.

Three days on, somewhat resuscitated, they arrived back with supplies for Mackintosh, Spencer-Smith and Wild. Wild, hearing the dogs, staggered from the tent, his sledge harness already on, and, despite his hunger and weakness, coming to help pull the sledge.

The party set off again only to have Hayward fall ill. There was nothing for it but to put the two sickest men, Mackintosh and Spencer-Smith on sledges and to pull them. And this is what was done. Joyce, Richards and Wild dragged their human cargo over the soft snow, hardly able to move but determined to continue. Hayward staggered along as well as he could.

A week of this punishing routine saw them reach breaking-point. They simply didn't have the energy to go on and Mackintosh volunteered to be temporarily left behind.

On 9 March, while the men lay in their tent, Spencer-Smith died. He had been particularly ill through the night, complaining of chest pains and cold. The temperature was – 30 degrees. At six in the morning he stopped breathing.

Forty-eight hours later the four men reached Hut Point and on 16 March they returned for Mackintosh and brought him safely back to the hut.

Poignantly, Joyce would later recount how, even in the worst of times, he would look over his shoulder somehow hoping he might catch sight of Shackleton and his five companions gaining on them out of the blizzard. But an extraordinary undertaking had been completed: they had walked almost 1600 miles, over 200 days, with little to eat, poorly equipped, eventually sacrificing a life, but they had laid the depots as promised for a leader who would never reach them.

The unpredictability of the ice meant the men were forced to remain at Hut Point into early May. Mackintosh in particular was anxious to get back to Cape Evans to discover whether there was any news of the *Aurora*. The others were less inclined to move, fearing danger on the unstable ice. On 7 May, despite warnings from his comrades, Mackintosh insisted that he was moving and the following day he and Hayward set off, promising to return if they ran into trouble. The pair left the hut at 1 p.m. Two hours later a blizzard swept across the landscape, engulfing everything. Such was the ferocity of the storm that it was two days before the men trapped inside the hut could even begin to search for Mackintosh and Hayward.

What they found, when the weather cleared, were the tracks of the pair's footsteps on the ice. They followed the trail for two miles until it ended in broken ice.

There was the slight possibility that Mackintosh and Hayward had got across before the ice broke but it was a faint hope and one that was finally dashed two months later, when Joyce and his men reached Cape Evans to discover that neither Mackintosh nor Hayward had made it.

It was to be late December 1916 before a relief ship – the *Aurora* – set out to rescue the men from Cape Evans. Shackleton had, by then, gone through protracted and excruciating negotiations with the governments of Australia and New Zealand to organize the rescue. The lack of proper financial management in the original fitting of the *Aurora* meant that Shackleton was viewed as less than reliable by both governments. Neither was willing to give command of a ship they had overhauled and underwritten to a man who appeared so blasé with other people's money. Shackleton, on the other hand, was adamant that the stranded men were his responsibility and he was the one who would rescue them. He also insisted that the *Aurora* was his ship and he wasn't about to hand her over to anyone – debts or no debts.

Eventually, a compromise was reached and Shackleton sailed on the *Aurora* under a government appointee. His position on the ship wasn't an issue with Shackleton, he simply wanted to get to his men, and he was quite content to sail out of Port Chalmers on 20 December under the command of Captain John Davis, a man of Irish descent.

Three weeks later the *Aurora* reached Cape Royds. Shackleton described the scene:

'No sign of life at my old hut. We fired a distress signal no sign of life at Cape Evans hut. I went alone to our hut and found there a note unsigned dated Dec. 15. 1915 stating that

the party was housed at Cape Evans. There was no statement as to the safety of all hands
... on looking round I noticed Wilds name and Jacks in paint that was still wet. As the two
men were on the Barrier party they were the ones we were most anxious about.'

At Cape Evans, Richards, seeing the *Aurora*, told Joyce: 'Their shouts of "Ship ho!"
brought their comrades running and they shook each other by the hand, all worries and
troubles passed overboard.'

After reuniting with his comrades, and learning that Mackintosh and Hayward were
missing, Shackleton organized a search party, but no trace of the pair was found. Before
leaving the ice, a cross was erected in memory of Mackintosh, Hayward and Spencer-Smith,
and Shackleton had lines from Browning's 'Prospice' buried with the names of the three
men, in a container beneath the cross (this container was rediscovered in 1947 by an
American expedition):

> 'I was ever a fighter, so – one fight more,
> The best and the last!'

So the quotation from Browning began, and so the memories of the three were commemo-
rated by those who had miraculously survived on both sides of the continent. Shackleton had
indeed met his men again, but under circumstances none could have wished or imagined.

9

Shackleton and the Great War

1917–1921

Two and a half years had passed since Shackleton left England, and still the Great War raged across Europe. Antarctica had brought its own wars, defeats and victories and Shackleton now felt it was time to get back to England to the unfinished business of that other war. He was still as keen to fight for his country as he had been in 1914.

First were the practicalities of finishing the business of the expedition with visits to New Zealand and Australia. From New Zealand he wrote to Emily, talking of his fight against 'great odds and extraordinary conditions' of the previous years and about the 'feeling of power that I like' in the work in Antarctica. It was as if he felt a need to justify his own experiences in the face of the carnage in Europe.

Moving to Australia, he faced a barrage of criticism about the loose ends that had surrounded the *Aurora*. The broad consensus on the Australian relief committee was that he had been slovenly in his approach. Shackleton lost no time in telling the committee that he and his men had been 'treated unfairly' when they needed help. He pointed out that it was South American governments, which had come to the rescue. Australia and New Zealand, he maintained, had done little more than thwart him personally. The relief committee members were taken aback but as they listened they were impressed by Shackleton's conviction and what had seemed destined to be a difficult meeting ended with handshakes all round and an apology from the Australians.

On 20 March Shackleton addressed 11,000 people in Sydney. The crowd had come to see a hero and he didn't disappoint them. His subject was patriotism:

> 'To take your part in this war is not a matter merely of patriotism, not a matter merely of duty or of expediency; it is a matter of the saving of a man's soul and of a man's own opinion of himself … We lived long dark days in the South. The danger of the moment is a thing easy to meet, and the courage of the moment is in every man at some time. But I want to say to you that we lived through slow dead days of toil, of struggle, dark striving and anxiety; days that called not for heroism in the bright light of day, but simply for dogged persistent endeavour to do what the soul said was right. It is in the same spirit that we men of the British race have to face this war. What does the war mean to Australia? Everything. It means as much to you as though the enemy was actually beating down your gate. This summons to fight is a call imperative to the manhood within you … For this call to fight means to men more than ease, more than money, more than love of woman, more even than duty; it means the chance to prove ourselves the captains of our own soul.'

Potent as Shackleton's words were, they were as much about his own view of life as they were about the war effort. The ideals of heroism, patriotism and fighting the good fight were the same that had driven him south. The concept of looking into your soul and finding a personal truth by which to steer had long been part of his credo.

Leaving Australia, Shackleton travelled to San Francisco on the first leg of his journey back to England. There he was offered an extensive lecture tour of the United States. He turned it down, saying he wanted to be home again and settled, instead, for a month. Following a heart-warming welcome in San Francisco, he set off on a short lecture trip. In Tacoma he reduced his fee to avoid a loss to the woman who had organized the lecture. The sole advertising she had done, according to Shackleton, was to hire 'a boozy looking old man carrying a banner, evidently from some fancy dress performance they had once, covered with white cotton wool to represent snow … He was leaning up against a lamppost covered with cotton wool.' Better moments came at well-attended lectures in New York and Chicago, arranged by the American Geographical Society.

In England Emily awaited her husband's return with some trepidation. She had long ago recognized that suburban life was not for him: 'I know it would bore Ernest to be here for any length of time – but the children have been very happy ... I only hope he will get something to do – that will interest him – as he could never be happy in a quiet domestic life.'

Shackleton himself was adamant that his presence in England would make a difference to the war effort. He had done what he could in terms of raising morale in New Zealand and Australia. Now he could hardly wait to become part of the war machine. The adventure of Antarctica was behind him, the challenge of the war lay ahead. By this time, thirty of his comrades were fighting and one, Tim MacCarthy, was dead.

When he reached England in late May he was summoned to Buckingham Palace to see the king and to give an account of the expedition. That done, he set about tidying up outstanding business. He also spent time getting to know his children again, eager to make up for lost time. But the details of domesticity were a mystery to him. Returning from an expedition where survival depended on discipline, he found the relaxed attitude to authority that Emily had encouraged in the children impossible to understand. Used to dealing with men who obeyed his commands without questioning, he became agitated with children who ignored or challenged him. Emily acted as a buffer – trying to explain her thinking to him and pointing out that she was the one who had had to deal with the day-to-day details of the children's lives and this was her way of doing it.

To add to his dissatisfaction, the possibility of an office job in London, co-ordinating food supplies for the Allies, proved less than appealing. The thought of a desk job was offputting and he saw that 'in some quarters (it might) be thought I was avoiding the active side of the war'.

He spent much of his time in London, a compromise which suited Emily and himself. From there he could be the loving, concerned and absent father and husband, writing and telephoning to see that all was well. And from there he could continue his friendship with the actress Rosalind Chetwynd who, as Rosa Lynd, was then on the London stage. She lived in Park Lane where Shackleton was a regular visitor. He and Rosalind had first met more

EHS in North Russia in 1918: 'A sailor dressed up as a soldier.'

than a decade earlier, when she was a neighbour of Frank Shackleton. Their relationship, though interrupted by his expeditions, had continued and now that Shackleton was back in London the pair met regularly.

Photographs of Shackleton taken after his return from Antarctica and over the following three years show a man growing prematurely old. His health was a factor in this decline but there's something else in the face and the figure, signs of a man going to seed. The face is a disappointed one. In an age when victory was quintessential, he was a man who had never quite managed to win.

Worst of all, while war raged about him, a war of which he wanted to be a part, he was marooned on an island of debt-paying and problem-solving for an expedition that was already over. The past was his constant companion, the future a worrying uncertainty.

Shackleton had also begun to drink. Never comfortable with alcohol, it now seemed to offer a way out of his troubles. It may have been a temporary escape, but he recognized its dangers and regularly went on the wagon.

By July he had paid all the men involved in the trans-Antarctic expedition and felt free to seek real war work. But he met with antipathy from many of those he expected to welcome his enthusiasm. Those who had been most critical of his going south at the outbreak of the war were now unwilling to make use of his expertise.

He put forward several proposals, mostly in relation to the Russian front where, he felt, his experience would be especially useful. Finally, in September 1917, he was given a job under Sir Edward Carson in the Department of Information.

Carson was a fellow-Irishman, a barrister and an Ulster Unionist MP. In the legal world his main claim to fame was his involvement in the Oscar Wilde libel trial in 1895, where he represented the Marquess of Queensberry and won. In the world of politics Carson was the leading defender of Ulster Unionism in particular and Irish Unionism in general. In 1910 he had become head of the Unionist Party. In September 1912 he was instrumental in organizing the signing of Ulster's Solemn League and Covenant, a further stand against Home Rule by almost half a million Ulster Unionists. A year later 500 delegates of the Ulster Unionist Council elected him Chairman of the Provisional Government of Ulster. With the outbreak of war he was brought into the Cabinet and now, as Minister without Portfolio, he found a use for Shackleton – the former Unionist candidate in Scotland.

He was to travel to South America and investigate German propaganda agencies there and help to spread British propaganda. His high standing in South America would, he was told, be a great help. This wasn't the work he had expected but it was work – unpaid into the bargain – and he took it.

His lack of salary he dismissed with, 'It did not matter.'

Before he left, he was summoned again by the king, this time to Sandringham, to lecture on the trans-Antarctic expedition. Shackleton had spent the previous months trying, unsuccessfully, to have Polar medals awarded to those of his comrades whom he regarded as meriting them. The Admiralty, however, was against the idea, arguing that such awards would be frivolous in a time of war. Using his sway with royalty, he now got the awards for all but four of the men – Holness, McNeish, Stephenson and Vincent – not because they were refused but because Shackleton decided none deserved a nomination. In each case, he argued, the men had not come up to the standards he demanded of his crew. For Harry McNeish, in particular, the carpenter whose work had fitted the *James Caird* againt the worst excesses of a stormy sea, the decision was particularly wounding.

On 17 October Shackleton set sail for Buenos Aires via New York. Leaving home was followed by the familiar pattern of regret and a sense of wasted opportunity. He wrote to Emily:

'I was happy really happy this time when all was right between us, and now I do not feel far away though I am missing you: I think darling that you are wonderful in many ways

and the more I think about you the more I see what a wonderful wife you have been to me I suppose darling that I am a funny curious sort of wanderer but take this [from] me I have been far happier at home these last few months than ever before ... I think our children are just sweet in all their ways and I am proud of them of each in some particular way ... I can only tell you that I love you.'

Shackleton had fallen in love with Emily Dorman on shore leave; he'd courted her on shore leave; he'd married her during one of his most prolonged periods ashore and he'd lived his life with her between expeditions. Whether this was what she had expected, it was what she grew to accept and what she, probably, saw as the best way of keeping the marriage alive. Shackleton's life had been one of travelling hopefully, his arrivals home were bound to be a disappointment, and the best love he could offer was what came from afar.

Holness, Vincent, How, Stephenson, Blackborow, McLeod, possibly 22 June 1915. Holness, Vincent and Stephenson, as well as McNeish, were the only Endurance crew members not included in the list of Polar Medals published in The Times on 16 February 1918.

His work in South America involved him in intelligence gathering on German propaganda efforts and countering with British information. While in Buenos Aires he was ill a number of times, finding the heat unbearable. He was also fighting a tendency towards binge drinking. As it happened, his posting there was to be short and in March 1918 he was recalled to London.

The summer was spent in England and only in August was he allowed to do what he had wanted since his return from America. He was given charge of the winter equipment for the North Russian expedition. The job-description was vague but this, the authorities believed, was the best way to deal with Shackleton. His free spirit might have been an advantage in Antarctica but it was seen as a definite obstacle when it came to army life.

The north Russian campaign was one of the more complicated and least effective of the war. Russia itself was in the throes of a civil war and the British government was anxious to keep the White Russians on its side. The Revolution had seen the new Russian government make peace with the Germans early in 1918 and one of the Revolutionaries' chief problems was in bringing the remnants of the White army under control. For the British government, however, the important issue was the maintaining of a presence in north Russia and the holding of Spitsbergen.

Spitsbergen was under Norwegian control but the new Russian government was willing to support German claims to the area. For the British, Spitsbergen was a valuable watch-point on the Arctic entry to the Atlantic but they couldn't afford to send an overt military force to what was a neutral, Norwegian area. Instead, they used the cover of the Northern Exploration Company to pursue their interests. Shackleton was invited to join the company and travel to Spitsbergen as part of the venture.

Apart from its political significance, the company, in which he had been given shares as part of his employment contract, had hopes of mining gold, coal and iron in the area and, as ever, Shackleton was looking for the opportunity to make his fortune.

With his old friends Frank Wild and James McIlroy on board, Shackleton left Aberdeen for Norway early in August. Having reached Tromso, he became ill with a suspected heart attack. Despite McIlroy's offer, he refused to undergo a medical examination.

His gradual recovery coincided with his recall to London by the War Office. His new orders were to organize and accompany the shipment of equipment to Murmansk to relieve an expeditionary group, which had arrived in June. He would travel there with the rank of major. At Murmansk he would join 150 Canadian soldiers trained in Arctic survival. As far as the war effort was concerned, his time, it appeared, had come.

Shackleton's commanding officer in Russia was General Charles Maynard. Maynard was less than impressed by what he had heard of Shackleton before his arrival. He had expected a man who was difficult, if not impossible, to get on with. Once he got to know Shackleton his impression changed: 'From the moment of his arrival to the time of his departure ... he gave me of his very best, and his loyalty from start to finish was absolute. He fitted at once into the niche awaiting him.'

Reunited with Hussey, Macklin, Worsley and Stenhouse, Shackleton was, suddenly, optimistic again. Ill health, disappointment, financial worries were all put aside as adventure took centre stage.

With no particular task that he could call his own, he took charge of organizing the camp and was popular with most of the men – officers and rank and file soldiers. He looked after clothing, rations and equipment but he never saw action.

On 17 May 1918 he wrote one of his affectionate letters home, to Cecily at school at Rodean: 'Do you think they would take me as a janitor at Rodean or could I come as a Professor of Ice and Snow? Your tottering aged Daddy Ernest Shackleton.' And, on 26 October, from Syrea: 'I hope girlie that you are putting in some good work at school this term ... Work and punctuality and being tidy are three good things and after a little attention all this comes naturally.'

In November the war proper ended and a month later he returned to London with Maynard, to try to get further supplies for the men in Russia. While in England he spent a short time with his family but on Christmas Day he and Maynard set sail again.

In January the Murmansk force was mustered to travel to Archangel, a distance of 150 miles, to fight the Bolsheviks. Shackleton was suddenly busy arranging provisions, packing sledges and giving advice, but to his disappointment, he was not included in the actual party.

The reality was brought home to him. He might play at soldiering but he was not regarded as a soldier. They might use his talents but they would never see him as an equal on the battlefield. The adventure of war, which was to have followed the great adventure

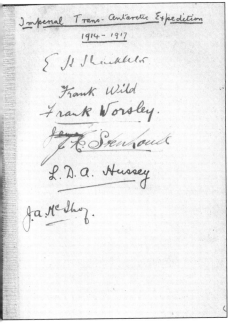

in Antarctica, was proving to be nothing more than a peripheral service to those in the thick of the action.

At times he was saddened by this, at other times angered, feeling the gifts he possessed were subordinated by those who knew less about the business of survival in an Arctic landscape than he did.

While anger had to be curtailed in camp, it found expression in his letters: 'Sometimes I ... feel ... part of my youth is slipping away from me and that nothing matters,' he wrote to Emily. 'I want to upset everybody's calm and peace of mind when I meet calm and contented people. I feel I am no use to anyone unless I am outfacing the storm.'

The war ended without his seeing any action. In February he resigned his position in the army but he believed his financial security might still lie in north Russia. He planned to use the destitution of the population as a foundation from which they, he and the British government might benefit. He would establish a company, raise capital and send supplies of clothing and other essentials to the impoverished people of the area. In return, the North Russian government would give him a 99-year lease on sections of Murmansk, which would then be developed for British interests. Furthermore, his company would be given exploration rights for minerals and the right to use White Sea ports for trading. Everybody would prosper, everybody would be happy.

Finance was the key to the plan, as it was to most things in Shackleton's life. He was convinced that the required money, somewhere in the region of £2,000,000, could be raised without difficulty; the opportunities were clear to him and would, he assumed, be so to potential investors. He met the Assistant Governor-General of the area and the plan

Inscriptions at front of South: EHS, F. Wild, F. Worsley, J.R. Stenhouse (1887–1941) was Chief Officer of the Aurora 1914–1915. He served with distinction in both wars. Leonard Hussey, who provided cheerful music with his banjo on the Endurance and the Quest, accompanied Shackleton's body after his death to Montevideo and then back to Grytviken for the burial. James Archibald McIlroy was surgeon on the Endurance and later on the Quest. His parents were from Greencastle, County Antrim, and they moved to Birmingham. Later James worked as a ship's doctor; he had a colourful love life but died a bachelor.

appeared to be making headway. Returning to England in March, he poured his energie into the enterprise but North Russia was to fall to the Revolutionaries before anything came of the great design.

While the North Russian possibilities were being explored, he needed to continue to make a living. During the summer of 1919 he returned to the dreaded lecture circuit Though thoroughly sick of lecturing, it served the dual purpose of raising money and keeping him away from home.

In November *South*, his account of the trans-Antarctic expedition, was published and the response was extremely positive and sales good. A claim, however, from the executors of one of his benefactors meant that the money coming from the sales was diverted to the benefactor's estate, and Shackleton never saw a penny of the profits.

Some money did come from the sales of rights to the film he had made of the Antarctic expedition but again this was confused by his allocating some of these rights to Ernest Joyce and then finding himself at loggerheads with Joyce about what exactly had been agreed.

In December he began a series of lectures and slide-shows at the Philharmonic Hall in Portland Street, London. The series was to run for five months with two lectures a day, accompanied by the showing of the film. Attendance was mediocre but the series made him a living. One can only imagine the absolute tedium of re-telling the same stories over and over, often to a half-empty house.

Yet, this was to be the spur that saw him turn his attention to a grander escape from rows of peering faces. He would return to being an explorer and leave behind the second-hand life of talking about it.

His newest plan was to move north, to explore the unexplored Beaufort Sea and, possibly, to try for the North Pole. Alexander Macklin became his confidant. In February 1920 he wrote to the Royal Geographical Society and they approved the idea but suggested he approach the Canadian government. By the time he had finished his lecture series in May he'd been in touch with the Canadians and they, too, were supportive. Both *The Times* and the *Daily Mail* offered to help with pre- and post-expedition publicity and by the summer's end Shackleton was busy plotting and planning. He drew up a prospectus to raise interest in, and money for, his latest scheme.

If the lecture series in the Philharmonic had seemed like an endless echo to Shackleton, his plans for the Arctic trip must have sounded similar to those who knew him. He was counting on the support of a few wealthy backers, rather than trying to draw small amounts from a wide number of people. He contacted the Admiralty in the hope that they would fit out the expedition vessel, and hoped the British government would assist with funding. And *The Times* carried the public announcement of Shackleton's latest plan of adventure.

The dawn of 1921 brought a rush of activity. In January he was in Norway looking at a whaling ship, the *Foca I*. In February the details of the expedition were published, outlining plans to take twelve men and to collect 150 huskies at Hudson Bay and then to travel on, via Baffin Bay, into Lancaster Sound and so to the Beaufort Sea.

At the end of February he went to Canada and received the blessing of the Canadian government. A month later his plans had altered slightly and he informed Hugh Robert Mill that he was going to take fifteen men in total on the trip. By then he had renamed the ship the *Quest* and was preparing for a second visit to Canada in April. Now there was no time for monotony, no doubts about age and stimulation. He might not be going south again but he was going.

Shackleton arrived back in England from Canada on 19 May and nine days later Macklin set off for Canada to collect the dogs. Just over three weeks on Macklin found himself in Winnipeg with a new Canadian government and a shift in policy on the question of expeditions. Money was tight in Canada and none would be wasted on fripperies like Arctic exploration.

Within days Macklin received a wire from Shackleton, telling him to return home and informing him that the *Quest* would 'carry out Antarctic coast survey and Southern islands exploration'. He had decided that an expedition would go ahead – the destination was no longer the important part. The ship had been bought, much of the money was in, the men were standing by. He would once more head south.

10

The Quest

1921–1922

◆

The *Quest* expedition was Shackleton's last great throw of the dice. Aged forty-seven, he was still a reasonably young man but his energy was not what it had been. In his enthusiasm to ensure it went ahead, he attempted to interest as many people in as wide a prospectus as could be managed.

For the economists among his audience he maintained there was money to be made in the sub-Antarctic from exploiting everything from coal, oil, phosphate and nickel deposits to guano, pearl fishing, whaling and sealing.

For the geographers there was the possibility of finding lost islands, improving charts and mapping 2000 miles of the coast of Enderby Land.

For marine biologists there was the promise of what dredging work might reveal.

For meteorologists there was the prospect of finding good sites for wireless and meteorology stations.

And, for the emerging Air Ministry there was the undertaking to look for suitable airfield locations.

In the matter of finance, Shackleton was, for once, blessed. His old school friend John Quiller Rowett, who had shared his walks home from school in Dulwich and who had gone on to make a fortune in the rum business, undertook to pay whatever Shackleton hadn't managed to raise towards the Antarctic expedition. This was a gesture of extraordinary

Shackleton, Rowett and Wild in 1921. John Quiller Rowett (1876-1924), an old Dulwich College friend, was the main backer of the Shackleton-Rowett expedition in the Quest *having made money supplying rum to the Royal Navy.*

generosity and, although Shackleton offered to repay the money from whatever books, lectures and films that followed the *Quest* expedition, Rowett must have known the money might never materialize. He agreed that Shackleton should be allowed to go ahead on his own terms. Those, as Shackleton had outlined, were that he would 'have an absolute veto on everything ... I am opposed as a matter of principle root and branch, with the interference of Committees.'

While the *Quest* was a smaller ship than the *Endurance*, too small in the view of Hugh Robert Mill, Shackleton got to work on fitting her out with all the modern paraphernalia he could muster. This aspect of the expedition caught the attention of the press and the public, and a stream of stories appeared in newspapers outlining the range of gadgets on board the ship. Everything, from the electrically heated crow's nest to the most up to date wireless se to the electric Odograph which would record the *Quest's* course and speeds, became th focus of the reporters' attention. Mill thought Shackleton was attempting too much in ship that, while equipped with modern conveniences, was ill suited to the difficult work tha lay ahead.

Some geographers were resistant to the use of modern equipment in expedition work particularly where its use drew public attention. Sir Clements Markham had believed tha anything that caught the imagination of the masses must be suspect.

But for that very public, of which the scientists and geographers were so suspicious Shackleton was a light in the darkness that followed the Great War. So many hopes had die and been buried in the battlefields of Europe that it seemed there might never be anothe dream to displace the nightmare of loss and death. And now here was the man the peopl loved undertaking another adventure, pursuing his dream with such conviction that peopl couldn't but believe he would succeed.

Shackleton thrived on the image of himself as the explorer. He told the *Daily Graphic* 'I go exploring because I like it and because it's my job ... So I return to the wild again an again until, I suppose, in the end the wild will win.'

Like an old cricket team, they reassembled for another tilt at a prize that had long elude them, Shackleton naming the names: Worsley as captain; Wild and McIlroy appearing back from Africa in answer to the call; James Dell, who had missed the *Endurance* expeditio through illness, and D.G. Jeffrey, who'd missed it because of the war, were there.

Charles Green, the cook who'd kept body and soul together on the *Endurance*, was back in the galley, and Alfred Kerr, another *Endurance* man, was signed as second engineer Leonard Hussey, now qualified as a doctor, was on board, as was Alexander Macklin James Dell and Thomas McLeod made up the eleventh and twelfth men of the old boys network. Shackleton was at the helm of a crew he knew and trusted, and who knew anc trusted him.

And there were new men, too. Hubert Wilkins, who had first met Shackleton in 1912 was taken as a biologist, and Roderick Carr, who had made his acquaintance in Russia, was entrusted with responsibility for flying the plane which Shackleton planned to take. Both

Wilkins, who had an interest in aircraft, and Carr worked on the design of the 80-horse-power monoplane which was to be another of the innovations that would make this expedition so unique.

There was another radical difference that raised hackles on many fronts. Emily Shackleton had become involved in the Girl Guide movement and, when the *Daily Mail* proposed offering a place on the *Quest* to a Boy Scout, she wholeheartedly endorsed the idea.

The newspaper's advertisement drew almost 1700 applications and these were whittled down to a manageable ten, who were then interviewed on 18 August 1921 by Shackleton himself. The telegrams sent out the following day to the families of the unsuccessful applicants told the whole story. 'Shackleton selecting Marr and Mooney, but wanted to take the lot.' Unable to choose between Norman Mooney and James Marr, he opted to take both.

This publicity stunt drew criticism from those who already thought the serious scientific nature of the *Quest* expedition was being overshadowed by an insatiable desire for publicity.

Choosing two young men who had no experience of life at sea, no particular gifts to bring to the expedition and were, simply, a source of newspaper columns, before the ship set sail, was definitely at odds with Shackleton's care in surrounding himself with tried and trusted comrades. As it happened, by the time the *Quest* reached Madeira, Mooney had fallen so ill with seasickness that Shackleton decided he was unfit to continue his adventure and should return home.

As with previous expeditions, the ship was on view to the public as a fund-raiser for charity. Given the wealth of gadgetry on board and the pressure to get her fitted in time, however, the public had to content themselves with viewing the *Quest* from the quayside.

Shackleton's relationship with the Admiralty continued to be patchy. They offered him assistance in installing the radio on the *Quest* and made maps available. But this was done only after he had paid just over £200 for borrowed instruments, which had gone down on the *Endurance*.

Preceding the *Quest's* departure, finances were in place, the public was behind Shackleton, even the Admiralty and the Royal Geographical Society had rowed in, granted without any great enthusiasm and with qualms about the company Shackleton was keeping.

Yet the expedition lacked focus, not just in the diversity of its objectives but in Shackleton's approach. He was looking forward to the adventure but was also unwell, suffering from back, shoulder and chest pains, and tiredness. Shortly before they sailed, Hussey insisted (taking him to see a specialist at King's Hospital in London about constant pains in his fee The specialist diagnosed nothing more serious than flat feet and suggested that Shackleto wear supports in his boots. Otherwise, he was given a clean bill of health.

Emily, noting that he was not in particularly good shape and worried by his chron tiredness also insisted he see a specialist but, according to McIlroy, Shackleton 'examine the specialist instead of the specialist examining him' and put his lack of energy down middle age.

Many things less serious than a life-threatening illness could have explained the ach and pains. He was not as fit as he had been and he was a heavy smoker. The years since h last expedition saw him drinking more than he ought and taking less exercise than h might. He lived under constant stress – both personally and financially, in his marriage an the promises of repayment from unwritten books, unmade films and undelivered lectures

EHS, his wife Emily and their children, Cecily, Raymond and Eddie, aboard the Quest *15 August 1921; that summer he was based with his family at 14 Milnthorpe Road, Eastbourne, Sussex.*

Of course, there were other facto which wore Shackleton down. His time in the Antarctic had been demanding physically and mentally. The *Enduranc* trip took a huge amount out of him and the constant sniping which followe had eaten into his confidence. Th *Quest* expedition, in spite of all th great ambitions riding on it, might b viewed as aimless, and Shackleto knew this. It had none of the drivin focus of its predecessors. It could b seen as a simple escape from England and a promise of almost inevitable disappointment.

There were no circumstances in which all its ambitions could be met, rather the expeditio was an end in itself, a last voyage to be followed by the inevitable anticlimax of real life.

So often, Shackleton had set off with his beloved Browning's lines in his head, 'when th fight begins within himself, a man's worth something'. But this time there was little of tha fight in his heart.

Yet, as the day of departure grew closer, something of the old adventurer returned to haunt the body of the man and he was, if only briefly, the shining giant of England. *The Times* wrote of his spirit turning 'old men into wistful youths' and, it continued 'There is nothing for us to do but wish him good luck.'

On 18 September the *Quest* left London for Plymouth. This time there was no war to distract from the farewell and the quays were thronged with crowds wishing the ship and her crew

EHS bids farewell – looking frail with cigarette in hand, saying goodbye for the last time.

185

Quest in the Pool of London, summer 1921. An uncomfortable mover on the sea, this small Norwegian sealer, built in 1917, was finally claimed by the ice north of Newfoundland in 1962.

bon voyage. Shackleton rejoined the ship in Plymouth and, following a farewell dinner hosted by Rowett, the *Quest* set sail on 24 September. Shackleton wrote: '... shore and sea are still and in the calm lazy gathering dusk on a glassy sea we move on the long Quest. Providence is with us even now ... I turn from the glooming mystic immensity of the sea and looking at the decks of the *Quest* am roused from dreams of what may be in the future to the needs of the moment.'

What he didn't record was an observation made to the Harbourmaster in Portsmouth. As they passed a buoy, with its slowly tolling bell, McIlroy overheard Shackleton say: 'That's my death knell.'

Whatever about the troubles that lay ahead, those first days at sea were a time of tranquillity and relaxation after the manic preparations of previous months. Three days into the voyage he noted in his diary that he had 'stopped the wireless operator from taking in the news last night it is of no importance to us now in a little world of our own'.

These moments of serenity, however, proved illusory. Not only was the *Quest* small and heavily laden, but she was much slower than Shackleton had expected. Eight knots per hour had been promised but, even in calm conditions, the little ship was finding it difficult to maintain five and a half. Within five days of leaving Portsmouth Shackleton realized he would have to alter his plans, as his diary entry of 28 September records:

'*[The Quest] must be treated as a five knot vessel ... I am tied to time for the ice ... I can see that our decks need to be absolutely clear when we are in the roaring forties. Her foremast also gives me anxiety ... The main thing is that I may have to curtail our island programme in order to get to the Cape in time ... Everyone is cheerful which is a blessing all singing and enjoying themselves though pretty well wet: several are a bit sick ... These are just random thoughts: but borne in on one as it all being so different from the other strain of preparation: it is a blessing that this time I have not the financial worry or strain.*'

EHS and Worsley, one of the last photographs of them together. The New Zealander Frank Worsley (1872-1943) was a superb navigator and seaman who made the boat journey from Elephant Island to South Georgia possible.

After encountering stormy weather in the Bay of Biscay, the *Quest* developed a knock in the engine. There was nothing for it but to put into port in Lisbon. Although the crew could ill afford this loss of time and the added expense, there was no alternative, the work had to be done and so, on 2 October the ship berthed and work began on her engines.

A week later she was making for Madeira where she docked 16 October. Having come through particularly bad storms, Shackleton decided that the photographer Bee Mason and the scout Mooney, who'd shown little sign of recovery from severe seasickness, should return home. Nor was this loss of two crewmen the greatest of the problems blown in on the gales. The rigging of the ship had been strained and constant buffeting had bent the crankshaft. Writing from Madeira, Shackleton recounted his problems to Emily and continued: 'This is a lonely life after all ... I miss you ... and I love you.'

187

At St Vincent, in the Cape Verde Islands, Gerald Lysaght left the *Quest*, as planned, to return to England, and Shackleton wrote to Emily telling her he felt ill but reassuring her that in a couple of days he'd be back to his old self.

The next leg of the expedition ran more smoothly, but Shackleton decided to dock in Rio de Janeiro for a full overhaul, to find a remedy for the recurring engine problems.

The Atlantic crossing was made in calm hot weather, to the delight of all but the stokers. As she steamed, Shackleton organized the repainting of the ship – changing the colours from yellow and white to black and grey.

On 22 November the *Quest* arrived in Rio and there she was to stay for almost four weeks. The work she underwent was major. The engines were stripped and repaired. The rigging was fixed and extensions were built to the deck-house.

The crew went in various directions, some remaining in Rio, some journeying farther afield. Wilkins and Douglas travelled ahead by steamer to do research work on South Georgia until the *Quest* called to collect them.

Captain Sharpus, who worked in Wilson's shipyard where the *Quest* had gone for repairs, recalled the stress the ship was causing Shackleton. 'Everything in the engine room of that ship seemed to be wrong ... I knew he was worried almost to death. I dreaded him meeting ... the ship's engineer or ... our engineer ... for fear they'd tell him some new trouble. I could see by his face it hurt him so. All his hopes and ambitions seemed centred in that little ship, and she seemed to let him down so much that I got to hate the damned boat.'

Shackleton's days were spent at the shipyard 'on an island baking hot with mosquitoes and clanging hammers all day', and many of his nights in Rio were occupied by 'some long drawn out function' and 'all the time I am mad to get away'.

The added delay led Shackleton to the decision not to visit Cape Town, even though some of his equipment, including essential parts for the aeroplane, had been sent there for collection. He had been told the *Quest*'s engines were not up to heavy work in the ice and the choices were stark. Go south as soon as possible and do as much as could be done as quickly as possible, or abandon the expedition.

By now, much of the *Quest*'s planned itinerary had been changed and it was decided she would sail south with three new crewmen – Young, Argles and Naisbitt, a South African, a Canadian and an Englishman. Naisbitt recalled his interview with Shackleton in Rio. He had arrived wearing a suit and a hat and Shackleton asked 'if I had ever done a day's work in my life. I said I had served in the Navy four years and that I was fond of sport … He asked if I realized I might have to carry meals from the galley to the forward mess, the little ship rolling and pitching in heavy seas and the decks awash most of the time. I told him I was sure I could do the job. He asked me

Rio de Janiero November-December 1921, probably the last photograph of Shackleton on land. He never liked the heat, and the stress was increased by troubles with the ship's engines and his own heart.

what I was doing in Rio and I told him. Then he seemed to hesitate and endeavoured to discourage me: thinking no doubt I was throwing away my commercial career but he saw I was keen.'

Writing from Rio, Shackleton admitted the state of his mental health to Emily:

'I have been in a whirl and strain ever since we came in: Everything seemed to go wrong twice the engines had to be altered … altogether it has been hell. Now it is 110 degrees in the shade … I only just write this to say that you must not worry about me and that my health is really all right … I am going to take no risks in the ice so don't worry … I am doing my best.'

There was something particularly forlorn in that last phrase. Shackleton had never been one to talk of doing his best, rather he had been the one who got things done in spite of everything. His P.S. was to prove closer to the truth: 'Darling I am a little tired but all right you seem always young.'

It was 16 December.

The following evening Shackleton and Captain Sharpus were working on accounts on board the *Quest*. Most of the men were ashore, enjoying a final evening of freedom before their departure the following day. When a boat came to take Sharpus back to shore, Shackleton, who had been feeling unwell, asked if he might accompany him and get some air. He spent the night on land and the following day, when Macklin came to check on him, he claimed to have recovered from what was simply a fainting spell due to the hot weather. He refused to undergo any medical examination. Sharpus, however, maintained that Shackleton had suffered a heart attack and both doctors, Macklin and McIlroy, set sail on 18 December, uncertain about the true state of their leader's health. Shackleton warned them not to talk about his illness and insisted that he was completely better. Both men advised him to rest and, surprisingly, he didn't argue.

Macklin noted in his diary that Shackleton was subdued and seemed to want to talk more than he had formerly done, yet he was uncertain about what he would do when the *Quest* got south. Macklin wrote, 'I do not quite understand his enigmatical attitude – I wonder what we really shall do.'

To see Shackleton uncertain about where the *Quest* would go and how she would spend the winter and what exactly the expedition would achieve was alarming for Macklin and those who had previously travelled with him. Something was not right with the Boss, but he dismissed the concerns of those about him.

Another worrying trait was Shackleton's recent practice of opening a bottle of champagne each morning, a startling change for a man who had frowned on the use of alcohol on board ship, other than on festive occasions.

To reduce the Boss's workload, Macklin suggested that responsibility for the running of the ship might, to some extent, be delegated to Worsley and Wild – both experienced men. Shackleton listened without arguing, but continued his own workload.

Everything about the expedition – the immensity of the undertaking, Shackleton's attempt to cover as many angles as possible, the publicity of taking the two boy scouts on board, even the decision to go south when the Canadian Arctic Expedition was cancelled – spoke of desperation.

A fine, bright, calm Christmas Eve gave way to a Christmas Day that saw a full force gale pummelling the ship. Christmas dinner was cancelled and Green supplied the men with sandwiches and cocoa. The wind and rain continued through the night into the following day, and the calmer weather, when it came, brought news that one of the fresh water tanks had leaked and was dry. Another raging storm blew up on 27 December. Shackleton had already been on watch or on call through the Christmas Day gale and now continued on the bridge. His own cabin had been flooded and what sleep he took was taken in snatches in the wardroom. The storm, he said, was the worst he had ever endured and, by the time it abated on the 28th he and everyone on board was drained. But the *Quest* had one final trick to play.

No sooner had the weather improved than Kerr, the Second Engineer, discovered a leak in the ship's furnace. At best it meant a reduction in speed until they reached South Georgia. At worst it might mean the end of the expedition. To the exhausted Shackleton it was another kick when his spirit was already down.

Christopher Naisbitt was to witness a side of Shackleton that was rarely seen. 'When the Boss is annoyed about something it seems to upset him altogether – nothing is right. At mealtimes there is something to complain about – the plates have not been warmed for the hot dishes – his macaroni cheese is not sufficiently crisp – or something else is wrong. Capt. Hussey seems to be a very useful man in this direction ... he generally administers the right dope for a boisterous Irish spirit and after a while you find Dr Jekyll climbing out of Mr Hyde.'

Shackleton was suffering from constant back and face pains, and the heavy weather through which the ship was passing meant there was no time to sleep properly.

On 1 January 1922, as the weather at last improved, he returned to his diary, which had been ignored during the gales: 'The year has begun kindly for us: it is curious how a certain date becomes a factor and milestone in ones life: Christmas Day in the raging gale seemed out of place I dared not hope that today would be as it was: Anxiety has been probing deeply into me: for until the very end of the year things have gone awry ..."There are two points in the adventures of the diver" one when a beggar, he prepares to plunge one when a prince he rises with his pearl.'

He wasn't the only anxious one. Macklin and McIlroy were watching the Boss carefully. Both knew his physical problems, and both knew he wasn't taking their advice.

For Shackleton, this return to the southern ocean cut through the freezing wastes of memory. On 2 January he spotted an iceberg and wrote about 'the years that have gone since in the pride of young manhood I first went forth to the fight I grow old and tired but must always lead'.

There is sense of enormus foreboding and heavy-heartedness in this and later diary entries, as though the cold bright waters and rising icebergs were no longer sufficient to lighten the closing shadows.

Continuing fine weather and then the sighting of South Georgia on 4 January saw Shackleton's pessimism lift somewhat and he, Wild and Worsley surveyed the outline of their old haunts. As the day wore on Shackleton took the *Quest* into Grytviken harbour and anchored her where the *Endurance* had once dropped anchor. Later he went ashore and revisited the scenes of his former adventure, spending time with the station manager, Jacobsen, and rambling around the familiar places before returning to the ship and promising that, on the morrow, the crew would celebrate the Christmas Day they had missed in the storm.

That night Shackleton played a few hands of cards with McIlroy before telling the doctor he was tired and going to his cabin. Once there, he wrote in his diary: '... after 16 days of turmoil and anxiety: on a peaceful sunshiny day we came to anchor in Gryviken [sic]. How familiar the coast seemed as we passed down ... Now we must speed all we can but the prospect is not too bright for labour is scarce. The old smell of dead whale permeates every-thing: It is a strange and curious place. Douglas and Wilkins are at different ends of the island. A wonderful evening. "In the darkening twilight I saw a lone star hover, gem like above the bay."'

The shadow was about to envelop him.

Just after two o'clock on the morning of 5 January, Macklin answered a whistle call from Shackleton's cabin. He spoke with the Boss and then went back to his watch. A short time afterwards the whistle sounded again and Macklin returned to the cabin. In his diary he recorded the remaining events of those early hours:

'He told me that he was suffering from pains in the back & bad facial neuralgia. He wished for some drug that would produce immediate relief. He said he had taken 3 tablets of aspirin & that they had done him no good. I noticed he was covered in only one blanket & as the night was cold I said "You should be more warmly covered. I will get you my blanket" which I did & tucked it all around him. He was impatient however for some drug to immediately relieve him of pain & to give him sleep. I left him & went to the medicine cupboard & got 10 minims of Chlorodyne, which I gave him in water. He did not take it at once but said "put it down there while I talk to you". He then said I do not believe that aspirin is any good it takes too long to act, will that stuff of yours act

EHS death cabin on the Quest. *Later occupied by Wild.*

quickly." I told him "yes". He asked "what is the cause of this trouble of mine" & I told him, as I had told him many times before, that he had been overdoing things, & that it was no good expecting any single dose of medicine to put him right, but that it was much more important to try & lead a more regular life, get sleep regularly, have a good daily motion of the bowels & have a regular simple diet. He replied "You're always wanting me to give

193

up things, what is it I ought to give up". I replied "chiefly alcohol Boss I don't think it agrees with you". He then said "I can feel the pain coming again give me the medicine quickly". He swallowed it but immediately had a very severe paroxysm during which he died. I stopped by him till I saw that all was hopeless & then went to McIlroy for it flashed through my mind that his death would cause a sensation & that there might be an inquiry & said "Mick come at once and see the Boss he is dying." He came but on entering the room said as soon as he saw him "Yes! He's gone". Naturally it staggered us & for a few moments we said & did nothing. Then we woke up Wild & told him, & later Worsley. On my way to McIlroy I also woke Hussey & told him to get a hypodermic injection of ether ready at once but did not give it as it would have been quite useless. Death is a terrible thing & I can never get used to it, but this was much more so, as can easily be understood. The cause of death is, I feel perfectly sure, angina pectoris. I laid him out & fixed things up, turned out the lamp, which was burning, & shut the door.'

It wasn't until breakfast time that the crew was called together by Wild. Some of them thought the expedition was being abandoned due to lack of money. When they had gathered, Wild spoke. 'Boys,' he said, 'I've got some sad news for you. The Boss died suddenly at three o'clock this morning. The expedition will carry on.'

Later in the morning, Macklin, McIlroy and Wild went ashore to notify the local magistrate of Shackleton's death and to arrange for a death certificate. Even then nothing went

Grytviken and Quest *in King Edward Cove, South Georgia. Shackleton's final anchorage.*

smoothly. As there was no wireless on South Georgia and the set on the *Quest* was not functioning, Wild was delegated to go to Leith where the *Albuera* was anchored, and have her send out the news as soon as she sailed within range of a wireless station. This was to be only the first of many decisions and changes of mind that would follow in the wake of his death.

Shackleton's body was sewn into canvas and taken to the hospital in Grytviken where, on 7 January, his remains were injected with formalin and Hussey arranged for the body to be carried by steamer to Montevideo and thence to England. He would accompany the remains while the rest of the crew went on with the expedition, under Wild's command, something they knew Shackleton would have wanted.

On 19 January the body left South Georgia aboard the *Professor Gruvel,* arriving in Montevideo ten days later. As ever, the Uruguayans were fulsome in their honouring of Shackleton. They had fêted him in life and so they showed their respect for him in death.

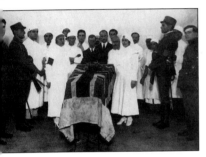

EHS's coffin, nurses and Hussey (centre left), in the Military Hospital, Montevideo, where Shackleton's body lay for two weeks until the memorial service. The nurses kept fresh red and white roses from the hospital garden on his coffin.

Crew of the Quest building a memorial cairn on King Edward Point after returning to Grytviken in April 1922.

His coffin was greeted by one hundred cadets and taken, draped in the Union Jack, to the military hospital. There, a guard of honour stood by it day and night and fresh roses were placed on it daily by the hospital staff.

As soon as the news of her husband's death, and the planned return of his body reached Emily, she decided that the appropriate place for his burial was the place where he had died, the island that had been so important to him and that had now claimed him. Recognizing better than most, that south was where Shackleton's soul was drawn, she had no doubt that south was where his body belonged and she asked the Uruguayan authorities to return her husband's body for burial to South Georgia.

Once the request reached Uruguay, the President, Baltasar Brum, ordered full military honours for the re-embarkation of the coffin. Writing of Shackleton, he referred to his 'magnificent ... humanity ... in an age of warlike heroism he was the hero, calm and strong, who left behind him neither death nor grief'.

195

On St Valentine's day Shackleton's remains were brought to the Holy Trinity Church and on 15 February the president, ministers of the government and foreign dignitaries attended a memorial service. After the service, Shackleton's coffin was placed on a gun carriage and a salute fired.

On the quays, the coffin was formally handed over to the British *chargé d'affaires*, Edward Hope Vere, and taken on board the British streamer *Woodville*. The following morning a Uruguayan cruiser, the *Uruguay*, accompanied the steamer to the limit of the country's territorial waters where another gun salute saw her on her way. On 27 February Shackleton's body arrived back on South Georgia in a blizzard.

On 5 March a service was held in the Lutheran church in Grytviken, led by a Mr Binnie, the local English magistrate. The church was crowded, as the church on Uruguay had been, but this time the congregation was made up of sailors, station workers, whaling men and local people. Afterwards Shackleton's coffin was carried across the rough South Georgian ground and laid to rest at last.

There were wreaths from the British and Uruguayan governments and one from the people of South Georgia made by a Mrs Aarberg, the only woman on the island. The crew of the *Quest*, then steaming south through the ice, was represented by Leonard Hussey. A plain wooden cross stood above the grave. Its simplicity, the final homecoming of the sailor from the sea, was more eloquent than the accolades and editorials that followed his death.

On 6 April, a month after Shackleton's burial, the *Quest* returned to South Georgia and his comrades built a stone cairn on a site overlooking the harbour in Grytviken. Macklin wrote in his diary: 'Wild took the cross which Dell had made & which Kerr and Smith had secured into a drum, & erected it in the cairn. The cairn with the cross forms a conspicuous mark. I think this is as "the Boss" would have had it himself, standing lonely in an island far from civilisation, surrounded by stormy tempestuous seas, & in the vicinity of one of his greatest exploits. It is likely to be seen by few, but the few who see it are men who themselves lead hard lives, & who are able to appreciate better than those at home, the work which he accomplished.'

11

The Legend

◆

Shackleton's death, a quiet passing that had none of the elements of the heroic posthumously foisted on Scott's memory, was regretted and forgotten beyond the circle of his family and friends. In death, as in life, he was an outsider. Had his body been brought back to England there would, doubtless, have been an enormous and communal outpouring of grief, but that too is a transient thing. The public, who had loved him and made him its own, mourned his passing. For a time, some of Browning's words from 'The Lost Leader' were particularly apposite:

> 'We that had loved him so, followed him, honoured him,
> Lived in his mild and magnificent eye,
> Learned his great language, caught his clear accents,
> Made him our pattern to live and to die.'

But the 1920s were a difficult time for the working people of England, those very people who had taken Shackleton to their hearts. Post-war England was no longer filled with the optimism that had taken the country into a world war, and the smell of victory was little different from the smell of defeat. Most families carried with them the grief for lost sons and fathers, brothers and husbands, and the struggle for survival left little time or energy for remembering dead champions.

Unveiling of rugged granite headstone by Governor of the Falklands, Arnold Hodson, 25 February 1928. Carved by Stewart McGlashen, Edinburgh, the inscription reads, 'I hold that a man should strive to the uttermost for his life's set prize', adapted from a poem by Robert Browning, 'The Statue and the Bust', which correctly reads: 'Let a man contend to the uttermost for his life's set prize, be that what it will.'

In Ireland, newly independent but in the throes of a civil war, Shackleton was never likely to be viewed heroically. Despite his triumphant return as a lecturer in the previous decade and his roots by birth, childhood and family history in the country, there was little empathy in the new state with a man seen as British, a man who had carried the Union Jack to Antarctica.

In Britain, where his memory might have been cherished, his standing in death as in life was beyond the pale. He had never played the establishment game and while individual geographers admired his spirit, the Royal Geographical Society already had one dead hero on its hands and an Englishman at that.

Shackleton's true home was on that no man's land of ice and snow where nationality meant nothing and comradeship meant everything. His final resting-place, among the whalers and sailors of northern Europe, displaced men whose ambitions had been washed up on the bleak shores of South Georgia, was chillingly appropriate.

After the rush to praise, a public silence descended. Behind the scenes, however, a committee was established to gather funds for Emily and the children and for Shackleton's mother and two of his sisters, whom he had been supporting at the time of his death.

Hugh Robert Mill, one of Shackleton's closest friends and greatest admirers, set to work on a biography. He was well placed to write the book, knowing Shackleton and being one of his confidantes and having Emily's assistance in preparing the work. He, also, brought a sense of objectivity in the assessment of Shackleton's life.

Following the publication of Mill's book, *The Life of Sir Ernest Shackleton*, in April 1923, there were other memorials. A headstone was erected in South Georgia in 1928. In 1932 a statue was

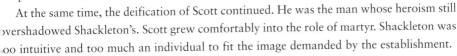

Shackleton's statue by Charles Jagger, unveiled in January 1932. Originally designed for a plinth, it was placed in a niche in the buildings of the Royal Geographical Society at a busy junction of Exhibition Road and Kensington Gore, London.

unveiled by the Marquis of Zetland, but gradually the memory of Shackleton faded from the public consciousness.

At the same time, the deification of Scott continued. He was the man whose heroism still overshadowed Shackleton's. Scott grew comfortably into the role of martyr. Shackleton was too intuitive and too much an individual to fit the image demanded by the establishment.

While one of his great strengths was the technical planning of supplies for expeditions, when it came to decision-making on the ground, Shackleton's intuition was the basis for almost everything. And, once that intuition had been followed, responsibility and loyalty were expected and given as an integral part of the comradeship he developed with his crew. Recognizing their enthusiasm and affection, Shackleton would lead only to places from which he felt he could safely return. His men were not expendable. Much has been made of the poetic side of Shackleton's nature and it is true that he saw himself literally and metaphorically in the role of poet adventurer. He never allowed his poetic vision to cloud his common sense, however, and in that regard he was much less limited in his vision than Scott.

Leonard Hussey was to write of him: 'He would often say to me when some particularly brave or daring act was brought to his notice, " ... the quality that I look for most is optimism especially optimism in the face of reverses and apparent defeat. Optimism is true moral courage." '

Nor was Shackleton some kind of early twentieth-century saint. He was fiercely independent but he never shirked responsibility for his decisions. His comrades were well aware of his fallibility and he never sought to disguise it.

Nowhere was this aspect of the man more evident than in his personal life, whose complexity makes him even more intriguing. It was this complexity as much as anything that allowed Emily to live with his foibles and without his practical support. She recognized that, most of the time, he gave what he could.

As soon as Emily was his, her love became secondary to his ambition. He would say that he wished to keep her in the style she deserved but there was never a time when he allowed shortage of money to stop his travelling. Indeed, as the years went by, he would grow to depend on her for his financial security.

The onset of middle age and the certainty of his decreasing physical strength were painful propositions for Shackleton. Life was running ahead of him and he could no longer keep pace with it. For a man whose time had been spent in the pursuit of physical fulfilment, this was alarming. The older he grew, the more he fought against age.

The adoration of women was one of the temporary stays against decay. He was not alone in his inability to love only one woman but that inability did nothing to assuage his constant feelings of deep guilt. He believed that love, like financial security, would always be found somewhere else.

Shackleton's death and his subsequent demotion to supporting Scott meant that much of the complexity of his personality and life was forgotten. Not until the 1950s, and the appearance of Margery and James Fisher's book, *Shackleton*, in 1957, and Alfred Lansing's *Endurance* in 1959, did the revival of interest in the explorer begin.

Both Roland Huntford's *Shackleton*, published in 1985, and Caroline Alexander's *The Endurance. Shackleton's Legendary Antarctic Expedition*, which appeared in 1999, added greatly to the understanding and rehabilitation of the man.

Ironically, at a time when Scott's star appears to be fading, Shackleton's is brighter than ever. He is the one most often chosen by people as the person they would like to have travelled with to the Antarctic. Shackleton has recently been taken up as an icon by management firms who regularly refer to him as the perfect example of the ideal manager, the man who got all his crew back safely from each of his expeditions. Shackleton hated the notion of management by numbers. This transformation into some kind of super man-manager does him an enormous disservice. Worst of all, it ignores his troubled heart. Shackleton was not a type, he was a man, embued with bravery but flawed.

Failure, as much as anything, made him the man he was. He saw little that was glorious in his decision to abandon an expedition that had all but reached the Pole or in the struggle to get his men back safely from the *Endurance* fiasco. These events were traumatic and forced him to dig deep into his spiritual and physical reserves. Had Shackleton been the icon that management gurus wish to make him he would have been a great deal less a man and a great deal less interesting.

His diary entry for 9 January 1909 – the farthest South entry – reads in part: '... the icy gale cut us to the bone, we looked south with our powerful glasses, but could see nothing but the dead white snow plain. There was no break in the plateau as it extended towards the Pole, and we feel sure that the goal we have failed to reach lies on this plain ... Homeward bound at last. Whatever regrets may be, we have done our best.' The realism and the philosophy of the man are there, understated but patent – disappointment, determination, survival.

The Royal Geographical Society and the Admiralty were the corporate sectors of Shackleton's time, against which he fought for the right of individuals, he and his comrades. He led by example. There was an expectation, an unspoken demand, that those same comrades give as much as they could. For those who didn't, he had little sympathy.

The truth about Shackleton is that he was human, not super-human. His dreams did not come true, he was not the person he would like to have been. For most of his life he carried the expectations of and responsibility for his parents, sisters and wayward brother. He was an outsider and, as he grew older, on the periphery of the lives of his wife and children. His restlessness never allowed him to find peace with himself. He loved life and he lived it to the last breath he drew, but his romantic spirit was never satisfied.

Only in death did he find the peace he searched for and the recognition that was fleeting in his lifetime. And only in death did he reach that place that always just eluded his grasp, where no further demands could be made on his energy and vision.

Speaking in Sydney in March 1917, he gave what might well serve as his epitaph:

> '*Death is a very little thing – the smallest thing in the world. I can tell you that, for I have come face to face with death ... I know that death scarcely weighs in the scale against a man's appointed task. Perhaps in the quiet hours of night, when you think over the things I have said, you will feel the little snakes of doubt twisting in your heart. I have known them. Put them aside. If we have to die, we will die in the pride of manhood, our eyes on the goal and our hearts beating time to the instinct within us.*'

Above: Eleanor Shackleton (1879-1960) at her birthplace Kilkea House in 1958. She described how she and her other brothers and sisters were born in the front room upstairs. (Courtesy Richard Greene) Centre: Edward Arthur Alexander, Baron Shackleton of Burley KG, PC, OBE, FRS (1911-94) in 1988. Younger son of Ernest Shackleton; distinguished parliamentarian in the Commons and the Lords, where he became Labour Leader of the House; explorer, writer, businessman, President of the Royal Geographical Society, with long-standing interests in science and the South Atlantic, especially the Falklands. Right: Dr Jan Piggott, Keeper of Archives at Dulwich College; in 2000 he organized a remarkable exhibition on Shackleton at Dulwich, editing Shackleton, The Antarctic and Endurance to accompany the exhibition. (Courtesy Judith Faulkner) Hon. Alexandra Shackleton only daughter of Lord Shackleton; President of the James Caird Society who has done much to promote the memory of her grandfather. Harding Dunnett (1909-2000), lifelong devotee of Sir Ernest Shackleton, both of whom were past pupils of Dulwich College; founder and chairman of the James Caird Society.

At the opening of the exhibition The Endurance. Shackleton's Legendary Antarctic Expedition, *Peabody Essex Museum, Salem, Massachusetts, June 2000 – left to right: Conrad Anker, Californian mountaineer, participant in* Shackleton's Antarctic Adventure IMAX *film; Jonathan Shackleton; Caroline Alexander, whose book,* Mrs Chippy's Last Expedition (1997), *led to the publication in 1998 of her* The Endurance. Shackleton's Legendary Antarctic Expedition *to accompany the remarkable Shackleton exhibition at the American Museum of Natural History in New York in 1999. This started a wave of worldwide interest in Shackleton.*

Bibliography & Recommended Reading

ALEXANDER, Caroline, *Mrs Chippy's Last Expedition: The Remarkable Journal of Shackleton's Polar-Bound Cat* (HarperCollins, New York, 1997).

——, *The* Endurance. *Shackleton's Legendary Expedition* (Bloomsbury, London 1998). Excellent selection of well reproduced Hurley photos and good text.

AMUNDSEN, Roald, *My Life as an Explorer* (New York 1928).

BARRINGTON, Amy, *The Barringtons* (Ponsonby and Gibbs, Dublin 1917).

BEGBIE, Harold, *Shackleton – A Memory* (Mills & Boon, London 1922).

BICKELL, Lennard, *Shackleton's Forgotten Argonauts* (Macmillan, Australia 1982). Account of often-overlooked Ross Sea Party of Shackleton's Imperial Trans-Antarctic Expedition.

CROSSLEY, Louise, *Explore Antarctica* (Cambridge University Press 1995). Good slim introduction to Antarctica.

DUNNETT, Harding, *Shackleton's Boat* (Neville and Harding 1996). Complete history of the *James Caird* by Shackleton expert who was at Dulwich College when Shackleton was on his *Quest* expedition.

FISHER, Margery and James, *Shackleton* (James Barrie, London 1957). Sensible, well-documented biography of Shackleton, completed when a number of his crewmen were still alive.

GWYNN, Stephen, *Captain Scott* (John Lane, London 1929).

HARTWIG, G., *The Polar World* (Longmans, Green, & Co.,London 1874).

HEACOK, Kim, *Shackleton. The Antartcic Challenge* (National Geographic, New York 1999).

HEADLAND, Robert, *Chronological List of Antarctic Expeditions and Related Events* (Cambridge University Press 1989). Mine of carefully documented information; new edition expected soon.

HUNTFORD, Roland, *Scott and Amundsen* (Hodder and Stoughton, London 1979). Pro-Amundsen and anti-Scott.

——, *Shackleton* (Hodder and Stoughton, London 1985). Comprehensive biography written by an admirer.

HURLEY, Frank, *South with* Endurance. *The Photographs of Frank Hurley* (Bloomsbury, London 2001). Definitive collection of Hurley's *Endurance* photographs with contributions on the man, the photographs and the photographer.

HUSSEY, Leonard, *South with Shackleton* (Samson Low, London 1949). Interesting reflections on the 'Boss' by the only crew member at Shackleton's burial.

LANSING, Alfred, Endurance, *Shackleton's Incredible Voyage* (Hodder and Stoughton, London 1959). Great account of this extraordinary journey, widely read in the USA.

LOCKE, Stephen, *George Marston: Shackleton's Antarctic Artist* (Hampshire County Council 2000).

LYNCH, Wayne, *Penguins of the World* (Firefly Books, Canada 1997).

MARKHAM, Albert, *The Life of Sir Clements R. Markham* (John Murray, London 1917).

MILL, Hugh Robert, *The Life of Sir Ernest Shackleton* (Heinemann, London 1923). First biography written in close consultation with Shackleton's family.

MILLS, Leif, *Frank Wild* (Caedmon of Whitby, North Yorkshire 1999). Useful life of Shackleton's most doughty travelling companion, who also went south with Scott and Mawson.

MORRELL, Margot and Stephanie CAPPARELL, *Shackleton's Way. Leadership lessons from the Great Antarctic Explorer* (Viking, New York 2001). Good analysis from modern business viewpoint of what made Shackleton such an outstanding leader.

NEWMAN, Stanley (ed.), *Shackleton's Lieutenant* (Polar Publications, Aukland 1990). *Nimrod* diary of Aeneas Mackintosh.

PIGGOTT, Jan. *Shackleton. The* Antarctic *and* Endurance (Dulwich College 2000). Five essays by experts, and a superbly produced catalogue for an exhibition about Shackleton.

READER'S DIGEST. *Great Stories from the Frozen Continent* (New York 1998). Useful reference book.

RICHARDS, Richard. *The Ross Sea Shore Party 1914-1917.* (Scott Polar Research Institute, Cambridge 1962). Valuable as one of only two first-hand accounts of this part of the Imperial Trans-Antarctic Expedition.

ROSOVE, Michael, *Antarctica 1772-1922. Freestanding Publications through 1999*; (Adelie Books, California 2001). Excellent new bibliography and standard reference work.

RUBIN, Jeff, *Antarctica* (Lonely Planet Guide, Melbourne 2000). Useful guide for the visitor to Antarctica.

SCOTT, Robert F., *The Voyage of the 'Discovery'* (John Murray, London 1905).

—— (ed.), *The South Polar Times*, Volume 1 (London 1907).

SHACKLETON, Ernest, *The Heart of the Antarctic* (Heinemann, London 1909). Shackleton's own account of the 1907-1909 *Nimrod* expedition.

——, *South* (Heinemann, London 1919). Shackleton's own account of his *Endurance* expedition.

SHACKLETON, Jonathan. *The Shackletons of Ballitore [1580-1987]* (Private, 1988). Brief history of Irish branch of the family, with genealogical sheets.

SMITH, Michael, *An Unsung Hero – Tom Crean* (Collins, Cork 2000). Great tribute to a remarkable man, from his humble beginnings in County Kerry. Served with Scott and Shackleton.

SOPER, Tony, *Antarctica – A guide to the Wildlife* (Bradt Travel Guides, Bucks UK 2000). Best pocket guide to Antarctic wildlife, illustrated by Captain Scott's granddaughter.

SPUFFORD, Francis, *I May Be Some Time* (Faber & Faber, London 1996). Philosophical essay about British obsession with frozen places.

THOMSON, John, *Shackleton's Captain – A Biography of Frank Worsley* (Mosaic Press, Toronto 1999).

WILD, Frank, *Shackleton's Last Voyage. The Story of the* Quest (Cassell, London 1923).

WILSON, David and ELDER, D.B., *Cheltenham in Antarctica* (Reardon, Cheltenham 2000). Biography of David's great uncle Edward (Ted) Wilson. Good information and illustrations.

WORSLEY, Frank, *Shackleton's Boat Journey* (Hodder and Stoughton, London 1933). Excellent account by navigator of the *James Caird*.

Recommended websites

www.antarctic-circle.org   www.ernestshackleton.net   www.jamescairdsociety.com   www.70south.com

Acknowledgments

Jonathan and John have been assisted by many experts and institutions. We especially thank the following:

In travels to Antarctica: Tony Soper and Anna Sutcliffe, Geoff Green and Angela Holmes, and Dave Burkitt a Port Lockroy.

In Ireland: Richard and Claudia Greene, Kevin Hannafin, Kevin Kenny, Noel Lambe, Brendan O'Brien and th Crean family, Joe O'Farrell, Frank and Seamus Taaffe, Margaret O'Riordan at the Athy Heritage Centre, and th late Richard and Mary Shackleton.

In the United Kingdom: Robert Headland, Archivist and Curator, Lucy Martin and Phillipa Smith her predecesso as Photographic Library Manager at the Scott Polar Research Institute, Cambridge, for the use of their archive Daphne Knott and her colleagues at the National Maritime Museum, London; Andrew Tathum and Sarah Stron at the Royal Geographical Society, London, for the use of their archives; Valerie Mattingley of National Geographi Society UK; Tom Lamb of Christie's, London; John Blackborow, Bob Burton, Rod Downie (BAS), Wendy Drive the late Harding Dunnett, David Harding, Dr Jan Piggott at Dulwich College, Roger Putt, Hon. Alexandr Shackleton, John and Sally Sparks, David Wilson, and many others.

In the United States: Charles and Miranda Shackleton, Regina Daly and Rob Stephenson.

Illustration Credits

Index

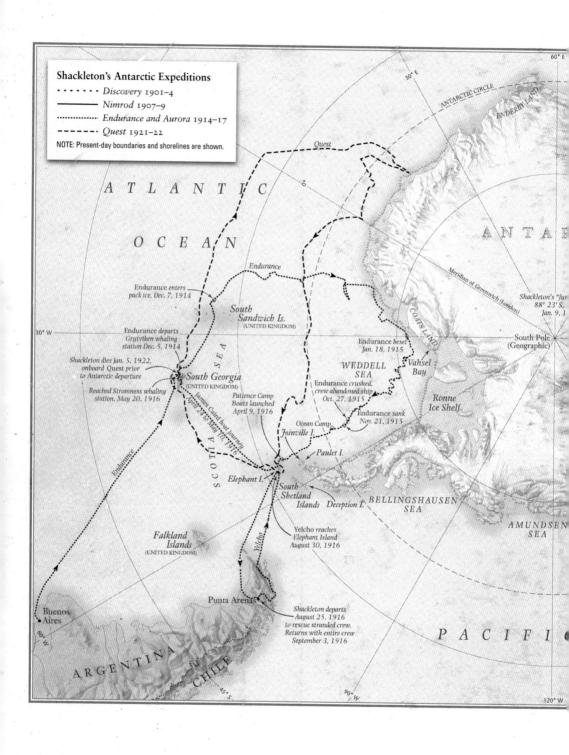

Shackleton's Antarctic Expeditions

· · · · · · · *Discovery 1901–4*
———— *Nimrod 1907–9*
············· *Endurance and Aurora 1914–17*
– – – – *Quest 1921–22*

NOTE: Present-day boundaries and shorelines are shown.

Quest

ATLANTIC

OCEAN

ANTARCTIC CIRCLE

ENDERBY LAND

ANTAR

Endurance

Endurance enters
pack ice, Dec. 7, 1914

South
Sandwich Is.
(UNITED KINGDOM)

Endurance departs
Grytviken whaling
station Dec. 5, 1914

30° W

Shackleton dies Jan. 5, 1922,
onboard Quest prior
to Antarctic departure

Reached Stromness whaling
station, May 20, 1916

South Georgia
(UNITED KINGDOM)

Endurance

James Caird boat journey
April 24 to May 10, 1916

S C O T I A

S E A

Patience Camp
Boats launched
April 9, 1916

Ocean Camp

Joinville I.

Paulet I.

Elephant I.

South
Shetland
Islands   Deception I.

Yelcho

Yelcho reaches
Elephant Island
August 30, 1916

Falkland
Islands
(UNITED KINGDOM)

60° E

30° E

Meridian of Greenwich (London)

COATS LAND

Endurance beset
Jan. 18, 1915

WEDDELL
SEA

Vahsel
Bay

Endurance crushed,
crew abandoned ship
Oct. 27, 1915

Endurance sank
Nov. 21, 1915

Shackleton's "fur
88° 23' S,
Jan. 9, 1

South Pole
(Geographic)

Ronne
Ice Shelf

BELLINGSHAUSEN
SEA

AMUNDSEN
SEA

Buenos
Aires

60° W

Punta Arenas

Shackleton departs
August 25, 1916
to rescue stranded crew.
Returns with entire crew
September 3, 1916

PACIFIC

ARGENTINA

CHILE

45° S

90° W

120° W